ISBN 0521 099315

D1637523

SELECTED WRITINGS
OF
DANIEL
DEFOE

Edited by
JAMES T. BOULTON

Professor of English Studies, University of
Birmingham

CAMBRIDGE UNIVERSITY PRESS

Published by the Syndics of the Cambridge University Press
Bentley House, 200 Euston Road, London NW1 2DB
American Branch: 32 East 57th Street, New York, N.Y.10022

First published by B. T. Batsford Ltd 1965
Reprinted by Cambridge University Press 1975

ISBNS
0 521 20713 4 hard covers
0 521 09931 5 paperback

First printed in Great Britain
by William Clowes and Sons Ltd, London and Beccles

Reprinted in Great Britain
at the University Printing House, Cambridge
(Euan Phillips, University Printer)

Contents

Preface   VII

Acknowledgment   VIII

Note on the Text   IX

Defoe's Life: A Chronological Survey   X

Introduction   I

The Selections

FROM AN ESSAY UPON PROJECTS   23

AN ARGUMENT SHEWING, THAT A STANDING ARMY...   35

FROM THE TRUE-BORN ENGLISHMAN   51

FROM LEGION'S MEMORIAL   82

THE SHORTEST-WAY WITH THE DISSENTERS   86

FROM A HYMN TO THE PILLORY   100

Letter to Robert Harley   110

FROM A REVIEW   112

A TRUE RELATION OF THE APPARITION OF ONE MRS
    VEAL   132

Letters to Robert Harley   142

AND WHAT IF THE PRETENDER SHOULD COME?   147

AN APPEAL TO HONOUR AND JUSTICE   165

FROM THE FAMILY INSTRUCTOR   196

Letter to Charles de la Faye   208

FROM MEMOIRS OF A CAVALIER   211

FROM THE COMPLETE ENGLISH TRADESMAN   225

FROM THE HISTORY OF THE PYRATES: OF CAPTAIN
    BELLAMY   239

FROM THE COMPLEAT ENGLISH GENTLEMAN   247

Letter to Henry Baker   258

Notes   261

Preface

Paradoxically Defoe is diminished by his popularity as the author of a handful of important novels, since the remainder of his voluminous writings suffer undue neglect. Fully to understand him he should be taken whole but his authorship of over 500 publications—the *Review*, which normally appeared thrice weekly for over nine years, counting as one—renders this feat wellnigh impossible. The purpose of this selection, then, is to enable the reader to make or renew the acquaintance of Defoe on some of his favourite topics such as trade and politics, manners and morality, in poetry as well as in prose, and in works like *A True Relation of the Apparition of One Mrs Veal* and *Memoirs of a Cavalier* which are characteristic blends of fact and fiction. Equipped with the insights possible from this sample, the reader—it is hoped—will return to the major novels with a keener appreciation of their distinctive quality and a livelier sense of their author and his defiant adherence to 'Reason', 'Nature', and 'Experience'.

Both as man and novelist Defoe has received a great deal of critical attention over the last 40 years. His language and rhetoric have, however, been relatively disregarded; for this reason the introductory essay is devoted to these aspects of his achievement. For biographical and other critical data the reader should consult the list of books given overleaf.

Acknowledgment

Thanks are due to Professor George R. Healey, editor of *The Letters of Daniel Defoe*, and the Clarendon Press, for permission to reproduce the text of six letters. Acknowledgment is also due to the Trustees of the British Museum for permission to reproduce the facsimile of Defoe's handwriting on page XII.

The editor would also like to express his appreciation of the assistance so generously given during the preparation of this volume by Professor G. Aylmer, Mr W. R. Chalmers, Mr G. Eltringham, Mr P. Russell-Gebbett, Professor J. Sutherland, and the Librarian and his staff of Nottingham University Library. A special word of gratitude is due to Professor Kinsley for his very helpful reading of the introductory essay in draft form, and to the late Professor Vivian de Sola Pinto, for his wise counsel on this as well as on many other previous occasions. Acknowledgment must, finally, be made of the immeasurable benefit derived from the authors and editors of the works listed below:

Healey, G. H. (ed.)	*The Meditations of Daniel Defoe* (Cummington, Mass.), 1946
	The Letters of Daniel Defoe (Oxford), 1955
Lee, W.	*Daniel Defoe: Life and Recently Discovered Writings*, 1869
Novak, M.	*Economics and the Fiction of Daniel Defoe* (Berkeley), 1962
	Defoe and the Nature of Man (Oxford), 1963
Moore, J. R.	*Daniel Defoe* (Chicago), 1958
	A Checklist of the Writings of Defoe (Indiana), 1960
Morley, H.	*The Earlier Life and the Chief Earlier Works of Daniel Defoe*, 1889
Payne, W. L.	*The Best of Defoe's Review* (Columbia), 1951

Secord, A. W.		*Studies in the Narrative Method of Daniel Defoe* (Urbana), 1924
	(ed.)	*A Review of the Affairs of France* (Facsimile Text Society, New York), 22 vols., 1938
		Robert Drury's Journal and Other Studies (Urbana), 1961
Sutherland, J.		*Defoe*, 1937
Watt, I.		*The Rise of the Novel*, 1957

Note on the Text

Except where otherwise indicated all texts are based on the first editions. Other than the correction of obvious errors and the expansion, where possible, of Defoe's abbreviations and contractions, no textual changes have been introduced.

For references to Defoe's novels the edition of *The Works of Defoe* by G. H. Maynadier (Boston, 1903) has been used.

The place of publication of all works quoted is London unless stated otherwise.

Defoe's Life:
A Chronological Survey

1660	Daniel Foe born in London; son of a tallow-chandler
c. 1671–9	Pupil of Rev. James Fisher (Dorking), and then at Rev. Charles Morton's Dissenting Academy (Newington Green) in preparation for the Presbyterian ministry
c. 1682	Established as a merchant in the hosiery trade
1684	Married Mary Tuffley; received a dowry of £3,700
1685	Brief involvement as a supporter of Monmouth's rebellion
1685–92	Merchant dealing in wine, tobacco and other merchandise; travelled extensively in Europe (probably in France, Holland, Italy and Spain)
1688	Published first extant (though possibly his third) political tract: *A Letter to a Dissenter from his Friend at the Hague*
1692	Bankrupt for £17,000; agreed to pay his creditors in full
1697–1701	Agent for William III in England and Scotland
1701	*The True-Born Englishman*
1702	*The Shortest-Way with the Dissenters*
1703	Arrested on account of *The Shortest-Way* (January); he stood in the pillory (29–31 July). His imprisonment led to the failure of his brick and tile factory. Robert Harley (the moderate Tory Minister) arranged for Defoe's release
1703–14	Government agent under Harley, serving as pamphleteer, reporter and adviser; he travelled widely in England and Scotland, and actively promoted the Anglo-Scottish Union

1704–14	Wrote the *Review*
1708	Fall of Harley; succeeded by Sidney, Earl of Godolphin, whom Defoe served
1710	Resumed service to Harley who was again leading the Ministry
1713	Twice arrested, for debt and for publishing ironical pamphlets in support of the Hanoverian succession; released on both occasions through governmental influence.
1714	Accession of George I; fall of the Tory Ministry. Defoe served under Whig Ministries until 1730
1715	*An Appeal to Honour and Justice*, an autobiographical justification of Defoe's previous conduct under Tory Ministries
1719	*Robinson Crusoe*
1722	*Moll Flanders*
1722	*A Journal of the Plague Year*
1722	*Colonel Jack*
1724	*Roxana*
1724	*A Tour Thro' the Whole Island of Great Britain*
1731	Last publication: *An Effectual Scheme for the Immediate Preventing of Street Robberies*
1731	Defoe died (24 April)

Pardom me My L: to believ yo Lordships favour to me has at least so much share in y Conduct of it, if not in y Substance, that I am Perswaded I can not be More Obliged to y Donor, than to your Lordships Singular Goodness, which tho' I can not deserve, yet I shall allways Sencibly Reflect on, & Improve, And I should be doubly blest, if Providence would put it into my hands, to Render yo Lordship Some service suited to y Sence I have of yo Lordships Extra ordinary Favour.

And yet I am yo Lordships Most Humble Peticoner, That if Possible I may kno' the Originalls of this Munificence, sure That hand That can Suppose me to Merit so much Regard, Must believ me fitt to be trusted wth the knowlege of my benefactor, and Uncapable of Discovering any Part of it, That should be Conceal'd; But I submitt this to yo Lordship and the Persons Concern'd.

I Frankly Acknowlege to ya Lordship, and to y Unknown Rewarders of my Mean Performances, That I do not see y Merit they are thus pleas'd to value, the most I wish and wch I hope I can answer for is, That I shall allwayes Preserv the Homely Despicable Title of an Honest Man, If this will recomend me, yo Lordship shall Never be asham'd of giving me that Title, Nor my Enemys be able by fear or Reward to make me other wise.

In all other things I justly Apprehend yo Lordships Disappointment and That yo Lship will find little Else in Me worth yo Notice.

I am

May it Please yo Lordship

yo Lships Highly Oblig'd

Most Humble and Most Obedt Servt

Daniel De Foe

Facsimile of Defoe's handwriting

INTRODUCTION
Daniel Defoe: His Language and Rhetoric

It is characteristic of Defoe that his *Essay upon Literature* should be concerned mainly with technology, with the making of books rather than the writing of them. He demonstrates how printing developed and thus led to 'the spreading of useful Knowledge in the World, making the Accession to it cheap and easy'.[1] His principal discussions of literary style and language occur not in prefaces, critical essays or treatises such as those by Dryden, Addison, Pope or Dennis; appropriately they are to be found in works such as the *Essay upon Projects* and *The Complete English Tradesman*. Their objectives were severely practical. In the first Defoe instructed his age in ways of improving society —by organizing the banking system, the building of roads or the treatment of lunatics. One of his proposals—in complete harmony with the current interest in linguistic problems—was for the founding of an Academy on the lines of the Parisian model established by Richelieu; since the aim of the institution would be to 'refine the *English* Tongue' (p. 29), he was justified in including a discussion of language.[2] The 'complete tradesman', for his part, needed to know how to write business letters, what literary manner to adopt, or how to use technical terminology; thus a consideration of style and language was again proper to Defoe's practical aim. Style, indeed, for Defoe was not an end in itself; it was, as Locke said of language, a means to communicate 'thoughts or ideas to another' and 'thereby to convey the knowledge of things'.[3]

Language was (in this essentially Baconian tradition) for intelligently directed use: hence swearing (against which Defoe inveighed

[1] *Op. cit.* (1726), p. 114. (Note: references to extracts from Defoe's writings included in the Selection printed below are incorporated in the text of the Introduction.)

[2] Dryden had called for a British Academy under royal patronage in the dedication to *Troilus and Cressida* (1679).

[3] *An Essay concerning Human Understanding* (1690), III, x, 23.

in the *Essay upon Projects*) was 'senseless and foolish' because it consisted of words which 'signify nothing' and led to the 'superfluous crowding in of insignificant words more than are needed to express the thing intended'.[4] Defoe might well have said with Gulliver that his 'principal Design was to inform, and not to amuse'; he might also have claimed to make language (like the Brobdingnagians their mathematics) 'wholly applied to what may be useful in Life'.[5] And usefulness presupposed intelligibility, that 'free, plain, honest way of laying things open', essential to 'a right Information of things'.[6]

> The tradesmen need not be offended at my condemning them *as it were* to a plain and homely stile; easy, plain, and familiar language is the beauty of speech in general, and is the excellency of all writing, on whatever subject, or to whatever persons they are we write or speak. The end of speech is that men might understand one another's meaning; certainly that speech, or that way of speaking which is most easily understood, is the best way of speaking. If any man was to ask me, which would be supposed to be a perfect stile, or language, I would answer, that in which a man speaking to five hundred people, of all common and various capacities, idiots or lunaticks excepted, should be understood by them all in the same manner with one another; and in the same sense which the speaker intended to be understood, this would certainly be a most perfect stile. (p. 227).

Such a 'perfect stile' makes no provision for irony; nor does it allow for the sort of delight the cultivated reader of *Gulliver's Travels* derived from a close attention to those stylistic devices which were designed to hoodwink the less perceptive. In Defoe's view all readers of normal intelligence should respond 'in the same manner with one another'. He obviously did not bargain for the use to which Swift would put the 'Trading Stile' in the *Modest Proposal*; he was, in his own words, 'a Plain Dealer'[7] and his kind of plainness, while it was perfectly suited to his purpose on most occasions, precluded that ironic detachment that Swift could command. Defoe himself required it in

---

[4] *Op. cit.* (1697), pp. 130–1.

[5] *Gulliver's Travels* (1726), IV, xii; II, vii.

[6] *Review* (Edinburgh edn.), VI, 127, pp. 505–6. (For comparable views expressed by earlier seventeenth-century writers on the need for 'a plain, easie artificial Stile . . . to treat of Things', see R. F. Jones, *The Seventeenth Century* (Stanford, 1951), pp. 75–110.)

[7] *Ibid.*, VI, 4, p. 14.

The Shortest-Way with the Dissenters; his lack of it was one cause of the misunderstanding which greeted that pamphlet (see p. 87).

To write ironically with success a writer needs to be alert to two audiences: those who will recognize the ironic intention and enjoy the joke, and those who are the object of the satire and are deceived by it. This implies that the ironist has ranged himself with those of his readers who share his superior values, intelligence and literary sensibility; together they look down on the benighted mob. This vantage point Defoe did not share. His Dissenting background engaged his sympathies with those who, on the political and social planes, were struggling to assert their rights, rather than with those whose struggle was to maintain an inherited position and traditional privileges. His education at Revd. Charles Morton's Dissenting Academy, with its emphasis on the vernacular and modern languages, mathematics, geography, and similar subjects with a practical, cash value, cut him off from the classical tradition instinctively assumed by the Tory satirists.[8] And his commercial activities, as well as his experience of business failure, ranged him with the 'Artizans, Countrymen, and Merchants' whose language the Royal Society preferred 'before that of Wits, and Scholars'.[9] Defoe, then, wrote 'to serve the World' not through any superior amusement shared with the Pharisees, but through informing, cajoling, and generally educating the Scribes. The 'Mathematical plainness' of language celebrated by Bishop Sprat was his proper medium.

This plainness was not only functional; it was not only a highly serviceable tool for one who did not distinguish between the life of a commercial, practical world where vulgar speech prevails, and the portrayal of that world in literature; this literary manner also had moral connotations of great moment for Defoe. He was in no doubt that a man's language and his morality were closely related, a fact which emerges from his treatment of the 'Wits and Scholars' mentioned by Sprat. He had no time for the wits (especially the 'Wit turn'd Tradesman'); he described them as 'the Froth and Flutter of the

[8] For a discussion of seventeenth-century advocates of the vernacular—especially Bacon and George Snell—see R. F. Jones, *The Triumph of the English Language* (1953), ch. X.

[9] Thomas Sprat, *History of the Royal Society* (1667), p. 113.

Creation' (p. 238) and made a sharp distinction between them and men of wisdom or common sense. The question of the scholar's use of language was treated with greater seriousness. Defoe's judgment on 'meer Learned Men' was harsh: their education in Latin makes them 'dull, awkward, and heavy in delivering themselves'(p. 254); there are 'many great Scholars whose *English* has been far from Polite' (p. 29); and Defoe is (like Swift) especially distrustful of clergy, doctors, and lawyers because they rely on 'Habits of Speech' peculiar to their professions (p. 29). This last criticism is both moral and literary. Such men are 'full of Stiffness' in their use of words; they also betray a pride in being different from normal men, an arrogant contempt for ordinary speech which is the basis of honest social intercourse, and a reluctance to share their knowledge with the common man. For his part Defoe asserted his reverence for 'the general vulgar sense' of language in the *Serious Reflections of Robinson Crusoe*;[10] the very high proportion of words ot Anglo-Saxon origin in Defoe's vocabulary confirmed it. In the *Serious Reflections* his view of the interdependence of style and morality is made patently clear. He is discussing honesty and remarks:

> The plainness I profess, both in style and method, seems to me to have some suitable analogy to the subject, honesty, and therefore is abolutely necessary to be strictly followed; and I must own, I am the better reconciled, on this very account, to a natural infirmity of homely plain writing, in that I think the plainness of expression, which I am condemned to, will give no disadvantage to my subject, since honesty shows the more beautiful, and the more like honesty, when artifice is dismissed, and she is honestly seen by her own light only; likewise the same sincerity is required in the reader, and he that reads this essay without honesty, will never understand it right.[11]

Stylistic plainness, then, is both appropriate to the subject and a warranty of honest purpose; a man who writes clearly and directly, who is 'plain and explicit' (p. 228), can be trusted. The standpoint assumed is identical with that common in everyday life—that one can judge a man's trustworthiness by his honest face and plain speaking, and if he is one to 'smile and smile' you will know him for a villain. Defoe fully

[10] *Robinson Crusoe*, III, 26.

[11] *Ibid.*, III, 26–7. (Defoe's reasoning in this passage closely resembles that found in attacks on pulpit eloquence in the Restoration period. See R. F. Jones's article on that subject, reprinted in his *Seventeenth Century*, pp. 111–42.)

accepted the logic of his statement in the *Review* concerning a letter from one of his readers:

> The Honesty and Plainess of the Stile of this Letter, I hope will offend no body, but rather convince any Man of the Genuine Native Sincerity of the Man.[12]

For Defoe 'plain English and plain dealing' were inseparable.[13]

'Plain English' meant the language of the everyday world where man was moulded by circumstances which tested his courage, sense and ingenuity; the world which made Moll a thief and a prostitute, Colonel Jack a pickpocket, and turned Roxana 'from a lady of pleasure', into 'a woman of business'. The diction, imagery, and pro-verbial wisdom employed by these characters were a guarantee of the authenticity of their autobiographical narratives; they were intended to reinforce the claim that these accounts were direct transcripts of human experience. The same linguistic features are to be found in Defoe's other writings which were invariably concerned with the actual world of affairs.

His principles, formed by contact with this practical world, were largely unsophisticated as befitted the 'Plain Dealer'; his language was appropriately unaffected. Like Swift in *The Tale of a Tub* or *The Conduct of the Allies*, Defoe could reduce complex issues to a simple formula: man's needs consist of 'Three things, *Money*, *Friends*, and *Health*' and without them 'he Dies in a Ditch, or in some worse place, *an Hospital*' (p. 24); 'Self-destruction is the effect of Cowardice in the highest extream' (p. 24); again, in political matters, 'Wisdom, Safety, and Peace' reside solely in 'the Golden Mean';[14] and on his favourite subject of trade—'Trade is the Life of a Nation's Wealth . . . Trade makes the whole World live by, and depend upon one another; Trade makes barren climates fruitful, thinly-inhabited countries populous . . .'[15]—he is well stocked with simple certainties. This is not to suggest that the man was a simpleton or that no serious thought lay behind his ingenuous formulae. Professor Novak (in *Defoe and the Nature of Man*) gives an account of the 'ideological basis of some of Defoe's best themes

[12] *Op. cit.*, III, 94, p. 375.
[13] *Essay upon Projects*, p. 28.
[14] *Review*, IV, 141, p. 561.
[15] *Ibid.*, IV, 6, p. 23.

and stories', and in so doing he reveals a wider reading in traditional and recent philosophy on Defoe's part than is apparent at first sight. But it is still true that Defoe's reader is invariably aware of writing which, as Coleridge said of Junius, was designed to make a stir in the coffee-house, the lobby of the House of Commons, or a public meeting rather than to be satisfying 'for the closet of a Sidney, or for a House of Lords such as it was in the time of Lord Bacon'.[16] And the language he adopted was fitting: direct, unsophisticated, and lucid.

Defoe expresses anger with a crude vigour: swearing is 'a Vomit of the Brain' and as impertinent 'as if a man shou'd *Fart* before a Justice, or *talk Bawdy* before the Queen' (p. 31). This is the robust speech of the market-place, given extra pungency by the writer's earthy imagination and his closeness to readers who would share his contempt for the *beau monde* among whom swearing was voguish. A shared scorn for families who gloried in their ancient lineage similarly accounts for the robust vulgarity of his description of 'That Het'rogeneous Thing, *An Englishman*':

> In eager Rapes, and furious Lust begot,
> Betwixt a Painted Britton and a Scot:
> Whose gend'ring Offspring quickly learnt to bow,
> And yoke their Heifers to the Roman Plough:
> From whence a Mongrel half-bred Race there came ... (p. 63)

It accounts too for the deliberately coarse lines which follow the Prologue for the opening of the Haymarket Theatre (pp. 117–8); Defoe lowers his tone and language to communicate with greater strength his contempt for the attitudes expressed in Sir Samuel Garth's verses. The frequent and conventionally elevated claims for the Restoration theatre were so much bombast to Defoe and the normal reader of the *Review*. But there is other than this kind of (pejorative) vulgarity in Defoe's writing; also to be reckoned with is his invigorating use of common speech. For example, he uses a harsh-sounding colloquialism (biblical in origin) to add toughness to the centre of a line in *The True-Born Englishman*: 'Fools out of favour grudge at Knaves in Place' (p. 54); idiomatic remarks frequently appear in the poem to show contempt—'Fate jumbl'd them together, *God knows how*', 'Lords, whose

---

[16] *Coleridge's Miscellaneous Criticism*, ed. T. M. Raysor (1936), p. 314.

Parents were the *Lord knows who*' (pp. 64, 66); the younger brother in
The Family Instructor uses a lively vulgarism when he says that his
father 'will go thro' stitch with what he has begun' (p. 202); and, judged
by standards of stylistic refinement, Defoe's prose often suffers from
the clumsiness which is permissible in conversation but not in print.

Much has been made of this clumsiness and of Defoe's prolixity. Ian
Watt rightly observes that economy and compactness require labour;
they reduce an author's speed of writing and consequently diminish
his financial gain when diffuseness is economically profitable.[17] Defoe,
it is true, does not discipline the popular orator's tendency to repeat
himself, to heap illustration on illustration, and to add details that are
strictly superfluous. On the other hand, he does not multiply words to
achieve a superficial literary grace or indulge the copious and figur-
ative language of the early romances; each detail, separately considered, is relevant; what he cannot restrain is that fascination—which
communicates itself to his audience—with observed facts of human behaviour and environment. When, therefore, he insists that he is 'no
Man of Circumlocution, but loves to come directly to the point',[18]
his claim is justified only in one particular sense: that he does not write
with premeditation; relying on a native sensitivity to word and cadence, he writes at the behest of feeling and common sense. Yet too
much can be made of Defoe's stylistic deficiencies; the consequence is
to underrate his literary sensibility.

This would be a serious fault. Not infrequently in *The True-Born
Englishman* the overt lack of refinement obscures Defoe's command of
that 'ease and quickness' which Locke thought essential to verbal communication. Of the so-called true-born Englishman he remarks:

> *His own dear Praises close the ample speech,*
> *Tells you how Wise he is;* that is, how Rich:
> For Wealth is Wisdom; he that's Rich is wise;
> And all men Learned Poverty despise. (p. 68)

These lines have a vigour worthy of Pope; their phrasing and cadence
are controlled; and the result is a memorable, trenchant statement of
a view expressed by Pope himself as well as by Johnson. Similarly in

[17] *The Rise of the Novel* (Penguin, 1963), pp. 58–9.
[18] *Review*, VIII, 91, p. 365.

the reference to Charles II—'Throughout his Lazy, Long, Lascivious Reign' (p. 62)—the alliteration and length of line appropriately reinforce the surface meaning. Again, his hearty contempt for the pillory and the tyranny it symbolized is amply conveyed in the vivid, pithy descriptions which stay in the mind long after other details of the poem fade. The pillory is by turns the 'State *Machin*', the '*Stool of State*', the '*State-Trap* of the law', '*Great Engine*', a 'swelling Stage', a 'Theater', 'the Satyr of the Age', the '*Speaking Trumpet* of Men's Fame', the '*Herald of Reproach*', and finally, 'the Bug-bear of the Law'. There is not only imaginative resourcefulness here, but also an understanding of the political value of the easily-remembered, quotable catchphrase that summarizes a shared attitude. The pairs of alliterative words—'Prejudices and Passions', 'causeless Curses', Ballads and Balderdash'—to be found occasionally in the prose serve an analogous purpose. Furthermore, though Defoe is well known for the length and disorder of his sentences in which clauses—to adapt a remark by Coleridge—sometimes seem to 'have the same connection with each other that marbles have in a bag; they touch without adhering'[19]—his skill in the short sentence or aphorism should not be disregarded:

> There is the Christianity and Justice by which I have been treated; and this Injustice is the thing that I complain of. (p. 181).
> The tradesman that is a lover of pleasure, shall be a poor man. (p. 230).
> Business neglected is business lost. (p. 231).
> Pleasure is a thief to business. (p. 231).

Defoe was certainly conscious of the value of pungent compression; that the aphorisms have a biblical source (as is the case with 'the tradesman that is a lover of pleasure, shall be a poor man') or are proverbial in form, merely underlines the fact that he dealt primarily in familiar, traditional ways of thinking and speaking. It should not be assumed however, that Defoe was unaware of formal stylistic devices: he can use antithesis; where the object is concrete, such as money or the pillory, he apostrophizes skilfully (pp. 101, 122–4); and he makes effective use of a series of rhetorical questions to force home incontestable truths and at the same time convey his own surprise that the truths require stating at

[19] *Inquiring Spirit*, ed. K. Coburn (1951), p. 183.

all (pp. 40, 232). And no man can more evocatively communicate the deep satisfactions associated with the practical world. One thinks of those experienced by Crusoe or Roxana, of the quiet pleasure of 'H.F.' the saddler in the *Journal of the Plague Year*, when 'the people began to walk the streets again' after the plague, or of this sentence from *The Complete English Tradesman*:

> To a complete tradesman there is no pleasure equal to that of being in his business, no delight equal to that of seeing himself thrive, to see trade flow in upon him, and to be satisfied that he goes on prosperously. (p. 231).

'*Names and Things directly I proclaim*' (p. 75): so says Britannia in *The True-Born Englishman*; and she speaks for Defoe. The real world fascinated him: hence the enthusiasm in his writing on money and trade, on projects, pirates, or immediate political issues; hence too the realistic environments he creates for his characters in the novels, in the *Memoirs of a Cavalier*, and in the dramatized incidents which illustrate his arguments whether they concern pensions for seamen or the qualities essential to a complete gentleman. Whatever the matter under consideration it is presented in a tone and style which emphasize its direct relevance to the world of 'things'. Defoe is invariably concerned with what he can make seem practicable—this is, for example, the touchstone for his case in the *Argument Shewing, That a Standing Army . . .*, and for his proposals in the *Essay upon Projects*. Indeed his handling of any question involved the firm assumption that an argument based on incontrovertible facts, frankly stated, will induce belief. Quite bluntly, after referring to some historical facts in the 'Explanatory Preface' to *The True-Born Englishman*, he continues: 'This is so plain, that he who is ignorant of it, is too dull to be talk'd with' (p.52). When he remarks 'The reason is plain . . .' (p. 42), or, in *Mrs Veal*, 'This relation is Matter of Fact, and attended with such Circumstances as may induce any Reasonable man to believe it' (p. 134), the premise is the same in each case. It is equally operative in the novels. Having shown the circumstances in which Colonel Jack was brought up, or the difficulties which beset Moll or Roxana at the beginning of their careers; having shown the pressure of 'necessity' which drove them to crime; Defoe assumes that the logic of the events he describes will induce belief in the historical reality of his characters.

9

The prose proper to this demonstration was lucid, unsophisticated, and unornamented, but tough and flexible; it had a close relationship with common speech while revealing sufficient control to convince the audience of the writer's reliability. Defoe had to show—to adapt his words from the *Review*—that he was both a man of action and a man of sense (p. 116). An excellent example of his prose, containing all these essential features, is *Legion's Memorial*. Its imperative clarity conveys the barely-restrained anger and determination of 'the People of England' as they warn their representatives in the House of Commons:

> You are not above the People's Resentments, they that made you Members, may reduce you to the same Rank from whence they chose you; and may give you a Taste of their abused Kindness, in Terms you may not be pleased with. (p. 84).

This level is sustained; we feel that the petition originates with a public which thinks, speaks and writes in simple, unequivocal terms. As a consequence the commonplace biblical quotation at the end—'*Our Name is Legion, and we are many*'—takes on a threatening power. The words are no longer a cliché blunted by continual use; they become a token of strength vitalized and substantiated by the tone of the language in the preceding pages.

As with Swift in the *Drapier's Letters*, Junius or Tom Paine, Defoe's authority in such a pamphlet and elsewhere comes mainly from the assurance carried by his prose that he was personally involved alongside his readers in the world he wrote about. It was for him predominantly a business world in which facts and figures were highly important, where technical terms from old or developing trades were increasingly current, or where politics were significant to the extent that they altered the actual conditions in which men lived and worked. This is where literature and popular art of all ages, but especially his own, put the emphasis. Swift's bitterness about the political situation in Ireland (in the *Short View of the State of Ireland*) was expressed in terms of its degrading effects on the lives of Irishmen; Hogarth in 'Gin Lane' vilified the morality of a society which allowed the sale of cheap gin and thereby promoted a coarsening brutality among its poor; and Defoe was anti-imperialistic because further conquests would merely increase

the nation's burdens without enlarging its trade.[20] There were theo-
retical considerations behind each of these attitudes—Defoe makes frequent reference to the principles he supports—but in each case the
author emphasized their practical significance. I have mentioned
Defoe's reliance on facts; his use of arithmetical computations—in
Crusoe, the *Journal of the Plague Year*, or the *Essay upon Projects*—is
well known; and the frequency with which he resorts to technical
terms is borne in on any editor of his works. The *Essay upon Projects*
reveals his familiarity with the jargon of a variety of trades and
professions; his *History of the Pyrates* shows him at ease with terms
associated with piracy and seamanship; while in *The Complete English
Tradesman* he instructs his readers that they should be conversant with
the language of their own and cognate trades. 'Plain writing' in the
commercial world includes the jargon of the appropriate trade. For his
own part Defoe takes Locke's advice to explain any term which is 'very
material in the discourse and . . . is liable to any doubtfulness or mistake'.[21] It is as if he had followed Lord Falkland's practice (commended by Swift in the *Letter to a Young Gentleman*) 'that when he
doubted whether a Word were perfectly intelligible or no, he used to
consult one of his Lady's Chambermaids . . . and by her Judgment was
guided whether to receive or reject it'.

'For the good of the common People of the Nation':[22] this was
Defoe's objective and his audience. For his didacticism—"'tis more for
your Service to make you wise, than merry'[23]—to have maximum
effect, his literary manner must necessarily keep his readers in contin-
uous and close touch with the life of the world to which the counsel
applied. Facts, figures, technical terms were employed with this purpose. So was his imagery: it did not transfigure the world but presented it plain. Defoe's imagination was not one which could transform
the commonplace by bringing it into juxtaposition with other areas of
experience so as to illuminate the nature of both and give a pleasurable
shock to the reader. His writing is barren of imagery one finds in

[20] See *Review*, IV, 101.
[21] *Essay concerning Human Understanding*, III, xi, 12.
[22] *A Short Narrative of the Life and Actions of his Grace John, D. of Marlborough*
(1711), p. 21.
[23] *Review*, VI, 34, p. 133.

Hardy's *Return of the Native*, for example, where an old man, as 'white-headed as a mountain', is walking along a white road that bisects the heath 'like the parting line on a head of black hair';[24] moss-covered roots would not, for Defoe, look like 'hands wearing green gloves' as they did for Hardy.[25] Here the commonplace details lose their ordinariness through the imaginative fusion effected in the author's mind. Defoe is much closer to the Swift who, when giving 'the *plain Story of the Fact*' in the Drapier's fourth letter, finds that 'Cordials must be frequently apply'd to weak Constitutions, *Political* as well as *Natural*'; he is reminded of 'the last Howls of a Dog dissected alive' by the vociferous protests of Mr Wood; and the proposals of one of Wood's 'Adherents' are 'like a *Dutch* Reckoning' where, if the charges are disputed, 'the Landlord shall bring it up every Time with new Additions'. Such writing does not transfigure reality; like Defoe's ironic remark that, were the Pretender to succeed to the throne, all problems associated with parliamentary government would be 'cur'd as effectually as a Feaver is cur'd by cutting off the Head, or as a Halter cures the Bleeding at the Nose' (pp. 161–2), it brings the reader sharply back to it. The arguments developed by Swift and Defoe are, so they would have us believe, directly relevant to a world where landlords overcharge, medical remedies are uncertain, and executions common. Similar observations are prompted by Defoe's comment that the reputation of honest projectors is sullied by the dishonest, 'like Cuckolds [who] bear the reproach of other Peoples Crimes' (p. 24); or by the assertion that the freeholder is the man with most to fear from a standing army 'as he is most concern'd for the Safety of a Ship, who has a Cargo on her Bottom' (p. 38); or by the excited rush of metaphors applied by 'Mr Review' to money—'the great wheel in the vast Machine of Politick Motion, the vehicle of Providence, the great Medium of Conveyance, in which all the Physick of the secret Dispensation in human Affairs is administred' (pp. 122–3). The ideas reinforced by such writing are certainly made vivid, but the pleasure derived from the imagery is different in kind from that given by Hardy's; it has a rhetorical rather than a poetic purpose. It assures us that Defoe has his feet on the ground,

24 *Op. cit.* (1878), I, ii.
25 *The Woodlanders* (1887), ch. VII.

that his wisdom is that of a man who knows life to the bone and is trustworthy.

He would have agreed with Lord Kames (with certain reservations about the word 'amusement') that 'abstract or general terms have no good effect in any composition for amusement; because it is only of particular objects that images can be formed.'[26] The 'particular objects' on which Defoe draws are instructive in themselves; they reveal much about his dominant interests and the experience which provided the bond between his audience and himself. In the non-fictional works, as would be expected, he relies most heavily on the world of trade—the skills of diamond-polishers, bricklayers, carpenters, weavers, cloth merchants, silversmiths and the like; agriculture supplies countless analogies, many of them proverbial in kind; war, the sea, and the Bible do likewise. Through the imagery we are also made conscious of the significance of Wren's architecture to readers of the *Review*,[27] the notoriety of the criminal Jack Sheppard (p. 232), the 'fine Paintings' and 'fine brocaded Silk' which appear to have been status symbols for the rich tradesman (p. 237), the prevalence of coining (p. 30), or the fame of the Vicar of Bray (p. 192). We are involved in a world intensely active and richly varied, a predominantly workaday existence, sometimes coarse but invariably vigorous; above all it abounds with concrete objects from ordinary life. Where there is evidence of Defoe's handling of source-material for his own purpose, it leads to the same conclusions. A sentence from the account of the battle of Leipzig in the *Swedish Intelligencer* (quoted by Professor Secord in *Robert Drury's Journal and Other Studies*) provides one example:

> The foremost rank falling on their knees; the second stepping forward; and the third rank standing right up, and all giving fire together they poured so much lead at one instant . . . that their ranks were much broken with it.[28]

When Defoe uses these details in the *Memoirs of a Cavalier* he writes:

> the Scottish brigades giving fire three ranks at a time over one another's heads, poured in their shot so thick that the enemy were cut down like grass before a scythe.

[26] *Elements of Criticism* (1763 edn.), III, 198–9.
[27] See *op. cit.*, I, 35, p. 153.
[28] A. W. Secord, *op. cit.* (Urbana, 1961), p. 99.

Another brief remark (concerning Gustavus Adolphus's crossing of the river Lech) from the same source—'the small and great shot go off incessantly on both sides all this while'[29]—reappears in the *Memoirs* as, 'the cannon and musket bullets flew like hail'. Not only does Defoe show greater economy in the first extract, and greater particularity in the second; in both cases the similes bring the incidents within the scope of common experience.

A good deal of his imagery is, like this, strongly reminiscent of the type found in proverbs; that this is also true of the novels recalls the claim made earlier about the close relationship between the actual world and the world of Defoe's fiction. The observation that we do not know where fact ends and fiction begins in the *Journal of the Plague Year* or, before Professor Secord made his analysis of sources, in the *Memoirs of a Cavalier*, has of course frequently been made. But an examination of imagery reveals more cogently that the voices of Defoe the novelist and Defoe the journalist were identical; the kind of image he considered appropriate for rhetorical works reappears in the fictional autobiographies. The common denominator is the image drawn from natural phenomena or commonplace activities; from, in other words, that everyday existence which is at once the source and the test of proverbial wisdom. 'The Author has put his Hand to the Plow', Defoe says in the Preface to *The True-Born Englishman*; a butcher (in the election comedy from the *Review*) drivels 'like a Boar' (p. 128); the malicious attribution of pamphlets to Defoe is 'a flail' against which there is no defence (p. 189); and the Cavalier, not having eaten for 30 hours, was 'ravenous as a hound' (p. 223). Proverbs abound—John Tutchin was 'kick'd about from Pillars unto Posts' (p. 69), and the prudent tradesman 'lets no Irons burn, and yet lets no Irons cool' (p. 236); phrases occur which are proverbial in cast if not strictly so in origin—'Poverty makes Thieves as bare Walls make giddy Housewives' (p. 130); and fables are quoted or alluded to. Imagery characteristic of the novels is of the same order. Intellectually Roxana is 'as sharp as a hawk'; Amy is as faithful to her 'as the skin to [her] back'; she comes to see that 'the highest tide has its ebb'; her resolution is 'as swift as lightning'; and her merchant-husband feels 'like a fish out of water' when deprived of his commercial

---

[29] *Ibid.*, pp. 104–5.

activities.[30] Similarly, for Moll, marriage is a 'lottery' or 'a leap in the dark';[31] for his part Crusoe bakes his earthenware vessels 'as hard as stone and as red as a tile', his method being the same 'as the children [who] make dirt pies or as a woman would make pies that never learned to make paste'.[32] There is, it is clear, no fundamental difference. The same phrases, symptomatic of Defoe's whole morality, are to be found in both the novels and the non-fiction. '*An Estate's a Pond*, but *a Trade's a spring*' conveys the pride of the rising middle class in the ever-increasing wealth of the prosperous tradesman and in his superiority over men of inherited property; it occurs with equal propriety in the *Complete English Tradesman* (p. 233) and in the history of that 'woman of business', Roxana.[33] And the most famous of all Defoean phrases, 'Give me not Poverty lest I Steal', with its attendant plea, 'Lead me not into temptation'—the first as well as the second of biblical origin—appears in the *Review* (p. 131) and also in *Moll Flanders*, *Colonel Jack* and, allusively, in *Robinson Crusoe*.[34] The world, with its rewards and its terrors, was ever present to Defoe; whether as journalist addressing himself directly to his audience or as novelist addressing them through a created character, his vision of it demanded language and imagery which were basically the same.

Both, like his predilection for dramatizing, reveal the man who instinctively drew on his own and his readers' experience of everyday living. 'I do not find it easy to express what I mean without putting down the very words, at least not so as to be very intelligible.'[35] The remark is instructive. It is Defoe's justification for illustrating the stupidity of swearing by giving a snatch of lively conversation, in the *Essay upon Projects*. To remind people, to confront them with what they know of human behaviour, and to make them scrutinize it honestly, sometimes severely and sometimes sympathetically: this was his intention. 'The reason of my telling you this story, is to let you see . . .': so he says in *The Great Law of Subordination Consider'd*.[36] And we are

[30] *Roxana* (1724), I, 3, 33, 160; II, 52, 65.
[31] *Moll Flanders* (1722), I, 98–9.
[32] *Robinson Crusoe*, I, 135.
[33] *Roxana*, I, 258.
[34] *Moll Flanders*, I, 266; *Colonel Jack* (1722) I, 251; *Robinson Crusoe*, I, 3.
[35] *Essay upon Projects*, Preface.
[36] *Op. cit.* (1724), p. 112.

constantly being made to 'see': in the *Essay upon Projects* how merchant seamen respond to a request to fight a privateer when they have no guarantee of pension rights if they are wounded (p. 26); in the *Argument* how treacherous the militia were capable of being (p. 49); in *The True-Born Englishman* how the unscrupulous tradesman, like Sir Charles Duncombe, was allowed by contemporary morality to prosper through ingratitude and sharp practice—a portrait worthy of comparison with Pope's Sir Balaam (p. 77–80); or, in *The Compleat English Gentleman* how boorish was the behaviour of the man without education (pp. 250–2). 'I don't know any-thing can give you a more perfect *Idea* of the Behaviour of these sort of People', he remarks of the labouring poor in *The Great Law*, and immediately there follow concrete examples of human actions.[37] It is a technique in constant use. The 'Idea' is thus carried alive to his audience and, moreover, he avoids what, according to Matthew Arnold, 'is *not* interesting':

> that which does not add to our knowledge of any kind; that which is vaguely conceived and loosely drawn; a representation which is general, indeterminate, and faint, instead of being particular, precise, and firm.[38]

An 'Idea' was not meaningful to Defoe in metaphysical terms—he shows himself little concerned with the mystery lying behind the outward signs of human nature—but in its visible repercussions. 'I am most entertained with those Actions which give me a Light into the Nature of Man':[39] hence his preoccupation with the real, the direct transcript of human experience, rather than with the fabricated, 'imaginary' example. It is clear, for instance, that—unlike that purveyor of pious instruction, Mrs Sherwood, a century later—Defoe derived greater pleasure from recording the conversation of the rebellious children in *The Family Instructor* than that of their rather priggish brother and sister. Equally, while he sympathized with the scorn of the younger brother for the ignorance of the elder, in *The Compleat English Gentleman*, it is the latter whose retorts are the more forceful; it is he who is brilliantly caught in his contempt for the parson:

[37] *Ibid.*, p. 113.
[38] *Poems* (1853), Preface.
[39] *A Collection of Miscellany Letters, Selected out of Mist's Weekly Journal* (1722–7), III, 198.

'Is it not your business to work for your bread, and is not that your trade? Is not the pulpit your shop, and is not this your apron, Mr Book Beater?' Here he took up [the] chaplain's scarf and gave it a twirle into his face. (p. 252).

The imperfect rather than the 'complete' gentleman was closer to Defoe's experience of human nature and like the central characters in the novels, more honestly reflected the world of fact.

The recording of relatively brief dramatic moments is Defoe's forte, in the novels as in other work. 'But I am gone too far in this Part. I return to my own Story': the tone and phrase might well be found in any of the novels; they come from the autobiographical *Appeal to Honour and Justice* (p. 171). They are the prelude to Defoe's account of his imprisonment (after *The Shortest-Way with the Dissenters*) and his release through the efforts of Robert Harley, the moderate Tory Minister. We are presented with a 'scene': Defoe 'friendless and distress'd'; the cryptic message, '*Pray ask that Gentleman, what I can do for him?*' from 'a Person of Honour'; Defoe's refusal to answer it at once; and then, 'I immediately took my Pen and Ink, and writ the Story of the Blind Man in the Gospel ... *Lord that I may receive my Sight*'. The incident is vividly from life; there is the action described in the biblical story within the telling of the larger prison scene; and Defoe has subtly maintained the mystery of the original experience. Or with a single word he gives verisimilitude to an event: Godolphin 'receiv'd me with great Freedom, and told me smiling ...' (p. 173). This is the kind of detail that adds authenticity. The skill with which Defoe orders the detail of time, place and circumstance in *Mrs Veal* to lead up to the dramatic moment—'Mrs *Veal* Dyed the 7th of *September* at 12 a Clock at Noon' (p. 138)—has been sufficiently commented upon elsewhere; the *Memoirs of a Cavalier* has been underestimated in this respect. The graphic account of the crossing of the river Lech by Gustavus Adolphus, in that work, rests on the unfolding of the situation detail by detail: what men did and why, their hopes and fears, their conversation, are all recounted so as to create suspense and hold one's attention (pp. 213–16). Similarly, the admirable narration of the Cavalier's adventures when he is on the run after Marston Moor, fighting a guerrilla, rearguard action over unknown terrain, dressing up in peasant costume to become a spy in enemy Leeds—all hangs on Defoe's ability to place the reader imaginatively in the Cavalier's position so that he encounters his anxieties, shares his decisions and their consequences (pp. 216–24). Everything turns on control of particulars. The Cavalier develops as an interesting character throughout his *Memoirs*, and again it is on minutiae that this depends: on, for example, the authenticating detail that, when he dresses as a peasant, he has 'a white cap on [his] head, and a fork on [his] shoulder'; his companion, masquerading as a woman, wears 'a russet gown and petticoat'; and it is a 'white loaf', not merely bread, which the Cavalier is given to eat.

For dramatic vigour of a coarse, anecdotal kind, 'Mr Review's' description of the election scene is his most memorable *tour de force* (pp. 124–9). More vivid than Johnson's account of the progress of a petition in his pamphlet *The False Alarm*, the passage reminds one of Hogarth and Fielding. The scene is peopled in their manner with a few principal actors and many subsidiary figures to crowd the situation in order to catch the confusion, bustle and the essential comedy of life. Defoe draws our attention to a crowd of people, in the yard of the Greyhound Inn, who are initially distinguished only in general terms by their actions. Then more precisely we are confronted with a specific group at a table in a particular place and they are identified by their trades. Finally we focus on the central actor, Sir William, and the response to him of the crowd previously sketched. The literary experience is analogous to 'reading' one of Hogarth's 'Election' series. Like Fielding, too, Defoe is excited by habits of speech; his enjoyment of the rural coarseness is matched only by his delight in the knockabout farce between Sir William and the butcher whose vote is being canvassed. The level of behaviour is animal: Defoe is inferring that men are reduced to this through the corrupt electioneering system. There is, then, a rumbustious pleasure in the activities depicted. There is also a moral purpose—to show would-be parliamentarians how ludicrous and often ineffectual are their efforts to capture votes; indeed 'to show the Gentlemen their own Picture *in little*.' One feels too that Defoe could have remarked of this scene as he did of his anecdote illustrating the need for seamen's pensions: 'If I shou'd turn this suppos'd Example into a real History, and Name [the persons involved] . . . it wou'd be too plain to be contradicted' (p. 26).

He certainly would have claimed that he had written a 'parable', a term he applied to *Pilgrim's Progress*, his own *Family Instructor*, and we may think not wholly justifiably, to *Robinson Crusoe*.[40]

> Things seem to appear more lively to the Understanding, and to make a stronger Impression upon the Mind, when they are insinuated under the Cover of some Symbol or Allegory, especially where the Moral is good, and the Application obvious and easy.[41]

This statement not only throws fresh light on the importance of dramatization to Defoe; it also reminds us forcibly that he was a didactic writer. Like Swift, Defoe rarely wrote without a specific purpose; both could have claimed with 'Mr Review': 'he writes to serve the World, not to please them.'[42] The dictum must be viewed with caution, nevertheless it should make us alert to Defoe's rhetorical purpose. The rhetorician is, after all, present in *Mrs Veal* as much as in a pamphlet formally presenting a thesis like the *Argument Shewing, That a Standing Army* . . .; he is as keen to establish the truth of his account in the first as he is to secure acceptance of his case in the second. Throughout *Mrs Veal* he is insisting on the veracity of the story. He begins, in the Preface, by tracing the pedigree of his sources as well as the honesty and intelligence of his informant; he proceeds to underline the reliability of the main witness, Mrs Bargrave, and—through circumstantial detail, realistic because haphazard conversation, corroborative evidence from a servant, and the like—carefully to build up an accurate case; this, in turn, he claims convinced what amounts to a jury of 'sceptical' no less than 'judicious' observers. Furthermore the witness who called Mrs Bargrave 'a great Lyar' is discredited by evidence of his dishonesty, thus providing a sharp contrast with the integrity both of Mrs Bargrave and of the narrator himself; he has demonstrated his readiness to tell all the facts though they may occasionally (but not damagingly) be to Mrs Bargrave's discredit. The material is organized, then, to secure not only dramatic intensity but also rational conviction. The latter is more obviously Defoe's aim in the *Argument*. There—as in *The True-Born Englishman*—he signposts his readers through a considerable body of factual evidence by providing summaries at significant points, by

[40] *Robinson Crusoe*, III, 107–8.
[41] *A Collection of Miscellany Letters*, IV, 210.
[42] *Review*, III, Introduction, p. 4.

occasionally narrowing the focus of his argument to retain the audience's attention and prove his own clarity of mind, and by conducting his case at all times in simple language. He assumed that what is reasonable should be plain, what is plain should achieve conviction.

The Shortest-Way with the Dissenters and its sequel. *A Hymn to the Pillory*, required persuasive techniques of a totally different order. The object of the first was to satirize the High Anglicans in general and their epitome, Dr Henry Sacheverell, in particular. Defoe's method was to assume the rôle of such a man but to exaggerate the latter's contemptuous loathing of the Dissenters to such a degree that the pamphlet would be recognized for what it was—a magnificent irony. That the expectation was not realized points not so much to a wrong choice of method—though the extremism of Sacheverell was really beyond exaggeration—as to a too complete identification between Defoe and his *persona*. Imaginatively he *became* a High Anglican and spoke so authentically in his tones that the pamphlet was accepted at its face-value. Yet it remains a satiric masterpiece. In a tone of arrogant superiority and confidence the speaker sees the opportunity to exterminate the Dissenters—the 'heretical Weed of Sedition'—as a 'Divine occasion' with 'Providence' ready to lend a hand; he presumes to tell Queen Anne what she 'ought to do' as head of the Church, and part of her duty is to break her promises to the nonconformists; he even, by implication, identifies in turn Charles I and the Anglican Church with Christ Himself. We are being given, indeed, a first-class study in monomania. Defoe admirably catches the note of hysteria in the speaker's voice; he restricts his sources of imagery, makes him repeat words, metaphors and catchphrases so as to reinforce the impression of an *idée fixe;* and he allows him proudly to quote Scipio's (in mistake for Cato's) call for the destruction of Carthage, thereby associating him with another monomaniac.

> When a Man's Fancy gets *astride* on his Reason, when Imagination is at Cuffs with the Senses, and common Understanding, as well as common Sense, is Kickt out of Doors; the first Proselyte he makes, is Himself.

This man depicted by Swift in *A Tale of a Tub* is the one Defoe presents in action in *The Shortest-Way*. He creates a fanatical extremist who is powerless to see 'the object as in itself it really is', a man to be contemplated as a strange phenomenon rather than to be taken seriously. A magnificent achievement, then, and Defoe came close to repeating it in the person of the Jacobite 'author' of *And What if the Pretender Should Come?* eleven years later.

The *Hymn to the Pillory* demanded yet another kind of imaginative leap. The poem takes the form of an address to the pillory by the crowd who watched Defoe in the '*State-Trap* of the Law' and to whom the work was sold on that occasion late in July 1703. In other words it created a dramatic out of an actual situation: it made the crowd articulate and provided them with a point of view towards the scene in which they were actors. Defoe—like others named in the verses— becomes an 'object' in his own poem. A further inversion of the normal occurs in the argument of the *Hymn* which closely parallels that expressed in Pope's line, 'Nothing is Sacred now but Villany':[43] that in a time when the pillory punishes the innocent and allows the guilty to go free, traditional morality has been subverted.

> *Justice with Change of Int'rest Learns to bow,*
> *And what was Merit once, is Murther now* (p. 101).

The poem vigorously expresses this single theme; there is no equivocation or compromise. This, of course, is part of its rhetorical strength as popular art; so are the references to easily recognizable facts, Defoe's persuasive assumption that all ordinary citizens are united against corrupt men in power or privileged positions, and the general impression he creates that he is using the idiom of the common man. Implicitly, then, he claimed to be the voice of the people; the enthusiastic reception of his poem demonstrated how accurately he had gauged the response of his audience.

The awareness of an audience, often of a particular kind—the *Appeal to Honour and Justice*, for example, was directed at George I's Whig government whereas *And What if the Pretender Should Come?* was intended to 'open the Eyes of the poor ignorant Country People' (p. 179) —is a hallmark of Defoe's writing in whatever mode. Frequently his awareness was explicit. He knew as well as Johnson that 'the Stage but echoes back the publick Voice,[44] and said so openly in the *Review*-paper

---

[43] *Epilogue to the Satires* (1738), I, 170.
[44] *Prologue at the opening of the Theatre in Drury Lane* 1747.

on the opening of the Haymarket Theatre (pp. 114–18); in the poem, *Reformation of Manners*, he showed his recognition of the public's taste for the 'Lewdness' of Rochester rather than the 'Sublime' of Milton;[45] and in the *Essay on the History and Reality of Apparitions* he noted ironically that he must avoid quoting Scripture if he is to 'talk politely'.[46] Few writers have understood their audiences more completely than Defoe; few have addressed them with greater courage or, when the occasion required, defiance; and few have given them a greater variety of literary pleasures than this 'Master of Common Sense in the publick Affairs' (p. 185). There is little wonder that the people of Coketown in Dickens's *Hard Times* 'took Defoe to their bosoms'.[47] Above all he had learned to credit his readers with those qualities of the honest projector which he himself possessed in such an eminent degree: 'Sense, Honesty, and Ingenuity' (p. 25).

45 *Op. cit.* (1702), p. 59.
46 *Op. cit.* (1727), p. 42.
47 *Op. cit.* (1854), I, viii.

An Essay Upon Projects   1697

This was the first work publicly acknowledged by Defoe: the Preface is signed 'D.F.'. It was a tract for the times, for what he calls the *'Projecting Age'*. In the Introduction he tries to account for 'such a multitude of Projectors more than usual', and properly stresses the impetus provided by war and the development of stock companies; as additional factors he might have cited the rebuilding of London after the Great Fire, the increasing use of industrial machinery, the expansion of overseas trade, or the growing interest in natural science. Defoe himself had a permanent interest in 'projecting'. He had already invested disastrously in an effort to exploit Joseph Williams's newly-invented diving-bell; he took part in a scheme to raise civet cats in England to break the Dutch monopoly; and the brick and tile factory, being developed concurrently with the writing of the *Essay*, was a project which flourished until he was gaoled over *The Shortest-Way with the Dissenters*. A later proposal for establishing South American colonies is to be found in a letter to Robert Harley, 23 July 1711 (*Letters*, ed. G. H. Healey, pp. 345–9). The absurdities inevitably associated with 'projecting' were satirized by Swift in *Gulliver's Travels*, through the Grand Academy of Lagado; they were also turned to brilliant account in his *Modest Proposal*.

An Essay Upon Projects

Of Projectors

Man is the worst of all God's Creatures to shift for himself; no other Animal is ever starv'd to death; Nature without, has provided them both Food and Cloaths; and Nature within, has plac'd an Instinct that never fails to direct them to proper means for a supply; but Man must either *Work or Starve, Slave or Dye*; he has indeed Reason given him to direct him, and few who follow the Dictates of that Reason come to such unhappy Exigencies; but when by the Errors of a Man's Youth he has reduc'd himself to such a degree of Distress, as to be absolutely without Three things, *Money, Friends*, and *Health*, he Dies in a Ditch, or in some worse place, *an Hospital*.

Ten thousand ways there are to bring a Man to this, and but very few to bring him out again.

Death is the universal Deliverer, and therefore some who want Courage to bear what they see before 'em, *Hang themselves for fear*; for certainly Self-destruction is the effect of Cowardice in the highest extream.

Others break the Bounds of Laws to satisfy that general Law of Nature, and turn open Thieves, House-breakers, Highway-men, Clippers,[1] Coiners, &c. till they run the length of the Gallows, and get a Deliverance the nearest way at St. *Tyburn*.

Others being masters of more Cunning than their Neighbours, turn their Thoughts to Private Methods of Trick and Cheat, a Modern way of Thieving, every jot as Criminal, and in some degree worse than the other, by which honest men are gull'd with fair pretences to part from their Money, and then left to take their Course with the Author, who sculks behind the curtain of a Protection,[2] or in the *Mint* or *Friars*,[3] and bids defiance as well to Honesty as the Law.

Others yet urg'd by the same necessity, turn their thoughts to Honest Invention, founded upon the Platform of Ingenuity and Integrity.

These two last sorts are those we call *Projectors*; and as there was always *more Geese than Swans*, the number of the latter are very inconsiderable in comparison of the former; and as the greater number denominates the less, the just Contempt we have of the former sort, bespatters the other, who like Cuckolds bear the reproach of other Peoples Crimes.

A meer Projector then is a Contemptible thing, driven by his own desperate Fortune to such a Streight, that he must be deliver'd by a Miracle, or Starve; and when he has beat his Brains for some such Miracle in vain, he finds no remedy but to paint up some Bauble or other, *as Players make Puppets talk big*, to show like a strange thing, and then cry it up for a New Invention, gets a Patent for it, divides it into Shares, and *they must be Sold*; ways and means are not wanting to Swell the new Whim to a vast Magnitude; Thousands, and Hundreds of thousands are the least of his discourse, and sometimes Millions; till the Ambition of some honest Coxcomb is wheedl'd to part with his Money for it, and then

Nascitur ridiculus mus.[4]

the Adventurer is left to carry on the Project, and the Projector laughs at him. The *Diver* shall walk at the bottom of the *Thames*; the *Saltpeter-Maker* shall Build *Tom T[ur]ds* Pond into Houses;[5] the Engineers Build Models and Wind-mills to draw Water, till Funds are rais'd to carry it on, by Men who have more Money than Brains, and then *good night Patent and Invention*; the Projector has done his business, and is gone.

But the Honest Projector is he, who having by fair and plain principles of Sense, Honesty, and Ingenuity, brought any Contrivance to a suitable Perfec-tion, makes out what he pretends to, picks no body's pocket, put his Project in Execution, and contents himself with the real Produce, as the profit of his Invention.

*   *   *   *

Of Seamen

Sailors are *Les Enfans Perdus*, the *Forlorn hope of the World*; they are Fellows that bid Defiance to Terror, and maintain a constant War with the Elements; who by the Magick of their Art, Trade in the very confines of Death, and are always posted within shot, as I may say, of the Grave: 'Tis true, their familiarity with Danger makes them despise it, for which, I hope, no body will say they are the wiser; and Custom has so harden'd them, that we find them the worst of Men, tho' always in view of their last Moment.

I have observ'd one great Error in the Custom of *England*, relating to these sort of People, and which this way of *Friendly-Society*[6] wou'd be a Remedy for.

If a Seaman who Enters himself, or is Press'd into the King's Service, be by any Accident Wounded or Disabled, to Recompence him for the Loss, he receives a Pension during Life, which the Sailors call *Smart-Money*, and is proportioned to their Hurt, as for the Loss of an Eye, Arm, Leg, or Finger, and the like; and as 'tis a very Honourable thing, so 'tis but reasonable, That a Poor Man who loses his Limbs (which are his Estate) in the Service of the Government, and is thereby disabled from his Labour to get his Bread, shou'd be provided for, and not suffer'd to Beg or Starve for want of those Limbs he lost in the Service of his Country.

But if you come to the Seamen in the Merchants Service, not the least Provision is made; which has been the Loss of many a good Ship, with many a Rich Cargo, which wou'd otherwise have been Sav'd.

And the Sailors are in the Right of it too: *For Instance*: A Merchant Ship coming home from the *Indies*, perhaps very Rich, meets with a Privateer (not so Strong but that She might Fight him, and perhaps get off); the Captain calls up his Crew, tells them, *Gentlemen, You see how 'tis, I don't question but we may Clear our selves of this Caper, if you will Stand by Me*. One of the Crew, as willing to Fight as the rest, and as far from a Coward as the Captain, but endow'd with a little more Wit than his Fellows, Replies, *Noble Captain, We are all willing to Fight, and don't question but to Beat him off; but here is the Case, If we are Taken, we shall be set on Shore, and then sent Home, and Lose, perhaps, our Cloaths, and a little Pay; but if we fight and Beat the Privateer, perhaps Half a Score of us may be Wounded and Lose our Limbs, and then we are Undone and our Families; if you will Sign an Obligation to us, That the Owners, or Merchants, shall allow a Pension to such as are Maim'd, that we may not Fight for the Ship, and go a Begging our selves, we will bring off the Ship, or Sink by her side, otherwise I am not willing to Fight, for my part.* The Captain cannot do this; so they Strike, and the Ship and Cargo is Lost.

If I shou'd turn this suppos'd Example into a real History, and Name the Ship and the Captain that did so, it wou'd be too plain to be contradicted.

Wherefore, for the Encouragement of Sailors in the Service of the Merchant, I wou'd have a *Friendly-Society* Erected for Seamen; wherein all Sailors, or Seafaring-men, Entring their Names, Places of Abode, and the Voyages they go upon, at an *Office of Ensurance for Seamen*, and Paying there a certain small Quarteridge, of 1 s. per Quarter, shou'd have a Seal'd Certificate from the Governors of the said Office, for the Articles hereafter mentioned.

If any such Seaman, either in Fight, or by any other Accident at Sea, come to be disabled, he shou'd receive from the said Office the following Sums of Money, either in Pension for Life, or Ready Money, as he pleas'd.

		l.		*l.*	
	An Eye	25		2	
	Both Eyes	100		8	
	One Leg	50		4	
	Both Legs	80		6	
For the	Right Hand	80	or	6	*Per Ann.*
Loss of	Left Hand	50		4	for Life.
	Right Arm	100		8	
	Left Arm	80		6	
	Both Hands	160		12	
	Both Arms	200		16	

Any Broken Arm, or Leg, or Thigh, towards the
Cure ———— ———— ———— ———— ———— 10 *l.*
If taken by the *Turks*, 50 *l.* towards his Ransom.
If he become Infirm and Unable to go to Sea, or
Maintain himself, by Age or Sickness, 6 *l. per Ann.*
To their Wives if they are Kill'd or Drown'd, 50 *l.*[7]

In Consideration of this, every Seaman Subscribing to the Society, shall Agree to Pay to the Receipt of the said Office, his *Quota* of the Sum to be Paid, whenever, and as often as such Claims are made; the Claims to be Enter'd into the Office, and upon sufficient Proof made, the Governors to Regulate the Division, and Publish it in Print.

*   *   *   *

Of Academies

We have in *England* fewer of these than in any part of the World, at least where Learning is in so much esteem. But to make amends, the two great Seminaries we have, are without comparison the *Greatest*, I won't say the *Best* in the World; and tho' much might be said here concerning Universities in general, and Foreign Academies in particular, I content my self with noting that part in which we seem defective. The *French*, who justly value themselves upon erecting the most Celebrated Academy of *Europe*,[8] owe the Lustre of it very much to the great Encouragement the Kings of *France* have given to it. And one of the Members making a Speech at his Entrance, tells you, *That 'tis not the least of the Glories of their Invincible Monarch, to have engross'd all the Learning of the World in that Sublime Body.*

The peculiar Study of the Academy of *Paris*, has been to Refine and Correct their own Language; which they have done to that happy degree, that we see it now spoken in all the Courts of *Christendom*, as the Language allow'd to be most universal.

I had the Honour once to be a Member of a small Society, who seem'd to offer at this Noble Design in *England*. But the Greatness of the Work, and the Modesty of the Gentlemen concern'd, prevail'd with them to desist an Enterprize which appear'd too great for Private Hands to undertake. We want indeed a *Richlieu* to commence such a Work: For I am persuaded, were there such a *Genius* in our Kingdom to lead the way, there wou'd not want Capacities who cou'd carry on the Work to a Glory equal to all that has gone before them. The *English* Tongue is a Subject not at all less worthy the Labour of such a Society than the *French*, and capable of a much greater Perfection. The Learned among the *French* will own, That the Comprehensiveness of Expression is a Glory in which the *English* Tongue not only Equals but Excels its Neighbours; *Rapin*, St. *Evremont*, and the most Eminent *French* Authors have acknowledg'd it: And my Lord *Roscommon*,[9] who is allow'd to be a good Judge of *English*, because he wrote it as exactly as any ever did, expresses what I mean, in these Lines;

> "For *who did ever in* French *Authors see*
> "*The Comprehensive* English *Energy?*
> "*The weighty* Bullion *of one* Sterling *Line,*
> "*Drawn to* French Wire *wou'd through whole Pages shine.*

"And if our Neighbours will yield us, as their greatest Critick has done, "the Preference for Sublimity and Nobleness of Stile, we will willingly quit "all Pretensions to their Insignificant Gaiety.[10]

'Tis great pity that a Subject so Noble shou'd not have some as Noble to attempt it: And for a Method, what greater can be set before us, than the Academy of *Paris?* Which, to give the *French* their due, stands foremost among all the Great Attempts in the Learned Part of the World.

The present King of *England*,[11] of whom we have seen the whole World writing *Panegyricks* and *Encomiums*, and whom his Enemies, when their Interest does not silence them, are apt to say more of than ourselves; as in the War he has given surprizing Instances of a Greatness of Spirit more than common; so in Peace, I dare say, with Submission, he shall never have an Opportunity to illustrate his Memory more, than by such a Foundation: By which he shall have Opportunity to darken the Glory of the *French* King in Peace, as he has by his daring Attempts in the War.

Nothing but Pride loves to be flatter'd, and that only as 'tis a Vice which blinds us to our own Imperfections. I think Princes as particularly unhappy in having their Good Actions magnify'd, as their Evil Actions cover'd: But King *William*, who has already won Praise by the Steps of dangerous Virtue, seems reserv'd for some Actions which are above the Touch of Flattery, whose Praise is in themselves.

And such wou'd this be: And because I am speaking of a Work which seems to be proper only for the Hand of the King himself, I shall not presume to carry on this Chapter to the Model, as I have done in other Subjects. Only thus far;

That a Society be erected by the King himself, *if his Majesty thought fit*, and composed of none but Persons of the first Figure in Learning; and 'twere to be wish'd our Gentry were so much Lovers of Learning, that Birth might always be join'd with Capacity.[12]

The Work of this Society shou'd be to encourage Polite Learning, to polish and refine the *English* Tongue, and advance the so much neglected Faculty of Correct Language, to establish Purity and Propriety of Stile, and to purge it from all the Irregular Additions that Ignorance and Affectation have introduc'd; and all those Innovations in Speech, if I may call them such, which some Dogmatic Writers have the confidence to foster upon their Native Language, as if their Authority were sufficient to make their own Fancy legitimate.

By such a Society I dare say the true Glory of our *English* Stile wou'd appear; and among all the Learned Part of the World, be esteem'd, as it really is, the Noblest and most Comprehensive of all the Vulgar Languages in the World.

Into this Society should be admitted none but Persons Eminent for Learning, and yet none, or but very few, whose Business or Trade was Learning: For I may be allow'd, I suppose, to say, We have seen many great Scholars, meer Learned Men, and Graduates in the last Degree of Study, whose *English* has been far from Polite, full of Stiffness and Affectation, hard Words, and long unusual Coupling of *Syllables* and Sentences, which sound harsh and untuneable to the Ear, and shock the Reader both in Expression and Understanding.

In short, There should be room in this Society for neither *Clergymen, Physician*, or *Lawyer*. Not that I wou'd put an Affront upon the Learning of any of those Honourable Employments, much less upon their Persons: But if I do think that their several Professions do naturally and severally prescribe Habits of Speech to them peculiar to their Practice, and prejudicial to the Study I speak of, I believe I do them no wrong. Nor do I deny but there may be, and now are among some of all those Professions, Men of Stile and Language, great Masters of *English*, whom few men will undertake to Correct; and where such do at any time appear, their extraordinary Merit shou'd find them a Place in this

Society; but it shou'd be rare, and upon very extraordinary Occasions, that such be admitted.

I wou'd therefore have this Society wholly compos'd of Gentlemen; whereof Twelve to be of the Nobility, if possible, and Twelve Private Gentlemen, and a Class of Twelve to be left open for meer Merit, let it be found in who or what sort it would, which should lye as the Crown of their Study, who have done something eminent to deserve it. The Voice of this Society should be sufficient Authority for the Usage of Words, and sufficient also to expose the Innovations of other mens Fancies; they shou'd preside with a Sort of Judicature over the Learning of the Age, and have liberty to Correct and Censure the Exorbitance of Writers, especially of Translators. The Reputation of this Society wou'd be enough to make them the allow'd Judges of Stile and Language; and no Author wou'd have the Impudence to Coin without their Authority. *Custom*, which is now our best Authority for Words, wou'd always have its Original here, and not be allow'd without it. There shou'd be no more occasion to search for Derivations and Constructions, and 'twou'd be as Criminal then to *Coin Words, as Money*.

The Exercises of this Society wou'd be Lectures on the *English* Tongue, Essays on the Nature, Original, Usage, Authorities and Differences of Words, on the Propriety, Purity, and *Cadence of Stile*, and of the Politeness and *Manner* in Writing; Reflections upon Irregular Usages, and Corrections of Erroneous Customs in Words; and in short, every thing that wou'd appear necessary to the bringing our *English* Tongue to a due Perfection, and our Gentlemen to a Capacity of Writing like themselves; to banish Pride and Pedantry, and silence the Impudence and Impertinence of Young Authors, whose Ambition is to be known, tho' it be by their Folly.

I ask leave here for a Thought or two about that Inundation Custom has made upon our Language and Discourse by *Familiar Swearing*; and I place it here, because Custom has so far prevail'd in this foolish Vice, that a man's Discourse is hardly agreeable without it; and some have taken upon them to say, *It is pity it shou'd not be lawful, 'tis such a Grace in a man's Speech, and adds so much Vigour to his Language.*

I desire to be understood right, and that by Swearing I mean all those Cursory Oaths, Curses, Execrations, Imprecations, Asseverations, and by whatsoever other Names they are distinguish'd, which are us'd in Vehemence of Discourse, in the Mouths almost of all men more or less, of what sort soever. . . .

'Tis a senseless, foolish, ridiculous Practice; 'tis a Mean to no manner of End; 'tis Words spoken which signify nothing; 'tis Folly acted for the sake of Folly, which is a thing even the Devil himself don't practice: The Devil does evil, we say, but it is for some design, either to seduce others, or, as some Divines say, from a Principle of Enmity to his Maker: Men Steal for Gain, and Murther to gratify their Avarice or Revenge; Whoredoms and Ravishments, Adulteries and Sodomy, are committed to please a vicious Appetite,[13] and have always alluring Objects; and generally all Vices have some previous Cause, and some some visible Tendency; but this, of all Vicious Practices, seems the most Nonsensical and Ridiculous; there is neither Pleasure nor Profit; no Design pursued, no Lust gratified, but is a mere Frenzy of the Tongue, a Vomit of the Brain, which works by putting a Contrary upon the Course of Nature.

Again, other Vices men find some Reason or other to give for, or Excuses to palliate; men plead Want, to extenuate Theft; and strong Provocations, to excuse Murthers; *and many a lame Excuse they will bring for Whoring*; but this sordid Habit, even those that practise it will own to be a Crime, and make no Excuse for it; and the most I cou'd ever hear a man say for it, was, That *he cou'd not help it.*

Besides, as 'tis an inexcusable Impertinence, so 'tis a Breach upon Good Manners and Conversation, for a man to impose the Clamour of his Oaths upon the Company he converses with; if there be any one person in the Company that does not approve the way, 'tis an imposing upon him with a freedom beyond Civility; as if a man shou'd *Fart* before a Justice, or *talk Bawdy* before the Queen, or the like.

To suppress this, Laws, Acts of Parliaments, and Proclamations, are Bawbles and Banters, the Laughter of the Lewd Party, and never had, as I cou'd perceive, any Influence upon the Practice; nor are any of our Magistrates fond or forward of putting them in execution.

It must be Example, not Penalties, must sink this Crime; and if the Gentlemen of *England* wou'd once drop it as a Mode, the Vice is so foolish and ridiculous in it self, 'twou'd soon grow odious and out of fashion.

This Work such an Academy might begin; and I believe nothing wou'd so soon explode the Practice, as the Publick Discouragement of it by such a Society. Where all our Customs and Habits both in Speech and Behaviour, shou'd receive an Authority. All the Disputes about Precedency of Wit, with the Manners, Customs, and Usages of the Theatre wou'd be decided here; Plays shou'd pass here before they were Acted, and the Criticks might give their Censures, and damn at their pleasure; nothing wou'd ever dye which once receiv'd Life at this Original: The Two Theatres[14] might end their Jangle, and dispute for Priority no more; Wit and Real Worth shou'd decide the Controversy, and here shou'd be the *Infallible Judge.*

Under this Head of *Academies*, I might bring in a Project for

An Academy for Women

I have often thought of it as one of the most barbarous Customs in the world, considering us as a Civiliz'd and a Christian Countrey, that we deny the advantages of Learning to Women. We reproach the Sex every day with Folly and Impertinence, while I am confident, had they the advantages of Education equal to us, they wou'd be guilty of less than our selves.

One wou'd wonder indeed how it shou'd happen that Women are conversible at all, since they are only beholding to Natural Parts for all their Knowledge. Their Youth is spent to teach them to Stitch and Sow, or make Bawbles: They are taught to Read indeed, and perhaps to Write their Names, or so; and that is the heighth of a Woman's Education. And I wou'd but ask any who slight the Sex for their Understanding, What is a Man (a Gentleman, I mean) good for, that is taught no more ?

I need not give Instances, or examine the Character of a Gentleman with a good Estate, and of a good Family, and with tolerable Parts, and examine what Figure he makes for want of Education.[15]

The Soul is plac'd in the Body like a rough Diamond, and must be polish'd, or the Lustre of it will never appear: And 'tis manifest, that as the Rational Soul distinguishes us from Brutes, so Education carries on the distinction, and makes some less brutish than others: This is too evident to need any demonstration. But why then shou'd Women be deni'd the benefit of Instruction ? If Knowledge and Understanding had been useless additions to the Sex, God Almighty wou'd never have given them Capacities; for he made nothing needless: Besides, I wou'd ask such, What they can see in Ignorance, that they shou'd think it a necessary Ornament to a Woman? Or how much worse is a Wise Woman than a Fool? Or what has the Woman done to forfeit the Privilege of being taught? Does she plague us with her Pride and Impertinence? Why did we not let her learn, that she might have had more Wit? Shall we upbraid Women with Folly, when 'tis only the Error of this inhuman Custom, that hindred them being made wiser?

The Capacities of Women are suppos'd to be greater, and their Senses quicker than those of the Men; and what they might be capable of being bred to, is plain from some Instances of Female-Wit, which this Age is not without; which upbraids us with Injustice, and looks as if we deni'd Women the advantages of Education, for fear they shou'd *vye* with the Men in their Improvements.

To remove this Objection, and that Women might have at least a needful Opportunity of Education in all sorts of Useful Learning, I propose the Draugh of an Academy for that purpose.

I know 'tis dangerous to make Publick Appearances of the Sex; they are not either to be *confin'd* or *expos'd*; the first will disagree with their Inclinations, and the last with their Reputations; and therefore it is somewhat difficult; and I doubt a Method propos'd by an Ingenious Lady,[16] in a little Book, call'd, *Advice to the Ladies*, would be found impracticable. For, saving my Respect to the Sex, the Levity, which perhaps is a little peculiar to them, at least in their Youth, will not bear the Restraint; and I am satisfi'd, nothing but the heighth of Bigotry can keep up a Nunnery: Women are extravagantly desirous of going to Heaven, and will punish their *Pretty Bodies* to get thither; but nothing else will do it; and even in that case sometimes it falls out that *Nature will prevail*.

When I talk therefore of an Academy for Women, I mean both the Model, the Teaching, and the Government, different from what is propos'd by that Ingenious Lady, for whose Proposal I have a very great Esteem, and also a great Opinion of her Wit; different too from all sorts of Religious Confinement, and above all, from *Vows of Celibacy*.

Wherefore the Academy I propose should differ but little from Publick Schools, wherein such Ladies as were willing to study, shou'd have all the advantages of Learning suitable to their Genius. . . .

The Persons who Enter, shou'd be taught all sorts of Breeding suitable to both their Genius and their Quality; and in particular, *Musick* and *Dancing*, which it wou'd be cruelty to bar the Sex of, because they are their Darlings: But besides this, they shou'd be taught Languages, as particularly *French* and *Italian*; and I wou'd venture the Injury of giving a Woman more Tongues than one.

They shou'd, as a particular Study, be taught all the Graces of Speech, and all the necessary Air of Conversation; which our common Education is so defective in, that I need not expose it: They shou'd be brought to read Books, and especially History, and so to read as to make them understand the World, and be able to know and judge of things when they hear of them.

To such whose Genius wou'd lead them to it, I wou'd deny no sort of Learning; but the chief thing in general is to cultivate the Understandings of the Sex, that they may be capable of all sorts of Conversation; that their Parts and Judgments being improv'd, they may be as Profitable in their Conversation as they are Pleasant.

Women, in my observation, have little or no difference in them, but as they are, or are not distinguish'd by Education. Tempers indeed may in some degree influence them, but the main distinguishing part is their Breeding.

The whole Sex are generally Quick and Sharp: I believe I may be allow'd to say generally so; for you rarely see them lumpish and heavy when they are Children, as Boys will often be. If a Woman be well-bred, and taught the proper Management of her Natural Wit, she proves generally very sensible and retentive: And without partiality, a Woman of Sense and Manners is the Finest and most Delicate Part of God's Creation; the Glory of her Maker, and the great Instance of his singular regard to Man, his Darling Creature, to whom he gave the best Gift either God could bestow, or man receive: And 'tis the sordid'st Piece of Folly and Ingratitude in the world, to withhold from the Sex the due Lustre which the advantages of Education gives to the Natural Beauty of their Minds.

A Woman well Bred and well Taught, furnish'd with the additional Accomplishments of Knowledge and Behaviour, *is a Creature without comparison*; her Society is the Emblem of sublimer Enjoyments; her Person is Angelick, and her Conversation heavenly; she is all Softness and Sweetness, Peace, Love, Wit, and Delight: She is every way suitable to the sublimest Wish; and the man that has such a one to his Portion, has nothing to do but to rejoice in her, and be thankful.

An Argument Shewing, that a Standing Army, with Consent of Parliament, is not Inconsistent with a Free Government   1698

After a war which had exhausted both antagonists, France and England signed the Treaty of Ryswick on 20 September 1697. Louis XIV, however, was determined to increase his military strength in order to take advantage of the situation which would follow the expected death of Charles II of Spain; William III was equally determined—if Parliament agreed—to keep England in military readiness to meet such a threat. But Parliament strongly resisted the idea of a standing army in time of peace. The issue was debated by various pamphleteers, among the most able being John Trenchard and Walter Moyle whose *Argument shewing that a Standing Army is inconsistent with a Free Government* appeared in December 1697. In the same month Defoe replied with *Some Reflections on a Pamphlet lately Publish'd*. Further contributions to the debate included Defoe's second pamphlet (published anonymously) which is printed below. It is one of Defoe's finest pieces of political rhetoric, admirably designed to appeal to the freeholders to whom it was primarily addressed.

The Preface

The Present Pen and Ink War rais'd against a Standing Army, has more ill Consequences in it, than are at first Sight to be Discern'd. The Pretence is specious, and the cry of Liberty is very pleasing; but the Principle is Mortally Contagious and Destructive of the Essential Safety of the Kingdom; Liberty and Property, are the Glorious Attributes of the English Nation; and the dearer they are to us, the less Danger we are in of Loosing them; but I cou'd never yet see it prov'd, that the danger of loosing them by a small Army was such as we shou'd expose our selves to all the World for it. Some People talk so big of our own Strength, that they think England able to Defend it self against all the World. I presume such talk without Book; I think the prudentest Course is to prevent the Trial, and that is only to hold the Ballance of Europe as the King now does; and if there be a War to keep it abroad. How these Gentlemen will do that with a Militia, I shou'd be glad to see Proposed; 'tis not the King of England alone, but the Sword of England in the Hand of the King, that gives Laws of Peace and War now to Europe; And those who would thus write the Sword out of his Hand in time of Peace, bid the fairest of any Men in the World to renew the War.

The Arguments against an Army have been strongly urg'd; and the Authors with an unusual Assurance, Boast already of their Conquest, tho' their Armour is not yet put off. I think their Triumph goes before their Victory; and if Books and Writing will not, God be thanked the Parliament will Confute them, by taking care to maintain such Forces, and no more, as they think needful for our safety abroad, without danger at home, and leaving it to time to make it appear, that such an Army, with Consent of Parliament, is not inconsistent with a Free Government, &c.

An Argument shewing, that a Standing Army, with Consent of Parliament, is not Inconsistent with a Free Government, &c.

In the Great Debates about a Standing Army; and in all the Arguments us'd on one side and t'other, in the Case it seems to me, that both Parties are Guilty of running into the Extreams of the Controversie.

Some have taken up such terrible Notions of an Army, that take it how you will, call it what you will; be it Rais'd, Paid or Commanded by whom you will, and let the Circumstances be alter'd never so much, the Term is synonimous, an Army is an Army; and if they don't Enslave us, the Thanks is not to our good Conduct; for so many Soldiers, so many Masters: They may do it if they will; and if they do not do it now, they may do it in another Reign, when a King shall arise who knows not *Joseph,* and therefore the Risque is not to be run by any means: From hence they draw the Consequence, *That a Standing Army is Inconsistent with a Free Government,* &c. which is the Title to the Argument.

This we find back'd by a Discourse of *Militia's,* and by a Second part of the Argument,[1] &c. and all these Three, which seem to me to be wrote by the same Hand, agree in this Point in General, That the War being at an end, *no forces at all* are to be kept in Pay, *no Men* to be Maintained whose Profession is bearing Arms, whose Commission is to Kill and Slay, as he has it in *the Second Part;* but they must be Dismist, as Men for whom there is no more Occasion against an Enemy, and are dangerous to be kept up, least they find Occasion against our selves.

The Advocates for the Necessity of a *Standing Army,* seem to make light of all these Fears and Jealousies; and Plead the Circumstances of the Kingdom, with Relation to our Leagues and Confederacys abroad, the Strength of our Neighbours, a Pretender to the Crown in Being, the Uncertainties of Leagues, and the like, as Arguments to prove an Army necessary. I must own these are no Arguments any longer than those Circumstances continue, and therefore can amount to no more than to argue the necessity of an Army for a time, which time none of them has ventured to Assign, nor to say how, being once Establish'd, we shall be sure to be rid of them, in case a new King shou'd succeed before the time be expir'd, who may not value our Liberty at the rate his present Majesty has done.

I desire calmly to consider both these Extreams, and if it be possible, to find out the safe *Medium* which may please us all.

If there be any Person who has an ill Design in pushing thus against the Soldery, I am not to expect, that less than a Disbanding the whole Army will satisfie him; but such who have no other End than preserving our Liberties entire, *and leaving them so to Posterity,* will be satisfied with what they know is sufficient to that End; *for he who is not content with what will fully answer the End he proposes, has some other End than that which he proposes.* I make no Reflections upon any Party, but I propose to direct this Discourse to the Honest well meaning English-Freeholder, who has a share in the *Terra firma,* and therefore is concern'd to preserve Freedom to the Inhabitant that loves his Liberty better than his Life, and won't sell it for Money; and this is the Man who has the most

37

reason to fear a Standing Army, for he has something to loose; as he is most concern'd for the Safety of a Ship, who has a Cargo on her Bottom.

This Man is the hardest to be made believe that he cannot be safe without an Army, because he finds he is not easie with one. To this Man all the sad Instances of the Slavery of Nations, by Standing Armies, stand as so many Buoys to warn him of the Rocks which other Free Nations have split upon; and therefore 'tis to this Man we are to speak.

And in order to state the Case right, we are to distinguish first between *England* formerly, and *England* now; between a Standing Army able to enslave the Nation, and a certain Body of Forces enough to make us safe.

England now is in sundry Circumstances, different from *England* formerly, with respect to the Manner of Fighting, the Circumstances of our Neighbours, and of our Selves; and there are some Reasons why a Militia are not, and perhaps I might make it out cannot be made fit for the Uses of the present Wars. In the ancient Times of *England*'s Power, we were for many years the Invaders of our Neighbours, and quite out of fear of Invasions at home; but before we arriv'd to that Magnitude in the World, 'tis to be observed we were hardly ever invaded, but we were conquer'd, *William* the Conqueror was the last; and if the Spaniard did not do the same, 'twas because God set the Elements in Battel array against them, and they were prevented bringing over the Prince of *Parma*'s[2] Army; which if they had done, 'twould have gone very hard with us; but we owe it wholly to Providence.

I believe it may be said, that from that Time to this Day, the Kingdom has never been without some Standing Troops of Souldiers entertain'd in pay, and always either kept at Home or employ'd Abroad; and yet no evil Consequence follow'd, nor do I meet with any Votes of the Parliament against them as Grievances, or Motions made to Disband them, till the Days of King *Charles* the First. Queen *Elizabeth*, tho' she had no *Guard du Corps*, yet she had her *Guards du Terres*. She had even to her last hour several Armies, *I may call them*, in Pay among Forreign States and Princes, which upon any visible Occasion were ready to be call'd Home. King *James* the First had the same in *Holland*, in the Service of *Gustavus Adolphus* King of *Sweden*, and in the Unfortunate Service of the King of *Bohemia*; and that Scotch Regiment, known by the name of *Douglass*'s Regiment, have been, (*they say*) a Regiment Two hundred and fifty Years. King *Charles* the First had the same in the several Expeditions for the Relief of *Rochel*,[3] and that fatal Descent upon the Isle of *Rhe*,[4] and in his Expeditions into *Scotland*; and they would do well to reconcile their Discourse to it self, who say in one place, *If King* Charles *had had Five thousand Men, the Nation had never struck one stroak for their Liberties;* and in another, *That the Parliament were like to have been petitioned out of doors by an Army a hundred and fifty Miles off, tho' there was a Scotch Army at the Heels of them:* for to me it appears that King *Charles* the First had an Army then, and would have kept it, but that he had not the Purse to pay them, of which more may be said hereafter.

But *England* now stands in another Posture, our Peace at Home seems secure, and I believe it is so; but to maintain our Peace abroad, 'tis necessary to enter into Leagues and Confederacies: Here is one Neighbour grown too great for all the rest; *as they are single States or Kingdoms,* and therefore to mate him, several must joyn for mutual Assistance, according to the Scotch Law of Duelling, *that if one can't beat you ten shall.* These Alliances are under certain Stipulations and Agreements, with what Strength and in what Places, to aid and assist one another; and to perform these Stipulations, something of Force must be at hand if occasion require. That these Confederacies are of absolute and indispensible necessity, to preserve the Peace of a weaker against a stronger Prince, past Experience has taught us too plainly to need an Argument.

There is another constant Maxim of the present State of the War; and that is, *carry the War into your Enemies Country, and always keep it out of your own.* This is an Article has been very much opposed 'tis true; and some, who knew no better, would talk much of the fruitless Expence of a War abroad; as if it was not worth while to defend your Confederates Country, to make it a Barrier to your own. This is too weak an Argument also to need any trouble about; but this again makes it absolutely necessary to have always some Troops ready to send to the assistance of those Confederates if they are invaded. Thus at the Peace of *Nimeguen,*[5] six Regiments were left in *Holland,* to continue there in time of Peace, to be ready in case of a Rupture. To say, that instead of this we will raise them for their assistance when wanted, would be something, if this potent Neighbour, were not the *French* King, whose Velocity of Motion the *Dutch* well remember in 1672.[6] But then, *say they,* we may send our Militia. First, *The King can't command them to go*; and Secondly, if he could, *no body wou'd accept them*; and if they would go, and would be accepted of, *they would be good for nothing*: If we have no Forces to assist a Confederate, who will value our Friendship, or assist us if we wanted it? To say we are Self-dependent, and shall never need the Assistance of our Neighbour, is to say what we are not sure of, and this is certain it is as needful to maintain the Reputation of *England* in the Esteem of our Neighbours, as 'tis to defend our Coasts in case of an Invasion; for keep up the Reputation of our Power, and we shall never be Invaded.

If our Defence from Insurrections or Invasions, were the only necessary part of a future War, I shou'd be the readier to grant the Point, and to think our Militia might be made useful; but our business is *Principiis Obsta*, to beat the Enemy before he comes to our own door. Our Business in case of a Rupture, is to aid our Confederate Princes, that they may be able to stand between us and

Danger: Our Business is to preserve *Flanders*, to Garrison the Frontier Towns, and be in the Field in Conjunction with the Confederate Armies: This is the way to prevent Invasions, and Descents: And when they can tell us that our Militia is proper for this work, then we will say something to it.

I'll suppose for once what I hope may never fall out, That a Rupture of this Peace shou'd happen, and the *French*, according to Custom, break suddenly into *Flanders*, and over-run it, and after that *Holland*, what Condition wou'd such a Neighbourhood of such a Prince, reduce us to? If it be answer'd again, Soldiers may be raised to assist them. I answer, as before, let those who say so, read the History of the *French* King's Irruption into *Holland* in the year 1672, where he conquer'd Sixty strong fortified Towns in six Weeks time: And tell me what it will be to the purpose to raise Men, to fight an Enemy after the Conquest is made?

'Twill not be amiss to observe here that the Reputation and Influence the *English* Nation has had abroad among the Princes of *Christendom*, has been always more or less according as the Power of the Prince, to aid and assist, or to injure and offend, was Esteem'd. Thus Queen *Elizabeth* carried her Reputation abroad by the Courage of her *English* Souldiers and Seamen; and on the contrary, what a ridiculous Figure did King *James*, with his *Beati Pacifici*, make in all the Courts of *Christendom*? How did the Spàniard and the Emperor *banter* and *buffoon* him? How was his Ambassador asham'd to treat for him, while Count *Colocedo*[7] told Count *Mansfield*,[8] *That his New Master* (meaning King *James*) *knew neither how to make Peace or War*? King *Charles* the First far'd much in the same manner: And how was it altered in the Case of *Oliver*?

> Tho' his Government did a Tyrant resemble;
> He made England Great, and her Enemies tremble.
>
> Dialogue of the Horses.[9]

And what is it places the present King at the Helm of the Confederacies? Why do they commit their Armies to his Charge, and appoint the Congress of their Plenipotentiaries at his Court? Why do Distressed Princes seek his Mediation, as the Dukes of *Holstein, Savoy*, and the like? Why did the Emperor and the King of *Spain* leave the whole Management of the Peace to him? 'Tis all the Reputation of his Conduct and the *English* Valour under him; and 'tis absolutely necessary to support this Character which *England* now bears in the World, for the great Advantages which may and will be made from it; and this Character can never Live, nor these Allyances be supported with no Force at Hand to perform the Conditions.

These are some Reasons why a Force is necessary, but the Question is, What Force? For I Grant, it does not follow from hence, that a great Army must be kept on Foot in time of Peace, as the Author of the Second Part of the Argument says is pleaded for.

Since then no Army, and a great Army, are Extreams equally dangerous, the one to our Liberty at Home, and the other to our Reputation Abroad, and the Safety of our Confederates; it remains to Inquire what *Medium* is to be found out; or in plain *English*, what Army may, with Safety to our Liberties, be Maintained in *England*, or what Means may be found out to make such an Army serviceable for the Defence of us and our Allies, and yet not dangerous to our Constitution.

That any Army at all can be Safe, *the Argument denies*, but that cannot be made out; a Thousand Men is an Army as much as 100000; as the *Spanish* Armado is call'd, *An Armado*, tho' they seldom fit out above Four Men of War; and on this Account I must crave leave to say, I do Confute the Assertion in the Title of the Argument, that a Standing Army is Inconsistent with a Free Government, and I shall further do it by the Authority of Parliament.

In the Claim of Right,[10] presented to the present King, and which he Swore to observe, as the *Pacta Conventa* of the Kingdom, it is declar'd, *in hac verba, That the Raising or Keeping a Standing Army within the Kingdom in time of Peace, unless it be by Consent of Parliament, is against Law.*

This plainly lays the whole stress of the thing, not against the thing it self, *A Standing Army,* nor against the Season, *in time of Peace,* but against the Circumstance, *Consent of Parliament*; and I think nothing is more Rational than to Conclude from thence, that a Standing Army in time of Peace, with Consent of Parliament, is not against Law, and I may go on, nor is not Inconsistent with a Free Government, nor Destructive of the *English* Monarchy.

There are Two Distinctions necessary therefore in the present Debate, to bring the Question to a narrow Compass.

First, *I distinguish between a Great Army and a small Army. And*
Secondly, *I distinguish between an Army kept on Foot without Consent of Parliament, and an Army with Consent of Parliament.*

And whereas we are told, an Army of Soldiers is an Army of Masters, and the Consent of Parliament don't alter it, but they may turn them out of doors who Rais'd them, as they did the Long Parliament. The First distinction answers that; for if a great Army may do it, a small Army can't; and then the Second Distinction regulates the First. For it cannot be supposed, but the Parliament when they give that Consent which can only make an Army Lawful, will not Consent to a larger Army then they can so Master, as that the liberties or People of *England,* shall never be in danger from them.

No Man will say this cannot be, because the Number may be supposed as small as you please; but to avoid the Sophistry of an Argument, I'll suppose the very Troops which we see the Parliament have not Voted to be Disbanded; that is, those which were on Foot before the Year 1680.[11] No Man will deny them to be a Standing Army, and yet sure no Man will imagine any danger to our Liberties from them.

We are ask'd, if you establish an Army, and a Revenue to pay them, *How shall we be sure they will not continue themselves*? But will any Man ask that Question of such an Army as this? Can Six Thousand Men tell the Nation they won't Disband, but will continue themselves, and then Raise Money to do it? Can they Exact it by Military Execution? If they can, *our Militia must be very despicable*. The keeping such a Remnant of an Army does not hinder but the Militia may be made as useful as you please; and the more useful you make it, the less danger from this Army: And however it may have been the Business of our Kings to make the Militia as useless as they could, the present King never shew'd any Tokens of such a Design. Nor is it more than will be needful, for 6000 Men by themselves won't do, if the Invasion we speak of should ever be attempted. What has been said of the Appearance of the People on the *Purbeck fancied Invasion*,[12] was very true; but I must say, had it been a true One of Forty Thousand Regular Troops, all that Appearance cou'd have done nothing, but have drove the Country in order to starve them, and then have run away: I am apt enough to grant what has been said of the Impracticableness of any Invasion upon us, while we are Masters at Sea; but I am sure the Defence of *England's* Peace, lies in making War in *Flanders*. Queen *Elizabeth* found it so, her way to beat the *Spaniards*, was by helping the *Dutch* to do it. And she as much Defended *England* in aiding Prince *Maurice*, to win the Great Battel of *Newport*,[13] as she did in Defeating their *Invincible Armado*. *Oliver Cromwel* took the same Course; for he no sooner declared War against *Spain*, but he Embark'd his Army for *Flanders*: The late King *Charles* did the same against the *French*, when after the Peace of *Nimeguen*, Six Regiments of *English* and *Scots* were always left in the Service of the *Dutch*, and the present War is a further Testimony: For where has it been Fought, not in *England*, God be thanked, but in *Flanders*? And what are the Terms of the Peace, but more Frontier Towns in *Flanders*? And what is the Great Barrier of this Peace, but *Flanders*; the Consequence of this may be guess'd by the Answer King *William* gave when Prince of *Orange*, in the late Treaty of *Nimeguen*; when, to make the Terms the easier, 'twas offered, *That a Satisfaction shou'd be made to him by the* French, *for his Lands in* Luxemburgh; to which the Prince reply'd, *He would part with all his Lands in* Luxemburgh *to get the* Spaniards *one good Frontier Town in* Flanders. The reason is plain; for every one of those Towns, tho' they were immediately the *Spaniards*, were really Bulwarks to keep the *French* the further off from his own Country; and thus it is now: And how our Militia can have any share in this part of the War, I cannot imagine. It seems strange to me to reconcile the Arguments made use of to magnifie the Serviceableness of the Militia, and the Arguments to enforce the Dread of a Standing Army; for they stand like two Batteries one against another, where the Shot from one dismounts the Cannon of the other: *If a small Army may enslave us, our Militia are good for nothing; if good for nothing, they cannot defend us,* and then an Army is necessary: *If they are good, and are able to defend us, then a small Army can never hurt us,* for what may defend us Abroad, may defend us at Home; and I wonder this is not consider'd. And what is plainer in the World than that the Parliament of *England* have all along agreed to this Point, That a Standing Army in time of Peace, *with Consent of Parliament,* is not against Law. The Establishment of the Forces in the time of K. *Charles* II. was not as I remember ever objected against in Parliament, at least we may say the Parliament permitted them if they did not establish them: And the Present Parliament seems enclin'd to continue the Army on the same foot, so far as may be suppos'd from their Vote to disband all the Forces raised since 1680. To affirm then, *That a Standing Army,* (without any of the former Distinctions) *is Inconsistent,* &c. is to argue against the General Sense of the Nation, the Permission of the Parliament for 50 years past, and the Present apparent Resolutions of the best Composed House that perhaps ever entred within those Walls.

To this House the whole Nation has left the Case, to act as they see cause; to them we have committed the Charge of our Liberties, nay the King himself has only told them His Opinion, with the Reasons for it, *without leading them at all*; and the Article of the *Claim of Right* is left in full force: For this Consent of Parliament is now left the whole and sole Judge,[14] Whether *an Army* or *no Army*; and if it Votes an Army, 'tis left still the sole Judge of the Quantity, *how many,*or *how few.*

Here it remains to enquire the direct Meaning of those words, *Unless it be by Consent of Parliament,* and I humbly suppose they may, among other things, include these Particulars.

1. *That they be rais'd and continued not by a Tacit, but Explicite Consent of Parliament; or, to speak directly, by an Act of Parliament.*
2. *That they be continued no longer than such Explicite Consent shall limit and appoint.*

If these two Heads are granted in the word *Consent,* I am bold to affirm, Such an *Army is not Inconsistent with a Free Government,* &c.

I am as positively assur'd of the Safety of our Liberties under the Conduct of King and Parliament, while they concur, *as I am of the Salvation of Believers by the Passion of our Saviour*; and I hardly think 'tis fit for a private Man to impose his positive Rules on them for Method, any more than 'tis to limit the Holy Spirit, whose free Agency is beyond his Power: For the King, Lords and Commons, can never err while they agree; nor is an Army of 20 or 40000 Men *either* a Scarcrow enough to enslave us, while under that Union.

If this be allow'd, then the Question before us is, What may conduce to make the Harmony between the King, Lords and Commons eternal? And so the Debate about an Army ceases.

But to leave that Question, since Frailty attends the best of Persons, and Kings have their *faux Pas*, as well as other Men, we cannot expect the Harmony to be immortal; and therefore to provide for the worst, our Parliaments have made their own Consent the only Clause that can make an Army Legitimate: But to say that an Army directly as an Army, without these Distinctions, is destructive of the *English* Monarchy, and Inconsistent with a Free Government, *&c.* is to say then that the Parliament can destroy the *English* Monarchy, and can Establish that which is Inconsistent with a Free Government; which is ridiculous. But then we are told, that *the Power of the Sword was first placed in the Lords or Barons, and how they serv'd the King in his Wars with themselves and their Vassals, and that the King had no Power to Invade the Priviledges of the Barons, having no other Forces than the Vassals of his own Demeasnes to follow him:* And this Form is applauded as an extraordinary Constitution, *because there is no other Limitation of a Monarchy of any Signification than such as places the Sword in the hand of the Subject: And all such Governments where the Prince has the Power of the Sword, tho' the People have the Power of the Purse, are no more Monarchies but Tyrannies: For not only that Government is tyrannical which is tyrannically exercis'd, but all Governments are tyrannical which have not in their Constitution sufficient Security against the Arbitrary Power of their Prince*; that is, which have not the Power of the Sword to Imploy against him if need be.

Thus we come to the Argument: Which is not how many Troops may be allow'd, or how long; but in short, *No Mercenary-Troops at all can be maintain'd without Destroying our Constitution, and Metamorphizing our Government into a Tyranny.*

I admire how the Maintainer of this Basis came to omit giving us an Account of another Part of History very needful to examine, in handing down the True Notion of Government in this Nation *viz.* of Parliaments. To supply which, and to make way for what follows, I must take leave to tell the Reader, that about the time, when this Service by Villenage and Vassalage began to be resented by the People, and by Peace and Trade they grew rich, and the Power of the Barons being too great, frequent Commotions, Civil Wars, and Battels, were the Consequence, nay sometimes without concerning the King in the Quarrel: One Nobleman would Invade another, in which the weakest suffered most, *and the poor Man's Blood was the Price of all*; the People obtain'd Priviledges of their own, and oblig'd the King and the Barons to accept of an *Equilibrium*; this we call a Parliament: And from this the Due Ballance, we have so much heard of is deduced. I need not lead my Reader to the Times and Circumstances of this, but this Due Ballance is the Foundation on which we now stand, and which the Author of the Argument so highly applaudes as the best in the World; and I appeal to all Men to judge if this Ballance be not a much nobler Constitution in all its Points, than the old *Gothick* Model of Government.

In that the Tyranny of the Barons was intollerable, the Misery and Slavery of the Common People insupportable, their Blood and Labour was at the absolute Will of the Lord, *and often sacrifice to their private Quarrels:* They were as much at his beck as his Pack of Hounds were at the Sound of his Horne; whether it was to march against a Forreign Enemy, or *against their own Natural Prince:* So that this was but exchanging one Tyrant for Three hundred, for so many the Barons of *England* were accounted at least. And this was the Effect of the Security vested in the People, against the Arbitrary Power of the King; which was to say the Barons took care to maintain their own Tyranny, and to prevent the Kings Tyrannizing over them.

But 'tis said, *the Barons growing poor by the Luxury of the Times, and the Common People growing rich, they exchang'd their Vassalage for Leases, Rents, Fines, and the like.* They did so, and thereby became entituled to the Service of themselves; and so overthrew the Settlement, and from hence came a *House of Commons:* And I hope *England* has reason to value the Alteration. Let them that think not reflect on the Freedoms the Commons enjoy in *Poland*, where the *Gothick* Institution remains, and they will be satisfied.

In this Establishment of a Parliament, the Sword is indeed trusted in the Hands of the King, and *the Purse in the Hands of the People*; the People cannot make Peace or War without the King, nor the King cannot raise or maintain an Army without the People; and this is the True Ballance.

But we are told, *The Power of the Purse is not a sufficient Security without the Power of the Sword:* What! not against Ten thousand Men? To answer this, 'tis necessary to examine how far the Power of the Sword is in the Hands of the People already, and next whether the Matter of Fact be true.

I say the Sword is in part in the Hands of the People already, by the Militia, who, as the Argument says *are the People themselves*. And how are they Ballanc'd? 'Tis true, they are Commissioned by the King, but they may refuse to meet twice, till the first Pay is reimburst to the Countrey: And where shall the King Raise it without a Parliament? that very Militia would prevent him. So that our Law therein Authorizing the Militia to refuse the Command of the King, tacitly puts the Sword into the Hands of the People.

I come now to Examine the Matter of Fact, *That the Purse is not an Equivalent to the Sword,* which I deny to be true; and here 'twill be necessary to Examine, How often our Kings of *England* have Raised Armies on their own Heads, but have been forced to Disband them for want of Moneys, nay, have been forced to call a Parliament to Raise Money to Disband them.

King *Charles* the First is an Instance of both these; for his First Army against the *Scots* he was forced to Dismiss for want of Pay; and then was forced to call a Parliament to Pay and Dismiss the *Scots*; and tho' he had an Army in the Field at the Pacification, and a Church Army too, yet he durst not attempt to Raise Money by them.

I am therefore to affirm, *that the Power of the Purse is an Equivalent to the Power of the Sword;* and I believe I can make it appear, if I may be allowed to instance in those numerous Armies which *Gaspar Coligny,* Admiral of *France,* and *Henry* the Fourth King of *Navar,* and *William* the First P. of Orange brought out of *Germany* into *France,* and into the Low Countries, which all vanished, and could attempt nothing for want of a Purse to maintain them: But to come nearer, what made the Efforts of King *Charles* all Abortive, but *Want of the Purse?* Time was, he had the Sword in his Hand, when the Duke of *Buckingham* went on those Fruitless Voyages to *Rochell,* and himself afterwards to *Scotland,* he had Forces on Foot, a great many more than Five Thousand, which the Argument mentions, but he had not the Purse, at last he attempted to take it without a Parliament, *and that Ruin'd him.* King *Charles* the Second found the Power of the Purse, so much out-ballanced the Power of the Sword, that he sat still, and let the Parliament Disband his Army for him, *almost whether he would or no.*

Besides the Power of the Purse in *England,* differs from what the same thing is in other Countries, because 'tis so Sacred a thing, that *no King ever touch'd at it but he found his Ruine in it.* Nay, 'tis so odious to the Nation, that whoever attempts it, must at the same time be able to make an Entire Conquest or nothing.

If then neither *the Consent of Parliament,* nor the *smallness of an Army proposed,* nor the Power of *the Sword in the Hands of the Militia,* which are the People themselves, nor *the Power of the Purse,* are not a sufficient Ballance against the Arbitrary Power of the King, what shall we say? Are Ten Thousand Men in Arms, without Money, without Parliament Authority, hem'd in with the whole Militia of *England*, and *Dam'd by the Laws?* Are they of such Force as to break our Constitution? I cannot see any reason for such a Thought. The Parliament of *England* is a Body, of whom we may say, *That no Weapon Formed against them cou'd ever Prosper*; and they know their own Strength, and they know what Force is needful, and what hurtful, and they will certainly maintain the *First* and Disband the *Last*.

It may be said here, *'Tis not the fear of Ten Thousand Men, 'tis not the matter of an Army, but 'tis the Thing it self; grant a Revenue for Life, and the next King will call it,* My Revenue, *and so grant an Army for this King, and the next will say,* Give Me my Army.

To which I Answer, That these things have been no oftner ask'd in Parliament than deny'd; and we have so many Instances in our late Times of *the Power of the Purse,* that it seems strange to me, that it should not be allowed to be a sufficient Ballance.

King *Charles* the Second, as I hinted before, was very loath to part with his Army Rais'd in 1676, but he was forced to it for want of Money to pay them; he durst not try whether when *Money had Raised an Army, an Army cou'd not Raise Money*. 'Tis true, his Revenues were large, but Frugality was not his Talent, and that ruin'd the Design. King *James* the Second was a good Husband, and that very Husbandry had almost Ruin'd the Nation; for his Revenues being well managed, he maintain'd an Army out of it. For 'tis well known, the Parliament never gave him a Penny towards it; but he never attempted to make his Army Raise any Money; if he had, 'tis probable his Work had been sooner done than it was.

But pray let us Examine abroad, if *the Purse has not Governed all the Wars of* Europe. The *Spaniards* were once the most powerful People in *Europe*; their Infantry were in the Days of the Prince of *Parma*, the most Invincible Troops in the World. The *Dutch*, who were then his Subjects, and on whom he had Levied immense Sums of Money, had the 10th Penny demanded of them, and the Demand back'd by a great Army of these very *Spaniards*, which, among many other Reasons caused them to Revolt. The Duke *D'Alva*[15] afterwards attempted for his Master to raise this Tax by his Army, by which he lost the whole *Netherlands*, who are now the Richest People in the World; and the *Spaniard* is now become the meanest and most despicable People in *Europe*, and that only because they are the Poorest.

The present War is another Instance, which having lasted Eight Years, is at last brought to this Conclusion, *That he who had the longest Sword has yielded to them who had the longest Purse.*

The late King *Charles* the First, is another most lively Instance of this Matter, to what lamentable Shifts did he drive himself? and how many despicable Steps did he take, rather than call a Parliament, which he hated to think of. And yet, tho' he had an Army on Foot, he was forced to do it, *or starve all his Men*; had it been to be done, he wou'd have done it. 'Tis true, 'twas said the Earl of *Strafford* propos'd a Scheme, *to bring over an Army out of* Ireland, *to force* England *to his Terms;* but the Experiment was thought too desperate to be attempted, and the very Project Ruin'd the Projector; such an ill Fate attends every Contrivance against the Parliament of *England*.

But I think I need go no further on that Head: The Power of Raising Money is wholly in the Parliament, as a Ballance to the Power of Raising Men, which is in the King; and all the Reply I can meet with is, *That this Ballance signifies nothing, for an Army can Raise Money, as well as Money Raise an Army; to which I Answer,* besides what has been said already; *I do not think it practicable in* England: The greatest Armies, in the Hands of the greatest Tyrants we ever had in *England*, never durst attempt it. We find several Kings in *England* have attempted to Raise Money without a Parliament, and have tryed all the means they could to bring it to pass; and they need not go back to *Richard* the Second, to *Edward* the Second, to *Edward* the Fourth, to *Henry* the Eighth, or to *Charles* the First, to remind the Reader of what all Men who know any thing of History are acquainted with: But not a King ever yet attempted to Raise Money, by Military Execution, or Billetting Soldiers upon the Country. King *James* the Second had the greatest Army and the best, as to Discipline, that any King ever had; *and his desperate Attempts on our Liberties show'd his good Will,* yet he never came to that Point. I won't deny, but that our Kings have been willing to have Armies at Hand, to back them in their Arbitrary Proceedings, and the Subjects may have been aw'd by them from a more early Resentment; but I must observe, that all the Invasion of our Rights, and all the Arbitrary Methods of our Governors, has been under pretences of Law. King *Charles* the First Levy'd Ship-Money as his due, and the Proclamations for that purpose cite the pretended Law, that in Case of Danger from a Foreign Enemy, Ships shou'd be fitted out to Defend us, and all Men were bound to contribute to the Charge; *Coat* and *Conduct Money*[16] had the like Pretences; Charters were subverted by *Quo Warrantoes,*[17] and Proceedings at Law; Patriots were Murther'd under Formal Prosecutions, and all was pretended to be done legally.

I know but one Instance in all our *English* Story, where the Souldery were employ'd as Souldiers, in open Defyance of Law, to destroy the Peoples Liberties by a Military Absolute Power, and that stands as an Everlasting Brand of Infamy upon our Militia; and is an Instance to prove, beyond the Power of a Reply, *That even our Militia, under a bad Government, let them be our selves, and the People, and all those fine things never so much* are under ill Officers and ill Management, *as dangerous as any Souldery whatever*, will be as Insolent, and do the Drudgery of a Tyrant as effectually.

In the Year [1682] when Mr. *Dubois* and Mr. *Papillon*, a Member of the Present Parliament, were chosen Sheriffs of *London*, and Sir *John Moor*, under pretence of the Authority of the Chair, pretended to nominate one Sheriff himself, and leave the City to choose but one, and confirm the Choice of the Mayor, the Citizens struggled for their Right, and stood firm to their Choice, and several Adjournments were made to bring over the Majority of the Livery, but in vain:[18] At length the Day came when the Sheriffs were to be sworn, and when the Livery-men assembled at *Guild hall* to swear their Sheriffs, they found the Hall Garrison'd with a Company of Trained-Bands under Lieutenant Coll. *Quiney*, a Citizen himself, and most of the Soldiers, Citizens and Inhabitants; and by this Force the Ancient Livery-men were shut out, and several of them thrown down, and insolently used, and the Sheriffs thrust away from the Hustings, and who the Lord Mayor pleased was Sworn in an open Defiance of the Laws of the Kingdom, and Priviledges of the City. *This was done by the Militia to their Everlasting Glory*, and I do not remember the like done by a Standing Army of Mercenaries, in this Age at least. Nor is a Military Tyranny practicable in *England*, if we consider the power the Laws have given to the Civil Magistrate, unless you at the same time imagine that Army large enough to subdue the whole *English* Nation at once, which if it can be effected by such an Army as the Parliament now seem enclined to permit, we are in a very mean Condition.

I know it may be objected here, that the Forces which were on Foot before 1680, are not the Army in Debate, and that the Design of the Court was to have a much greater Force.

I do not know that, but this I know, that *those Forces were an Army*, and the Design of all these Oponents of an Army is in so many words, against *any Army at all*, small as well as great; a Tenet absolutely destructive of the present Interest of *England*, and of the Treaties and Alliances made by His Majesty with the Princes and States of *Europe*, who depend so much on his Aid in Guard of the present Peace.

The Power of making Peace or War is vested in the King: 'Tis part of his Prerogative, but 'tis implicitly in the People, because their Negative as to Payment, does really Influence all those Actions. Now If when the King makes War, the Subject shou'd refuse to assist him, the whole Nation would be ruin'd: Suppose in the Leagues and Confederacies His Present Majesty is engag'd in for the Maintenance of the present Peace, all the Confederates are bound in case of a Breach to assist one another with so many Men, say Ten thousand for the *English* Quota, more or less, where shall they be found? *Must they stay till they are Rais'd?* To what purpose would it be then for any Confederate to depend upon *England* for Assistance?

It may be said indeed, if you are so engag'd by Leagues or Treaties, you may hire Foreign Troops to assist till you can raise them. This Answer leads to several things which would take up too much room here.

Foreign Troops require Two things to procure them; Time to Negotiate for them, which may not be to be spar'd, for they may be almost as soon rais'd; Time for their March from *Germany*, for there are none nearer to be hir'd, and Money to Hire them, which must be had by Parliament, or the King must have it ready: If by Parliament, that is a longer way still; if without, that opens a worse Gate to Slavery than t'other: For if a King have Money, he can raise Men or hire Men when he will; and you are in as much danger then, and more than you can be in now from a Standing Army: So that since giving Money is the same thing as giving Men, as it appear'd in the late K. *James*'s Reign, both must be prevented, or both may be allow'd.

But the Parliament we see needs no Instructions in this Matter, and therefore are providing to reduce the Forces to the same *Quota* they were in before 1680, by which means all the fear of Invading our Liberties will be at an end, the Army being so very small that 'tis impossible, and yet the King will have always a Force at hand to assist his Neighbours, or defend himself till more can be Raised. The Forces before 1680 were an Army, and if they were an Army by Consent of Parliament, they were a Legal Army; and if they were Legal, then they were not inconsistent *with a Free Government, &c.* for nothing can be Inconsistent with *a Free Government*, which is done according to the Laws of that Government: And if a *Standing Army* has been in *England* Legally, then I have proved, *That a Standing Army is not Inconsistent with a Free Government, &c.*

FINIS

The True-Born Englishman
A Satyr   1701

The argument over a standing army (which provoked Defoe's pamphlet printed above) frequently prompted bitter attacks on William III's attempt to retain the services of his Dutch Guards; a parliamentary resolution reducing the army to about 8,000 men stipulated that these were 'to consist of his Majesty's natural born subjects'. The motive behind this censure was largely jealousy of the foreigner; it caused William serious concern and led him at least to contemplate abdication. The controversy continued both inside Parliament and outside. On 1 August 1700 there appeared what Defoe later described (see p. 168) as 'a vile abhorred Pamphlet, in very ill verse, written by one Mr Tutchin, and call'd *The Foreigners*'. Defoe was 'filled with a kind of Rage'; his common sense as well as his loyalty to William were affronted; and in January 1701 he published (anonymously) the poem printed below. It was an immediate success; ten genuine and many more spurious editions were printed in 1701. Defoe claimed that the poem gained him the personal friendship of the King; it certainly established a public reputation which he was proud to display on the title-pages of subsequent publications—'By the Author of The True-Born Englishman'.

The text used here is that of the first edition. The extract from the 'Explanatory Preface' comes from the ninth edition (1701) in which it first appeared. Footnotes printed in the text were supplied by Defoe in the original. (For the full text, ed. A. C. Guthkelch, see *Essays and Studies*, IV (1913), 101–50.)

The True-Born Englishman
A Satyr

An Explanatory Preface

... *The Intent of the Satyr is pointed at the Vanity of those who talk of their Antiquity, and value themselves upon their Pedigree, their Ancient Families, and being* True Born; *whereas 'tis impossible we shou'd be* True Born; *and if we could, shou'd have lost by the Bargain.*

These sort of People, who Call themselves True Born, *and tell long Stories of their Families, and like a Nobleman of* Venice, *Think a Foreigner ought not to walk on the same side of the Street with them, are own'd to be meant in this* Satyr. *What they wou'd infer from their long Original, I know not, nor is it easy to make out whether they are the better, or the worse for their Ancestors: Our* English Nation *may value themselves for their* Wit, Wealth, *and* Courage, *and I believe few Nations will dispute it with them; but for long Originals, and Ancient* True Born *Families of* English, *I wou'd advise them to wave the Discourse. A* True English *Man is one that deserves a Character, and I have no where lessened him, that I know of; but as for a* True Born English *Man, I confess I do not understand him.*

From hence I only infer, That an English Man, *of all Men ought not to despise* Foreigners *as such, and I think the Inference is just, since* what they are to day, we were yesterday, and to morrow they will be like us. *If Foreigners Misbehave in their several Stations and Employments,* I have nothing to do with that; *the Laws are open to Punish them equally with Natives, and let them have no Favour.*

But when I see the Town full of Lampoons and Invectives against Dutchmen, Only because they are Foreigners, *and the King Reproached and Insulted by Insolent Pedants, and Ballad-making Poets, for employing Foreigners; and for being a Foreigner himself, I confess my self mov'd by it to remind our Nation of their own Original, thereby to let them see what a Banter is put upon our selves in it; since speaking of* Englishmen ab Origine, *we are really all Foreigners our selves.*

I could go on to prove 'tis also Impolitick in us to discourage Foreigners; since 'tis easy to make it appear that the Multitudes of Foreign Nations who have took Sanctuary here, have been the greatest Additions to the Wealth and Strength of the Nation; the great Essential whereof is the Number of its Inhabitants: Nor would this Nation have ever arriv'd to the Degree of Wealth and Glory it now boasts of, if the addition of Foreign Nations both as to Manufactures and Arms had not been helpful to it. This is so plain, that he who is ignorant of it, is too dull to be talk'd with.

52

The Satyr therefore I must allow to be just, till I am otherwise convinc'd; because nothing can be more ridiculous, than to hear our People boast of that Antiquity, which if it had been true, would have left us in so much worse a Condition than we are in now: Whereas we ought rather to boast among our Neighbours, that we are a part of themselves, of the same Original as they, but better'd by our Climate, and like our Language and Manufactures, deriv'd from them, and improv'd by us to a Perfection greater than they can pretend to. . . .

The Preface

The End of Satyr is Reformation: And the Author, tho he doubts the Work of Conversion is at a general Stop, has put his Hand to the Plow.

I expect a Storm of Ill Language from the Fury of the Town, and especially from those whose English Talent it is to Rail: And without being taken for a Conjurer, I may venture to foretell, That I shall be Cavil'd at about my Mean Stile, Rough Verse, *and* Incorrect Language; *Things I might indeed have taken more Care in. But the Book is Printed; and tho I see some Faults, 'tis too late to mend them. And this is all I think needful to say to them.*

Possibly somebody may take me for a Dutchman, *in which they are mistaken: But I am one that would be glad to see* Englishmen *behave themselves better to Strangers, and to Governors also; that one might not be reproach'd in Foreign Countries, for belonging to a* Nation that wants Manners.

I assure you, Gentlemen, *Strangers use us better abroad; and we can give no reason but our Ill Nature for the contrary here.*

Methinks an Englishman, *who is so proud of being call'd A* Goodfellow, *shou'd be civil: And it cannot be denied but we are in many Cases, and particularly to Strangers, the Churlishest People alive.*

As to Vices, who can dispute our Intemperance, *while an* Honest Drunken Fellow *is a Character in a man's Praise? All our Reformations are Banters, and will be so, till our Magistrates and Gentry Reform themselves by way of Example; then, and not till then, they may be expected to punish others without blushing.*

As to our Ingratitude, I desire to be understood of that particular People, who pretending to be Protestants, have all along endeavour'd to reduce the Liberties and Religion of this Nation into the Hands of King James *and his Popish Powers: Together with such who enjoy the Peace and Protection of the present Government, and yet abuse and affront the King who procur'd it, and openly profess their Uneasiness under him:*

53

These, by whatever Names or Titles they are dignified or distinguished, are the People aim'd at: Nor do I disown, but that it is so much the Temper of an Englishman to abuse his Benefactor, that I could be glad to see it rectified.

They who think I have been guilty of any Error, in exposing the Crimes of my own Countrymen to themselves, may among many honest Instances of the like nature, find the same thing in Mr. Cowly, in his Imitation of the second Olympick Ode of Pindar: His Words are these;

> But in this Thankless World, the Givers
> Are envi'd even by th' Receivers:
> 'Tis now the Cheap and Frugal Fashion,
> Rather to hide than pay an Obligation.
> Nay, 'tis much worse than so;
> It now an *Artifice* doth grow,
> *Wrongs* and *Outrages* to do,
> Lest men should think we *Owe*.

The Introduction

Speak, *Satyr*; for there's none can tell like thee,
Whether' tis Folly, Pride, or Knavery,
That makes this discontented Land appear
Less happy now in Times of Peace,[1] than War:
Why Civil Feuds disturb the Nation more   5
Than all our Bloody Wars have done before.

Fools out of Favour grudge at Knaves in Place,
And men are always honest in Disgrace:
The Court-Preferments make men Knaves in course:
But they which wou'd be in them wou'd be worse.   10
'Tis not at Foreigners that we repine,
Wou'd Foreigners their Perquisites resign:
The Grand Contention's plainly to be seen,
To get some men put out, and some put in.
For this our S[enato]rs make long Harangues,   15
And florid M[embe]rs whet their polish'd Tongues.
Statesmen are always sick of one Disease;
And a good Pension gives them present Ease.

That's the Specifick makes them all content
With any King, and any Government.   20
Good Patriots at Court-Abuses rail,
And all the Nation's Grievances bewail:
But when the *Sov'reign Balsam*'s once appli'd,
The Zealot never fails to change his Side.
And when he must the *Golden Key*[2] resign,   25
The *Railing Spirit* comes about again.

   Who shall this Bubbl'd[3] *Nation disabuse,*
While they their own Felicities refuse?
Who at the Wars have made such mighty Pother,
And now are falling out with one another: 30
With needless Fears the Jealous Nation fill,
And always have been sav'd against their Will:
Who Fifty Millions *Sterling* have disburs'd,
To be with Peace and too much Plenty curs'd.
Who their Old Monarch eagerly undo,   35
And yet uneasily obey the New.
Search, *Satyr*, search, a deep Incision make;
The Poyson's strong, the Antidote's too weak.
'Tis pointed Truth must manage this Dispute,
And down-right English *Englishmen* confute.   40

   Whet thy just Anger at the Nation's Pride;
And with keen Phrase repel the Vicious Tide.
To *Englishmen* their own beginnings show,
And ask them why they slight their Neighbours so.
Go back to Elder Times, and Ages past,   45
And Nations into long Oblivion cast;
To Old *Britannia*'s Youthful Days retire,
And there for *True-Born Englishmen* enquire.
Britannia freely will disown the Name,
And hardly knows her self from whence they came: 50
Wonders that They of all men shou'd pretend
To *Birth* and *Blood*, and for a Name contend.
Go back to Causes where our Follies dwell,
And fetch the dark Original from Hell:
Speak, *Satyr*, for there's none like thee can tell.   55

The True-Born Englishman

PART I

*Wherever God erects a House of Prayer,
The Devil always builds a Chappel there:[4]
And 'twill be found upon Examination,
The latter has the largest Congregation:
For ever since he first debauch'd the Mind,   60
He made a perfect Conquest of Mankind.
With Uniformity of Service, he
Reigns with a general Aristocracy.
No Noncomforming Sects disturb his Reign,
For of his Yoak there's very few complain.   65
He knows the Genius and the Inclination,
And matches proper Sins for ev'ry Nation.
He needs no Standing-Army Government;
He always rules us by our own Consent:
His Laws are easy, and his gentle Sway   70
Makes it exceeding pleasant to obey.
The List of his Vicegerents and Commanders,
Outdoes your *Caesars*, or your *Alexanders*.
They never fail of his Infernal Aid,
And he's as certain ne're to be betray'd.   75
Through all the World they spread his vast Command,
And Death's Eternal Empire's maintain'd.
They rule so politickly and so well,
As if they were L[ords] J[ustices] of Hell.
Duly divided to debauch Mankind,   80
And plant Infernal Dictates in his Mind.
    Pride, the First Peer, and President of Hell,
To his share *Spain*, the largest Province, fell.
The subtile Prince thought fittest to bestow
On these the Golden Mines of *Mexico*;   85
With all the Silver Mountains of *Peru*;
Wealth which would in wise hands the World undo:[5]
Because he knew their Genius was such;
Too Lazy and too Haughty to be Rich.

*An *English* Proverb, *Where God has a Church, the Devil has a Chappel.*

So proud a People, so above their Fate,   90
That if reduc'd to beg, they'll beg in State.
Lavish of Money, to be counted Brave,
And Proudly starve, because they scorn to save.
Never was Nation in the World before,
So very Rich, and yet so very Poor.   95

   Lust chose the Torrid Zone of *Italy*,
Where Blood ferments in Rapes and Sodomy:
Where swelling Veins o'reflow with living Streams,
With Heat impregnate from *Vesuvian* Flames:
Whose flowing Sulphur forms Infernal Lakes,   100
And human Body of the Soil partakes.
There Nature ever burns with hot Desires,
Fann'd with Luxuriant Air from Subterranean Fires:
Here undisturb'd in Floods of scalding Lust,
Th' Infernal King reigns with Infernal Gust.   105

   Drunk'ness, the Darling Favourite of Hell,
Chose *Germany* to rule; and rules so well,
No Subjects more obsequiously obey,
None please so well, or are so pleas'd as they.
The cunning Artist manages so well,   110
He lets them Bow to Heav'n, and Drink to Hell.
If but to Wine and him they Homage pay,
He cares not to what Deity they Pray,
What God they worship most, or in what way.
Whether by *Luther*, *Calvin*, or by *Rome*,   115
They sail for Heav'n, by Wine he steers them home.

   Ungovern'd Passion settled first in *France*,
Where Mankind lives in haste, and thrives by Chance.
A *Dancing Nation*, Fickle and Untrue:
Have oft undone themselves, and others too: 120
Prompt the Infernal Dictates to obey,
And in Hell's Favour none more great than they.

   The *Pagan* World he blindly leads away,
And Personally rules with Arbitrary Sway:
The Mask thrown off, *Plain Devil* his Title stands;   125
And what elsewhere he Tempts, he there Commands.

There with full Gust th' Ambition of his Mind
Governs, as he of old in Heav'n design'd.
Worshipp'd as God, his *Painim Altars* smoke,
Embru'd with Blood of those that him Invoke.   130

The rest by Deputies he rules as well,
And plants the distant Colonies of Hell.
By them his secret Power he maintains,
And binds the World in his Infernal Chains.

By Zeal the *Irish*; and the *Rush* by Folly: 135
Fury the *Dane*: The *Swede* by Melancholly:
By stupid Ignorance, the *Muscovite*:
The *Chinese* by a *Child of Hell*, call'd Wit:
Wealth makes the *Persian* too Effeminate:
And Poverty the *Tartars* Desperate: 140
The *Turks* and *Moors* by *Mah'met* he subdues:
And God has giv'n him leave to rule the Jews:
Rage rules the *Portuguese*; and Fraud the *Scotch*:
Revenge the *Pole*; and Avarice the *Dutch*.

Satyr be kind, and draw a silent Veil,   145
Thy *Native England*'s Vices to conceal:
Or if that Task's impossible to do,
At least be just, and show her Virtues too;
Too Great the first, Alas! the last too Few.

England unknown as yet, unpeopled lay,   150
Happy, had she remain'd so to this day,
And not to ev'ry Nation been a Prey.
Her Open Harbours, and her Fertile Plains,
The Merchants Glory these, and those the Swains,
To ev'ry Barbarous Nation have betray'd her,   155
Who conquer her as oft as they Invade her.
So Beauty guarded but by Innocence,
That ruins her which should be her Defence.

Ingratitude, a Devil of *Black Renown*,
Possess'd her very early for his own.   160
An Ugly, Surly, Sullen, Selfish Spirit,
Who Satan's worst Perfections does inherit:

Second to him in Malice and in Force,
All *Devil without*, and all within him *Worse*.

  He made her First-born Race to be so rude,   165
And suffer'd her to be so oft subdu'd:
By sev'ral Crowds of Wandring Thieves o're-run,
Often unpeopl'd, and as oft undone.
While ev'ry Nation that her Pow'rs reduc'd,
Their Languages and Manners introduc'd.   170
From whose mixt Relicks our compounded Breed,
By Spurious Generation does succeed;
Making a Race uncertain and unev'n,
Deriv'd from all the Nations under Heav'n.

  The *Romans* first with *Julius Caesar* came,   175
Including all the Nations of that Name,
Gauls, Greeks, and *Lombards*; and by Computation,
Auxiliaries or Slaves of ev'ry Nation.
With *Hengist, Saxons; Danes* with *Sueno* came,
In search of Plunder, not in search of Fame.   180
Scots, Picts, and *Irish* from th' *Hibernian* Shore:
And Conqu'ring *William* brought the *Normans* o're.

  All these their Barb'rous Offspring left behind,
The Dregs of Armies, they of all Mankind;
Blended with *Britains* who before were here,   185
Of whom the *Welsh* ha' blest the Character.

  From this Amphibious Ill-born Mob began
That vain ill-natur'd thing, an Englishman.
The Customs, Sirnames, Languages, and Manners,
Of all these Nations are their own Explainers: 190
Whose Relicks are so lasting and so strong,
They ha' left a *Shiboleth* upon our Tongue;
By which with easy search you may distinguish
Your *Roman-Saxon-Danish-Norman* English.

  The great Invading* *Norman* let us know   195
What Conquerors in After-Times might do.

**Wm the Conq.*

To ev'ry* *Musqueteer* he brought to Town,
He gave the Lands which never were his own.
When first the *English* Crown he did obtain,
He did not send his *Dutchmen* home again.   200
No Reassumptions in his Reign were known,
D'avenant[6] might there ha' let his Book alone.
No Parliament his Army cou'd disband;
He rais'd no Money, for he paid in Land.
He gave his Legions their Eternal Station,   205
And made them all Freeholders of the Nation.
He canton'd out the Country to his Men,
And ev'ry Soldier was a Denizen.
The Rascals thus enrich'd, he call'd them *Lords,*
To please their Upstart Pride with new-made Words;   210
And *Doomsday-Book* his Tyranny records.

And here begins the Ancient Pedigree
That so exalts our Poor Nobility:
'Tis that from some *French* Trooper they derive,
Who with the *Norman* Bastard did arrive: 215
The Trophies of the Families appear;
Some show the Sword, the Bow, and some the Spear,
Which their Great Ancestor, *forsooth,* did wear.
These in the Heralds Register remain,
Their Noble Mean Extraction to explain.   220
Yet who the Hero was, no man can tell,
Whether a Drummer or a Colonel:
The silent Record blushes to reveal
Their Undescended Dark Original.

But grant the best, How came the Change to pass;   225
A *True-Born Englishman* of *Norman* Race?
A *Turkish* Horse can show more History,
To prove his Well-descended Family.
Conquest, as by the† Moderns 'tis exprest,
May give a Title to the Lands possest: 230
But that the Longest Sword shou'd be so Civil,
To make a *Frenchman English,* that's the Devil.

*Or Archer.
†Dr. Sherl[ock] *De Facto.*[7]

These are the Heroes that despise the *Dutch*,
And rail at new-come Foreigners so much;
Forgetting that themselves are all deriv'd   235
From the most Scoundrel Race that ever liv'd.
A horrid Medly of Thieves and Drones,
Who ransack'd Kingdoms, and dispeopl'd Towns.
The *Pict* and Painted *Britain*, Treach'rous *Scot*,
By Hunger, Theft, and Rapine, hither brought.   240
Norwegian Pirates, Buccaneering *Danes*,
Whose Red-hair'd Offspring ev'ry where remains.
Who join'd with *Norman-French*, compound the Breed
From whence your *True-Born Englishmen* proceed.

And lest by Length of Time it be pretended,   245
The Climate may this Modern Breed ha' mended,
Wise Providence, to keep us where we are,
Mixes us daily with exceeding Care:
We have been *Europe*'s Sink, *the Jakes* where she
Voids all her Offal Out-cast Progeny.   250
From our Fifth *Henry*'s time, the Strolling Bands
Of banish'd Fugitives from Neighb'ring Lands,
Have here a certain Sanctuary found:
The Eternal Refuge of the Vagabond.
Where in but half a common Age of Time,   255
Borr'wing new Blood and Manners from the Clime,
Proudly they learn all Mankind to contemn,
And all their Race are *True-Born Englishmen*.

Dutch, Walloons, Flemings, Irishmen, and *Scots,*
Vaudois and *Valtolins,* and *Hugonots,*   260
In good Queen *Bess*'s Charitable Reign,
Suppli'd us with Three hundred thousand Men.
Religion, *God we thank thee,* sent them hither,
Priests, Protestants, the Devil and all together:
Of all Professions, and of ev'ry Trade,   265
All that were persecuted or afraid;
Whether for Debt or other Crimes they fled,
David at *Hackelah*[8] was still their Head.

The Offspring of this Miscellaneous Crowd,
Had not their new Plantations long enjoy'd,   270
But they grew *Englishmen*, and rais'd their Votes
At Foreign Shoals of *Interloping Scots*.
The *Royal Branch from *Pict-land* did succeed,
With Troops of *Scots* and Scabs from *North-by-Tweed*.
The Seven first Years of his Pacifick Reign,   275
Made him and half his Nation *Englishmen*.
Scots from the *Northern* Frozen Banks of *Tay*,
With Packs and Plods came *Whigging* all away:
Thick as the Locusts which in *Egypt* swarm'd,
With Pride and hungry Hopes compleatly arm'd: 280
With Native Truth, Diseases, and No Money,
Plunder'd our *Canaan* of the Milk and Honey.
Here they grew quickly Lords and Gentlemen,
And all their Race are *True-Born Englishmen*.

The Civil Wars, the common Purgative,   285
Which always use to make the Nation thrive,
Made way for all that strolling Congregation,
Which throng'd in Pious† *Ch[arle]s*'s Restoration.
The *Royal Refugee* our Breed restores,
With *Foreign Courtiers*, and with *Foreign Whores*:   290
And carefully repeopled us again,
Throughout his Lazy, Long, Lascivious Reign,
With such a blest and True-born *English* Fry,
As much Illustrates our Nobility.
A Gratitude which will so black appear,   295
As future Ages must abhor to hear:
When they look back on all that Crimson Flood,
Which stream'd in *Lindsey*'s, and *Caernarvon*'s Blood:
Bold *Strafford, Cambridge, Capel, Lucas, Lisle*,[9]
Who crown'd in Death his Father's Fun'ral Pile.   300
The Loss of whom, in order to supply
With True-Born *English* Nobility,
Six Bastard Dukes survive his Luscious Reign,[10]
The Labours of *Italian C[astlemai]n*,[11]
French P[ortsmout]h,[12] *Tabby S[co]t*,[13] and *Cambrian*.[14]   305

*K[ing] J[ames] I.
†K[ing] C[harles] II.

Besides the Num'rous Bright and Virgin Throng,
Whose Female Glories shade them from my Song.

    This Offspring, if one Age they multiply,
May half the House with *English* Peers supply:
There with true *English* Pride they may contemn   310
S[chomber]g[15] and P[ortlan]d,[16] new-made Noblemen.

    French Cooks, *Scotch* Pedlars, and *Italian* Whores,
Were all made Lords, or Lords Progenitors.
Beggars and Bastards by his new Creation,
Much multipli'd the Peerage of the Nation;   315
Who will be all, e're one short Age runs o're,
As True-Born Lords as those we had before.

    Then to recruit the Commons he prepares,
And heal the latent Breaches of the Wars:
The Pious Purpose better to advance,   320
H' invites the banish'd Protestants of *France*:
Hither for God's sake and their own they fled,
Some for Religion came, and some for Bread:
Two hundred thousand Pair of Wooden Shooes,
Who, God be thank'd, had nothing left to lose;   325
To Heav'n's great Praise did for Religion fly,
To make us starve our Poor in Charity.
In ev'ry Port they plant their fruitful Train,
To get a Race of *True-Born Englishmen*:
Whose Children will, when riper Years they see,   330
Be as Ill-natur'd and as Proud as we:
Call themselves *English*, Foreigners despise,
Be surly like us all, and just as wise.

    Thus from a Mixture of all Kinds began,
That Het'rogeneous Thing, *An Englishman*:   335
In eager Rapes, and furious Lust begot,
Betwixt a Painted *Britton* and a *Scot*:
Whose gend'ring Offspring quickly learnt to bow,
And yoke their Heifers to the *Roman* Plough:
From whence a Mongrel half-bred Race there came,   340
With neither Name nor Nation, Speech or Fame.

In whose hot Veins new Mixtures quickly ran,
Infus'd betwixt a *Saxon* and a *Dane*.
While their Rank Daughters, to their Parents just,
Receiv'd all Nations with Promiscuous Lust.   345
This Nauseous Brood directly did contain
The well-extracted Blood of *Englishmen*.

Which Medly canton'd in a Heptarchy,
A Rhapsody of Nations to supply,
Among themselves maintain'd eternal Wars,   350
And still the Ladies lov'd the Conquerors.

The *Western* Angles all the rest subdu'd;
A bloody Nation, barbarous and rude:
Who by the Tenure of the Sword possest
One part of *Britain*, and subdu'd the rest.   355
And as great things denominate the small,
The Conqu'ring Part gave Title to the Whole.
The *Scot, Pict, Britain, Roman, Dane* submit,
And with the *English-Saxon* all unite:
And these the Mixture have so close pursu'd,   360
The very Name and Memory's subdu'd;
No *Roman* now, no *Britain* does remain;
Wales strove to separate, but strove in vain:
The silent Nations undistinguish'd fall,
And *Englishman*'s the common Name for all.   365
Fate jumbl'd them together, *God knows how*;
Whate're they were, they're *True-Born English* now.

The Wonder which remains is at our Pride,
To value that which all wise men deride.
For *Englishmen* to boast of Generation,   370
Cancels their Knowledge, and lampoons the Nation.
A *True-Born Englishman*'s a Contradiction,
In Speech an Irony, in Fact a Fiction.
A Banter made to be a Test of Fools,
Which those that use it justly ridicules.   375
A Metaphor invented to express
A man *a-kin* to all the Universe.

For as the *Scots*, as Learned Men ha' said,
Throughout the World their Wandring Seed ha' spread;
So open-handed *England*, 'tis believ'd,   380
Has all the Gleanings of the World receiv'd.

   Some think of *England* 'twas our Saviour meant,
The Gospel should to all the World be sent:
Since when the blessed Sound did hither reach,
They to all Nations might be said to Preach.   385

   'Tis well that Virtue gives Nobility,
Else God knows where we had our Gentry;
Since scarce one Family is left alive,
Which does not from some Foreigner derive.
Of Sixty thousand *English* Gentlemen,   390
Whose Names and Arms in Registers remain,
We challenge all our Heralds to declare
Ten Families which *English-Saxons* are.

   France justly boasts the Ancient Noble Line
Of *Bourbon*, *Mommorency*, and *Lorrain*.   395
The *Germans* too their House of *Austria* show,
And *Holland* their Invincible *Nassau*.
Lines which in Heraldry were Ancient grown,
Before the Name of *Englishman* was known.
Even *Scotland* too her Elder Glory shows,   400
Her *Gourdons*, *Hamiltons*, and her *Monroes*;
Dowglas, *Mackays*, and *Grahams*, Names well known,
Long before Ancient *England* knew her own.

   But *England*, Modern to the last degree,
Borrows or makes her own Nobility,   405
And yet she boldly boasts of Pedigree:
Repines that Foreigners are put upon her,
And talks of her Antiquity and Honour:
Her S[ackvi]lls, S[avi]ls, C[eci]ls, De[la]M[ee]rs,
M[ohu]ns and M[ontag]ues, D[ura]s and V[ee]rs,   410
Not one have *English* Names, yet all are *English* Peers.
Your H[oublo]ns, P[api]llons, and L[ethu]liers,
Pass now for True-Born *English* Knights and Squires,
And make good Senate-Members, or Lord-Mayors.

Wealth, howsoever got, in *England* makes   415
Lords of Mechanicks, Gentlemen of Rakes.
Antiquity and Birth are needless here;
'Tis Impudence and Money makes a P[ee]r.

Innumerable City-Knights we know,
From *Blewcoat Hospitals* and *Bridewell*[17] flow.   420
Draymen and Porters fill the City Chair,
And Footboys Magisterial Purple wear.
Fate has but very small Distinction set
Betwixt the *Counter* and the Coronet.
Tarpaulin Lords,[18] Pages of high Renown,   425
Rise up by Poor Mens Valour, not their own.
Great Families of yesterday we show,
And Lords, whose Parents were *the Lord knows who*.

PART II

The Breed's describ'd: Now, Satyr, if you can,
Their Temper show, for *Manners make the Man*.   430

... In their Religion they are so unev'n,   530
That each man goes *his own By-way to Heav'n*.
Tenacious of Mistakes to that degree,
That ev'ry man pursues it sep'rately,
And fancies none can find the Way but he:
So shy of one another they are grown,   535
As if they strove to get to Heav'n alone.
Rigid and Zealous, Positive and Grave,
And ev'ry Grace, but Charity, they have:
This makes them so ill-natur'd and Uncivil,
That all men think an *Englishman* the Devil.   540

Surly to Strangers, Froward to their Friend;
Submit to Love with a reluctant Mind;
Resolv'd to be ungrateful and unkind.
If by Necessity reduc'd to ask,
The Giver has the difficultest Task: 545
For what's bestow'd they awkwardly receive,

And always Take less freely than they Give.
The Obligation is their highest Grief;
And never love, where they accept Relief.
So sullen in their Sorrows, that 'tis known,   550
They'll rather dye than their Afflictions own:
And if reliev'd, it is too often true,
That they'll abuse their Benefactors too:
For in Distress their Haughty Stomach's such,
They hate to see themselves oblig'd too much.   555
Seldom contented, often in the wrong;
Hard to be pleas'd at all, and never long.[19]

If your Mistakes their Ill Opinion gain,
No Merit can their Favour reobtain:
And if they're not Vindictive in their Fury,   560
'Tis their unconstant Temper does secure ye:
Their Brain's so cool, their Passion seldom burns;
For all's condens'd before the Flame returns:
The Fermentation's of so weak a Matter,
The Humid damps the Fume, and runs it all to Water.   565
So tho the Inclination may be strong,
They're pleas'd by Fits, and never angry long.

Then if Good Nature shows some slender proof,
They never think they have Reward enough:
But like our *Modern Quakers* of the Town,   570
Expect your Manners, and return you none.

Friendship, th' abstracted Union of the Mind,
Which all men seek, but very few can find:
Of all the Nations in the Universe,
None talk on't more, or understand it less: 575
For if it does their Property annoy,
Their Property their Friendship will destroy.

As you discourse them, you shall hear them tell
All things in which they think they do excel:
No Panegyrick needs their Praise record;   580
An Englishman *ne're wants his own good word.*
His first Discourses gen'rally appear

67

Prologu'd with his own wondrous Character:
When, to illustrate his own good Name,
He never fails his Neighbour to defame: 585
And yet he really designs no wrong;
His Malice goes no further than his Tongue.
But pleas'd to Tattle, he delights to Rail,
To satisfy the Lech'ry of a Tale.
His own dear Praises close the ample Speech,   590
Tells you how Wise he is; *that is, how Rich:*
For Wealth is Wisdom; he that's Rich is wise;
And all men Learned Poverty despise.[20]
His Generosity comes next, and then
Concludes that he's a *True-Born Englishman*;   595
And they, 'tis known, are Generous and Free,
Forgetting, and Forgiving Injury:
Which may be true, thus rightly understood,
Forgiving Ill Turns, and Forgetting Good.

    Chearful in Labour when they've undertook it;   600
But out of Humour, when they're out of Pocket.
But if their Belly and their Pocket's full,
They may be Phlegmatick, but never Dull:
And if a Bottle does their Brains refine,
It makes their Wit as sparkling as their Wine.   605

    As for the general Vices which we find
They're guilty of in common with Mankind,
Satyr, forbear, and silently endure;
We must conceal the Crimes we cannot cure.
Nor shall my Verse the brighter Sex defame;   610
For *English* Beauty will preserve her Name.
Beyond dispute, Agreeable and Fair;
And Modester than other Nations are:
For where the Vice prevails, the great Temptation
Is want of Money, more than Inclination.[21]   615
In general, this only is allow'd,
They're something Noisy, and a little Proud.

    An *Englishman* is gentlest in Command;
Obedience is a Stranger in the Land:
Hardly subject to the Magistrate;   620

For Englishmen *do all Subjection hate.*
Humblest when Rich, but peevish when they're Poor;
And think whate're they have, they merit more.

    Shamwhig[22] pretends t' ha' serv'd the Government,
But baulk'd of due Reward, turns Malecontent.   625
For English *Christians always have regard*
To future Recompences of Reward.
His forfeit Liberty they did restore,
And gave him Bread, which he had not before.
But *True-Born English Shamwhig* lets them know,   630
His Merit must not lye neglected so.
As Proud as Poor, his Masters he'll defy;
And writes a *Piteous** *Satyr* upon *Honesty.*
Some think the Poem had been pretty good,
If he the Subject had but understood.   635
He got Five hundred Pence by this, and more,
As sure as he had ne're a Groat before.

    In Bus'ness next some Friends of his employ'd him;
And there he prov'd that Fame had not bely'd him:
His Benefactors quickly he abus'd,   640
And falsly to the Government accus'd:
But they, defended by their Innocence,
Ruin'd the Traytor in their own Defence.

    Thus kick'd about from Pillars unto Posts,
He whets his Pen against the Lord of Hosts: 645
Burlesques his God and King in Paltry Rhimes:
Against the *Dutch* turns Champion for the Times;
And Huffs the King, upon that very score,
On which he Panegyrick't him before.

    Unhappy *England,* hast thou none but such,   650
To plead thy Scoundrel Cause against the Dutch?
This moves their Scorn, and not their Indignation;
He that Lampoons the Dutch, *Burlesques the Nation.*

    The meanest *English* Plowman studies Law,
And keeps thereby the Magistrates in Awe: 655
*Satyr in Praise of Folly and Knavery.

Will boldly tell them what they ought to do,
And sometimes punish their Omissions too.

Their Liberty and Property's so dear,
They scorn their Laws or Governors to fear:
So bugbear'd with the Name of Slavery,   600
They can't submit to their own Liberty.
Restraint from Ill is Freedom to the Wise;
But Englishmen *do all Restraint despise.*
Slaves to the Liquor, Drudges to the Pots,
The Mob are Statesmen, and their Statesmen Sots.   665

Their Governors they count such dangerous things,
That 'tis their custom to affront their Kings:
So jealous of the Power their Kings posses'd,
They suffer neither Power nor Kings to rest.
The Bad with Force they eagerly subdue;   670
The Good with constant Clamours they pursue:
And did King Jesus reign, they'd murmur too.
A discontented Nation, and by far
Harder to rule in Times of Peace than War:
Easily set together by the Ears,   675
And full of causeless Jealousies and Fears:
Apt to revolt, and willing to rebel,
And never are contented when they're well.
No Government cou'd ever please them long,
Cou'd tye their Hands, or rectify their Tongue.   680
In this to Ancient Israel *well compar'd,*
Eternal Murmurs are among them heard.[23]

It was but lately that they were opprest,
Their Rights invaded, and their Laws supprest:
When nicely tender of their Liberty,   685
Lord ! what a Noise they made of Slavery.
In daily Tumults show'd their Discontent;
Lampoon'd their King, and mock'd his Government.
And if in Arms they did not first appear,
'Twas want of Force, and not for want of Fear.   690
In humbler Tone than *English* us'd to do,
At Foreign Hands for Foreign Aid they sue.

William *the Great Successor of* Nassau,
Their Prayers heard, and their Oppressions saw:
He saw and sav'd them: God and Him they prais'd;   695
To This their Thanks, to That their Trophies rais'd.
But glutted with their own Felicities,
They soon their New Deliverer despise;
Say all their Prayers back, their Joy disown,
Unsing their Thanks, and pull their Trophies down: 700
Their Harps of Praise are on the Willows hung;
For Englishmen *are ne're contented long.*

.   .   .   .

If all our former Grievances were feign'd,
King *James* has been abus'd, and we trepann'd;[24]   760
Bugbear'd with Popery and Power Despotick,
Tyrannick Government, and Leagues Exotick:
The Revolution's a Phanatick Plot,
W[*illiam*] a Tyrant, *S*[*underland*][25] a Sot:
A Factious Army and a Poyson'd Nation,   765
Unjustly forc'd King *James's* Abdiction.

But if he did the Subjects Rights invade,
Then he was punish'd only, not betray'd:
And punishing of Kings is no such Crime,
But Englishmen *ha' done it many a time.*   770

When Kings the Sword of Justice first lay down,
They are no Kings, though they possess the Crown.
Titles are Shadows, Crowns are empty things,
The Good of Subjects is the End of Kings;
To guide in War, and to protect in Peace: 775
Where Tyrants once commence, the Kings do cease:
For Arbitrary Power's so strange a thing,
It makes the *Tyrant,* and unmakes the *King.*
If Kings by Foreign Priests and Armies reign,
And Lawless Power against their Oaths maintain,   780
Then Subjects must ha' reason to complain.
If Oaths must bind us when our Kings do ill;

To call in Foreign Aid is to rebel.
By Force to circumscribe our Lawful Prince,
Is wilful Treason in the largest sense: 785
And they who once rebel, most certainly .
Their God, and King, and former Oaths defy.
If we allow no Male-Administration
Could cancel the Allegiance of the Nation;
Let all our Learned *Sons of Levi* try,   790
This Eccles'astick Riddle to unty:
How they could make a Step to Call the Prince,
And yet pretend to Oaths and Innocence.

By th' first Address they made beyond the Seas,
They're perjur'd in the most intense Degrees;   795
And without Scruple for the time to come,
May swear to all the Kings in *Christendom.*
And truly did our Kings consider all,
They'd never let the Clergy swear at all:
Their Politick Allegiance they'd refuse;   800
For Whores and Priests do never want excuse.

But if the *Mutual Contract* was dissolv'd,
The Doubt's explain'd, the Difficulty solv'd:
That Kings, when they descend to Tyranny,
Dissolve the Bond, and leave the Subject free.   805
The Government's ungirt when Justice dies,
And Constitutions are Non-Entities.
The Nation's all a Mob, there's no such thing
As Lords or Commons, Parliament or King.
A great promiscuous Crowd the Hydra lies,   810
Till Laws revive, and mutual Contact ties:
A Chaos free to chuse for their own share,
What Case of Government they please to wear:
If to a King they do the Reins commit,
All men are bound in Conscience to submit: 815
But then that King must by his Oath assent
To *Postulata's* of the Government;
Which if he breaks, he cuts off the Entail,
And Power retreats to its Original.

This Doctrine has the Sanction of Assent,   820
From Nature's Universal Parliament.
The Voice of Nations, and the Course of Things,
Allow that Laws superior are to Kings.
None but Delinquents would have Justice cease,
Knaves rail at Laws, as Soldiers rail at Peace: 825
For Justice is the End of Government,
As Reason is the Test of Argument.

No man was ever yet so void of Sense,
As to debate the Right of Self-Defence;
A Principle so grafted in the Mind,   830
With Nature born, and does like Nature bind:
Twisted with Reason, and with Nature too;
As neither one nor t'other can undo.[26]

Nor can this Right be less when National;
Reason which governs one, should govern all.   835
Whate're the Dialect of Courts may tell,
He that his Right demands, can ne're rebel.
Which Right, if 'tis by Governors deny'd,
May be procur'd by Force, or Foreign Aid.
For *Tyranny*'s a Nation's Term for Grief;   840
As Folks cry *Fire*, to hasten in Relief.
And when the hated word is heard about,
All men shou'd come to help the People out.

Thus *England* groan'd, *Britannia*'s Voice was heard;
And Great *Nassau* to rescue her, appear'd: 845
Call'd by the Universal Voice of Fate;
God and the Peoples Legal Magistrate.
Ye Heav'ns regard! Almighty *Jove* look down,
And view thy Injur'd Monarch on the Throne.
On their Ungrateful Heads due Vengeance take,   850
Who sought his Aid, and then his part forsake.
Witness, ye Powers! it was our Call alone,
Which now our Pride makes us asham'd to own.
Britannia's Troubles fetch'd him from afar,
To court the dreadful Casualties of War: 855

But where Requital never can be made,
Acknowlegment's a Tribute seldom paid.

He dwelt in Bright *Maria*'s Circling Arms,
Defended by the Magick of her Charms,
From Foreign Fears, and from Domestick Harms.   860
Ambition found no Fuel for her Fire,
He had what God cou'd give, or Man Desire.
Till *Pity* rowz'd him from his soft Repose,
His Life to unseen Hazards to expose:
Till *Pity* mov'd him in our Cause t' appear;   865
Pity! *that Word which now we hate to hear.*
But *English* Gratitude is always such,
To hate the Hand which does oblige too much.

Britannia's Cries gave Birth to his Intent,
And hardly gain'd his unforeseen Assent: 870
His boding Thoughts foretold him he should find
The People Fickle, Selfish, and Unkind.
Which Thought did to his Royal Heart appear
More dreadful than the Dangers of the War:
For nothing grates a Generous Mind so soon,   875
As base Returns for hearty Service done.

Satyr be silent, awfully prepare
Britannia's Song, and *William*'s Praise to hear.
Stand by, and let her chearfully rehearse
Her Grateful Vows in her Immortal Verse.   880
Loud Fame's Eternal Trumpet let her sound;
Listen ye distant Poles, and endless Round.
May the strong Blast the welcome News convey
As far as Sound can reach, or Spirit fly.
To *Neighb'ring Worlds*, if such there be, relate   885
Our Hero's Fame, for theirs to imitate.
To distant Worlds of Spirits let her rehearse:
For Spirits without the help of Voice converse.
May Angels hear the gladsome News on high,
Mixt with their everlasting Symphony.   890
And Hell it self stand in suspence to know
Whether it be the Fatal Blast, or no.

BRITANNIA

The Fame of Virtue 'tis for which I sound,
And Heroes with Immortal Triumphs crown'd.
Fame built on solid Virtue swifter flies,   895
Than Morning Light can spread my Eastern Skies.
The gath'ring Air returns the doubling Sound,
And lowd repeating Thunders force it round:
Echoes return from Caverns of the Deep:
Old Chaos dreams on't in Eternal Sleep.   900
Time hands it forward to its latest Urn,
From whence it never, never shall return,
Nothing is heard so far, or lasts so long;
'Tis heard by ev'ry Ear, and spoke by ev'ry Tongue.

My Hero, with the Sails of Honour furl'd,   905
Rises like the Great Genius of the World.
By Fate and Fame wisely prepar'd to be.
The Soul of War, and Life of Victory.
He spreads the Wings of Virtue on the Throne,
And ev'ry Wind of Glory fans them on.   910
Immortal Trophies dwell upon his Brow,
Fresh as the Garlands he has worn but now.

By different Steps the high Ascent he gains,
And differently that high Ascent maintains.
Princes for Pride and Lust of Rule make War,   915
And struggle for the Name of Conqueror.
Some fight for Fame, and some for Victory.
He Fights to Save, and Conquers to set Free.

Then seek no Phrase his Titles to conceal,
And hide with Words what Actions must reveal.   920
No Parallel from Hebrew Stories take,
Of God-like Kings my Similies to make:
No borrow'd Names conceal my living Theam;
But Names and Things directly I proclaim.
'Tis honest Merit does his Glory raise;   925
Whom that exalts, let no man fear to praise.
Of such a Subject no man need be shy;

Virtue's above the Reach of Flattery.
He needs no Character but his own Fame,
Nor any flattering Titles, but his Name.   930

·   ·   ·   ·   ·   ·   ·   ·   ·   ·   ·   ·   ·

We blame the K[ing] that he relies too much   1025
On Strangers, *Germans, Hugonots,* and *Dutch*;
And seldom does his great Affairs of State,
To *English* Counsellors communicate.
The Fact might very well be answer'd thus;
He has so often been betray'd by us,   1030
He must have been a Madman to rely
On *English* G[odolphi]ns²⁷ Fidelity.
For laying other Arguments aside,
This Thought might mortify our *English* Pride,
That Foreigners have faithfully obey'd him,   1035
And none but *Englishmen* have e're betray'd him.
They have our Ships and Merchants bought and sold,
And barter'd *English* Blood for Foreign Gold.
First to the *French* they sold our *Turky*-Fleet,²⁸
And Injur'd *Talmarsh* next at *Camaret.*²⁹   1040
The King himself is shelter'd from their Snares,
Not by his Merit, but the Crown he wears.
Experience tells us 'tis the *English* way,
Their Benefactors always to betray.

And lest Examples should be too remote,   1045
A Modern Magistrate of Famous Note,³⁰
Shall give you his own History by Rote.
I'll make it out, deny it he that can,
His Worship is a True-born *Englishman,*
In all the Latitude that Empty Word   1050
By Modern Acceptation's understood.
The Parish-Books his Great Descent record,
And now he hopes e're long to be a Lord.
And truly as things go, it wou'd be pity
But such as he bore Office in the City: 1055
While Robb'ry for Burnt-Offering he brings,
And gives to God what he has stole from Kings:

Great Monuments of Charity he raises,
'*And good* St. Magnus *whistles out his Praises.*
To City-Gaols he grants a Jubilee,   1060
And hires Huzza's from his own Mobile.[31]

Lately he wore the Golden Chain and Gown,
With which Equipt he thus harangu'd the Town.

Sir C[harle]s D[uncom]b's Fine Speech, &c.[32]

With Clouted Iron Shooes and Sheepskin Breeches,
More Rags than Manners, and more Dirt than Riches: 1065
From driving Cows and Calves to *Layton*-Market,
While of my Greatness there appear'd no Spark yet,
Behold I come, to let you see the Pride
With which Exalted Beggars always ride.

Born to the Needful Labours of the Plow,   1070
The Cart-Whip grace't me as the Chain does now.
Nature and Fate in doubt what course to take,
Whether I shou'd a Lord or Plough-Boy make;
Kindly at last resolv'd they wou'd promote me,
And first *a Knave,* and then *a Knight* they vote me.   1075
What Fate appointed, Nature did prepare,
And furnish'd me with an exceeding Care.
To fit me for what they design'd to have me;
And ev'ry Gift *but Honesty* they gave me.

And thus Equipt, to this Proud Town I came,   1080
In quest of Bread, and not in quest of Fame.
Blind to my future Fate, an humble Boy,
Free from the *Guilt and Glory* I enjoy.
The Hopes which my Ambition entertain'd,
Were in the Name of *Foot-Boy* all contain'd.   1085
The Greatest Heights from Small Beginnings rise;
The Gods were Great on Earth, before they reach'd the Skies.

B[ack]well, the Generous Temper of whose Mind,
Was always to be bountiful inclin'd:

Whether by his Ill Fate or Fancy led,   1090
First took me up, and furnish'd me with Bread.
The little Services he put me to,
Seem'd Labours rather than were truly so.
But always my Advancement he design'd;
For 'twas his very Nature to be kind.   1095
Large was his Soul, his Temper ever Free;
The best of Masters and of Men to me.
And I who was before decreed by Fate,
To be made Infamous as well as Great,
With an obsequious Diligence obey'd him,   1100
Till trusted with his All, and then betray'd him.

All his past Kindnesses I trampled on,
Ruin'd his Fortunes to erect my own.
So Vipers in the Bosom bred, begin
To hiss at that Hand first which took them in.   1105
With eager Treach'ry I his Fall pursu'd,
And my first Trophies were *Ingratitude.*

Ingratitude's the worst of Human Guilt,
The basest Action Mankind can commit;
Which like the Sin against the Holy Ghost,   1110
Has least of Honour, and of Guilt the most.
Distinguish'd from all other Crimes by this,
That 'tis a Crime which no man will confess.
That Sin alone, which shou'd not be forgiv'n
On Earth, altho perhaps it may in Heav'n.   1115

Thus my first Benefactor I o'rethrew;
And how shou'd I be to a second true?
The Publick Trust came next into my Care,
And I to use them scurvily prepare:
My Needy Sov'reign Lord I play'd upon,   1120
And Lent him many a Thousand of his own;
For which, great Int'rests I took care to charge,
And so my Ill-got Wealth became so large.

My Predecessor *Judas* was a Fool,
Fitter to ha' been whipt, and sent to School,   1125

Than Sell a Saviour: Had I been at hand,
His Master had not been so cheap Trepann'd;
I wou'd ha' made the eager *Jews* ha' found,
For Thirty Pieces, Thirty thousand Pound.

My Cousin *Ziba*,[33] of Immortal Fame, 1130
(Ziba *and I shall never want a Name:*)
First-born of Treason, nobly did advance
His Master's Fall, for his Inheritance.
By whose keen Arts old *David* first began
To break his Sacred Oath to *Jonathan:* 1135
The Good Old King, 'tis thought, was very loth
To break his Word, and therefore broke his Oath.
Ziba's a Traytor of some Quality,
Yet *Ziba* might ha' been inform'd by me:
Had I been there, he ne're had been content 1140
With half th' Estate, nor half the Government.

In our late Revolution 'twas thought strange,
That I of all mankind shou'd like the Change:
But they who wondered at it, never knew,
That in it I did my Old Game pursue: 1145
Nor had they heard of Twenty thousand Pound,
Which ne're was lost, yet never cou'd be found.

Thus all things in their turn to Sale I bring,
God and my Master first, and then the King:
Till by successful Villanies made bold, 1150
I thought to turn the Nation into Gold;
And so to Forg[er]y my Hand I bent,
Not doubting I could gull the Government;
But there was ruffl'd by the Parliament.
And if I 'scap'd th' Unhappy Tree to climb, 1155
'Twas want of Law, and not for want of Crime.

But my *Old Friend, who printed in my Face
A needful Competence of *English* Brass,
Having more business yet for me to do,
And loth to lose his Trusty Servant so, 1160

* *The Devil.*

79

Manag'd the matter with such Art and Skill,
As sav'd his Hero, and threw out the B[il]l.[34]

And now I'm grac'd with unexpected Honours,
For which I'll certainly abuse the Donors:
Knighted, and made a Tribune of the People,   1165
Whose Laws and Properties I'm like to keep well:
The *Custos Rotulorum* of the City,
And Captain of the Guards of their *Banditti*.[35]
Surrounded by my Catchpoles, I declare
Against the Needy Debtor open War.   1170
I hang poor Thieves for stealing of your Pelf,
And suffer none to rob you, but my self.

The King commanded me to help Reform ye,[36]
And how I'll do't, Miss—[37] shall inform ye.
I keep the best Seraglio in the Nation,   1175
And hope in time to bring it into Fashion.
No *Brimstone-Whore* need fear the Lash from me,
That part I'll leave to Brother *Jeffery*.[38]
Our Gallants need not go abroad to *Rome*,
I'll keep a Whoring Jubilee at home.   1180
Whoring's the Darling of my Inclination;
A'n't I a Magistrate for Reformation?
For this my Praise is sung by ev'ry Bard,
For which *Bridewell* wou'd be a just Reward.
In Print my Panegyricks fill the Street,   1185
And hir'd Gaol-birds their Huzza's repeat.
Some Charities contriv'd to make a show,
Have taught the Needy Rabble to do so:
Whose empty Noise is a Mechanick Fame,
Since for Sir *Belzebub* they'd do the same.   1190

The Conclusion

Then let us boast of Ancestors no more,
Or Deeds of Heroes done in days of Yore,

In latent Records of the Ages past,
Behind the Rear of Time, in long Oblivion plac'd.
For if our Virtues must in Lines descend,   1195
The Merit with the Families would end:
And Intermixtures would most fatal grow;
For Vice would be Hereditary too;
The Tainted Blood wou'd of necessity,
Involuntary Wickedness convey.   1200

Vice, like Ill Nature, for an Age or two,
May seem a Generation to pursue;
But Virtue seldom does regard the Breed;
Fools do the Wise, and Wise Men Fools succeed.

What is't to us, what Ancestors we had?   1205
If Good, what better? or what worse, if Bad?
Examples are for Imitation set,
Yet all men follow Virtue with Regret.

Cou'd but our Ancestors retrieve their Fate,
And see their Offspring thus degenerate;   1210
How we contend for Birth and Names unknown,
And build on their past Actions, not our own;
They'd cancel Records, and their Tombs deface,
And openly disown the vile degenerate Race:
For Fame of Families is all a Cheat,   1215
'Tis Personal Virtue only makes us great.

FINIS

Legion's Memorial [1701]

The ingratitude of the nation and Parliament's reluctance to meet William's demands for military readiness had been attacked by Defoe in works such as those printed above. On 29 April 1701 five representatives of the freeholders of Kent presented 'The Kentish Petition' to Parliament urging immediate action—'that our religion and safety may be effectually provided for'—in view of the potential danger from France. The Tory Commons, suspecting a Whig plot, gaoled the petitioners. But their triumph was brief. On 14 May Defoe, 'guarded with about sixteen men of quality', presented the Speaker, Robert Harley, with *Legion's Memorial to the House of Commons* in which the nation's right to control their representatives is bluntly asserted. One tradition has it that Defoe was disguised as a woman when he presented the *Memorial*; whatever the truth about this his defiant courage was manifest. He was undoubtedly acting, in one capacity, as a partisan Whig but the occasion also allowed him to act as the spokesman for a troubled nation in a way that makes relevant Dryden's remark (of Sir Fopling Flutter) in the Epilogue to Etherege's *The Man of Mode*: 'Legion's his name, a people in a man'. Popular acclaim, shared with the Kentish petitioners on their release from gaol when Parliament rose, was his proper reward.

Legion's Memorial

Begin: Mr. S[peake]r.

The inclosed Memorial you are charged with, in the Behalf of many Thousands of the good People of England.

There is neither Popish, Jacobite, Seditious, Court, or Party Interest concern'd in it; but Honesty and Truth.

You are commanded by Two Hundred Thousand Englishmen, to deliver it to the H[ouse]e of C[ommon]s, and to inform them that it is no Banter, but serious Truth; and a serious Regard to it is expected; nothing but Justice, and their Duty is required, and it is required by them who have both a Right to require, and Power to compel, viz. the People of England.

We could have come to the House, strong enough to oblige them to hear us, but we have avoided any Tumults, not desiring to embroil, but to save our native Country.

If you refuse to communicate it to them, you will find cause in a short Time to repent it.

To R[ober]t H[arle]y, Esq.; S[peake]r to the H[ous]e of C[ommon]s,
These

THE MEMORIAL

To the K[night]s, C[ommon]s, and B[urgesse]s in P[arliamen]t
Assembled.

A Memorial from the Gentlemen, Free-holders, and Inhabitants of the Counties of ——— in Behalf of themselves, and many Thousands of the good People of England.

Gentlemen,

It were to be wished you were Men of that Temper, and possessed of so much Honour, as to bear with the Truth, tho' it be against you; especially from us who have so much Right to tell it to you; but since, even Petitions to you from your Masters, (for such are the People who chose you) are so haughtily received, as with the committing the Authors to illegal Custody; you must give us leave

83

to give you this fair Notice of your Misbehaviour, without exposing our Names.

If you think fit to rectify your Errors, you will do well, and possibly may hear no more of us; but if not assure yourselves the Nation will not long hide their Resentments. And tho' there are no stated Proceeding to bring you to your Du y, yet the great Law of Reason, says, and all Nations allow, that whatever Power is above Law, is burthensome and tyrannical; and may be reduced by *Extrajudicial* Methods: You are not above the People's Resentments, they that made you Members, may reduce you to the same Rank from whence they chose you; and may give you a Taste of their abused Kindness, in Terms you may not be pleased with.

[Then follow fifteen grievances concerning the abuse of Habeas Corpus, the contempt shown for the petition of the gentlemen of Kent, the partial administration of justice, 'saucy and indecent Reproaches upon his Majesty's Person' in the Commons, the moral depravity of Members, etc.]

Wherefore, in the said Prospect of the impending Ruin of our native Country, while Parliaments (which ought to be the Security and Defence of our Laws and Constitution) betray their Trust, and abuse the People whom they should protect: And no other way being left us, but *that force* which we are very loath to make use of, that Posterity may know we did not insensibly fall under the Tyranny of a prevailing Party, We do hereby claim and declare,

1. That is it the undoubted Right of the People of *England*, in case their Representatives in Parliament do not proceed according to their Duty, and the People's Interest, to inform them of their Dislike, disown their Actions, and to direct them to such Things as they think fit, either by Petition, Address, Proposal, Memorial, or any other peaceable Way.

2. That the *House of Commons*, separately and otherwise than by Bill legally passed into an Act, have no legal Power to suspend or dispense with the Laws of the Land, any more than the King has by his Prerogative.

3. That the *House of Commons* has no legal Power to imprison any Person, or commit them to Custody of Serjeants, or otherwise (their own Members except) but ought to address the King, to cause any Person, on good Grounds, to be apprehended; which Person so apprehended, ought to have the Benefit of the *Habeas Corpus* Act, and be fairly brought to Tryal, by due Course of Law.

4. That if the *House of Commons*, in Breach of the Laws and Liberties of the People, do betray the Trust reposed in them, and act negligently or arbitrarily and illegally, it is the undoubted Right of the People of *England* to call them to an Account for the same, and by Convention, Assembly or Force, may proceed against them as Traitors and Betrayers of their Country.

These Things we think proper to declare, as the unquestioned Right of the

People of *England*, whom you serve, and in Pursuance of that Right, (avoiding the Ceremony of petitioning our Inferiors, for such you are by your present Circumstances, as the Person *sent* is less than the Sender.) We do publicly Protest against all your foresaid illegal Actions, and in the Name of ourselves, and of the good People of *England*, do require and demand

1. That all the Publick just Debts of the Nation be forthwith paid and discharged.

2. That all Persons *illegally imprisoned*, as aforesaid, be either immediately discharged, or admitted to Bail, as by Law they ought to be; and the Liberty of the Subject recognized and restored.

3. That *J[oh]n H[o]w*[1] aforesaid, be obliged to ask his Majesty Pardon for his vile Reflections, or be immediately expelled the House.

4. That the growing Power of *France* be taken into Consideration; the Succession of the Emperor to the Crown of *Spain* supported, our *Protestant* Neighbours protected, as the true Interest of *England*, and the *Protestant Religion* requires.

5. That the *French* King be obliged to quit *Flanders*, or that his Majesty be addressed to declare War against him.

6. That *suitable Supplies* be granted to his Majesty, for the putting all these necessary Things in Execution, and that care be taken, that such Taxes as are raised, may be more equally assessed and collected, and scandalous Deficiencies prevented.

7. That the *Thanks of the House* may be given to those Gentlemen, who so gallantly appeared in the Behalf of their Country, with the *Kentish* Petition, and have been so scandalously used for it.

Thus, *Gentlemen*, you have your Duty laid before you, which it is hoped you will think of; but if you continue to neglect it, you may expect to be treated according to the Resentments of an *injur'd Nation; for Englishmen* are no more to be Slaves to *Parliaments*, than to a King.

Our Name is Legion, and we are many.[2]

POSTSCRIPT

If you require to have this Memorial signed with our Names, it shall be done on your first Orders, and personally *presented.*

The Shortest-Way with the Dissenters: or Proposals for the Establishment of the Church

1702

In November 1702 a Bill was introduced into the Commons 'to Prevent Occasional Conformity', a Tory move to curb the political power of Dissenters (by forbidding the practice of periodic conformity with the Established Church to qualify for public office) and thus weaken their allies, the Whigs. The Queen had seemed to countenance such tactics by her first speech from the throne (May 1702) in which she declared her firm adherence to 'the interests and religion of the Church of England'. The Commons passed the Bill within a month; it was on the point of being sent to the Lords; political feeling was running high—and Defoe struck. *The Shortest-Way* appeared on 1 December. Its purpose was to satirize the extreme Tory view expressed in Dr Henry Sacheverell's famous 'Oxford sermon' (June 1702) which advised the Church 'to hang out the bloody flag of defiance against the Dissenters' (see Sutherland, *Defoe*, p. 279). Defoe's satiric method was to exaggerate such an attitude in order to expose its folly and to show the High Tories:

1. That 'tis Nonsense to go round about, and tell us of the Crimes of the *Dissenters*, to prepare the World to believe they are not fit to Live in a Humane Society, that they are Enemies to the Government, and Law, to the Queen, and the Public Peace, and the like; the *shortest way*, and the soonest, wou'd be to tell us plainly that they wou'd have them all Hang'd, Banish'd and Destroyed.
2. But withal to acquaint those Gentlemen who fancy the time is come to bring it to pass, that they are mistaken; for that when the thing they mean is put into plain *English*, the whole Nation replies with the *Assyrian* Captain, *Is thy Servant a Dog, that he shou'd do these things?* (*A Brief Explanation of a Late Pamphlet, entituled, The Shortest Way with the Dissenters*, [1703], p. 3).

The *Brief Explanation* rightly claims that men like Sacheverell had 'said the same things [as expressed in *The Shortest-Way*] in terms very little darker' – but Defoe's irony misfired. It was hailed by the Tories as a pungent expression of their case; it was denounced by the Dissenters whose cause it aimed to serve; though Defoe felt that 'if any man take the pains seriously to reflect upon the Contents, the Nature of the Thing and the Manner of the Stile, it seems Impossible to imagine it should pass for anything but an Irony' (*Brief Explanation*, p. 1). When the true intention of the pamphlet was recognized, the Government acted quickly. On 3 January 1703 a warrant was issued for Defoe's arrest; he was eventually caught and imprisoned in May. Yet his success was assured: he had exposed the follies of the extremists; he was known as the author of one of the most celebrated pamphlets ever written; and he had come to the attention of Robert Harley the moderate Tory politician, who was to be his protector for over a decade.

The Shortest-Way with the Dissenters, &c.

Sir *Roger L'Estrange* tells us a Story in his Collection of Fables, of the Cock and the Horses. The Cock was gotten to Roost in the Stable, among the Horses, and there being no Racks, or other Conveniences for him, it seems, he was forc'd to roost upon the Ground; the Horses jostling about for room, and putting the Cock in danger of his Life, he gives them this grave Advice; *Pray Gentlefolks let us stand still, for fear we should tread upon one another.*[1]

THERE are some People in the World, who now they are *unpearcht*, and reduc'd to an Equality with other People, and under strong and very just Apprehensions of being further treated as they deserve, begin with *Aesop's* Cock, to Preach up Peace and Union, and the Christian Duties of Moderation, forgetting, that when they had the Power in their Hands, those Graces were Strangers in their Gates.

It is now near Fourteen Years, that the Glory and Peace of the purest and most flourishing Church in the World[2] has been Eclips'd, Buffetted, and Disturb'd, by a sort of Men, who God in his Providence has suffer'd to insult over her, and bring her down; these have been the Days of her Humiliation and Tribulation: She has born with an invincible Patience the Reproach of the Wicked, and God has at last heard her Prayers, and deliver'd her from the Oppression of the Stranger.

And now they find their Day is over, their Power gone, and the Throne of this Nation possest by a Royal, *English*, True, and ever Constant Member of, and Friend to the Church of *England*. Now they find that they are in danger of the Church of *England*'s just Resentments; now they cry out *Peace, Union, Forbearance*, and *Charity*, as if the Church had not too long harbour'd her Enemies under her Wing, and nourish'd the viperous Brood, till they hiss and fly in the Face of the Mother that cherish'd them.

No Gentlemen, the Time of Mercy is past, your *Day of Grace is over*; you shou'd have practis'd Peace, and Moderation, and Charity, if you expected any your selves.

We have heard none of this Lesson for Fourteen Years past: We have been huff'd and bully'd with your Act of Tolleration;[3] you have told us that you are the *Church establish'd by Law*, as well as others; have set up your Canting-Synagogues at our Church-Doors, and the Church and her Members have been loaded with Reproaches, with Oaths, Associations, Abjurations, and what not; where has been the Mercy, the Forbearance, the Charity you have shewn to *tender Consciences of the Church of England*, that cou'd not take Oaths *as fast as you made 'em*; that having sworn Allegiance to their lawful and rightful King, cou'd not dispence with that Oath, *their King being still alive*, and swear to your new *Hodge-podge of a Dutch-Government*.[4] These ha' been turn'd out of their Livings, and they and their Families left to starve; their Estates double Tax'd, to carry on a War they had *no Hand in*, and you *got nothing by*: What Account can you give of the Multitudes you have forc'd to comply, against their Consciences, with your new *sophistical Politicks*, who like the new Converts in *France*, Sin because they can't Starve. And now the Tables are turn'd upon you, you *must not be Persecuted*, *'tis not a Christian Spirit*.

You have *Butcher'd* one King, *Depos'd* another King, and made a *mock King* of a Third; and yet you cou'd have the Face to expect to be employ'd and trusted by the Fourth; any body that did not know the Temper of your Party, wou'd stand amaz'd at the Impudence, as well as Folly, to think of it.

Your Management of your *Dutch Monarch*, whom you reduc'd to a meer *King of Cl[ub]s*, is enough to give any future Princes such an Idea of your Principles, as to warn them sufficiently from coming into your Clutches; and God be thank'd, the Queen is out of your Hands, knows you, and will have a care of you.

There is no doubt but the supreme Authority of a Nation has in its self a Power, *and a Right to that Power*, to execute the Laws upon any Part of that Nation it governs. The execution of the known Laws of the Land, and that with but a weak and gentle Hand neither, was all that the phanatical Party of this Land have ever call'd Persecution; this they have magnified to a height, that the Sufferings of the *Hugonots* in *France* were not to be compar'd with —— Now to execute the known Laws of a Nation upon those who transgress them, after having first been voluntarily consenting to the making those Laws, can never be call'd Persecution, but Justice. But Justice is always Violence to the Party offending, for every Man is Innocent in his own Eyes. The first execution of the Laws against the Dissenters in *England*, was in the Days of King *James* the First; and what did it amount to, truly, the worst they suffer'd, was at their own request, to let them go to *New-England*, and erect a new Collony,[5] and give them great Privileges, Grants, and suitable Powers, keep them under the Protection, and defend them against all Invaders, and receive no Taxes or Revenue from them. This was the cruelty of the Church of *England*, fatal Lenity! 'Twas the ruin of that excellent Prince, King *Charles* the First. Had King *James* sent all the

Puritans in *England* away to the *West-Indies*, we had been a national unmix'd Church; the Church of *England* had been kept undivided and entire.

To requite the Lenity of the Father, they take up Arms against the Son; Conquer, Pursue, Take, Imprison, and at last put to Death the anointed of God, and Destroy the very Being and Nature of Government, setting up a sordid Impostor, who had neither Title to Govern, nor Understanding to Manage, but supplied that want with Power, bloody and desperate Councils and Craft, without Conscience.

Had not King *James* the First witheld the full execution of the Laws; had he given them strict Justice, he had clear'd the Nation of them, and the Consequences had been plain; his *Son had never been murther'd by them*, nor the Monarchy overwhelm'd; 'twas *too much Mercy* shewn them, was the ruin of his Posterity, and the ruin of the Nation's Peace. One would think the Dissenters should not have the Face to believe that we are to be wheedl'd and canted into Peace and Toleration, when they know that they have once requited us with a civil War, and once with an intollerable and unrighteous Persecution for our former Civillity.

Nay, to encourage us to be Easy with them, 'tis apparent, that they never had the Upper-hand of the Church, but they treated her with all the Severity, with all the Reproach and Contempt as was possible: What Peace, and what Mercy did they shew the Loyal Gentry of the Church of *England* in the time of their Triumphant Common-wealth? How did they put all the Gentry of *England* to ransom, whether they were actually in Arms for the King or not, making People compound for their Estates, and starve their Families? How did they treat the Clergy of the Church of *England*, sequester'd the Ministers, devour'd the Patrimony of the Church, and divided the Spoil, by sharing the Church-Lands among their Soldiers, and turning her Clergy out to starve; just such Measure as they have mete, shou'd be measur'd to them again.

Charity and Love is the known Doctrine of the Church of *England*, and 'tis plain she has put it in practice towards the Dissenters, even beyond what they ought, till she has been wanting to her self, and in effect, unkind to her own Sons; particularly, in the too much Lenity of King *James* the First, mentioned before, had he so rooted the Puritans from the Face of the Land, which he had an opportunity, early to ha' done, they had not the Power to vex the Church, as since they have done.

IN the Days of King *Charles* the Second, how did the Church reward their bloody Doings with Lenity and Mercy, *except the barbarous Regicides of the pretended Court of Justice*; not a Soul suffer'd for all the Blood in an unnatural War: King *Charles* came in all Mercy and Love, cherish'd them, preferr'd them, employ'd them, witheld the rigour of the Law, and oftentimes, even against the Advice of his Parliament, gave them liberty of Conscience;[6] and how did they requite him with the villainous Contrivance to Depose and Murther him and his Successor at the *Rye-Plot*.[7]

KING *James*, as if Mercy was the inherent Quality of the Family, began his Reign with unusual Favour to them: Nor could their joining with the Duke of *Monmouth*[8] against him, move him to do himself Justice upon them; but that mistaken Prince thought to win them by Gentleness and Love, proclaim'd an universal Liberty[9] to them, and rather discountenanc'd the Church of *England* than them; how they requited him all the World knows.

THE late Reign is too fresh in the Memory of all the World to need a Comment; how under Pretence of joining with the Church in redressing some Grievances, they pusht things to that extremity, in conjunction with some mistaken Gentlemen, as to Depose the late King, as if the Grievance of the Nation cou'd not ha' been redress'd but by the absolute ruin of the Prince: Here's an Instance of their Temper, their Peace, and Charity. To what height they carried themselves during the Reign of a King of their own; how they crope[10] into all Places of Trust and Profit; how they insinuated into the Favour of the King, and were at first preferr'd to the highest Places in the Nation; how they engrost the Ministry, and *above all, how pitifully they Manag'd*, is too plain to need any Remarks.

BUT particularly, their Mercy and Charity, the Spirit of Union, they tell us so much of, has been remarkable in *Scotland*, if any Man wou'd see the Spirit of a Dissenter, let him look into *Scotland*; there they made an entire Conquest of the Church, trampled down the sacred Orders, and supprest the Episcopal Government,[11] with an absolute, and as they suppose, irretrievable Victory, tho', 'tis possible, *they may find themselves mistaken*: Now 'twou'd be a very proper Question to ask their *Impudent Advocate, the Observator*,[12] Pray how much Mercy and Favour did the Members of the Episcopal Church find in *Scotland*, from the *Scotch* Presbyterian-Government; and I shall undertake for the Church of *England*, that the Dissenters shall still receive as much here, tho' they deserve but little.

In a small Treatise *of the Sufferings of the Episcopal Clergy in Scotland*,[13] 'twill appear, what Usage they met with, how they not only lost their Livings, but in several Places, were plunder'd and abus'd in their Persons; the Ministers that cou'd not conform, turn'd out, with numerous Families, and no Maintenance, and hardly Charity enough left to relieve them with a bit of Bread; and the

Cruelties of the Party are innumerable, and not to be attempted in this short Piece.

And now to prevent the distant Cloud which they perceiv'd to hang over their Heads from *England*; with a true Presbyterian Policy, they put in for *a union of Nations*, that *England* might unite their Church with the Kirk of *Scotland*, and their Presbyterian Members sit in our House of Commons, and their Assembly of *Scotch* canting Long-Cloaks in our Convocation; what might ha' been, if our Phanatick, Whiggish-States-men had continu'd, God only knows; but we hope we are out of fear of that now.

'Tis alledg'd by some of the Faction, and they began to Bully us with it; that if we won't unite with them, they will not settle the Crown with us again, but when her Majesty dies, will chuse a King for themselves.

If they won't, we must make them, and 'tis not the first time we have let them know that we are able: The Crowns of these Kingdoms have not so far disowned the right of Succession, but they may retrieve it again, and if *Scotland* thinks to come off from a Successive to an Elective State of Government, *England* has not promised not to assist the right Heir, and put them into possession, without any regard to their ridiculous Settlements.

THESE are the Gentlemen, these their ways of treating the Church, both at home and abroad. Now let us examine the Reasons they pretend to give why we shou'd be favourable to them, why we should continue and tollerate them among us.

First, THEY are very Numerous, they say, they are a great Part of the Nation, and we cannot suppress them.

To this may be answer'd 1. THEY are not so Numerous as the Protestants in *France*, and yet the *French* King effectually clear'd the Nation of them at once,[14] and we don't find he misses them at home.

But I am not of the Opinion they are so Numerous as is pretended;[15] their Party is more Numerous than their Persons, and those mistaken People of the Church, who are misled and deluded by their wheedling Artifices, to join with them, make their Party the greater; but those will open their Eyes, when the Government shall set heartily about the work, and come off from them, as some Animals, which they say, always desert a House when 'tis likely to fall.

2dly. The more Numerous, the more Dangerous, and therefore the more need to suppress them; and God has suffer'd us to bear them as Goads in our sides, for not utterly extinguishing them long ago.

3dly. If we are to allow them, only because we cannot suppress them, then it ought to be tryed whether we can or no; and I am of Opinion 'tis easy to be done, and cou'd prescribe Ways and Means, if it were proper, but I doubt not but the Government will find effectual Methods for the rooting the Contagion from the Face of this Land.

ANOTHER Argument they use, which is this, That 'tis a time of War, and we have need to unite against the common Enemy.

WE answer, this common Enemy had been no Enemy, if they had not made him so; he was quiet, in peace, and no way disturb'd, or encroach'd upon us, and we know no reason we had to quarrel with him.

But further, We make no question but we are able to deal with this common Enemy without their help; but why must we unite with them because of the Enemy, will they go over to the Enemy, if we do not prevent it by a union with them—We are very well contented they shou'd; and make no question, we shall be ready to deal with them and the common Enemy too, and better without them than with them.

Besides, if we have a common Enemy, there is the more need to be secure against our private Enemies; if there is one common Enemy, we have the less need to have an Enemy in our Bowels.

'Twas a great Argument some People used against suppressing the Old-Money,[16] that 'twas a time of War, and 'twas too great a Risque for the Nation to run, if we shou'd not master it, we shou'd be undone; and yet the Sequel prov'd the Hazard was not so great, but it might be mastered; and the Success was answerable. The suppressing the Dissenters is not a harder Work, nor a Work of less necessity to the Publick; we can never enjoy a settled uninterrupted Union and Tranquility in this Nation, till the Spirit of Whiggisme, Faction, and Schism is melted down like the Old-Money.

To talk of the Difficulty, is to Frighten our selves with Chimæras and Notions of a Powerful Party, which are indeed a Party without Power; Difficulties often appear greater at a distance, than when they are search'd into with Judgment, and distinguish'd from the Vapours and Shadows that attend them.

We are not to be frightned with it; this Age is wiser than that, by all our own Experience, *and their's too*; King *Charles* the First, had early supprest this Party, if he had took more deliberate Measures. In short, 'tis not worth arguing, to talk of their Arms, their *Monmouths*, and *Shaftsburys*,[17] and *Argiles*[18] are gone, their *Dutch-Sanctuary* is at an end, Heaven has made way for their Destruction, and if we do not close with the Divine occasion, we are to blame our selves, and may remember that we had once an opportunity to serve the Church of *England*, by extirpating her implacable Enemies, and having let slip the Minute that Heaven presented, may experimentally[19] Complain, *Post est Occasio Calvo*.[20]

Here are some popular Objections in the way.

As first, THE Queen has promis'd them, to continue them in their tollerated Liberty; and has told us she will be a religious Observer of her Word.

WHAT her Majesty will do we cannot help, but what, as the Head of the Church, she ought to do, is another Case: Her Majesty has promised to Protect and Defend the Church of *England*,[21] and if she cannot effectually do that without the Destruction of the Dissenters, she must of course dispence with one Promise to comply with another. But to answer *this Cavil more effectually*: Her Majesty did never promise to maintain the Tolleration, to the Destruction of the Church; but it is upon supposition that it may be compatible with the well being and safety of the Church, which she had declar'd she would take especial Care of: Now if these two Interests clash, 'tis plain her Majesties Intentions are to Uphold, Protect, Defend, and Establish the Church, and this we conceive is impossible.

Perhaps it may be said, THAT the Church is in no immediate danger[22] from the Dissenters, and therefore 'tis time enough: But this is a weak Answer.

For first, IF a Danger be real, the Distance of it is no Argument against, but rather a Spur to quicken us to prevention, lest it be too late hereafter.

And 2dly, Here is the Opportunity, and the only one perhaps that ever the Church had to secure her self, and destroy her Enemies.

The Representatives of the Nation have now an Opportunity, the Time is come which all good Men ha' wish'd for, that the Gentlemen of *England* may serve the Church of *England*; now they are protected and encouraged by a Church of *England* Queen.

What will ye do for your Sister in the Day that she shall be spoken for.[23]

If ever you will establish the best Christian Church in the World.

If ever you will suppress the Spirit of Enthusiasm.

If ever you will free the Nation from the viperous Brood that have so long suck'd the Blood of their Mother.

If you will leave your Posterity free from Faction and Rebellion, this is the time.

This is the time to pull up this heretical Weed of Sedition, that has so long disturb'd the Peace of our Church, and poisoned the good Corn.

BUT, says another Hot and Cold Objector, this is renewing Fire and Faggot, reviving the Act *De Heret. Comburendo*:[24] This will be Cruelty in its Nature, and Barbarous to all the World.

I answer, 'TIS Cruelty to kill a Snake or a Toad in cold Blood, but the Poyson of their Nature makes it a Charity to our Neighbours, to destroy those Creatures, not for any personal Injury receiv'd, but for prevention; not for the Evil they have done, but the Evil they may do.

Serpents, Toads, Vipers, &c. are noxious to the Body, and poison the sensative Life; these poyson the Soul, corrupt our Posterity, ensnare our Children, destroy the Vitals of our Happyness, our future Felicity, and contaminate the whole Mass.

Shall any Law be given to such wild Creatures: Some Beasts are for Sport, and the Huntsmen give them advantages of Ground; but some are knock'd on Head by all possible ways of Violence and Surprize.

I do not prescribe Fire and Faggot, but as *Scipio* said of *Carthage, D[e]lenda est Carthago*;[25] they are to be rooted out of this Nation, if ever we will live in Peace, serve God, or enjoy our own: As for the Manner, I leave it to those Hands who have a right to execute God's Justice on the Nation's and the Church's Enemies.

BUT if we must be frighted from this Justice, under the specious Pretences, and odious Sense of Cruelty, nothing will be effected: 'Twill be more Barbarous and Cruel to our own Children, and dear Posterity, when they shall reproach their Fathers, as we do ours, and tell us, 'You had an Opportunity to root out 'this cursed Race from the World, under the Favour and Protection of a true '*English* Queen; and out of your foolish Pity you spared them, because, for-'sooth, you would not be Cruel, and now our Church is supprest and perse-'cuted, our Religion trampl'd under Foot, our Estates plundred, our Persons 'imprisoned and dragg'd to Jails, Gibbets, and Scaffolds; your sparing this '*Amalakite* Race is our Destruction, your Mercy to them proves Cruelty to 'your poor Posterity.

HOW just will such Reflections be, when our Posterity shall fall under the merciless Clutches of this uncharitable Generation, when our Church shall be swallow'd up in Schism, Faction, Enthusiasme, and Confusion; when our Government shall be devolv'd upon Foreigners, and our Monarchy dwindled into a Republick.

'Twou'd be more rational for us, if we must spare this Generation, to summon our own to a general Massacre, and as we have brought them into the

World Free, send them out so, and not betray them to Destruction by our supine negligence, and then cry *it is Mercy*.

Moses was a merciful meek Man, and yet with what Fury did he run thro' the Camp, and cut the Throats of Three and thirty thousand of his dear *Israelites*, that were fallen into Idolatry;[26] what was the reason? 'twas Mercy to the rest, to make these be Examples, to prevent the Destruction of the whole Army.

How many Millions of future Souls we save from Infection and Delusion, if the present Race of poison'd Spirits were purg'd from the Face of the Land.

'TIS vain to trifle in this matter, the light foolish handling of them by Mulcts, Fines, *&c.* 'tis their Glory and their Advantage; if the Gallows instead of the Counter, and the Gallies instead of the Fines, were the Reward of going to a Conventicle, to preach or hear, there wou'd not be so many Sufferers, the Spirit of Martyrdom is over; they that will go to Church to be chosen Sheriffs and Mayors,[27] would go to forty Churches rather than be Hang'd.

If one severe Law were made, and punctually executed, that who ever was found at a Conventicle, shou'd be Banished the Nation, and the Preacher be Hang'd, we shou'd soon see an end of the Tale, they wou'd all come to Church; and one Age wou'd make us all One again.

TO talk of 5*s*, a Month for not coming to the Sacrament, and 1*s. per* Week for not coming to Church, this is such a way of converting People as never was known, this is selling them a Liberty to transgress for so much Money: If it be not a Crime, why don't we give them full Licence? And if it be, no Price ought to compound for the committing it, for that is selling a Liberty to People to sin against God and the Government.

If it be a Crime of the highest Consequence, both against the Peace and Welfare of the Nation, the Glory of God, the Good of the Church, and the Happyness of the Soul, let us rank it among capital Offences, and let it receive a Punishment in proportion to it.

We Hang Men for Trifles, and Banish them for things not worth naming, but an Offence against God and the Church, against the Welfare of the World, and the Dignity of Religion, shall be bought off for 5*s*. this is such a shame to a Christian Government, that 'tis with regret I transmit it to Posterity.

IF Men sin against God, affront his Ordinances, rebell against his Church, and disobey the Precepts of their Superiors, let them suffer as such capital Crimes deserve, so will Religion flourish, and this divided Nation be once again united.

And yet the Title of Barbarous and Cruel will soon be taken off from this

Law too. I am not supposing that all the Dissenters in *England* shou'd be Hang'd or Banish'd, but as in cases of Rebellions and Insurrections, if a few of the Ring-leaders suffer, the Multitude are dismist, so a few obstinate People being made Examples, there's no doubt but the Severity of the Law would find a stop in the Compliance of the Multitude.

To make the reasonableness of this matter out of question, and more unanswerably plain, let us examine for what it is that this Nation is divided into Parties and Factions, and let us see how they can justify a Separation, or we of the Church of *England* can justify our bearing the Insults and Inconveniences of the Party.

ONE of their Leading Pastors, and a Man of as much Learning as most among them, in his Answer to a Pamphlet, entituled, *An Enquiry into the occasional Conformity,*[28] hath these Words, P. 27 *Do the Religion of the Church and the Meeting-houses make two Religions? Wherein do they differ? The Substance of the same Religion is common to them both; and the Modes and Accidents are the things in which only they differ.* P. 28 *Thirty-nine Articles are given us for the summary of our Religion, Thirty-six contain the Substance of it, wherein we agree; Three the additional Appendices, about which we have some differences.*[29]

Now, if as by their own acknowledgment, the Church of *England* is a true Church, and the Difference between them is only a few *Modes and Accidents,* Why shou'd we expect that they will suffer Gallows and Gallies, corporeal Punishment and Banishment for these Trifles; there is no question but they will be wiser; even their own Principles won't bear them out in it, they will certainly comply with the Laws, and with Reason, and tho' at the first, Severity may seem hard, the next Age will feel nothing of it; the Contagion will be rooted out; the Disease being cur'd, there will be no need of the Operation, but if they should venture to transgress, and fall into the Pit, all the World must condemn their Obstinacy, as being without Ground from their own Principles.

Thus the Pretence of Cruelty will be taken off, and the Party actually supprest, and the Disquiets they have so often brought upon the Nation, prevented.

THEIR Numbers, and their Wealth, makes them Haughty, and that is so far from being an Argument to perswade us to forbear them, that 'tis a Warning to us, without any more delay, to reconcile them to the Unity of the Church, or remove them from us.

AT present, Heaven be prais'd, they are not so Formidable as they have been, and 'tis our own fault if ever we suffer them to be so; Providence, and the Church of *England*, seems to join in this particular, that now the Destroyers of the Nations Peace may be overturn'd, and to this end the present Opportunity seems to be put into our Hands.

To this end her present Majesty seems reserv'd to enjoy the Crown, that the Ecclesiastick as well as Civil Rights of the Nation may be restor'd by her Hand.

To this end the Face of Affairs have receiv'd such a Turn in the process of a few Months, as never has been before; the leading Men of the Nation, the universal Cry of the People, the unanimous Request of the Clergy, agree in this, that the Deliverance of our Church is at hand.

For this end has Providence given us such a Parliament, such a Convocation, such a Gentry, and such a Queen as we never had before.

AND what may be the Consequences of a Neglect of such Opportunities? The Succession of the Crown has but a dark Prospect, another *Dutch* Turn[30] may make the Hopes of it ridiculous, and the Practice impossible: Be the House of our future Princes never so well inclin'd, they will be Foreigners; and many Years will be spent in suiting the Genius of Strangers to the Crown, and to the Interests of the Nation; and how many Ages it may be before the *English* Throne be filled with so much Zeal and Candour, so much Tenderness, and hearty Affection to the Church, as we see it now cover'd with, who can imagine.

'Tis high time then for the Friends of the Church of *England*, to think of Building up, and Establishing her, in such a manner, that she may be no more Invaded by Foreigners, nor Divided by Factions, Schisms, and Error.

IF this cou'd be done by gentle and easy Methods, I shou'd be glad, but the Wound is coroded, the Vitals begin to mortifie, and nothing but Amputation of Members can compleat the Cure; all the ways of Tenderness and Compassion, all perswasive Arguments have been made use of in vain.

THE Humour of the Dissenters has so encreas'd among the People, that they hold the Church in Defiance, and the House of God is an Abomination among them: Nay, they have brought up their Posterity in such pre-possest Aversions to our Holy Religion, that the ignorant Mob think we are all Idolaters, and Worshippers of *Baal*; and account it a Sin to come within the Walls of our Churches.

The primitive Christians were not more shie of a Heathen-Temple, or of Meat offer'd to Idols, nor the *Jews* of Swine's-Flesh, than some of our Dissenters are of the Church, and the Divine Service solemnized therein.

THIS Obstinacy must be rooted out with the Profession of it; while the Generation are left at Liberty daily to affront God Almighty, and Dishonour his Holy Worship, we are wanting in our Duty to God, and our Mother the Church of *England*.

How can we answer it to God, to the Church, and to our Posterity, to leave them entangled with Fanaticisme, Error, and Obstinacy, in the Bowels of the Nation; to leave them an Enemy in their Streets, that in time may involve them in the same Crimes, and endanger the utter Extirpation of Religion in the Nation.

WHAT's the Difference betwixt this, and being subjected to the Power of the Church of *Rome*, from whence we have reform'd? If one be an extreme on one Hand, and one on another, 'tis equally destructive to the Truth, to have Errors settled among us, let them be of what Nature they will.

Both are Enemies of our Church, and of our Peace, and why shou'd it not be as criminal to admit an Enthusiast[31] as a Jesuit? Why shou'd the *Papist* with his Seven Sacraments be worse than the *Quaker* with no Sacraments at all? Why shou'd Religious-houses be more intollerable than Meeting-houses— Alas the Church of *England*! What with Popery on one Hand, and Schismaticks on the other; how has she been Crucify'd between two Thieves.

Now *let us Crucifie the Thieves*. Let her Foundations be establish'd upon the Destruction of her Enemies: The Doors of Mercy being always open to the returning Part of the deluded People: Let the Obstinate be rul'd with the Rod of Iron.

Let all true Sons of so Holy an Oppressed Mother, exasperated by her Afflictions, harden their Hearts against those who have oppress'd her.

And may God Almighty put it into the Hearts of all the Friends of Truth, to lift up a Standard against Pride and Antichrist, that the Posterity of the Sons of Error may be rooted out from the Face of this Land for ever——

FINIS

A Hymn to the Pillory   1703

After his arrest on 20 May 1703, on the Earl of Nottingham's warrant, for publishing *The Shortest-Way*, Defoe was released on bail. He rejected the advice of friends (to which he alludes near the end of the *Hymn*) to break bail; he returned to Newgate and, on 7 July, was sentenced to a fine of 200 marks, to find sureties of good behaviour for seven years, and to stand three times in the pillory. Nottingham deferred the pillorying in the hope of extracting evidence against leading Whigs, but Defoe refused to 'sell his Friends'; he was put in the pillory on 29, 30 and 31 July. It was a punishment he feared: prisoners had been maimed, even killed, by hostile crowds. However, his courage was equal to the occasion: as he stood in the '*State-Trap* of the Law' the *Hymn* was being sold among the onlookers. It was a calculated appeal to mob-emotion; audaciously it defied the men in power, with the result that, instead of attacking him, the crowd encouraged Defoe with their sympathy. The appeal above the law to their common humanity had triumphed.

A Hymn to the Pillory

Hail *Hi'roglyphick* State *Machin*,
Contriv'd to Punish Fancy in:
Men that are Men, in thee can feel no Pain,
And all thy *Insignificants* Disdain.
    Contempt, that false New Word for shame,   5
    Is without Crime an empty Name.
    A Shadow to Amuse Mankind,
But never frights the Wise or Well-fix'd Mind:
    Vertue despises Humane Scorn,
    And Scandals Innocence adorn.   10

    Exalted on thy *Stool of State*,
What Prospect do I see of Sov'reign Fate;
    How th' *Inscrutables* of Providence,
    Differ from our contracted Sence;
    Here by the Errors of the Town,   15
    The Fools look out and Knaves look on.
Persons or Crimes find here the same respect,
    And Vice does Vertue oft Correct,
    The undistinguish'd Fury of the Street,
    Which Mob and Malice Mankind Greet: 20
    No Byass can the Rabble draw,
But *Dirt* throws *Dirt* without respect to Merit, or to Law.

Sometimes the *Air of Scandal* to maintain,
Villains look from thy Lofty Loops in Vain:
But who can judge of Crimes by Punishment,   25
Where Parties Rule, and L[aw]s Subservient.
Justice with Change of Int'rest Learns to bow,
And what was Merit once, is Murther now:
Actions receive their Tincture from the Times,
And as they change are Vertues made or Crimes.   30
    Thou art the *State-Trap* of the Law,

But neither can keep Knaves, nor Honest Men in Awe;
 These are too hard'nd in Offence,
 And those upheld by Innocence.

How have thy opening Vacancy receiv'd,   35
In every Age the Criminals of State?
 And how has Mankind been deceiv'd,
 When they distinguish Crimes by Fate?
Tell us, *Great Engine*, how to understand,
Or reconcile the Justice of the Land;   40
How *Bastwick*, *Pryn*, *Hunt*, *Hollingsby* and *Pye*,[1]
 Men of unspotted Honesty;
 Men that had Learning, Wit and Sence,
 And more than most Men have had since,
Could equal Title to thee claim,   45
With *Oats* and *Fuller*,[2] Men of later Fame:
 Even the Learned *Selden*[3] saw,
 A Prospect of thee, thro' the Law:
He had thy *Lofty Pinnacles* in view,
But so much Honour never was thy due: 50
Had the Great *Selden* Triumph'd on thy Stage,
 Selden the Honour of his Age;
 No Man wou'd ever shun thee more,
Or grudge to stand where *Selden* stood before.

 Thou art no shame to Truth and Honesty,   55
Nor is the Character of such defac'd by thee,
 Who suffer by Oppressive Injury.
 Shame, like the Exhalations of the Sun,
 Falls back where first the motion was begun:
And they who for no Crime shall on thy Brows appear,   60
Bear less Reproach than they who plac'd 'em there.

But if Contempt is on thy Face entail'd,
 Disgrace it self shall be asham'd;
Scandal shall blush that it has not prevail'd,
 To blast the Man it has defam'd.   65
Let all that merit equal Punishment,
Stand there with him, and we are all Content.

There would the Fam'd S[achevere]ll[4] stand,
With Trumpet of Sedition in his Hand,
Sounding the first *Crusado* in the Land.   70
    He from a Church of *England* Pulpit first
        All his Dissenting Brethren Curst;
        Doom'd them to Satan for a Prey,
        And first found out *the shortest way*;
With him the Wise Vice-Chancellor o'th 'Press.[5]   75
Who, tho' our Printers Licences defy,
        Willing to show his forwardness,
        Bless'd it with his Authority;
He gave the Churche's Sanction to the Work,
As *Popes* bless Colours for Troops which fight the *Turk*.   80
    Doctors in scandall these are grown,
For *Red-hot Zeal* and Furious Learning known:
Professors in Reproach and highly fit,
For *Juno*'s Academy, *Billingsgate*.[6]
    Thou like a True-born *English* Tool,   85
        Hast from their Composition stole,
And now art like to smart for being a Fool:
And as of *English* Men, 'twas always ment,
They'r better to Improve than to Invent;
    Upon their Model thou hast made,   90
    A Monster makes the World afraid.
    With them let all the States-men stand,
    Who Guide us with unsteady hand:
    Who Armies, Fleet, and Men betray;
    And Ruine all *the shortest way*.   95
    Let all those Souldiers stand in sight,
Who're Willing to be paid and not to fight.
Agents, and Collonels, who false Musters bring,
To Cheat your Country first, and then your King:
Bring all your *Coward Captains* of the Fleet;   100
Lord! What a Crowd will there be when they meet?

    They who let *Pointi* 'scape to *Brest*,
With all the Gods of *Cartagena* Blest.[7]
    Those who betray'd our *Turkey* Fleet;
Or Injur'd *Talmash* Sold at *Camaret*.[8]   105
    Who miss'd the Squadron from *Thouloon*,

103

And always came too late or else too soon;[9]
All these are Heroes whose great Actions Claim,
Immortal Honour to their Dying Fame;
    And ought not to have been Denyed,   110
On thy great Counterscarp, to have their Valour try'd.

Why have not these upon thy swelling Stage,
Tasted the keener Justice of the Age;
If 'tis because their Crimes are too remote,
Whom leaden-footed Justice has forgot?   115
    Let's view the modern Scenes of Fame,
If Men and Management are not the same;
        When Fleets go out with Money, and with Men,
        Just time enough to venture home again?
Navyes prepar'd to guard th' insulted Coast,   120
    And Convoys settl'd when Our Ships are lost.
    Some Heroes lately come from Sea,
If they were paid their Due, should stand with thee;
    Papers too, should their Deeds relate,
To prove the Justice of their Fate: 125
Their Deeds of War at *Port Saint Mary*'s done,
And see the Trophy's by them, which they won:
Let Or[mon]d's Declaration there appear,
He'd certainly be pleas'd to see 'em there.
    Let some good Limner represent,   130
    The ravish'd Nuns, the plunder'd Town,
    The *English* Honour how mispent;
The shameful coming back, and little done.[10]

    The *Vigo* Men[11] should next appear,
    To Triumph on thy Theater;   135
They, who on board the Great Galoons had been,
Who rob'd the *Spaniards* first, and then the Queen:
Set up their praises to their Valour due,
How Eighty Sail, had beaten Twenty two.
    Two Troopers so, and one Dragoon,   140
Conquer'd a *Spanish* Boy, a Pampalone.[12]
    Yet let them Or[mon]d's Conduct own,
Who beat them first on Shore, or little had been done:
    What unknown spoils from thence are come,

How much was brought away, *How little home.*   145
If all the Thieves should on thy Scaffold stand
    Who rob'd their Masters in Command:
    The Multitude would soon outdo,
    The City Crouds of Lord Mayor's show.

.   .   .   .

When all these Heroes have past once thy Stage,
And thou hast been the Satyr of the Age;
Wait then a while for all those Sons of Fame,   275
Whom present Pow'r has made too great to name:
Fenc'd from thy hands, they keep our Verse in Awe,
Too great for Satyr, and too great for Law.
    As they their Commands lay down,
They all shall pay their Homage to thy Cloudy Throne: 280
    And till within thy reach they be,
    Exalt them in Effigie.

    The Martyr of the by-past Reign,
For whom new Oaths have been prepar'd in vain;
She[rloc]k's Disciple first by him trepan'd,   285
He for a K[nave] and they for F[ool]s should stand
Tho' some affirm he ought to be Excus'd,
    Since to this Day he had refus'd;
And this was all the Frailty of his Life,
He Damn'd his Conscience, to oblige his Wife.[13]   290
But spare that Priest, whose tottering Conscience knew
That if he took but one, he'd Perjure two:
Bluntly resolv'd he wou'd not break 'em both,
And Swore by G[o]d he'd never take the Oath;
    Hang him, he can't be fit for thee,   295
    For his unusual Honesty.

    Thou *Speaking Trumpet* of Mens Fame,
    Enter in every Court thy Claim;
Demand 'em all, for they are all thy own,
Who Swear to Three Kings, but are true to none.   300
    Turn-Coats of all sides are thy due,

And he who once is false, is never true:
To Day can Swear, to Morrow can Abjure,
For Treachery's a Crime no Man can Cure:
Such without scruple, for the time to come,   305
May Swear to all the Kings in Christendom;
  But he's a Mad Man will rely
  Upon their lost Fidelity.

They that in vast Employments rob the State,
See them in *thy Embraces* meet their Fate;   310
Let not the Millions they by Fraud obtain,
Protect 'em from the Scandal, or the Pain:
  They who from Mean Beginnings grow
  To vast Estates, but God knows how;
  Who carry untold Sums away,   315
From little Places, with but little Pay:
  Who Costly Palaces Erect,
  The Thieves that built them to Protect;
The *Gardens, Grotto's, Fountains, Walks, and Groves*
Where Vice Triumphs in Pride, and Lawless Loves: 320
Where mighty Luxury and Drunk'ness Reign'd,
Profusely Spend what they Prophanely Gain'd:
Tell 'em there's *Mene Tekel's*¹⁴ on the Wall,
Tell 'em the *Nations Money* paid for all:
  Advance by double Front and show,   325
And let us both the Crimes and Persons know:
Place them aloft upon thy Throne,
Who slight the Nation's Business for their own;
Neglect their Posts, in spight of Double Pay,
And run us all in Debt *the Shortest Way*.   330

Great Pageant, Change thy Dirty Scene,
For on thy Steps some Ladies may be seen;
When Beauty stoops upon thy Stage to show
She laughs at all the Humble Fools below.
 Set *Sapho* there, whose Husband paid for Clothes   335
Two Hundred Pound a Week in *Furbulo's*:¹⁵
There in her Silks and Scarlets let her shine,
She's Beauteous all without, all Whore within.

Next let Gay *URANIA* Ride,
Her Coach and Six attending by her side: 340
    Long has she waited, but in vain,
    The City Homage to obtain:
The Sumptuous Harlot long'd t' Insult the *Chair*,
And Triumph o'er our City Beauties there.
Here let her Haughty Thoughts be Gratifi'd,   345
    In Triumph let her Ride;
    Let *DIADORA* next appear,
And all that want to know her, see her there.
What tho' she's not a *True Born English Wh*[o]*re?*
    French Harlots have been here before;   350
Let not the Pomp nor Grandeur of her State
    Prevent the Justice of her Fate,
But let her an Example now be made
To Foreign *Wh*[ore]*s* who spoil the English Trade.
Claim 'em, thou *Herald of Reproach,*   355
Who with uncommon Lewdness will Debauch;
Let *C——* upon thy Borders spend his Life,
'Till he Recants the Bargain with his Wife:
    And till this Riddle both Explain,
    How neither can themselves Contain;   360
How Nature can on both sides run so high,
As neither side can neither side supply:
    And so in Charity agree,
He keeps two Braces of Whores, two Stallions she.

    What need of *Satyr* to Reform the Town?   365
    Or Laws to keep our Vices down?
    Let 'em *to Thee* due Homage pay,
This will Reform us all *the Shortest Way.*
Let 'em *to thee* bring all the Knaves and Fools,
    Vertue will guide the rest by Rules: 370
They'll need no Treacherous Friends, no breach of Faith,
No Hir'd Evidence with their Infecting Breath;
    No Servants Masters to Betray,
    Or Knights o'th' Post,[16] who Swear for Pay;
No injur'd Author'l on thy Steps appear,   375
Nor such as *wou'd be Rogues,* but such *as are.*
    The first Intent of Laws

Was to Correct th' Effect, and check the Cause;
   And all the Ends of Punishment,
Were only Future Mischiefs to prevent. 380

   But Justice is Inverted when
     Those Engines of the Law,
Instead of pinching Vicious Men,
     Keep Honest ones in awe;
   Thy Business is, as all Men know, 385
To Punish Villains, not to make Men so.

   When ever then thou art prepar'd,
To prompt that Vice thou should'st Reward,
And by the Terrors of thy Grisly Face,
   Make Men turn Rogues to shun Disgrace; 390
The End of thy Creation is destroy'd,
   Justice expires of Course, and Law's made void.

   What are thy Terrors? that for fear of thee,
     Mankind should dare to sink their Honesty?
He's Bold to Impudence, that dare turn Knave, 395
     The Scandal of thy Company to save:
He that will Crimes he never knew confess,
Does more than if he knew those Crimes transgress:
     And he that fears thee more than to be base,
     May want a Heart, but does not want a Face. 400

   Thou like the Devil dost appear
Blacker than really thou art by far:
   A wild Chimerick Notion of Reproach,
Too little for a Crime, for none too much:
   Let none th' Indignity resent, 405
For Crime is all the shame of Punishment.
Thou Bug-bear of the Law stand up and speak,
   Thy long Misconstru'd Silence break,
Tell us who 'tis upon thy Ridge stands there,
   So full of Fault, and yet so void of Fear; 410
   And from the Paper in his Hat,
Let all Mankind be told for what:

Tell them it was because he was too bold,
And told those Truths, which shou'd not ha' been told.
    Extoll the Justice of the Land, 415
Who Punish what they will not understand.
      Tell them he stands Exalted there,
      For speaking what we wou'd not hear;
      And yet he might ha' been secure,
Had he said less, or woud' he ha' said more. 420
      Tell them that this is his Reward,
      And worse is yet for him prepar'd,
Because his Foolish Vertue was so nice
As not to sell his Friends, according to his Friends Advice;

      And thus he's an Example made, 425
    To make Men of their Honesty afraid,
      That for the time to come they may,
      More willingly their Friends betray;
Tell 'em the Men that plac'd him here,
Are Friends unto the Times, 430
      But at a loss to find his Guile,
      They can't commit his Crimes.

FINIS

Letter to Robert Harley

May–June 1704?

Sir

As I Took the freedome to Say to you So I Can Not but Repeat to your honor I am at a Loss how to behave my Self under the Goodness and Bounty of the Queen. Her Majtie Buyes my Small Services So Much too Dear[1] and leaves me So Much in the Dark as to my Own Merit That I am Strangely at a stand what to Say.

I have Enclos'd My humble Acknowlegemt to Her Majtie and Perticularly to my Ld Treasurer but when I am writeing to you Sir Pardon me to alter my Stile. I am Impatient to kno' what in my Small Service pleases and Engages. Pardon me Sir Tis a Necessary Enquiry for a Man in the Dark that I may Direct my Conduct and Push That Little Merit to a proper Extent.

Give me leav Sir as at first to Say I Can Not but Think Tho' her Majtie is Good, and My Ld Treasurer kind, yet my wheel within all These Wheels must be your Self, and There I Fix my Thankfullness as I have of a Long Time my hope—as God has Thus Mov'd you to Reliev a Distrest family, Tis my Sincere Petition to him, that he would Once Put it into my hand to Render you Some Such Signall Service, as might at least Express my Sence of it, and Encourage all Men of Power to Oblige and Espouse Gratefull and Sincere Minds.

Your farther Enquiry Into the Missfortunes and afflicting Circumstances That attend and Suppress me fills me with Some Surprise. What Providence has Reserv'd for me he Only knows, but Sure The Gulph is too Large for me to Get ashore again.

I have Stated the black Case. Tis a Mellancholly prospect Sir and My feares Suggest That Not less Than a Thousand Pounds will Entirely Free me.

Tis True and I am Satisfy'd 500*l* or 6 at Most Joyn'd to This I Now Reciev will Open the Door to Liberty and bind all The hands of Creditors That I may have Leisure to Raise The Rest [in] perhaps a year or Two, but the Summe is Too Large for me to Expect.[2]

Indeed This Debt is Rais'd by Doublings of Interest on bonds, The Length of Time haveing Encreased the Burthen. I was Riseing Fairly to Clear it all when the Publick Disaster you kno' of began, but Sir That Entirely blasted all my affaires, and I Can Easily Convince you was above 2500*l* Loss to me all at Once.[3]

I forbear to Say all the Moveing Things to you I Could on This head. All my prospects were built on a Manufacture I had Erected in Essex; all The late kings Bounty to me was Expended There. I Employ'd a hundred Poor Familys at work and it began to Pay me Very well. I Generally Made Six hundred pound profit per Annum.

I began to live, Took a Good House,[4] bought me Coach and horses a Second Time. I paid Large Debts Gradually, small Ones wholly, and Many a Creditor after composition whom I found poor and Decay'd I Sent for and Paid the Remaindr to tho' Actually Discharged.

But I was Ruin'd *The shortest way* and Now Sir had Not your Favour and her Majties Bounty Assisted it must ha' been One of the worst Sorts of Ruine. I do Not mean as to Bread; I firmly and I Thank God Comfortably Depend on the Divine Goodness That I shall Never want That, But a Large and Promiseing family, a Vertuous and Excellent Mother to Seaven Beautifull and hopefull Children, a woman whose fortunes I have Ruin'd, with whom I have had 3700*l*, and yet who in the worst of my afflictions when my Ld N. first Insulted her Then Tempted her,[5] scorn'd So much as to Move me to Complye with him, and Rather Encourag'd me to Oppose him.

Seaven Children Sir whose Education Calls on me to furnish Their heads if I Can not Their Purses, and which Debt if not paid Now Can Never be Compounded hereafter is to me a Moveing Article and helps Very often to make me Sad.

But Sir I am I Thank God Furnisht with Patience. I Never Despaird and In the Worst Condition allways believ'd I should be Carryed Thro' it, but which way, has been and yet Remaines a Mystery of Providence Unexpounded.

I beg heartly your Pardon for This Tedious Epistles. The Miserable are allways full of Their Own Cases and Think Nothing Impertinent. I write This for tis too Moveing for me to Speak it. I shall attend the Ordrs and houres you Appointed To morro' Even and am

Sir, your Most obedt Servt
[symbol][6]

I Presume to send the Enclos'd[7] Open for your Approbation. You will please to put a seal to it—

A Review   1704-13

Possibly the surest literary evidence of Defoe's interests and principles, as well as his personality, is the *Review*, a periodical which he sustained three times a week—except for a few months late in 1712 when the tax on periodicals forced him to publish twice a week—for over nine years. The very length of the *Review*'s career—nearly five times as long as the *Tatler*, *Spectator*, or *Guardian*—proves the man's tenacity of purpose, resourcefulness and courage.

> I have spoken neither for Gain, or the Hopes of it; neither to oblige or serve any one Party or Person in the world; on the Other Hand, I never did, or ever shall refrain speaking what my own Conscience dictates to me to be Truth (*Review*, VIII, 137).

Though in the main the *Review* supported Robert Harley's moderate Toryism this claim of essential independence cannot at least be disproved. It is certainly demonstrable that Defoe avoided party extremes; he frequently emphasized the danger of party strife and the need for national unity. Politics, both domestic and foreign, were perennial topics, as was trade, but so, as the occasion demanded, were the religious situation, the state of the theatre or of the Press. On every topic he was invariably provocative; overt amusement was confined to the short-lived 'Scandalous Club' or 'Miscellanea' sections, or the 'Little Review'; but for the most part he relied on intellectual stimulus. He was forthright, believing that the issues he treated were too serious for bantering or the mild satire purveyed by the *Spectator;* he recognized that his purpose could be achieved only by hammering away at ideas.

> My case differs from all your other writers [such as the *Spectator*]; they court you to read, invite you, propose to make you smile, and contrive to do it, that you may read and buy their Papers; I must force you to read [for] your Interest, your occasion, the Use you make of the Subjects I write on. (I [IX], 40, p. 80).

Indeed he told his readers in 1709, 'he thinks 'tis more for your service to make you wise, than merry' (IV, 34, p. 133).

His truthfulness was always a matter for pride—in 1710 he challenged any reader to reveal 'one Untruth in Seven Years Writing' (VII, 95, p. 377)—and accordingly his style was direct, bold and plain. In fact his comment on a letter from a correspondent may appropriately be applied to his own writing: 'The Honesty and Plainess of the Stile . . . I hope will offend no body, but rather convince any Man of the [writer's] Genuine Native Sincerity' (III, 94, p. 375).

A Review

Vol. II No. 26 Thursday, May 3, 1705

Digression upon Digression; (said the Printer, when he read the Copy of this Paper.) *Well*, Gentlemen, *the Cause is new, and the Author must give you the History of it.*

Nothing could have taken me off from the Weighty and Serious Subject of Peace, which I have so Earnestly pursued, and which I am pleas'd to say, has met with so general an Encouragement, but an Accident like this; and since it is but the Trespass of one Paper, I hope it may be Excused.

We have lately Erected at the Cost and Charges of several Pious Charitably Disposed Christians, a Noble and Magnificent Fabrick, near the *Hay-market*, in the Liberties of *Westminster*.¹

The Name of this Thing (for by its Outside, it is not to be Distinguish'd from a *French Church* or a Hall, or a Meeting-House, or any such usual Publick Building) is a Theater, or in *English*, a Play-House.

The Use and Design of this, is for the Encouragement of Wit, the Entertainment of the Ladies, *&c.* for the Representations, or Misrepresentations of Vice, for the Encouragement of Vertue; and, in short, to Contribute to the Exceeding Reformation of our Manners.

The Dimensions of this Noble Pile, its Beauty, its Stupendious Height, the Ornament and Magnificence of its Building, are Demonstrations of the Great Zeal of our Nobility and Gentry, to the Encouragement of Learning, and the Suppressing Vice and Immorality.

What tho' the Founders of this Structure may Complain of Deficient Funds for the Compleating the Building, and that some Gentlemens Names stand to the Roll, whose Money has not yet Encreased the Bank, and that there may be some Ground for the following Notes?

> The Fabrick's Finish'd, and the Builder's part
> Has shown the Reformation of his Art.
> Bless'd with Success, thus have their first Essays
> *Reform'd* their *Buildings*, not *Reform'd* their *Plays*.
> The Donor's Bounty may be well Design'd,
> But who can Guess the Model of the Mind?

> Never was Charity so Ill Employ'd,
> Vice so [En]courag'd, Vertue so Destroy'd;
> Never Foundation so abruptly laid,
> So Much Subscrib'd, and yet so little Paid.
> On Publick Faith the Fabrick they begin,
> And Vice it self is run in Debt to Sin.

After all, the Author has nothing to say to the Crime of a Play; nor am I so Narrow in my Opinion, as to think it is an Unlawful Action, either in the Player's *Acting*, or the Person's *Seeing* a Play, if it could be Abstracted from all the Unhappy Circumstances that attend our Theaters.

Nor am I so angry at the Gentlemen Concern'd in our Theaters, either as Poets, or Actors; I know 'tis the Taste of the Town, that will have everything mix'd with something Vicious, or will not be pleas'd with it. *D[am]n a Sober Dog, a serious Play is like a Game at Nothing*, and away they go; so that, in short, to Reform the Stage, would be not to Build it up, but to pull it down; and if nothing but Representations of Vertue, and Decrying Vice, should be the Dull Subject, the Wit would be lost, and the Labour too, and all the Players and Poets would be starv'd.

But, Gentlemen and Ladies, if you would have a Reformation in the Playhouse, you must Reform your Taste of Wit, and let the Poet see, you can Relish a Play, tho' there be neither Bawdy, nor Blasphemy in it.

If you find any foul Stuff, tho' wrap'd up in never so Clean Linen, Hiss it off the Stage, and show your Resentment at it, by that Blast which the Breath of an Auditory can give it.

If you find a Poet Insulting Heaven, by way of Suppressing Prophaneness, Bantering Vertue to Discourage Vice, Speaking Blasphemy with a Grace to Discountenance Irreligion, and Talking B[aw]dy, to set off your Modesty. Let the Impotent Buffoon know, by your Contempt of his rude Essay, that your Judgment is no more to be Impos'd upon, than your Senses; and that you can Distinguish the Performance from the Pretences.

If this were done, Players would be Distinguish'd by the Company; at a Lewd Light Entertainment, you would have no Body come, that have been used to Blushing; and at a Noble Sublime Piece of Wit, and True Invention, you would have Faces that never were seen there before.

Custom and Habit would bring Vertue into liking, and a Performance full of Instruction, and pointed with True Satyr, at every Thing Vicious, would be every Jot as Entertaining, as Farce full of Lewd and Vicious Emblems, Empty and Profane Similies.

This would Reform the Stage to your Hands, and you would find the Gentlemen of the Stage, are only Occasional Conformists to Vice, because they see you require it as Tradesmen that bring those Goods to Market that will Sell best.

I cannot be without so much Charity for our Players, as to believe this of them; they cannot be Men of Action, without being Men of Sence; and as they are the latter, they could not but be as well pleased with what was Clean, Handsome, and well Perform'd, when it came from the pure Channel of Honour and Vertue, as from the Black *Stygian* Lake of Nastiness and Corruption.

The Standard of Wit would thus be altered, we should have no Ill Plays Wrote, because they would please no Body; the Players would not Act them, because no Body would come to see them; the Booksellers would not Print them, because no Body would Buy.

In short, the Errors of the Stage, lie all in the Auditory; the Actors, and the Poets, are their Humble Servants, and being good Judges of what will please, are forc'd to Write and Act with all the Aggravations and Excesses possible, that they may not be Undone and Ruin'd, lose both their Reputation and their Employments.[2]

So easie a Thing would it be to Reform the Stage; so soon would a Mode of Vertue Ruine all the Manufacture of Vice in the Nation.

I had not Design'd to Introduce this into the World in so short an Abridgment, but that I find the first Prologue at the Opening our New House Publish'd this Day, in which I own a great deal of Wit, but so firmly built upon the Old Foundation of Vice and Prophaneness, that I cannot Imagine, but it is an Eternal Reflection upon the Auditory, to be pleas'd with it.

Comparing the Building to the Introduction of the World, and the Poet to the Creator, is Prophane, without Excuse: I confess, to say that Cathedrals and Churches were built from the Ages Ignorance, and bringing it down to this Age thus:

And Stages Thrive, as Churches did before,

Is Clenching[3] a Jest upon themselves; and I joyn with the Poet, that the Thriving of the Stage, is from the Ages Ignorance, especially while Unreform'd and Prophane.

I Conclude this Paper with the Copy of the Prologue, and a few hasty lines upon the same Subject, which are left to the Censure of the Readers.

PROLOGUE[4] *Spoken at the* First Opening *of the*
QUEEN'S New Theatre *in the* Hay-Market

Such was our Builder's Art, that soon as Nam'd,
This Fabrick, like the Infant-World, was Fram'd.

The Architect must on dull Order wait.
But 'tis the Poet only can Create.
None else, at Pleasure, can Duration give,
When Marble fails, the Muses Structures live.
The *Cyprian* Fane is now no longer seen,
Tho' Sacred to the Name of Love's Fair Queen.
Ev'n *Athens* scarce in Pompous Ruine stands,
Tho' finish'd by the Learn'd *Minerva*'s Hands.
More sure Presages from these Walls we find,
By Beauty founded,⁵ and by Wit design'd;
In the good Age of Ghostly Ignorance,
How did Cathedrals rise, and Zeal Advance?
The Merry Monks said *Orisons* at Ease,
Large were their Meals, and light their Penances;
Pardon for Sins was purchas'd with Estates,
And none but Rogues in Rags Dy'd Reprobates.
But now that Pious Pageantry's no more,
And Stages Thrive, as Churches did before.
Your own magnificence you here Survey,
Majestick Columns stand, where Dunghils lay,
And Carrs Triumphal rise from Carts of Hay.
Swains here are taught to hope, and Nymphs to fear,
And big *Almanzor*'s Fight, mock-*Blenheim*'s here.
Descending Goddesses Adorn our Scenes,
And quit their bright Abodes for Gilt Machines.
Shou'd *Jove*, for this fair *Circle*, leave his Throne,
He'd meet a Lightning fiercer than his own.
Tho' to the *Sun*, his tow'ring *Eagles* Rise,
They scarce cou'd bear the Lustre of these Eyes.

On the New Playhouse *in the* Hay-Market

A *Lay-stall*⁶ this, *Apollo* spoke the Word,
And straight arose a *Playhouse* from a T[urd].
Here *Whores* in *Hogstyes*, Vilely blended lay,
Just as in *Boxes*, at our *Lewder Play;*
The Stables have been Cleans'd, the Jakes made Clear,
Herculean Labours, ne'r will Purge us here.
   Some call this Metamorphosis a Jest,
And say, We're but a *Dunghill* still at best;

The Nastiness of all your Common-Shores,
Being far less Nauseous than our *Beaus* and *Whores.*
Bless us! (said I) What Monstrous Beast's a Man?
Whom Rules can never Guide, nor Art make Clean;
View but our Stately Pile, the *Columns* stand
Like some Great *Council Chamber* of the Land:
When Strangers View the Beauty and the State,
As they pass by, they ask *what Church* is that?
Thinking a Nation, so Devout as we,
Ne'r build such *Domes,* but to some Deity;
But when the *Salt Assembly*[7] once they View,
What Gods they Worship, how *Blaspheme the True;*
How Vice's Champions, Uncontroul'd within,
Roul in the very Excrements of Sin:
The *Horrid Emblems* so Exact appear,
That Hell's an Ass, to what's Transacted here.

Vol. III   No. 2   Thursday, January 3, 1706

Of Trade in General

Trade is a general Exchange of the Necessaries and Utensils of Life, from and between Person and Person, Place and Place.

The Principal Subjects of Trade are Included, in Provisions, House-Furniture, and Cloathing; and they are handed from Place to Place, by an Infinite and incessant Circulation; they are attended with a vast Variety of Handicrafts, to Furnish Tools to make Vessels to Convey, and Instruments to produce and preserve.

'Twould be Foreign to the Design of these Papers, to give an *Index* of the several Arts, into which Trade is thus subdivided. I shall go on farther upon the Generals, and then come to Particulars of another sort.

Generally speaking, all the Innumerables of Trade, come under these two Heads; Natural Produce, and Manufacture. The different Climates and Soil in the World, have, by the Wisdom and Direction of *Nature Natureing,* which I Call GOD, produc'd such differing Species of things, all of them in their kind equally Necessary, or at least Useful and Desirable; as insensibly preserves the Dependance, of the most Remote Parts of the World upon one another; and at least makes them useful to each other, and Contributing to one anothers Convenience, Necessity, or Delight.

And here I might digress to good purpose, in setting out, how the most Plentiful Country, receives from the most Barren; how every Nation has something to fetch from, and something to send to one another; every Nation something to spare, which another Country wants, and finds something wanting, another Country can spare; and this occasions Exchanging with those Countries, to the Advantage of both; and that we call TRADE. This necessarily implies Convenience for Portage, and that we call Navigation; and thus General Negoce began to be improv'd by Humane Industry, to Strange and Unaccountable Enlargements.

This Variety also, is not only Natural, but Artificial; and as the Climates and Soil, have produc'd in every Country different Growths or Species of things; so the differing Genius of the People of every Country, prompts them to different Improvements, and to different Customs. They Eat, Wear, and Dwell after differing Manners; and as all People, Tenacious of their own way, seek what qualifies them best to pursue it; they seek to Foreign Climates to furnish themselves, with what they cannot have so much to their purpose, or so suited to their occasions or Inclinations at Home; and this is again Revolv'd into necessary Correspondence, they must send to those Countries some Equivalent, to satisfie the People for what they take from them; and thus we are again brought home to *TRADE*.

To Examine this Variety a little, may not be Unpleasant, nor in its end Unprofitable to the Reader; because it will tend to open our particular Scenes of Trade, of which in Course, I shall come to Treat more Particularly and Largely, than perhaps is expected.

The Variety, both of the Produce and Manufactures of the several Countries, are the Foundations of Trade, and I Entitle Providence to it; not only as it is found in Nature, but as it is found in Customs and Consequences of things; for GOD in whose Infinite foreknowledge, all the Accidents of Time are always present, who is one Infinite Substantial Essential NOW, in which is no past or future, must be suppos'd to foreknow that Natural Causes consider'd, *and to Natural Causes, he had in his infinite Wisdom by Laws of Nature, submitted all the Variety of Consequences*; the Generations of the World, could not subsist in the Manner prescrib'd, without the Mutual Assistance, and Concurrence of one another. The bare Produce of the Earth, in many of our Neighbouring Countries, could by no means have Maintain'd the Numbers of People, which the Consequences of Trade have brought together. To Answer for this, Navigable Rivers, as well as a Navigable Sea, has made the Communication of Remote Parts Practicable; and Floaty Bodies are adapted for Vessels, that the Light

Bodies may bear the Heavy, and Goods that will not bear it, may be fenc'd from the Inconvenience of Weather, and preserv'd fit for Use and Convenience.

The Rivers and Roads, are as the Veins and Arteries, that Convey Wealth, like the Blood, to all the Parts of the World; and this Wealth is the Life of Kingdoms and Towns; the Support of their People, and Test of their Power.

I wonder sometimes, at the Ignorance of those People and Nations, whose Gentry pretend to Despise Families rais'd by Trade;[1] Why should that, which is the Wealth of the World, the Prosperity and Health of Kingdoms and Towns, be accounted Dishonourable?

If we Respect Trade, as it is understood by Merthandizing; it is certainly the most Noble, most instructive, and Improving of any way of Life. The Artificers or Handicrafts-Men, are indeed Slaves; the Gentlemen are the Plowmen of the Nation, but the Merchant is the Support, and Improver of Power, Learning, and Fortunes.

A True-Bred Merchant, is a Universal Scholar, his Learning Excells the meer Scholar in Greek and Latin, as much as that does the Illiterate Person, that cannot Write or Read: He Understands Languages without Books, Geography without Maps; his Journals and Trading-Voyages delineate the World; his Foreign Exchanges, Protests and Procurations, speak all Tongues; He sits in his Counting-House, and Converses with all Nations, and keeps up the most exquisite and extensive part of human Society in a Universal Correspondence.

He is qualified for all sorts of Employment in the State, by a General Knowledg of things and Men; he remits and draws such vast Sums, that he Transacts more Value than a large Exchequer.

By the Number of these, Cities, rise out of nothing, and decay again into Villages: If Trade abandons a Port; if the Merchants quit the place, it languishes of course, and dies like Man in a Consumption, insensibly; if these flock to a Town, Home-trade crowds upon them; Seamen increase; People flock in, and the Village soon becomes a City.

In Nations and Empires 'tis the same; what infinite Crowds of People flock into *Holland*; Cities without Number, and Towns thick like the Houses in other Countries, that the whole Country seems to be one populous City; People in such Multitude, that all the Land in the Country can't find Butter and Cheese for them; much less maintain them.

All these attend upon Trade; by Trade, they possess the World, and have greater Stocks of Goods in each Country's Growth, than the Countries from whence they have them can show.

Their Rivers are throng'd with Shipping like a Wood; their Naval Stores are inexhaustible; they can build a Navy, and fit it to Sea, sooner than any Nation in the World; and yet have neither the Timber or Plank, the Iron-Work or

Cordage, the Pitch or the Tar, the Hemp or the Rosin, in any part of the Country.

All this is done by Trade; the Merchant makes a wet Bog become a populous State; enriches Beggars, enobles Mechannicks, raises not Families only, but Towns, Cities, Provinces and Kingdoms.

How then can that be dishonourable; that in its kind is the support of the World, and by and from which Nations and Kingdoms are made to differ from one another; are made to excel one another, and be too strong, because too rich for one another.

The Merchant by his Correspondence reconciles that infinite Variety, which, as I noted, has by the Infinite Wisdom of Providence, been scattred over the Face of the World.

If *England* has Wool, and *Spain* has Oil; *Spain* sends her Oil over to *England* to enable *England* to work that Wool into Cloth, Bays, Sayes, Perpets and Stuffs; and so they may be sent over to *Spain* for their Clothing.

Has *Spain* Wine, *England* has her Beer and fine Ale, which in those Countries where there they have Wine, is justly esteem'd before it: And again, we send for their Wines to drink here, our Prelates enclining to seek those Liquors which we must fetch from abroad.

We Cloth all the Islands and Continent of *America*; and they in return, furnish us with Sugars and Tobaccoes, things by Custom becoming as useful to us, as our Cloths is to them: Trade carries the very Soil away, and transposes the World in Parts; removing Mountains, and carrying them over the Sea into other Countries; what a Quantity of the *Terra Firma* has been carried from *New-Castle* in *Coles*; whose Ashes lie mix'd with the Soil in most parts of the World; what Cavities and Chasms in the Bowels of the Earth have we made for our Tin, Lead and Iron, in the respective Countries of *Cornwal, Darby* and *Sussex*.

These we carry abroad, and with them we purchase and bring back the Woods of *Norway*; the Silks of *Italy* and *Turky*; the Wines and Brandies of *France*, the Wines, Oil, and Fruit of *Spain*; the Druggs of *Persia*; the Spices of *India*; the Sugars of *America*; the Toys and Gaiety of *China* and *Japan*.

An infinite Variety might here be run through; every Country Communicates to its other corresponding Country what they want; and these can spare them *vice versa*; receive from that Country again, what of their Growth these want; and not a Country so barren, so useless, but something is to be found there that can be had no where else.

All the World could not have thought of such an encreasing Trade, as has been establish'd in our Colonies of *America*; for Tobacco and Sugar and abundance of useful things; the Cocheneal, Cocoa, Bark and Drugs of *America*; the Elephants Teeth of *Africa*; the Fish of *Newfoundland* and *New-England*; the

Whales from uninhabitable *Greenland*, and the like; no Nation so hot or so cold, but it contributes something to another, by which Wealth is advanced, People benefited and imploy'd; and this in its true Original call'd, TRADE.

In the Pursuit of this Matter of General Trade, the Nature of the thing led Mankind to a Necessity of a General Medium of Trade; and the Original of this is found in this absolute Necessity: For example, one Country Demands more Goods from another, than it can pay for in Goods of its own Growth or Procuring, or than that Country will take in Exchange: now Trade labouring under this Dilemma, Necessity drove Men to form a Medium of Trade; something whose Value being always intrinsick, would be accepted every where, and that always must attend to form the Balance and pay the overplus; and this is, MONEY.

When this Money could not be either readily as to Time, or sufficiently as to Quantity, be procur'd; the Honour and Character of the Persons, raised from Experience of Probity and punctual Payment, made the Men easy; and in Confidence of the Integrity of the Person Trading, he will be content with to Morrow, which cannot with convenience be had to Day; and accordingly he stays the Day appointed, and then receives it; *and this we call CREDIT*; of both which in our ensuing Discourse.

Vol. IV   No. 106   Thursday, October 16, 1707

. . . O Money, Money! What an Influence hast thou on all the Affairs of the quarreling, huffing Part of this World, as well as upon the most plodding Part of it! Without Thee Parliaments may meet, and Councils sit, and Kings contrive, but it will all be to no Purpose, their Councils and Conclusions can never be put in Execution! Thou raisest Armies, fightest Battles, fittest out Fleets, takest Town, Kingdoms, and carriest on the great Affairs of the War; All Power, all Policy is supported by Thee, even Vice and Vertue act by thy Assistance, by Thee all the great things in the World are done, Thou makest Heroes, and crown'st the Actions of the mighty; *By Thee*, in one Sence Kings reign, Armies conquer, Princes grow Great, and Nations flourish.

Mighty *Neuter!* Thou great *Jack-a-both sides* of the World, how hast Thou brought all Things into Bondage to thy Tyranny? How art Thou the mighty WORD of this War, the great Wheel in the vast Machine of Politick Motion, the Vehicle of Providence, the great *Medium* of Conveyance, in which all the Physick of the secret Dispensation in human Affairs is administred, and by the Quantity of which it operates to Blessing or Cursing? Well art thou call'd *the God of this World*; for in thy Presence and Absence consists all the Heaven or Hell of human Affairs; for Thee, what will not Mankind do, what Hazards will they run, what Villanies perform? For Thee, Kings tyrannize, Subjects are oppress'd, Nations ruin'd, Fathers murther'd, Children abandon'd, Friends betray'd. Thou art the Charm that unlocks the Cabinet, unscrews Nature; for Thee, the Traytor fawns, the Parasite flatters, the Profligate swears, and the Hippocrite prays; for Thee, the Virgin prostitutes, the Honourable degenerates, the Wise Man turns Fool, the Honest Man a Knave, the Friend turns Traytor, the Brother turns a Stranger, Christians turn Heathens, and Mankind Devils.

Thou art the Test of Beauty, the Judge of Ornament, the Guide of the Fancy, the Index of Temper, and the Pole Star of the Affections; Thou makest Homely Things Fair, Old Things Young, Crooked Things Straight; Thou hast the great Remedy of Love, thou can'st give the Blind an Eye, the Lame a Leg, the Froward a Temper, and the Scandalous a Character; Thou makest Knaves honest, Whores chast, and Bullies Justices of the Peace; Thou creepest into all our Towns, Cities, Corporations, Court Houses, ay, and Churches too; Thou makest the Differences there between the Great and the Small, the High and the Low, and to thy Charge it is justly lay'd, why Sotts lead, Blockheads preach, Knaves govern, and Elected Fools make Aldermen and Mayors.

In the Armies, Thou workest Wonders too; there Thou makest the Coward fight, and the Brave run away: Thou givest Victory, and leadest Triumphs; all the Caps and Feathers stand upon thy Head, and Thou hast the Passing of all Commissions; Thou makest Mareschals of *France*, Governours of Provinces, and Lieutenant-Generals; Thou makest Bullies Admirals, Sodomites Captains of Men of War, Cowards Commodores, and Brutes Leaders of Men. For Thee, the poor Soldier strives to have his Brains beat out, the Officers court Thee through all the Paths of Death and Horror; for Thee the Generals shift Hands, serve any body, nobody, and every body; Thou makest Christians fight for the *Turks*, Thou hirest Servants to the Devil, nay to the very Czar of *Muscovy*.

For Thee, the Kings of the Earth raise War, and the Pot-sherds dash against one another. Thou art Ambition, for Pride is really nothing but Covetousness; 'tis for Thee the Mighty sell their Rest, their Peace, and their Souls in Quest of Crowns and Conquests. They talk sometimes of other Trifles, such as Liberty, Religion, and I know not what; but 'tis all for Thee, I never knew but two Exceptions in our Histories, *viz*, *Gustavus Adolphus*, and King *William*; Thou art the mighty Center of human Action, the great Rudder the World steers by, the vast Hinge the Globe turns on—O Money, Money, who can form [thy] Character!

And yet Thou necessary Evil, Thou has some Panegyrick due to Thee also, and they that rail most at Thee, seek thy Favour; Thou assistest the Injur'd to shake off their Chains, the Invaded to defend themselves, and the Oppressed to regain their Liberty, and Thou art equally necessary to one, as to the other. In thy Excesses and the Excursions of Men about Thee, consists all thy Scandal; Thou encouragest Vertue, rewardest Honesty, and art the Reward given to Man for his Labour, *under the Sun*; without thy help, Tyrants would never be dethroned, nor Ambition restrained, nor any of the Capital Diseases of the World cured.

And how art Thou to be obtain'd? How must we court thy Favour? Truly, just as the rest of the World does, where Thou art, we must seek Thee; where Thou art legally provided, thou shouldest be legally demanded; but where fraudulently, oppressively, or violently amass'd, by the same Violence Thou art to be lawfully seiz'd upon; such are Pyrates of Nature, and ought to be plunder'd for the publick Good, and if their Power cannot be subdued, you may doubtless use the best Means you can to remove out of their Possession, the Prisoner MONEY.

And this brings me down to the Times; Money is now the Business, raising Money is the Affair, Ways and Means is the *Word*; the Answer is ready, where Money is legally obtain'd, it must be legally obtain'd again; Subjects honestly labouring, honestly possessing, ought to be left quietly, enjoying what they are Masters of; and this is the Foundation of what we call Law, Liberty, and Property, and the like modern Words very much in Use; this is the End of Parliaments, Constitutions, Government and Obedience; and this is the true Foundation of Order in the World, and long may it be our Priviledge to maintain it.

Vol. V   No. 31   Tuesday, June 8, 1708

Well, Gentlemen, I have done with my Exhortation about your choosing *Tories*; your Elections are near over, and if you have been mad, you must reap as you have sown; if you have done well, you will fear no Envy; if you have done ill, you will deserve no Pity; the Issue must determine the thing.

But I cannot quit this Affair of Elections, before I take Notice a little of the general Behaviour of the Gentry and Persons of Quallity, in order to their Election—What is become of all our Comedians? Ah, *Rochester, Shadwel,*

Otway, Oldham,[1] where is your Genius? Certainly, no Subject ever deserv'd so much to be exposed, nothing can be so fruitful in Banter, or deserved more to be ridicul'd.

Here's a Knight of the Shire, and he rides round the Country to get Votes, and he is to be at such a Town on the Market Day to meet with the Country Freeholders. Two Country Men are going to that Market, and they hear the Great Man will be there, and they fall to talk of it as they go along; One's a Grasier, and has *a Cow to sell*; the Other's a Farmer, and he has a Sow and Piggs, and they fall to dialogue it as they go along.

Grasier: Neighbour J., what they say Sir *Thomas* will be at the Town today.

Farmer: What to speak about his Election I warrant ye, is'nt it?

Gra.: Ay, ay, zooks we mun all vote for him, they say, his Bayly was with all the Tenants t'other Day, and kiss'd all our Wives round, and said, my Landlord sent him; but they say, he shall come and kiss 'em himself, before they'll speak for him, they won't take it at second hand.

Far.: Your good Wives know their Landlord well enough; was it not he that kiss'd Farmer *M.*'s Wife, and put two Guineas into her Mouth, which serv'd to stop her Mouth, and make her Husband speak?

Gra.: My Landlord does all he can to get in, and yet he never could get half his own Tenants to vote for him.

Far.: He's too close fisted, he does nothing for poor Folks all the time, but just when he wants to be chosen.

Gra.: Well, well, we must make him pay for it then, and he shall pay for it, if he gets my Vote for all I am his Tenant; I pay him Rent enough for his Farm, and if he don't like it, I have a little Farm of my own, I [can] live without him; if he comes to speak to me, I'll be very plain with'n.

Far.: In troth so will I too; but what shall we say to him, will he give us any Money?

Gra.: I can't tell; but if he won't, Sir *William* will, and he sets up against him; the Greyhound is his House, and he spends his Money like a Prince; I'm resolv'd to go there, I know his Steward *Jeffery*.

Far.: Nay, I'll go to them both; a Body may get drink enough at both Houses, and Money too they say; I'll e'en get it of both of them, as long as it is to be had.

Gra.: No, no, M., that is not fair.

Far.: Fair, they are Rogues to give Money at all; if they will give their Money away, any Body may take it, mayn't they? I don't steal it from them.

Gra.: But they give it to get your Vote, and you promise to vote for them, and you must cheat one of them.

Far.: That's your Mistake now, Neighbour, for *Jeffery* was with me yesterday, and I am to have two Guineas of his Masters to day, and I made no positive Promise, but put him thus; why Mr. *Jeffery*, Sir *William* knows, I won't be against him, leave the rest to me; he pretends to understand me, and I shall promise just the same to Sir *Thomas* today, if I can get two Guineas more; and then when the Day comes, I'll e'en stay at home, and vote for no Body, and a'nt I as good as my Word?

By this Part of the Story Gentlemen may see how they are used, when they go underhand to bribe and buy Voices from the Country; they debauch the very Morals of the People, gull and cheat themselves, see themselves Bubbles to the poorest Clown, and are bound to stand still, and tho' they know it, say nothing.

Here are two Gentlemen in a Town on the Market Day, there they take up each of them a publick House; first the Alehouse Keeper, he bumboosels them, and charges all the Ale he has in the House twice over, so much a Barrel, whether 'tis drunk out or no; if his Worship does not like it, he does him wrong, for he has brought in all his Customers to vote for him; and Sir *William* sent his Gentleman to him, and would he but have espoused his Interest, he offer'd him all that, and ten Guineas for the Use of his House——. Well, there's no disputing, there's 150 *l.* to pay, and there is no Remedy.

Well, then here sits Sir *Thomas* all the Market Day, the Rooms are all full; here's two or three Butchers, there half a dozen Farmers; in another a Gang of such a Townsmen, and Up-Stairs a Parcel of their Wives; Sir *Thomas* has his Servants up and down the Town, and in every Gang among them fishing for Votes, and drinking with them; now he goes into this Room, then to that; here a drunken Butcher, gorg'd with his Ale, spues in his Worships Presence, there a Clown belches in his Face; here Farmer *Q*s Wife huffs his Steward, because Sir *Thomas* was not civil to her, that is, spoke to her to have her Husbands Vote, but did not put two Guineas into her Hand, and tells him, her Sons are both Freeholders, and what does Sir *Thomas* mean? There's an old Woman, she's out of Humour, and a going away, and what's the Matter?—No, nothing's the Matter, but my Dame goes away, and won't promise the Steward any thing; well, she's quite lost, and the Reason is never known, till it comes out among the Gossips in the Neighbourhood, and the Steward hears of it, that Sir *Thomas* spoke to her in the Street, and did not salute her Gentlewomanship, whereas he had kissed all the Goodies and Gammars in the upper Room; this Scene is at the Sign of the *Red Lyon*, Sir *Thomas*——knows where.

Shall we go over the Way now to Sir *William*——, he is at the *Greyhound*, as the Farmer told us just now; and pray Friends take it with you as you go, that this Farce now has the Misfortune to be so true a Jest, that really I can hardly find in my Heart to laugh at it.

Sir *William* is a jolly, frank, open handed Gentleman, whether *Whig* or *Tory*, I don't examine, that is not to the Purpose here; the Lesson is to them all, and either may make use of the Moral, while it would be their Wisdom to let alone the Fable.

Coming into the *Greyhound* Inn at ——, you find it a large House built on all Sides of a Square Yard, or in our common Dialect, *all round the Square*, the Rooms and Gallaries are all full of the Country People, and several Tables in the Yard, some quite drunk, some three quarters speed, all drinking, stinking, roaring, swearing, sleeping, spuing, etc. and all for Sir *William*.

At a Table on the right hand under a Shed, on the *North East* Corner of the Wall, just by a Kennel where the Fox is chain'd, I am the more particular, because perhaps Sir *William* may want those Directions to remember it by, tho' one would think he should not neither——. At this Table sits about half a dozen Country Fellows, Butchers, Tanners, Farmers, and *sike*² *like*, drunk enough you may be sure.

Sir *William*, as he visits the Rooms where his Freeholders are drinking, comes out into the Gallary, and they spy him; then first Huzza, and all upon their Feet shouting, a——, a——, naming his Name, Sir *William* salutes them from the Gallary, and down they sit to it again; by and by one drunker than the rest, he calls out to Sir *William*, that he drank his Health, then there's another Bow due from Sir *William*: But Sir *William*, says the Clown aloud, won't you come and drink with us? and then he wraps out a Great W[oun]ds, won't your Worship come and drink one Cup with your honest Freeholders, we are all Freeholders, and swears again by his Maker, and again all Freeholders, B[y]G[o]dD[amn] yea, Sir *William*, all Freeholders, won't your Worship drink with us?

Well, Sir *W.* honest Gentleman, he does not care for it; but he says, Ay, ay, Gentlemen, I'll come to you presently, and then he sends one of his Stewards or Agents, bids him go to them. Who a P[ox] sent you to us Goodman Gentleman, you are a Steward, you are a Slave; bring us Sir *William* or the young Esq.; d[amn] ye, we scorn to drink with any Body but your Master, Sirrah——. Well, Gentlemen, says the Steward, for he must not offend them, my Master will wait on you; then another begins with two or three Hiccups and Belches, why look you Mr. ——, to the Steward, we are all Men that have something of our own, Man, and if Sir *W.* won't drink with us, *look ye Sir*, d'ye see, and he won't drink wy us, *that is*, and if Sir *William*, *that is*, thinks himself, *d' ye see*, too good to drink, *that is*, with poor Country Folks, *d'ye see*, why then I'll tell ye, that Sir, *d' ye see*, we'll vote none, *that is*, come *Tom*, we'll be gone; No, pray Gentlemen, pray Gentlemen, my Master is coming——. Away he goes and tells Sir *William*, they are a going away, if his Worship does not come down.

Down comes Sir *William*——, and O then they are as joyful as Drunkenness and Oaths will let them be, and his Worship must sit down; and could I but give you a Picture now of the Baronet among the *Boors*; on one hand of him sits a Butcher, greasie as the Master of the Company, fat as a Bullock of 12 *l.* Price, drunk as a Drum, drivelling like a Boar, foaming at Mouth with a Pipe in his Jaws, and being in the open Yard, holds it so that the Wind carries the Smoak directly in Sir *William*'s Face; on the other hand sits a Tanner, not so fat, but twice as drunk as t'other, every now and then he lets a great Fart, and first drinks his Worship's Health, then spues upon his Stockings; a third gets up from the Lower End of the Table to make a Leg, and drink to his Worship; then comes so near him to give him the Flagon, that making his reeling Bow, he spills some of the Beer upon him, gives a great Belch in his Face, and so scratching his Head, waits till his Worship must drink after him, and give him the Pot again; and making his Leg again a little too low, runs forward, being as the Sailors call too much by the Head, and over sets Sir *William*'s Chair and all, and falls upon him, the rest get all up to help him up; and two or three of them dragging their Brother Beast off him, Sir *William* gets up himself, and his Man is fain to help them up one after another——. Well, then his Worship sits, there's no getting away from them; if he offers to stir away, what won't your Worship drink with us, we'll all vote for you, then a Hiccup and an Oath by their Maker, and every Word interleaved with Damnation and Curses——. Well, at last comes in the Farmer, we talk'd of with his Sow and Piggs; ho *M., M.*, you Dog cries the Butcher, for belike he was a Chairman, here come hither, here is Sir *William*—— (I cannot foul my Paper, nor your Mouths, *Readers*, with their Oaths and Blasphemies, but your Imagination will suggest them). Come hither, *M.*, you Dog, come hither; then the Tanner begins with an Oath to Sir *William*, that's a Freeholder, an't like your Worship, we'll make him vote for your Worship, and he was always for Sir *Thomas*, we'll make him be for you——. Come hither, *M.*, you Dog, won't ye drink with Sir *William* ——. Huzza, a Dottrel, a Dottrel,[3] or a any thing, *that's instead of his Worships Name, by the way.*

Well, *M.* comes and makes his Leg—and Sir *William* speaks to him for his Vote. Ha, ha, an't like your Worship, I han't promised any Body yet; I am as like as another not to be against your Worship, ha ha. And what hast got there Goodman *M.*, says Sir *William*, what hast brought to Market? a Sow and Piggs, an't please your Worship to buy them, it will do me a Kindness; the Butcher whispers Sir *William*, buy them, buy them, your Worship shall be sure of him then; well, says Sir *William*, buy them for me—If you give him a little more than they are worth, you understand the thing; up gets the Butcher, let's see them, *M.*, what shall Sir *William* give you for them? —*M.*, why I'll have three Mark for them —No, no, look you *M.*, that is too much; but you know Sir *William* stands for our Shire, you shall vote for him, and he shall take the Sow and Piggs, and leave the Price to us——. Well, well, I an't against him, I'll give you my Word for that.—*So they make the Bargain*, the Butcher comes back, Sir *William* I have bought the Sow and Piggs, and he promises; your Worship must give him three Mark for them; Sir *William* orders the Steward to pay the Money; the Sow and Piggs are worth about half the Money, the Fellow promises he won't be against Sir *William*, but never promises to vote for him; goes away after that to Sir *Thomas*, gets Ditto of him, and keeps his Word with both by voting for no Body.

I could carry this Scene on to the most sordid monstrous Excesses, to which I have been too much an Eye-Witness; but I leave the Gentlemen yoak'd with *Boors* stooping to all the meanest, and vilest, and most indecent things imaginable, nay, till one of the Brutes calls to him to reach the Chamber Pot over the Table to him; but this beastly Doing is enough to shew the Gentlemen their own Picture *in little*, when their Interest guides them to seek an Opportunity of getting into a Parliament House. What Men that can stoop to this are fit for, when they come there, is a Question admits of a farther Enquiry.

Vol. VIII   No. 75   Saturday, September 15, 1711

Abuses in Trade never encrease so much, as when Trade declines—Men in Business driven to innumerable Shifts and Subterfuges, to support their Affairs, invade Right, encroach upon Justice, and dishonour Themselves. Again, They undermine one another, Combine and Confederate against one another; enter into Engrossments, Monopolies, Combinations, *&c.* And, in short, they seem to make War upon Trade itself; and one Observation I have made in this Case, which I believe seldom fails; these Encroachments upon Trade, Combinations, and Engrossings, generally end in Bankruptcy; the Reason is evident, thriving Men are generally fair Dealers; I allow it to be true, that they thrive, because they are fair Dealers; but much more is it true, they are fair Dealers because they Thrive.

The World has a very unhappy Notion of Honesty, which they take up to the Prejudice of the Unhappy—Such a Man is a fair Merchant, a punctual Dealer, an honest Man, and a rich man—Ay, says one, that makes him a rich Man, God blesses him because he is an Honest Man—*It's a mistake,* God's blessing is the Effect of no Man's Merit—God's blessing may have made him a rich Man—*But why is he an honest Man, a fair Dealer, a punctual Merchant?* The Answer is plain, Because he is a rich Man—The Man's Circumstances are easie, his Trade answers, his Cash flows, and his Stock Encreases; this Man cannot be otherwise than Honest, he has no occasion to be a Knave—Cheating in such a Man ought to be Felony, and that without the Benefit of Clergy[1]—He has no Temptation, no wretched Necessity of Shifting and Tricking, which another Man flies to, to deliver himself from Ruin—The Man is not Rich, because he is Honest, but he is Honest because he is Rich.

Look to the foolish and injurious Notion of the Age; Men are K[nave]s that break, and no doubt many K[nave]s do break—But give me leave to say, Men are made K[nave]s by breaking; a certain Draper not far from his Neighbours, had it always in his Mouth, such a Man was a Rogue, such a Villain, such a Cheat—Why, Sir, says one—Why, he can't pay his Debts—If he had said won't pay his Debts, I had join'd with him; but to prevent my asking after his Abilities, he always added, every Man was a Rogue that was a Bankrupt, and in 6 Months, I found his Father's Name in the *Gazette*;[2] this made him a little Modester, and now he finds as much difficulty to keep his own out, as any Man in the Street has done this seven Year—Blessed be God, Honesty of Principle may remain under deep Disasters, all the K[nave]s are not yet broke, some stand behind their Counters still, and walk the *Change* still, who deserve more the Gallows, than the Miserable that shelter under the Fury of Creditors; and are only Honest now, because they are not under the Necessity of being otherwise.

And pray, Gentlemen, do not vouch too fast for your own Honesty; you that have not been try'd with Distresses and Disasters, ye know not what you are your selves—Many a Man that thinks himself as Honest as [his] Neighbours, will find himself as great a R[ogu]e as any of them all, when he comes to the push.

How many honest Gentlemen have we in *England* of good Estates and noble Circumstances, that would be Highway Men, and come to the Gallows, if they were poor? How many rich, current, punctual, fair Merchants now walk the *Exchange*, that would be errant K[nave]s if they came to be Bankrupt? Poverty makes Thieves, as bare Walls makes giddy Housewives; Distress makes K[nave]s of honest Men, and the Exigencies of Tradesmen, when in declining Circumstances, of which none can judge, and which none can express but these that have felt them, will make honest Men do that, which at another time their very Souls abhorr—I own to speak this with sad Experience, and am not asham'd to confess myself a Penitent—And *let him that thinketh he standeth take heed lest he fall.*[3]

Let the honestest Man in this Town tell me when he is sinking, when he sees his Family's Destruction in such an Arrest, or such a Seizure, and has his Friends Money by him, or has his Employers Effects in his Hand; Can he refrain making use of it—? Can he forbear any more than a Starving Man will forbear his Neighbours Loaf? Will the honestest Man of you all, if ye were drowning in the *Thames*, refuse to lay hold of your Neighbour who is in the same Condition, for fear he drown with you? Nay, will you not pull him down by the Hair of his Head, tread on him with your Feet, tho' you sink him to the Bottom, to get yourself out?—What shall we say?—*Give me not Poverty, lest I Steal*,[4] says the *Wiseman, that is,* if I am poor I shall be a Thief; I tell you all, Gentlemen, in your Poverty, the best of you all will rob your Neighbour; nay go farther, *as I said once on the like Occasion,* you will not only rob your Neighbour, but if in distress, you will EAT your Neighbour, *ay*, and say Grace to your Meat too—Distress removes from the Soul, all R[e]lation, Affection, Sense of Justice, and all the Obligations, either Moral or Religious, that secure one Man against another.

Not that I say or suggest the Distress makes the Violence Lawful; but I say it is a Tryal beyond the Ordinary Power of Humane Nature to withstand; and therefore that Excellent Petition of the Lord's Prayer, which I believe is most wanted, and the least thought of, ought to be every Moment in our Thoughts, *Lead us not into Temptation.*

But to return to my first Observation; I am of the Opinion, That the Honour of Trade in this Nation, is the most declin'd in this Age, of any Thing, *Religion excepted,* that can be observ'd—I believe I need not beg the Question, it will be easily granted—Tricking, Sharping, Shuffling, and all manner of *Chicane,* is crept into our Commerce, more than ever was known.

I have hinted above, that it is an evident signal of the decay of Trade—And the Reason is, that a decay of Trade is naturally the great Original and Parent of these Follies, which if Men were Thriving, and their Affairs easie, they would avoid: Men rob for Bread, Women whore for Bread; Necessity is the Parent of Crime; Ask the worst High-Way Man in the Nation, ask the lewdest Strumpet in the Town, if they would not willingly leave off the Trade, if they could live handsomely without it—And I dare say, not one but will acknowledge it.

A True Relation of the Apparition of One Mrs. Veal, the next day after her Death: to one Mrs. Bargrave at Canterbury, the 8th day of September, 1705 1706

> As there is a Converse of Spirits, an Intelligence, or call it what you please, between our Spirits embodied and cased up in Flesh, and the Spirits unembodied; ... why should it be thought so strange a thing, that those Spirits should be able to take upon them an Out-side or Case? ... If they can assume a visible Form, as I see no Reason to say they cannot, there is no room then to doubt of the Reality of their appearing; because what *may be* we cannot but believe sometimes *has been*, as what *has been*, we are sure may be. (*An Essay on the History and Reality of Apparitions* (1727), pp. 4-5.)

One of the reasons for Defoe's fascination with the story of Mrs Veal is provided by this passage; but we have also to reckon with the Defoe of such later works as the *Memoirs of a Cavalier* (1720) or *A Journal of the Plague Year* (1722)—the skilled and accurate reporter organizing evidence to secure a forceful literary impact. Accuracy, credibility and vividness were his chief aims and he took advantage of four existing accounts of the event at Canterbury to realize them. (For a recent appraisal of the earlier accounts see A. H. Scouten, 'At that Moment of Time', *Forum* (Ball State College, Indiana), II (1961), ii, 44-51.) It appears that he was faithful to his sources—for example he was reporting not inventing the women's interest in Drelincourt's *Christian's Defence against the Fears of Death;* to make his story more universally credible he changed Mrs Veal from a spirit seeking vengeance over a family grievance (as in the earliest account), into one who tries to comfort a distressed woman; and the literary method, which emphasizes circumstantial detail or introduces the precise moment of Mrs Veal's death with a dramatic rather than a strictly chronological timing, achieves vividness of narration.

The text, here printed from the earliest extant edition, may also be found in eighteenth-century reprints of Drelincourt's *Christian's Defence*—which reached its twenty-first edition in 1776—to which it was added in 1706. (The advertisement at the end of the text below reveals a publisher fully aware of Defoe's publicity value.)

The Preface

This relation is Matter of Fact, and attended with such Circumstances as may induce any Reasonable Man to believe it. It was sent by a Gentleman, a Justice of Peace at Maidstone in Kent, and a very Intelligent Person, to his Friend in London, as it is here Worded;[1] which Discourse is attested by a very sober and understanding Gentlewoman,[2] a Kinswoman of the said Gentlemans, who lives in Canterbury, within a few Doors of the House in which the within named Mrs. Bargrave lives; who believes his Kinswoman to be of so discerning a Spirit, as not to be put upon by any Fallacy, and who possitively assured him, that the whole Matter, as it is here Related and laid down, is what is really True; and what She her self had in the same Words (as near as may be) from Mrs. Bargraves own Mouth, who she knows had no Reason to Invent and publish such a Story, nor any design to forge and tell a Lye, being a Woman of much Honesty and Virtue, and her whole Life a Course as it were of Piety.[3] The use which we ought to make of it is, to consider, That there is a Life to come after this, and a Just God, who will retribute to every one according to the Deeds done in the Body; and therefore, to reflect upon our Past course of Life we have led in the World; That our Time is Short and Uncertain, and that if we would escape the Punishment of the Ungodly, and receive the Reward of the Righteous, which is the laying hold of Eternal Life, we ought for the time to come, to turn to God by a speedy Repentance, ceasing to do Evil and Learning to do Well: To seek after God Early, if happily he may be found of us, and lead such Lives for the future, as may be well pleasing in his sight.

A True Relation of the Apparition of One Mrs. Veal

This thing is so rare in all its Circumstances, and on so good Authority, that my Reading and Conversation has not given me any thing like it; it is fit to gratifie the most Ingenious and Serious Enquirer. Mrs. *Bargrave* is the Person to whom Mrs. *Veal* Appeared after her Death; she is my Intimate Friend,[4] and I can avouch for her Reputation, for these last fifteen or sixteen Years, on my own Knowledge; and I can confirm the Good Character she had from her Youth, to the time of my Acquaintance. Tho' since this Relation, she is Calumniated by some People, that are Friends to the Brother of Mrs. *Veal* who Appeared; who think the Relation of this Appearance to be a Reflection, and endeavour what they can to Blast Mrs. *Bargrave*'s Reputation; and to Laugh the Story out of Countenance. But the Circumstances thereof, and the Chearful Disposition of Mrs. *Bargrave*, notwithstanding the unheard of ill Usage of a very Wicked Husband, there is not the least sign of Dejection in her Face; nor did I ever hear her let fall a Desponding or Murmuring Expression; nay, not when actually under her Husbands Barbarity; which I have been Witness to, and several other Persons of undoubted Reputation.

Now you must know, that Mrs. *Veal* was a Maiden Gentlewoman of about 30 Years of Age, and for some Years last past, had been troubled with Fits; which were perceived coming on her, by her going off from her Discourse very abruptly, to some impertinence:[5] She was maintain'd by an only Brother, and kept his House in *Dover*. She was a very Pious Woman, and her Brother a very Sober Man to all appearance: But now he does all he can to Null or Quash the Story. Mrs. *Veal* was intimately acquainted with Mrs. *Bargrave* from her Childhood. Mrs. *Veals* Circumstances were then Mean; her Father did not take care of his Children as he ought, so that they were exposed to Hardships: And Mrs. *Bargrave* in those days, had as Unkind a Father, tho' She wanted for neither Food nor Cloathing, whilst Mrs. *Veal* wanted for both: So that it was in the Power of Mrs. *Bargrave* to be very much her Friend in several Instances, which mightily endear'd Mrs. *Veal*; insomuch that she would often say, Mrs. *Bargrave you are not only the Best, but the only Friend I have in the World; and no Circumstances of Life, shall ever dissolve my Friendship.* They would often Condole each others adverse Fortune, and read together, *Drelincourt upon Death*,[6] and other good Books: And so like two Christian Friends, they comforted each other under their Sorrow.

Sometime after, Mr. *Veals* Friends got him a Place in the Custom-House at *Dover*, which occasioned Mrs. *Veal* by little and little, to fall off from her Intimacy with Mrs. *Bargrave*, tho' there was never any such thing as a Quarrel; but an Indifferency came on by degrees, till at last Mrs. *Bargrave* had not seen her in two Years and a half; tho' above a Twelve Month of the time, Mrs. *Bargrave* had been absent from *Dover*, and this last half Year, has been in *Canterbury* about two Months of the time, dwelling in a House of her own.

In this House, on the Eighth of *September* last, *viz.* 1705, She was sitting alone in the Forenoon, thinking over her Unfortunate Life, and arguing her self into a due Resignation to Providence, tho' her condition seem'd hard. And said she, *I have been provided for hitherto, and doubt not but I shall be still; and am well satisfied, that my Afflictions shall end, when it is most fit for me:* And then took up her Sewing-Work, which she had no sooner done, but she hears a Knocking at the Door; she went to see who it was there, and this prov'd to be Mrs. *Veal*, her

Old Friend, who was in a Riding Habit: At that Moment of Time, the Clock struck Twelve at Noon.

Madam says Mrs. *Bargrave*, I am surprized to see you, you have been so long a stranger, but told her, she was glad to see her and offer'd to Salute her, which Mrs. *Veal* complyed with, till their Lips almost touched, and then Mrs. *Veal* drew her hand cross her own Eyes, and said, *I am not very well*, and so waved it. She told Mrs. *Bargrave*, she was going a Journey, and had a great mind to see her first: But says Mrs. *Bargrave*, *how came you to take a Journey alone? I am amaz'd at it, because I know you have so fond a Brother*. O! says Mrs. *Veal*, *I gave my Brother the Slip, and came away, because I had so great a Mind to see you before I took my Journy*. So Mrs. *Bargrave* went in with her, into another Room within the first, and Mrs. *Veal* sat her self down in an Elbow-chair, in which Mrs. *Bargrave* was sitting when she heard Mrs. *Veal* Knock. Then says Mrs. *Veal, My Dear Friend, I am come to renew our Old Friendship again, and to beg your Pardon for my breach of it, and if you can forgive me you are one of the best of Women*. O! says Mrs. *Bargrave, don't mention such a thing, I have not had an uneasie thought about it, I can easily forgive it*. What did you think of me says Mrs. *Veal?* Says Mrs. *Bargrave, I thought you were like the rest of the World, and that Prosperity had made you forget your self and me*. Then Mrs. *Veal* reminded Mrs. *Bargrave* of the many Friendly Offices she did her in former Days, and much of the Conversation they had with each other in the time of their Adversity; what Books they Read, and what Comfort in particular they received from *Drelincourt's Book of Death*, which was the best she said on that Subject, was ever Wrote. She also mentioned Dr. *Sherlock*,[7] and two *Dutch* Books which were Translated, Wrote upon Death, and several others: But *Drelincourt* she said, had the clearest Notions of Death, and of the Future State, of any who have handled that Subject. Then she asked Mrs. *Bargrave*, whether she had *Drelincourt*; she said yes. Says Mrs. *Veal* fetch it, and so Mrs. *Bargrave* goes up Stairs, and brings it down. Says Mrs. *Veal*, Dear Mrs. *Bargrave, If the Eyes of our Faith were as open as the Eyes of our Body, we should see numbers of Angels about us for our Guard: The Notions we have of Heaven now, are nothing like what it is, as* Drelincourt *says. Therefore be comforted under your Afflictions, and believe that the Almighty has a particular regard to you; and that your Afflictions are Marks of Gods Favour: And when they have done the business they were sent for, they shall be removed from you*. And believe me my Dear Friend, believe what I say to you, *One Minute of future Happiness will infinitely reward you for all your Sufferings. For I can never believe*, (and claps her Hand upon her Knee, with a great deal of Earnestness, which indeed ran through all her Discourse) *that ever God will suffer you to spend all your Days in this Afflicted State: But be assured, that your Afflictions shall leave you, or you them in a short time*. She spake in that Pathetical and Heavenly manner, that Mrs. *Bargrave*

wept several times; she was so deeply affected with it. Then Mrs. *Veal* mentioned Dr. *Hornecks Ascetick*,[8] at the end of which, he gives an account of the
Lives of the Primitive Christians. *Their Pattern she recommended to our Imitation;*
and said, *their Conversation was not like this of our Age. For now* (says she) *there is
nothing but frothy vain Discourse, which is far different from theirs. Theirs was to
Edification, and to Build one another up in the Faith: So that they were not as we are,
nor are we as they are; but* said she, *We might do as they did. There was a Hearty
Friendship among them, but where is it now to be found?* Says Mrs. Bargrave, *'tis
hard indeed to find a true Friend in these days.* Says Mrs. *Veal,* Mr. *Norris*[9] has a Fine
Coppy of Verses, call'd *Friendship in Perfection,* which I wonderfully admire,
have you seen the Book says Mrs. *Veal?* No, says Mrs. *Bargrave, but I have the
Verses of my own writing out. Have you,* says Mrs. *Veal, then fetch them;* which she
did from above Stairs, and offer'd them to Mrs. *Veal* to read, who refused, and
wav'd the thing, saying, *holding down her Head would make it ake,* and then de-
sired Mrs. *Bargrave* to read them to her, which she did. As they were admiring
Friendship, Mrs. *Veal* said, Dear Mrs. *Bargrave,* I shall love you for ever: In the
Verses, there is twice used the Word *Elysium.* Ah! says Mrs. *Veal, These Poets
have such Names for Heaven.* She would often draw her Hand cross her own
Eyes; and say, Mrs. *Bargrave Don't you think I am mightily impaired by my Fits?*
No, says Mrs. *Bargrave,* I think you look as well as ever I knew you.

After all this discourse, which the Apparition put in Words much finer than
Mrs. *Bargrave* said she could pretend to, and was much more than she can remember (for it cannot be thought, that an hour and three quarters Conversation could all be retained, tho' the main of it, she thinks she does.) She said to
Mrs. *Bargrave, she would have her write a Letter to her Brother, and tell him, she
would have him give Rings to such and such; and that there was a Purse of Gold in her
Cabinet, and that she would have Two Broad Pieces given to her Cousin Watson.*
Talking at this Rate, Mrs. *Bargrave* thought that a Fit was coming upon her, and
so placed her self in a Chair, just before her Knees, to keep her from falling to
the Ground, if her Fits should occasion it; for the Elbow Chair she thought
would keep her from falling on either side. And to divert Mrs. *Veal* as she
thought, she took hold of her Gown Sleeve several times, and commended it.
Mrs. *Veal* told her, it was a Scower'd Silk, and newly made up. But for all this
Mrs. *Veal* persisted in her Request, and told Mrs. *Bargrave* she must not deny
her: and she would have her tell her Brother all their Conversation, when she
had an opportunity. Dear Mrs. *Veal,* says Mrs. *Bargrave, this seems so impertinent,
that I cannot tell how to comply with it; and what a mortifying Story will our Conversation be to a Young Gentleman?* Well, says Mrs. *Veal, I must not be deny'd.*
Why, says Mrs. *Bargrave, 'tis much better methinks to do it your self,* No, says Mrs.
Veal; tho' it seems impertinent to you now, you will see more reason for it hereafter.

Mrs. *Bargrave* then to satisfie her importunity, was going to fetch a Pen and Ink; but Mrs. *Veal* said, *let it alone now, and do it when I am gone; but you must be sure to do it:* which was one of the last things she enjoin'd her at parting; and so she promised her.

Then Mrs. *Veal* asked for Mrs. *Bargraves* Daughter; she said she was not at home; but if you have a mind to see her says Mrs. *Bargrave*, I'le send for her. *Do,* says Mrs. *Veal.* On which she left her, and went to a Neighbours, to send for her; and by the Time Mrs. *Bargrave* was returning, Mrs *Veal* was got without the Door in the Street, in the face of the *Beast-Market*[10] on a Saturday (which is Market Day) and stood ready to part, as soon as Mrs. *Bargrave* came to her. She askt her, *why she was in such hast?* she said, *she must be going; tho' perhaps she might not go her journey till Monday.* And told *Mrs.* Bargrave *she hoped she should see her again, at her Cousin* Watsons *before she went whither she was a going.* Then she said, *she would not take her Leave of her,* and walk'd from Mrs. *Bargrave* in her view, till a turning interrupted the sight of her, which was three quarters after One in the Afternoon.

Mrs. *Veal* Dyed the 7th of *September* at 12 a Clock at Noon, of her Fits, and had not above four hours Senses before her Death, in which time she received the Sacrament. The next day after Mrs. *Veals* appearing being Sunday, Mrs. *Bargrave* was mightily indisposed with a Cold, and a Sore Throat, that she could not go out that day: but on Monday morning she sends a person to Captain *Watsons* to know if Mrs. *Veal* were there. They wondered at Mrs. *Bargraves* enquiry, and sent her Word, that she was not there, nor was expected. At this Answer Mrs. *Bargrave* told the Maid she had certainly mistook the Name, or made some blunder. And tho' she was ill, she put on her Hood, and went her self to Captain *Watsons*, tho' she knew none of the Family, to see if Mrs. *Veal* was there or not. They said, they wondered at her asking, for that she had not been in Town; they were sure, if she had, she would have been there. Says Mrs. *Bargrave, I am sure she was with me on Saturday almost two hours.* They said it was impossible, for they must have seen her if she had. In comes Captain *Watson*, while they were in Dispute, and said that Mrs. *Veal* was certainly Dead, and her Escocheons[11] were making. This strangely surprised Mrs. *Bargrave*, who went to the Person immediately who had the care of them, and found it true. Then she related the whole Story to Captain *Watsons* Family, and what Gown she had on, and how striped. And that Mrs. *Veal* told her it was Scowred. Then Mrs. *Watson* cry'd out, *you have seen her indeed, for none knew but* Mrs. *Veal and my self, that the Gown was Scowr'd;* and Mrs. *Watson* own'd that she described the Gown exactly; for, said she, *I helpt her to make it up.* This, Mrs *Watson* blaz'd all about the Town, and avouch'd the Demonstration of the Truth of Mrs. *Bargraves* seeing Mrs. *Veal's* Apparition. And Captain *Watson* carried two

Gentlemen immediately to Mrs. *Bargraves* House, to hear the Relation from her own Mouth. And then it spread so fast, that Gentlemen and Persons of Quality, the Judicious and Sceptical part of the World, flock't in upon her, which at last became such a Task, that she was forc'd to go out of the way. For they were in general, extreamly satisfyed of the truth of the thing; and plainly saw, that Mrs. *Bargrave* was no Hypochondriack, for she always appears with such a chearful Air, and pleasing Mien, that she has gain'd the favor and esteem of all the Gentry. And its thought a great favor if they can but get the Relation from her own Mouth. I should have told you before, that Mrs. *Veal* told Mrs. *Bargrave*, that her Sister and Brother in Law, were just come down from *London* to see her. Says Mrs. *Bargrave, how came you to order matters so strangely? it could not be helpt* said Mrs. *Veal*; and her Sister and Brother did come to see her, and entred the Town of *Dover*, just as Mrs. *Veal* was expiring.[12] Mrs. *Bargrave* asked her, whether she would not drink some Tea. Says Mrs. *Veal, I do not care if I do: But I'le Warrant this Mad Fellow* (meaning Mrs. *Bargraves* Husband,) *has broke all your Trinckets.* But, says Mrs. *Bargrave, I'le get something to Drink in for all that;* but Mrs. *Veal* wav'd it, and said, *it is no matter, let it alone,* and so it passed.

All the time I sat with Mrs. *Bargrave,* which was some Hours, she recollected fresh sayings of Mrs. *Veal.* And one material thing more she told Mrs. *Bargrave,* that Old Mr. *Breton* allowed Mrs. *Veal* Ten pounds a Year, which was a secret, and unknown to Mrs. *Bargrave,* till Mrs. *Veal* told it her. Mrs. *Bargrave* never varies in her Story, which puzzles those who doubt of the Truth, or are unwilling to believe it. A Servant in a Neighbours Yard adjoining to Mrs. *Bargraves* House, heard her talking to some body, an hour of the Time Mrs. *Veal* was with her. Mrs. *Bargrave* went out to her next Neighbours the very Moment she parted with Mrs. *Veal,* and told what Ravishing Conversation she had with an Old Friend, and told the whole of it. *Drelincourt's Book of Death* is, since this happened, Bought up strangely. And it is to be observed, that notwithstanding all this Trouble and Fatigue Mrs. *Bargrave* has undergone upon this Account, she never took the value of a Farthing, nor suffer'd her Daughter to take any thing of any Body, and therefore can have no Interest in telling the Story.

But Mr. *Veal* does what he can to stifle the matter, and said he would see Mrs. *Bargrave*; but yet it is certain matter fact, that he has been at Captain *Watsons* since the Death of his Sister, and yet never went near Mrs. *Bargrave*; and some of his Friends report her to be a great Lyar, and that she knew of Mr. *Breton's* Ten Pounds a Year. But the Person who pretends to say so, has the Reputation of a Notorious Lyar, among persons which I know to be of undoubted Repute. Now Mr. *Veal* is more a Gentleman, than to say she Lyes; but says, a bad Husband has Craz'd her. But she needs only to present her self, and it will effectually confute that Pretence. Mr. *Veal* says he ask'd his Sister on her Death Bed, whether she had a mind to dispose of any thing, and she said, No. Now what the things which Mrs. *Veals* Apparition would have disposed of, were so Trifling, and nothing of Justice aimed at in their disposal, that the design of it appears to me to be only in order to make Mrs. *Bargrave*, so to demonstrate the Truth of her Appearance, as to satisfie the World of the Reality thereof, as to what she had seen and heard: and to secure her Reputation among the Reasonable and understanding part of Mankind. And then again, Mr. *Veal* owns that there was a Purse of Gold; but it was not found in her Cabinet, but in a Comb-Box. This looks improbable, for that Mrs. *Watson* own'd that Mrs. *Veal* was so very careful of the Key of her Cabinet, that she would trust no Body with it. And if so, no doubt she would not trust her Gold out of it. And Mrs. *Veals* often drawing her hand over her Eyes, and asking Mrs. *Bargrave*, whether her Fits had not impair'd her; looks to me, as if she did it on purpose to remind Mrs. *Bargrave* of her Fits, to prepare her not to think it strange that she should put her upon Writing to her Brother to dispose of Rings and Gold, which lookt so much like a dying Persons Bequest; and it took accordingly with Mrs. *Bargrave*, as the effect of her Fits coming upon her; and was one of the many Instances of her Wonderful Love to her, and Care of her, that she should not be affrighted: which indeed appears in her whole management; particularly in her coming to her in the day time, waving the Salutation, and when she was alone; and then the manner of her parting, to prevent a second attempt to Salute her.

Now, why Mr. *Veal* should think this Relation a Reflection, (as 'tis plain he does by his endeavouring to stifle it) I can't imagine, because the Generality believe her to be a good Spirit, her Discourse was so Heavenly. Her two great Errands were to comfort Mrs. *Bargrave* in her Affliction, and to ask her Forgiveness for her Breach of Friendship, and with a Pious Discourse to encourage her. So that after all, to suppose that Mrs. *Bargrave* could Hatch such an Invention as this from *Friday-Noon*, till *Saturday-Noon*, (supposing that she knew of Mrs. *Veals* Death the very first Moment) without jumbling Circumstances, and without any Interest too; she must be more Witty, Fortunate, and Wicked too, than any indifferent Person I dare say, will allow. I asked Mrs. *Bargrave* several times, *If she was sure she felt the Gown.* She answered Modestly, *if my Senses be to be relied on, I am sure of it.* I asked her, *If she heard a Sound, when she clapt her Hand upon her Knee:* She said, *she did not remember she did:* And she said, *she Appeared to be as much a Substance as I did, who talked with her. And I may* said she, *be as soon persuaded that your Apparition is talking to me now, as that I did not really see her; for I was under no manner of Fear, I received her as a Friend, and parted with her as such. I would not,* says she, *give one Farthing to make any one believe it, I have no Interest in it; nothing but trouble is entail'd upon me for a long time for ought that I*

know: and had it not come to Light by Accident, it would never have been made Pub-
lick. But now she says, *she will make her own Private Use of it, and keep her self out*
of the way as much as she can. And so she has done since. She says, *she had a*
Gentleman who came thirty Miles to her to hear the Relation; and that she had told it
to a Room full of People at a time. Several particular Gentlemen have had the
Story from Mrs. *Bargraves* own Mouth.

This thing has very much affected me, and I am as well satisfied, as I am of the
best grounded Matter of Fact. And why should we dispute Matter of Fact, because we cannot solve things, of which we can have no certain or demonstrative
Notions, seems strange to me: Mrs. *Bargrave*'s Authority and Sincerity alone,
would have been undoubted in any other Case.

FINIS

Advertisement

Drelincourts's Book of the Consolations against the Fears of Death, *has been*
four times Printed[13] *already in English, of which many Thousands have been Sold, and*
not without great Applause: And its bearing so great a Character in this Relation, the
Impression is near Sold off.

Letters to Robert Harley

13 September 1706

Sir

I Was Comeing to Wait Upon you and Take your Last Instructions, when I Met with your Ordr to Dispatch[1] without any farther Conferences; Tis the More Afflicting to me because you are pleas'd to Signifye That Something Unhappy Relateing to your Self Sir is the Occasion, in which I Condole tho' I kno' Not Directly the Occasion—But on My Own Account Sir This is a Perticular Disaster because I had a great many Enquiries to make Sir in Ordr to my Conduct in The Affair I go Upon.

Not but That as Abraham went Chearfully Out Not knowing whither he went, Depending on him that Sent him, So Sir I Willingly go On, Entirely Depending that I shall have Such Instructions as shall Not Dissable me from Effectually Answering your Expectation.

I Onely Entreat your leav to Remind you, that as you have acquainted Her Majtie & My Ld Treasr with my goeing, The Success of my Journey is the More my Concerne, least want of Information Rendring me Useless, The want of Capascity or Dilligence, be judg'd the Reason of my Miscarriage.

Under these Anxious Thoughts I beg you to Considr Sir That I am without the heads of the Treaty,[2] without the Characters of the Gentlemen who were here, and without the knowledge of what has been Transacted In the Councils here, in Ordr to Dictate to me what I am to Observ.[3] Hence I shall Seem Ignorant, of the Sence of England, and of what is Expected here, or Intended from Hence, and Thus I shall be so far from knowing the people I go to That I shall appear Not to kno' those I Come from.

However, That if my Notions are wrong, I may be Set Right by your Instructions, I beg leav, tho' it be beginning at the wrong End, to Set Down how I Understand my present business—as foll.

1. To Inform My Self of the Measures Takeing Or Partys forming Against the Union and Applye my Self to prevent them.

2. In Conversation and by all Reasonable Methods to Dispose peoples minds to the Union.

3. By writing or Discourse, to Answer any Objections, Libells or Reflections on the Union, the English or the Court, Relateing to the Union.

4. To Remove the Jealousies and Uneasyness of people about Secret Designs here against the Kirk &c.

Sir I beg the Ordrs you please to give me may Mention if I am Right in my thoughts of these Things—and that you will give me as much light as possible in your farther pleasure Concerning my Conduct.

I Can Not Quit This without Mentioning the Matter of Expence. I Confess Sir when you Told me it is Out of your private, and that the governmt should be at no Charge, it straughtn'd my Thoughts and I am the More Limited in My Designs—Indeed Sir Ile put you to No Expence for Extravagancies, but in the Affair, if I am a good husband I shall ill Serv you.

If it be proper to print any thing there—Some Charge will attend it, and for Intelligence of things I would not be spareing.

I Entreat you to give me the proper limits of Expence, that I may not make you Uneasy on that score; for Tho' I hope I Need Not Assure you That what I shall Take shall not be Missapply'd, and That I shall bring nothing back, leaving any Consideration for me or Mine to your Usuall Goodness; yet I beg you will please to hint to me for my Governmt what you think fit on the head of Charges.

I have Recd Sir your bill of £25—and with the Uttmost Expedition have Equipt my Self as the Summe and the Time will permitt.

I Mention the first not Sir by way of Complaint, of any thing but my Own Missfortune—who haveing as I accquainted you before Parted with So much as horse, Sadele, bridle, pistols and Every thing,[4] I am Forc't to buy all New—Yet Refurnisht Sir with Two horses and all Necessarys, I Assure you I have No fear of highway men. *Cantabit Vacuus*[5]—is my Motto, and if I Reach N Castle I shall be in Condition Very Fitt to wait upon Mr Bell—[6]

As to Family, 7 Children— &c. Hei Mihi—

No Man Sir That Ever Serv'd you shall Trouble you less than I with Complaints of This Nature—But if I have been honest I Must be Naked, & am less Asham'd to Tell you So Than I should be to Tell you I am foresworn and have Made Reserves.

I Need Say No More. Sir you were pleasd Once to Make me hope Her Majtie would have Some Concern for me when free—I have Now Naked Liberty—and Can Not but Recomend the Circumstance to That Bounty which I Trust you will Move on my Account.

Thus Sir you have a Widdo' and Seaven Children On your hands, but A word I presume from you will Ease you of the burthen.

I Ask your Pardon for This Representation to which My Present Circumstance Compells. I shall be No More Importunate in That affair.

I have been Considering About Treating of Union in the Review and Unless your Judgemt and Ordrs Differ believ as I shall Mannage it, it Must be Usefull, but beg hints from you if you find it Otherwise.[7]

I Entreat Letters from you Directed to Alexa Goldsmith[8] to be left at Mr

Joseph Caters in Coventry where I shall be God Willing On Thursday or Fryday at Farthest.

If any thing supplimentall offers the Next post, For Ditto to be left at Mr John Drury, Bookseller in Nottingham, and the Next at Mr John Coninghams⁹ at Manchester.

Your Most Obedt &c

[symbol]

Pray Sir please to give me the positiv day the Parliament are to sit Down.¹⁰ sept 13 1706, just takeing horse.

26 November 1706

Sir

I Can Not Express to your Honr what a Cordial the favour of your Letter was to me After Such a strange and Surpriseing Silence. I Thank God my Faith in your Regard to me was too firmly Fix't to suffer me to Neglect my Duty, but I own I have been Undr Perplexitys and Discouragemts Inumerable. I shall Trouble you no More with them.

My Success here I am In hopes will Answer your Expectations, tho' the Difficultyes have been Infinite. If No Kirk Devills More Than we yet Meet with appear, I hope all will be well and I begin to See thoro' it.

If I Understand the Cautions you are pleasd to give me in your Letter, they Respect England as much as Scotland, And Indeed I am afraid of Erring Most that way, and am Therefore Very Wary.

Tho I will Not Answer for Success yet I Trust in Mannagemt you shall not be Uneasy at your Trusting me here. I have Compass't my First and Main step happily Enough, in That I am Perfectly Unsuspectd as Corresponding with anybody in England. I Converse with Presbyterian, Episcopall-Dissenter, papist and Non Juror, and I hope with Equall Circumspection. I flatter my Self you will have no Complaints of my Conduct. I have faithfull Emissaries in Every Company And I Talk to Everybody in Their Own way. To the Merchants I am about to Settle here in Trade, Building ships &c. With the Lawyers I Want to purchase a House and Land to bring my family & live Upon it (God knows where the Money is to pay for it). To day I am Goeing into Partnership with a Membr of parliamt in a Glass house, to morrow with Another in a Salt work. With the Glasgow Mutineers I am to be a fish Merchant, with the Aberdeen Men a woollen and with the Perth and western men a Linen Manufacturer, and still at the End of all Discourse the Union is the Essentiall and I am all to Every one that I may Gain some.

Again I am in the Morning at the Committee, in the Afternoon in the assembly. I am privy to all their folly, I wish I Could not Call it knavery, and am Entirely Confided in.

Youl Pardon me this Excursion on my Self And bear with This allay to it, that I Really have spent a great Deal of your Money and am like to do More—yet perhaps not So Much as by Mr Bells Account, Since he sent me in his last more and sooner than I Expected, of which however I am not the Worse husband and have about £20 yet in hand tho' the press Dreins me and I am something behind to it.

I Assure you Sir and Entreat you to believ me I am not in anything Extravagant in this sharping Dear place. But where the Design I am in presses me, Then Indeed I am not spareing—My Own Affaires I have Recommended to you but too often, and had not mentioned them Now tho' severely presst there, Onely to assure you I can not Relieve them from Hence Tho' My Wife wrott me last week she had been 10 dayes without Money—I submitt it all to that providence which when he sees Good will smile, & Till then I must wait—

I shall strictly observ your Directions and act with the Uttmost Caution in Every Thing. . . .

I am, Sir, Your Most Obedt Servt
D F

Edinb. Nov. 26. 1706

6 December 1710

Sir

I Wrott you Two letters the last Post, One to Mr Bateman[1] and One in Cover to a faithfull friend to Convey if possible to your Self and Reciv Some Notice of your haveing Recd Mine, for which I have been Indeed Very Anxious, and also to Reciev your further Commands.

The Notice here Sir that in 212 [Parliament] you have Personally Spoken Against 214 [the Pretender][2] has fixed the Character I have had the Honor to Spread here of your Steddy Zeal for the Revolution, and Confirmed what I hinted in My last that Lieutt Generall Maitland[3] had Avouch'd Publickly in your just Defence (Vizt): that No Man in Britain was a Greater Prop to the Constitution than your Self.

I was Very Glad to have So Good an Assistant in So great a piece of Justice to you Sir, who I think have Recd So Much Injury from Some, from whom you have Merited much better, and the Rather because it directly Contradicted what Dr Oldfield[4] had been bussy here in Spreading both of your Self and Even of your Great Mistress the Queen her Self.

Now the joy begins to be Visible among the honest people who were and still are firm to her Majties Person as Well as Governmt, but were Terrifyed with the Absurd Notions of all being to be Given up to the 214 [Pretender] Even by 233 [the Queen] her Self. It is not strange that a Thing So Ridiculous Should prevail if the assurance of those who Reported it were Considred, and that they had Obtaind to be Sent up to 212 [Parliament], where they had peremptorily Said it should be don.

This Sir will Satisfye her Majtie That the Intrest of the Pretender is too great here to be Slighted, and that Nothing but Discouragements of it from her Self can keep them in bounds; but if her Majtie Pleases on any Occasion to Express her being pleased with the Zeal of her Subjects Against the Pretender, it Would strike them here as with a blast from Heaven, and Weaken his Intrest More than an army of 10000 Men Could do.

As to the people here, I mean the presbyterians, they Come heartily into Her Majties Intrest. Neither do they Relish the Chagrin of Our 288 [Whigs] in 116 [England]. The Ambassador[5] who has Resided here from the 106 [Dissenters], and who has left his Mission here for 249 [Southwark], is gone back re Infecta, and his Negotiations have Made less Impression than indeed I Expected. In Short Sir, Nothing but the 214 [Pretender] and Encroachments of 109 [Episcopacy] can make them Uneasy. I Endeavour to Assure them, and Shall hereafter Give you Some Account of Mediums to preserv her Majties Intrest here and yet make all but the 161 [Jacobites] Easy also.

I am, Sir, Your Most Obliged Servt
C GUILOT[6]

117 [Edinburgh] Decemb. 6. 1710

And what if the Pretender should come? or, some Considerations of the Advantages and Real Consequences of the Pretender's Possessing the Crown of Great-Britain 1713

The Protestant succession to the English throne was, for Defoe, 'the great exemplification' of that English liberty which was founded on the Revolution and the Declaration of Right (*Review*, Preface to Vol. VI, March 1710). Thus the uncertainty of Queen Anne's health, and the conflicting claims of James Stuart and the House of Hanover, prompted Defoe to write three pamphlets in 1713. On 21 February appeared *Reasons Against the Succession of the House of Hanover;* possibly on 23 March the pamphlet printed below was published; and finally, in April, came *An Answer to a Question that No Body Thinks of. Viz. But what if the Queen should die?* The titles of the first two pamphlets make it plain that this is the Defoe of *The Shortest-Way*, that his intention was to persuade his readers to reject the Pretender by making absurdly exaggerated claims for him. He remarked in the *Review* (18 April 1713) that he had exposed 'the foolish senseless Advantages which some allege shall accrue to us by the admitting the Pretender'.

As with the *Shortest-Way*, the publication of the ironical pamphlets brought trouble in its wake. Although Defoe later claimed, 'The Books I have written are as plain a Satyr upon the Pretender and his Friends, as can be written, if they are view'd Impartially' (*Review*, 16 April 1713), his Whig enemies seized the opportunity to initiate a prosecution against him. Robert Harley came to his assistance once again;

Defoe's defiant writing in the *Review* (18 April 1713), while the affair was *sub judice*, added a further dimension of difficulty; but eventually, in November 1713, he secured a general pardon from the Queen. (On the whole affair, see *An Appeal to Honour and Justice*, below, pp. 178–84.)

And what if the Pretender should come? or, some Considerations, &c.

If the Danger of the Pretender is really so great as the Noise which some make about it seems to suppose, if the Hopes of his Coming are so well grounded, as some of his Friends seem to boast, it behoves us who are to be the Subjects of the Approaching Revolution, which his Success must necessarily bring with it, to apply ourselves seriously to examine what our Part will be in the Play, that so we may prepare ourselves to act as becomes us, both with Respect to the Government we are now under, and with Respect to the Government we may be under, when the Success he promises himself shall (if ever it shall) answer his Expectation.

In order to do this it is necessary to state, with what Plainness the Circumstances of the Case will admit, the several Appearances of the Thing itself. (1.) *As they are* offered to us by the respective Parties who are for or against it. (2.) *As they* really appear by an Impartial Deduction from them both, without the least Byass either to one Side or other; that so the People of *Britain* may settle and compose their Thoughts a little in this Great, and at present Popular Debate, and may neither be terrified or affrighted with Mischiefs, which have no Reason or Foundation in them, and which give no Ground for their Apprehensions; and on the other Hand, may not promise to themselves greater Things from the Pretender, if he should come hither, than he will be able to perform for them; in order to this we are to consider the Pretender in his Person, and in his Circumstances. (1.) The Person who we call the Pretender: It has been so much debated, and such strong Parties have been made on both Sides to prove or disprove the Legitimacy of his Birth, that it seems needless here to enter into that Dispute; the Author of the *Review*,[1] one of the most Furious Opposers of the Name and Interest of the Pretender, openly grants his Legitimacy, and pretends to argue against his Admission from Principles and Foundations of his own Forming; we shall let alone his Principles and Foundations here, as we do his Arguments, and only take him by the Handle which he fairly gives us, (*viz.*) that he grants *the Person of the Pretender Legitimate*; if this be so, if the Person we contend about be the Lawful true Son of King *James*'s Queen, the Dispute whether he be the Real Son of the King will be quite out of the Question; because by the Laws of *Great-Britain*, and of the whole World, a Child

Born in Wedlock shall inherit, as Heir of the Mother's Husband, whether Begotten by him, as his Real Father, or not. Now to come at the true Design of this Work, the Business is, to hear (as above) what either Side have to say to this Point. The Friends of his Birth and Succession argue upon it thus, if the Person be lawfully Begotten, *that is*, if Born really of the Body of the Queen *Dowager*, during the Life of King *James*, he was without any Exception his Lawful Son; **if** he was his Lawful Son, he was his Lawful Heir; **if** he was his Lawful Heir, why is he not our Lawful King? *Since* Hereditary Right is Indefeasible, and is lately acknowledged to be so; and that the Doctrine of Hereditary Right being Indefeasible, is a Church of *England* Doctrine ever received by the Church, and inseparable from the true Members of the Church, the contrary being the stigmatizing Character of Republicans, King-killers, Enemies to Monarchy, Presbyterians, and Phanaticks: The Enemies of the Birth and Succession of the Person called the Pretender argue upon it thus, *That* he is the Lawfully Begotten, or Son Born really of the Body of the Queen *Dowager* of the late King *James*, *they doubt*; and they are justified in doubting of it, because no sufficient Steps were taken in the proper Season of it, *either before his Birth*, to convince such Persons as were more immediately concerned to know the Truth of it, that the Queen was really with Child, which might have been done past all Contradiction at that Time, more than ever after: *Or at his Birth*, to have such Persons as were more immediately concern'd, *such as Her Present Majesty*, &c. thoroughly convinc'd of the Queen being really deliver'd of a Child, by being Present at the Time of the Queen's Labour and Delivery. This being omitted, which was the Affirmative, *say they*, which ought to have been proved, we ought not to be concerned in the Proof of the Negative, which by the Nature of the Thing could not be equally certain; and therefore we might be justly permitted to conclude, that the Child was a Spurious, Unfair Production, put upon the Nation; for which Reason we reject him, and have now, by a Legal and Just Authority, deposed his Father and him, and settled the Succession upon the House of *Hanover*, being Protestants.

The Matter of his Title standing thus, divides the Nation into Two Parties, one Side for, and the other against, the Succession, either of the Pretender, or the House of *Hanover*, and either Side calling the other the Pretender; so that if we were to use the Parties Language, we must say, one Side is for, and the other Side against, either of the *Pretenders*; what the Visible Probabilities of either of these Claims succeeding are, is not the Present Case; the Nation appears at this Time strangely agitated between the Fears of one Party, and the Hopes of the other, each extenuating and aggravating, as their several Parties and Affections guide them, by which the Publick Disorder is very much encreased; what either of them have to alledge is our present Work to enquire; but more particularly what are the real or pretended Advantages of the expected Reign of him, who we are allow'd to distinguish by the Name of **the Pretender;** for his Friends here would have very little to say to move us to receive him, if they were not able to lay before us such Prospects of National Advantages, and such Views of Prosperity, as would be sufficient to prevail with those who have their Eyes upon the Good of their Country, and of their Posterity after them.

That then a Case so Popular, and of so much Consequence as this is, may not want such due Supports as the Nature of the Thing will allow, and especially since the Advantages and good Consquences of the Thing itself are so many, and so easie to be seen as his Friends alledge; why should not the Good People of *Britain* be made easie, and their Fears be turned into Peaceable Satisfaction, by seeing that this Devil may not be so Black as he is Painted; and that the Noise made of the Pretender and the frightful Things said of his Coming, and of his being receiv'd here, may not be made greater Scarecrows to us, than they really are; and *after all that has been said*, **if** it should appear that the Advantages of the Pretender's Succession are really greater to us, and the Dangers less to us, than those of the Succession of *HANOVER*, then much of their Difficulties would be over, who standing Neuter as to Persons appear against the Pretender, only because they are made to believe strange and terrible Things of what shall befal the Nation in Case of his Coming in, *such as* Popery, Slavery, *French* Power, destroying of our Credit, and devouring our Funds, (as that Scandalous Scribler, the *Review*, has been labouring to suggest,) with many other Things which we shall endeavour to expose to you, as they deserve. **If** we say it should appear then that the Dangers and Disadvantages of the Pretender's Succession are less than those of the House of *HANOVER*, who, because of an Act of Parliament, you know must not be called *Pretenders*; then there will remain nothing more to be said on that Score, but the Debate must be of the Reasonableness and Justice on either Side, for their Admittance, and there we question not but the Side we are really pleading for will have the Advantage.

To begin then with that most Popular and Affrighting Argument now made Use of, as the Bugbear of the People, against several other Things besides Jacobitism, we mean **French Greatness:** It is most evident that the Fear of this must, by the Nature of the Thing, be effectually removed upon our receiving *the Pretender*; the Grounds and Reasons why *French* Greatness is rendred Formidable to us, and so much Weight supposed to be in it, that like the Name of *Scanderberg*,[2] we fright our very Children with it, lye only in this, that we suggest the King of *France* being a profest Enemy to the Peace, and the Liberty of *Great-Britain*, will most certainly, as soon as he can a little recover himself, exercise all that Formidable Power to put the Pretender upon us, and not only to place him upon the Throne of *Great-Britain*, but to Maintain and Hold him up in it, against all the Opposition, either of the People of *Britain*, or the Confederate Princes Leagued with the Elector of *Hanover*, who are in the Interest of his Claim, or of his Party. Now it is evident, that upon a Peaceable admitting this Person, whom they call the Pretender, to Receive and Enjoy the Crown here, all that Formidable Power becomes your Friend, and *the being so* must necessarily take off from it every Thing that is called Terrible; forasmuch as the greater Terror and Amusement[3] the Power we apprehend really carries with it, the greater is the Tranquility and Satisfaction which accrues to us, when we have the Friendship of that Power which was so Formidable to us before: The Power of *France* is represented at this Time very terrible, and the Writers who speak of it apply it warm to our Imaginations, as that from whence we ought justly to apprehend the Impossibility of keeping out the Pretender, and this, notwithstanding they allow themselves at the same Time to suppose all the Confederate Powers of *Europe* to be Engaged, as well by their own Interest, as by the New Treaties of Barrier and Guarantee,[4] to Support and to Assist the Claim of the Elector of *Hanover*, and his Party. Now if this Power be so Great, and so Formidable, as they alledge, will it not on the other Side add a Proportion of Encrease to our Satisfaction, that this Power will be wholly in Friendship and League with us; and engaged to concern itself for the quieting our Fears of other Foreign Invaders; forasmuch as having once concern'd itself to set the Person of the Pretender upon the Throne, it cannot be supposed but it shall be equally concern'd to Support and Maintain him in that Possession, as what will mightily conduce to the carrying on the other Projects of his Greatness and Glory with the rest of *Europe*; in which it will be very much his Interest to secure himself from any Opposition he might meet with from this Nation, or from such as might be rendred Powerful by our Assistance. An Eminent Instance we have of this in the Mighty Efforts the *French* Nation have made for Planting, and Preserving when Planted, a Grandson of *France* upon the Throne of *Spain*;[5] and how Eminent are the Advantages to *France* from the Success of that Undertaking; of what less Consequence then would it be to the August Monarchy of *France*, to Secure and Engage to himself the constant Friendship and Assistance of the Power of *Great-Britain*, which he would necessarily do, by the placing this Person upon the Throne, who would thereby in Gratitude be engaged to contribute his utmost in Return to the King of *France*, for the carrying on his Glorious Designs in the rest of *Europe*. While then we become thus necessary to the King of *France*, Reason dictates that he would be our Fast Friend, our Constant Confederate, our Allie, firmly engaged to Secure our Sovereign, and Protect our People from the Insults and Attempts of all the World: Being thus engaged reciprocally with the King of *France*, there must necessarily be an End of all the Fears and Jealousies, of all the Apprehensions and

Doubts, which now so Amuse us, and appear so Formidable to us from the Prospect of the Power and Greatness of *France*; then we shall on the contrary say to the World, the stronger the King of *France* is, the better for the King of *England*; and what is best for the King, must be so for his People; for it is a most unnatural Way of Arguing, to suppose the Interest of a King, and of his People, to be different from one another.

And is not this then an Advantage incomparably greater to *Britain*, when the Pretender shall be upon the Throne, than any we can propose to ourselves in the present uneasie Posture of Affairs, which it must be acknowledged we are in now, when we cannot sleep in Quiet, for the terrible Apprehensions of being over-run by the Formidable Power of *France*.

Let us also consider the many other Advantages which may accrue to this Nation, by a nearer Conjunction, and closer Union, with *France*, such as Encrease of Commerce, Encouragement of Manufactures, Ballance of Trade; every one knows how vast an Advantage we reaped by the *French* Trade in Former Times, and how many Hundred Thousand Pounds a Year we gain'd by it, when the Ballance of Trade between us and *France* run so many Millions of *Livres* Annually **against** the *French* by the vast Exportation of our Goods to them, and the small Import which we receiv'd from them again, and by the Constant Flux of Money in *Specie*, which we drew from them every Year, upon Court Occasions, to the inexpressible Benefit of the Nation, and Enriching of the Subject, of which we shall have Occasion to speak hereafter more fully.

In the mean Time it were to be wished that our People, who are so bugbear'd with Words, and terrified with the Name of *French*, *French Power*, *French Greatness*, and the like, as if *England* could not Subsist, and the Queen of *England* was not Able to keep upon Her Throne any longer than the King of *France* pleased, and that Her Majesty was going to be a meer Servant to the *French* King,[6] would consider that this is an unanswerable Argument for the Coming of the Pretender, that we may make this so Formidable Prince our Friend, have all his Power engaged in our Interest, and see him going on Hand in Hand with us, in the securing us against all Sorts of Encroachments whatsoever: For if the King of *France* be such an Invincible Mighty Monarch, that we are nothing in his Eyes, or in his Hands; and that neither *Britain*, or all the Friends *Britain* can make, are able to deliver us from him; then it must be our great Advantage to have the Pretender be our King, that we may be out of the Danger of this Formidable *French* Power, being our Enemy; and that on the other Hand, we may have so Potent, so Powerful, so Invincible, a Prince be our Friend. The Case is evidently laid down to every common Understanding, in the Example of *Spain*; *till now*, the *Spaniards* for many Ages have been over-run, and impoverished, by their continued Wars with the *French*, and it was not doubted but one Time or other they would have been entirely conquered by the King of *France*, and have become a meer Province of *France*; whereas now, having but consented to receive a King from the Hands of the invincible Monarch, they are made easie as to the former Danger they were always in, are now most safe under the Protection of *France*; and he who before was their Terror, is now their Safety, and being safe from him, it appears they are so from all the World.

Would it not then be the manifest Advantage of this Nation to be likewise secur'd from the dangerous Power of *France*, and make that Potentate our fast Friend, who it is so apparent we are not able to resist as an Enemy? This is reducing the *French* Power the softest Way, if not the best and shortest Way; for if it does not reduce the Power itself, it brings it into such a Circumstance, as that all the Terror of it is removed, and we embrace that as our Safety and Satisfaction, which really is, and ought to be, our Terror and Aversion; this must of Necessity be our great Advantage.

How strange is it that none of our People have yet thought of this Way of securing their Native Country from the Insults of *France*? Were but the Pretender once received as our King, we have no more Disputes with the King of *France*, he has no Pretence to Invade or Disturb us; what a quiet World would it be with us in such a Case, when the greatest Monarch in the Universe should be our fast Friend, and be in our Interest to prevent any of the Inconveniencies which might happen to us from the Disgust of other Neighbours, who may be dissatisfied with us upon other Accounts: As to the terrible Things which some People fright us, and themselves with, from the Influence which *French* Councils may have upon us, and of *French* Methods of Government being introduced among us; these we ought to esteem only Clamours and Noise, raised by a Party to amuse and affright us; for pray let us enquire a little into them, and see if there be any Reason for us to be so terrified at them; suppose they were really what is alledged, which we hope they are not; *for Example*, the absolute Dominion of the King of *France* over his Subjects, is such, say our People, as makes them Miserable; well, but let us examine then, are we not already miserable for Want of this Absolute Dominion? Are we not miserably divided? Is not our Government miserably weak? Are we not miserably subjected to the Rabbles and Mob? Nay, is not the very Crown mobb'd here every now and then, into whatever our Soveraign Lord the People demand? whereas on the contrary, we see *France* entirely united as one Man; no virulent Scriblers there dare Affront the Government; no Impertinent P[arlia]ments there disturb the Monarch with their Addresses and Representations; no Superiority of Laws restrain the Administration; no Insolent Lawyers talk of the Sacred Constitution, in Opposition to the more Sacred Prerogative; but all with Harmony and General Consent agree to Support the Majesty of their Prince, and with their Lives and Fortunes; (not in Complimenting Sham Addresses only, but in Reality, and effectually) Support the Glory of their Great Monarch. In doing this they are all united together so firmly, as if they had but one Heart, and one Mind, and that the King was the Soul of the Nation: What if they are *what we foolishly call* Slaves to the Absolute Will of their Prince? That Slavery to them is meer Liberty; they entertain no Notions of that foolish Thing **Liberty**, which we make so much Noise about; nor have they any Occasion of it, or any Use for it if they had it; they are as Industrious in Trade, as Vigorous in Pursuit of their Affairs, go on with as much Courage, and are as well satisfied when they have wrought hard 20 or 30 Years to get a little Money for the King to take away, as we are to get it for our Wives and Children; and as they plant Vines, and plow Lands, that the King and his Great Men may eat the Fruit thereof, they think it as great a Felicity as if they Eat it themselves. The Badge of their Poverty, which we make such a Noise of, and Insult them about so much, (*viz.*) their Wooden Shoes, their Peasants make nothing of it; they say they are as happy in their Wooden Shoes, as our People are with their Luxury and Drunkenness; besides, do not our Poor People wear Iron Shoes, and Leather Doublets, and where is the Odds between them? All the Business forsooth is this Trifle we call Liberty, which rather than be plagued with so much Strife and Dissention about it as we are, who would be troubled with? Now it is evident **the Peace** and *Union* which we should enjoy under the like Methods of Government here, which we hope for under the Happy Government of the Pretender, must needs be a full Equivalent for all the pretended Rights and Priviledges which we say we shall loose; and how will our Rights and Privileges be lost? Will they not rather be Centred in our Common Receptacle (*viz.*) the Sovereign, who is according to the King of *France*'s happy Government the Common Magazine of Universal Privilege, communicating it to, and preserving it for, the general Use of his Subjects, as their Safety and Happiness requires. Thus he protects their Commerce, encourages their Foreign Settlements, enlarges their Possessions Abroad, encreases their Manufactures, gives them Room for spreading their numerous Race over the World; at Home he rewards Arts and Sciences, cultivates Learning, employs innumerable Hands in the Labours of the State, and the like; what if it be true that all they Gain is at his Mercy? Does he take it away, except when needful, for the Support of his Glory and Grandeur, which is their Protection? Is it not apparent, that under all the Oppressions they talk so much of, the *French* are the Nation the most Improved and Encreased in Manufactures, in Navigation, in Commerce, within these 50 Years, of any Nation in the World? And here we pretend Liberty, Property, Constitutions, Rights of Subjects, and such Stuff as that, and with all these fine Gewgaws,[7] which we pretend propagate Trade, and encrease the Wealth of the Nation, we are every Day Declining, and become Poor; how long will this Nation be blinded by their own foolish Customs? And when will they learn to know, that the Absolute Government of a Vertuous Prince, who makes the Good of his People his Ultimate End, and esteems their Prosperity his Glory, is the Best, and most Godlike, Government in the World.

Let us then be no more rendred uneasie with the Notions, that with the Pretender we must entertain *French* Methods of Government, such as Tyranny and Arbitrary Power; Tyranny is no more Tyranny, when improv'd for the Subjects Advantage; perhaps when we have tried it we may find it as much for our Good many Ways, nay, and more too, than our present Exorbitant Liberties, especially unless we can make a better Use of them, and Enjoy them, without being always going by the Ears about them, as we see daily, not only with our Governours, but even with one another; a little *French Slavery*, though it be a frightful Word among us, *that is*, being made so by Custom, yet may do us a great deal of Good in the Main, as it may teach us not to *Over* (Under) *Value* our Liberties, when we have them, so much as sometimes we have done; and this is not one of the least Advantages which we shall gain by the Coming of the Pretender, and consequently one of the good Reasons why we should be very willing to receive him.

The next Thing which they fill us with Apprehensions of in the Coming of the Pretender, is the Influence of *French* Councils, which they Construe thus, (*viz.*) That the Pretender being restor'd here by the Assistance of *France*, will not only Rule us by *French* Methods, (*viz.*) by *French* Tyranny, but in Gratitude to his Restorer he will cause us to be always ready with *English* Blood and Treasure to Assist and Support the *French* Ambition in the Invasions he will ever be making upon *Europe*, and in the Oppressions of other Nations; till at last he obtain the Superiority over them all, and turn upon us too, devouring the Liberties of *Europe* in his so long purposed and resolved *Universal Monarchy*. As to the Gratitude of the Pretender to the King of *France*, why should you make that a Crime? Are not all People bound in Honour to retaliate Kindness? And would you have your Prince be ungrateful to him that brought him hither? By the same Rule you would expect he could be ungrateful to us that receive him; besides, if it be so great an Advantage to us to have him brought in, we shall be all concern'd also in Gratitude to the King of *France* for helping us to him; and sure we shall not decline making a suitable Return to him for the Kindness; and is this any Thing more than common? Did we not pay the *Dutch* Six Hundred Thousand Pound *Sterling* for assisting the Late King *William*? And did we not immediately Embark with them in the War against the King of *France*? And has not that Revolution cost the Nation One Hundred

Millions of *British* Money to Support it? And shall we grutch[8] to Support the Pretender, and his Benefactor, at the same Expence, if it should be needful, for carrying on the New Scheme of *French* Liberty, which when that Time comes may be in a likely and forward Way to prevail over the whole World, to the General Happiness of *Europe?*

There seems to be but one Thing more which those People, who make such a Clamour at the Fears of the Pretender, take hold of, and this is Religion; and they tell us, that not only *French* Government, and *French* Influence, but *French* Religion, that is to say, **Popery,** will come upon us; but these People know not what they talk of, for it is evident that they shall be so far from being loaden with Religion, that they will rather obtain that so long desired Happiness, of having no Religion at all. This we may easily make appear has been the Advantage which has been long labour'd for in this Nation; and as the Attainments we are arriv'd to of that Kind are very considerable already, so we cannot doubt but that if once the Pretender were settled quietly among us, an Absolute Subjection, as well of Religious Principles, as Civil Liberties, to the Disposal of the Sovereign, would take Place. This is an Advantage so fruitful of several other manifest Improvements, that though we have not Room in this Place to enlarge upon the Particulars, we cannot doubt but it must be a most grateful Piece of News to a great Part of the Nation, who have long groan'd under the Oppressions and cruel Severities of the Clergy, occasion'd by their own strict Lives, and rigorous Virtue, and their imposing such Austerities and Restraints upon the People; and in this Particular the Clamour of Slavery will appear very scandalous in the Nation, for the Slavery of Religion being taken off, and an Universal Freedom of Vice being introduced, what greater Liberty can we enjoy.[9]

But we have yet greater Advantages attending this Nation by the Coming of the Pretender than any we have yet taken Notice of; and though we have not Room in this short Tract to name them all, and enlarge upon them as the Case may require, yet we cannot omit such due Notice of them, as may serve to satisfie our Readers, and convince them, how much they ought to favour the Coming of the Pretender, as the great Benefit to the whole Nation; and therefore we shall begin with our Brethren of *Scotland*; and here we may tell them, that they, of all the Parts of this Island, shall receive the most evident Advantages, in that the setting the Pretender upon the Throne shall effectually set them free from the Bondage they now groan under, in their abhorr'd Subjection to *England* by the **Union**, *which* may, no question, be declar'd Void, and Dissolv'd, as a Violence upon the *Scottish* Nation,[10] as soon as ever the Pretender shall be Established upon the Throne; a few Words may serve to recommend this to the *Scots*, since we are very well satisfied we shall be sure to oblige every

Side there, by it: The Opposition all Sides made to the Union at the Time of the Transaction of the Union in the Parliament there, cannot but give us Reason to think thus; and the present Scruple, even the Presbyterians themselves make, of taking the Abjuration,[11] if they do not, as some pretend, assure us that the said Presbyterian Nonjurers are in the Interest of the Pretender, yet they undeniably prove, and put it out of all question, that they are ill-pleased with the Yoke of the Union, and would embrace every just Occasion of being quietly and freely discharged from the Fetters which they believe they bear by the said Union; now there is no Doubt to be made, but that upon the very first Appearance of the Pretender, the Antient Kingdom of *Scotland* should recover her former well-known Condition, we mean, of being perfectly free, and depending upon none but the King of *France*. **How** Inestimable an Advantage this will be to *Scotland* and how effectually he will Support and Defend the *Scots* against their Antient Enemies, the *English*, forasmuch as we have not Room to enlarge upon here, we may take Occasion to make out more particularly on another Occasion. But it may not be forgotten here, that the Union was not only justly Distasteful to the *Scots* themselves, but also to many Good Men, and Noble Patriots of the Church, some of whom entred their Protests against Passing and Confirming, or Ratifying the same, such as the late Lord *Hav[er]sham*,[12] and the Right Wise, and Right Noble, E[arl] of *Nott[ingham]*, whose Reasons for being against the said *Union, besides those they gave in the House of P[eer]s, which we do by no Means mean or reflect upon in the least in this Place;* we say, whose other Reasons for opposing the said Union were founded upon an Implacable Hatred to the *Scots* Kirk, which has been Established thereby: It may then not admit of any Question, but that they would think it a very great Advantage to be delivered from the same, as they would effectually be by the Coming of the Pretender; wherefore by the concurring Judgment of these Noble and Wise Persons who on that Account opposed the *Union*, the Coming of the Pretender must be an Inexpressible Advantage to this Nation; nor is the dissolving the Union so desirable a Thing, meerly as that Union was an Establishing among us a Wicked Schismatical Presbyterian Generation, and giving the Sanction of the Laws to their Odious Constitution, which we Esteem (you know) worse than Popery; but even on Civil Accounts, as particularly on Account of the P[eer]s of *Scotland*, who many of them think themselves Egregiously maltreated, and robb'd of their Birthright, as P[eer]s, and have express'd themselves so in a something Publick Manner.[13] Now we cannot think that any of these will be at all offended that all this New Establishment should be revoked; nay, we have heard it openly said, that the *Scots* are so little satisfied with the *Union* at this Time, that if it were now to be put to the Vote, as it was before, whether they should Unite with *England*, or no, there would not be one Man in Fifteen, throughout *Scotland*, that would Vote for it. *If then* it appears that the whole Nation thus seems to be averse to the Union, and by the Coming in of this most Glorious Pretender that Union will be in all Appearance dissolved, and the Nation freed from the Encumbrance of it, will any *Scots* Man, who is against the Union, refuse to be for the Pretender? Sure it cannot be; I know it is alledged, that they will lay aside their Discontent at the Union, and Unite together against the Pretender, because that is to Unite against Popery; we will not say what a few, who have their Eyes in their Heads, may do; but as the Generality of the People there are not so well reconciled together, as such a Thing requires, it is not unlikely that such a Uniting may be prevented, if the Pretender's Friends there can but play the Game of dividing them farther, as they should do; to which End it cannot but be very serviceable to them to have the real Advantages of receiving the Pretender laid before them, which is the true Intent and Meaning of the Present Undertaking.

But we have more and greater Advantages of the Coming of the Pretender, and such as no question will invite you to receive him with great Satisfaction and Applause; and it cannot be unnecessary to inform you, for your Direction in other Cases, how the Matter, as to Real and Imaginary Advantage, stands with the Nation in this Affair; and *First*, The Coming of the Pretender will at once put us all out of Debt. These Abomination-Whigs, and these Bloody Wars, carried on so long for little or nothing, *have*, as is evident to our Senses *now*, (whatever it was all along,) brought a heavy Debt upon the Nation; so that if what a known Author lately Published is true, the Government pays now almost Six Millions a Year to the Common People for Interest of Money; that is to say, the Usurers Eat up the Nation, and Devour Six Millions Yearly; which is paid, and must be paid now for a long Time, if some *kind Turn*, such as this of the Coming of the Pretender, or such like, does not help us out of it; the Weight of this is not only Great, insuperably Great, but most of it is entailed for a terrible Time, not only for our Age, but beyond the Age of our Grand-children, even for Ninety-nine Years: By how much the Consideration of this Debt is Intolerable and Afflicting to the last Degree, by so much the greater must the Obligation be to the Person, who will Ease the Nation of such a Burthen, and therefore we place it among the Principal Advantages which we are to receive from the Admission of the Pretender, that he will not fail to rid us of this Grievance, and by Methods peculiar to himself, deliver us from so great a Burthen as these Debts are now, and, unless he deliver us, are like to be to the Ages to come: Whither he will do this at once, by remitting most Graciously to the Nation the whole Payment, and consequently take off the Burthen, *Brevi Manu*, as with a Spunge wiping out the Infamous Score, leaving it to fall as Fate directs, or by prudent Degrees, we know not, nor is it our

Business to determine it here; no Doubt the doing it with a Jerk, as we call it, *Comme une Coup de Grace*, must be the most expeditious Way; nay, and the kindest Way of putting the Nation out of its Pain; for lingering Deaths are counted cruel; and tho' *Une coup d'Eclat* may make an Impression for the Present, yet the Astonishment is soonest over; besides, where is the Loss to the Nation in this Sense? Tho' the Money be stopt from the Subject on one Hand, if it be stopt to the Subjects on the other, the Nation Loses or Gains Nothing; we know it will be Answer'd, that it is unjust, and that Thousands of Families will be ruin'd, because they who Loose, will not be those who Gain. But what is this to the Purpose in a National Revolution; unjust! Alas! Is that an Argument? Go and ask the Pretender! Does not he say you have all done unjustly by him? And since the Nation in general loses Nothing, what Obligation has he to regard the particular Injury that some Families may sustain? And yet farther, is it not remarkable, that most Part of the Money is paid by the Cursed Party of Whigs, who from the Beginning officiously appear'd to keep him from his Right? And what Obligation has he upon him to concern himself for doing them Right in Particular, more than other People? But to avoid the Scandal of Partiality, there is another Thought offers to our View, which the Nation is beholding to a Particular Author for putting us in Mind of; if it be unjust that we should suppose the Pretender shall stop the Payment on both Sides, because it is doing the Whigs Wrong, since the Tories, who perhaps being chiefly Landed Men, pay the most Taxes; then, to keep up a just Ballance, he need only continue the Taxes to be paid in, and only stop the Annuities and Interest which are to be paid out. Thus both Sides having no Reason to Envy or Reproach one another with Hardships, or with suffering Unequally; they may every one lose their Proportion, and the Money may be laid up in the Hands of the New Sovereign, for the Good of the Nation.

This being thus happily proposed, we cannot pass over the great Advantages which would accrue to this Nation in such a Case, by having such a Mass of Money laid up in the *Exchequer* at the Absolute Command of a most Gracious *French* Sovereign. But as these Things are so Glorious, and so Great, as to admit of no compleat Explication in this short Tract, give us Leave, *O People* of *Great-Britain*, to lay before you a little Scetch of your future Felicity, under the Auspicious Reign of such a Glorious Prince, as we all hope, and believe, the Pretender to be. (1.) You are to allow, that by such a Just and Righteous shutting up of the *Exchequer* in about Seven Years Time, he may be supposed to have received about Forty Millions Sterling from his People, which not being to be found in *Specie* in the Kingdom, will, for the Benefit of Circulation, enable him to Treasure up Infinite Funds of Wealth in Foreign Banks, a prodigious Mass of Foreign Bullion, Gold, Jewels, and Plate, to be ready in the *Tower*, or elsewhere, to be issued upon Future Emergency, as Occasion may allow. This prodigious Wealth will necessarily have these happy Events, to the Infinite Satisfaction and Advantage of the whole Nation, and the Benefit of which I hope none will be so Unjust, or Ungrateful, to deny. (2.) It will for ever after deliver this Nation from the Burthen, the Expence, the Formality, and the Tyranny, of Parliaments. No one can perhaps at the first View be rightly sensible of the many Advantages of this Article, and from how many Mischiefs it will deliver this Nation. (3.) How the Countrey Gentlemen will be no longer harrass'd to come, at the Command of every Court Occasion, and upon every Summons by the Prince's Proclamation, from their Families, and other Occasions, whether they can be spared from their Wives, &c. or no, or whether they can trust their Wives behind them, or no; nay, whether they can spare Money or no for the Journey, or whether they must come *Carriage Paid* or no; *then* they will no more be unnecessarily exposed to Long and Hazardous Journeys, in the Depth of Winter, from the remotest Corners of the Island, to come to *London,* just to give away the Countrey's Money, and go Home again; all this will be dispenced with by the Kind and Gracious Management of the Pretender, when he, *God bless us,* shall be our more Gracious Sovereign. (4.) In the happy Consequence of the Demise of Parliaments, the Countrey will be eased of that intolerable Burthen of Travelling to Elections, sometimes in the Depth of Winter, sometimes in the Middle of their Harvest, whenever the Writs of Elections Arbitrarily Summons them. (5.) And with them the Poor Gentlemen will be eased of that abominable Grievance of the Nation, (*viz.*) the Expence of Elections, by which so many Gentlemen of Estates have been Ruin'd, so many innocent People, of honest Principles before, have been Debauched, and made Mercenary, Partial, Perjur'd, and been Blinded with Bribes, to Sell their Countrey and Liberties to who bids most. It is well known how often, and yet how in vain, this Distemper has been the constant Concern of Parliaments, for many Ages, to Cure, and to provide sufficient Remedies for. Now if ever the effectual Remedy for this is found out, to the inexpressible Advantage of the whole Nation; and this perhaps is the only Cure for it that the Nature of the Disease will admit of; what terrible Havock has this kind of Trade made among the Estates of the Gentry, and the Morals of the Common People? (6.) How also has it kept alive the Factions and Divisions of the Countrey People, keeping them in a Constant Agitation, and in Triennial Commotions? So that what with Forming New Interests, and Cultivating Old, the Heats and Animosities never cease among the People. But once set the Pretender upon the Throne, and let the Funds be but happily stopt, and paid into his Hands, that he may be in no more Need of a Parliament, and all these Distempers will be cur'd as effectually as a Feaver is cur'd by cutting off the Head, or as a Halter[14] cures the Bleeding at the Nose. How Infatuated then is this Nation, that they should so obstinately refuse a Prince, by the Nature of whose Circumstances, and the avowed Principles of whose Party, we are sure to obtain such Glorious Things, such Inestimable Advantages, Things which no Age, no Prince, no Attempt of Parties, or Endeavour, though often aim'd at of Ministers of State, have ever been able to procure for us. (7.) This Amassing of Treasure, by the stopping the Funds on one Hand, and the receiving the Taxes on the other, will effectually enable the Pretender to set up, and effectually maintain, that Glorious and so often-desir'd, Method of Government, *Au Coup de Cannon, Anglice*, a Standing Army. This we have the Authority of the Antient Borough of *Carlisle*, that it is the Safety of the Prince, and the Glory of the Nation, as appears by their Renowned Address to King *James* II.[15] Then we should see a new Face of our Nation, and *Britain* would no more be a naked Nation, as it has formerly been; then we should have Numerous and Gallant Armies surrounding a Martial Prince, ready to make the World, as well as his own Subjects, tremble; then our Inland Counties would appear full of Royal Fortifications, Citadels, Forts, and Strong Towns; the Beauty of the Kingdom, and Awe of Factious Rebels: It is a strange Thing that this Refractory People of ours could never be made sensible how much it is for the Glory and Safety of this Nation that we should be put into a Posture of Defence *against ourselves:* It has been often alledged, that *this Nation can never be ruin'd but with their own Consent:* If then we are our own Enemies, is it not highly requisite that we should be put in a Condition to have our Ruin prevented? And that since it is apparent we are no more fit to be trusted with our own Liberties, having a Natural and a National Propensity to destroy and undo ourselves, and may be brought to Consent to our own Ruin, we should have such Princes as for the future know how to restrain us, and how reasonable is it to allow them Forces *to do so?*

We might enlarge here upon the Great and Certain Advantages of this best of Governments, *a Standing Army*; we might go back to the *Persian, Grecian,* and *Roman* Empires, which had never arriv'd to such a Pitch of Glory if the People and Nations who they subdued had been able to Nose them with[16] such Trifles as what we call Constitution, National Right, Antient Privileges, *and the like*; we might descend also to particular Advantages of Government, which it is hoped we may attain to in *Britain* when the Pretender arrives, some of which are grown Obsolete, and out of Use, by Custom, and long Possession of those troublesome Things call'd Liberties; among these may be reckoned,

(1.) The whole Kingdom will be at once eased of that ridiculous Feather-caps[17] Expence of Militia and Train'd-bands, which serve for little else but to justifie the Picking the Peoples Pockets, with an Annual Tax of Trophy-Money,[18] and every now and then putting the City of *London*, and Parts Adjacent, to Ten Thousand Pound Charge, to beat Drums, and shoot Muskets, for nothing; when on the contrary, you shall in the Blessed Revolution we now invite you to have all this done *Gratis*, by the Standing Troops kept constantly in Pay; and your Lieutenancy may lay down their Commissions among the rest of *Non-Significants* of the Nation.

(2.) You shall be for ever out of Danger of being ridden again by the **Mob**, your Meeting-houses shall no more be the Subject of the enraged Rabbles; nor shall the *Bank* of *England* desire the Drums to beat at Midnight to raise a Guard for *Grocer's-Hall*;[19] your new Monarch will suffer none to Insult or Plunder the City *but himself*; and as the City itself shall never want Soldiers, *how should it, when the whole Kingdom shall become a Garrison?* The Money in the *Bank* shall always be defended by a strong Guard, who shall, whenever there is any Danger of its being too safe, convey it, for its Eminent Security, from *Grocer's-Alley* to the *Tower*, or to the *Exchequer*, where it shall not fail to be kept for the Advantage of the Publick.

(3.) Again, upon this happy Change we shall immediately be delivered from that most Infamous Practice of Stock-jobbing, of which so much has been said to so little Purpose; for the Funds being turned all into One General Stock, and the Prince being himself your Security, you may even write upon all your Companies, this General Phrase, (*viz.*) *No Transfer*, as they do when the Books are shut up at the *Bank*, or *East-India* House; so as all the Rivers of Water are swallowed up in the Sea, as One Ocean, to which they are all tending, so all these petty Cheats will be Ingulph'd at once in the General Ocean of State Trick, and the *Exchange-Alley-Men* may justly be said to Buy the *Bear-Skin*[20] ever after.

(4.) **Then** (which is a Blessing we fear we cannot hope for before) we may expect to be deliver'd from the Throng of Virulent and Contumatious Libels which now Infest our Streets; and the Libellers themselves being most exemplarily Punished, for a Terror to the rest, will not dare to affront the Government with Ballads and Balderdash; if an impudent Fellow dares lift up his Pen against the Authority and Power of his Prince, he shall instantly feel the Weight of that Power to crush him, which he ought before to have feared; and Pamphleteers shall then not be Whipped and Pillor'd, but Hang'd; and when Two or Three of them have suffered that Way, it is hoped those wholesome Severities may put an effectual stop to the Noise and Clamour they now make in the Nation; above all, the Hands of the Government will then be set free from the Fetters of Law; and it shall not be always necessary for the Ministers of State to proceed by all the Forms of the Courts of Justice, in such Cases, by which the Scriblers of the Age pretend to stand it out against the Government, and put their own Construction upon their Libels. But when these happy Days arrive, Juries and Judges shall find and determine in these, and all other Cases, bring Verdicts, and give Sentence, as the Prince in his Royal Justice shall direct.

We might enter here upon a long List of other happy Circumstances we shall all arrive to, and of great Advantages not here named, which the Coming in of the Pretender shall infallibly bring us to the Enjoyment of, particularly in Matters of Religion, Civil Right, Property and Commerce, but the needful Brevity of this Tract will not admit of it; we shall only add one Thing more, which gives Weight to all the rest, (*viz.*) That the Certainty of these Things, and of their being the Natural Consequences of the bringing in the Pretender, adds to the certain Felicity of that Reign. This Sums up the Happiness of the Pretender's Reign; we need not talk of Security, as the *Review* has done, and pretend he is not able to give us Security for the Performance of any Thing he promises; every Man that has any Sense of the Principles, Honour, and Justice of the Pretender, his Zeal for the *Roman* Catholick Cause, his Gratitude to his Benefactor, the *French* King, and his Love to the Glory and Happiness of his Native Countrey, must rest satisfied of his punctually performing all these Great Things for us; to ask him Security, would be not to Affront him only, but to Affront the whole Nation; *No Man can doubt him*; the Nature of the Thing allows that he must do us all that Kindness; he cannot be true to his own Reason without it; wherefore this Treaty *executes itself*, and appears so rational to believe, that whoever doubts it may be supposed to doubt even the Veracity of *James* the Just.

What unaccountable Folly then must those People be Guilty of, who stand so much in the Way of their own and their Countrey's Happiness, as to oppose, or pretend to argue against, the receiving this Glorious Prince, and would be for having *Dutch* Men and Foreigners forsooth to come, and all under the Notion of their being *PROTESTANTS?* To avoid and detect which Fallacy, we shall in our next Essay enter into the Examination of the Religion and Orthodox Principles of the Person of the Pretender, and doubt not to make it out, for the Satisfaction of all Tender Consciences, that he is a true Protestant of the Church of *England*, Establish'd by Law, and in that very Natural Primitive Sense of that Phrase as it was used by His Royal Predecessor, of Famous and Pious Memory, *Charles* II. ———— and as such, no doubt, he will endeavour for the Recovery of the Crown, which Crown, if he obtains it, you see what Glorious Things he may do for himself, and us.

Quam si Non Tenuit Magnis Tamen Excidit Ausis.[21]

F I N I S

An Appeal to Honour and Justice 1715

Like most men who have lived in the public eye and whose activities have revealed seemingly unworthy motives or required apparently devious conduct, Defoe was anxious to justify himself to the world. Hence the publication of this work—on 24 February 1715—which claimed to be (according to the title-page) 'a True Account of his Conduct in Publick Affairs'. In it Defoe appealed 'to the Honour and Justice of [his] worst Enemies' (p. 176) to clear him of the unsubstantiated charges frequently made against him; and he urgently hoped to be restored 'to the opinion of Sober and Impartial Men' (p. 194). His purpose, then, appears honourable, especially in a man whose distinction rested on personal achievement, not on inherited status. In fact, Defoe had other motives. The *Appeal* was also intended to explain and defend his public services under William and the last three Ministries of Queen Anne, so that he should be in good odour with the Whigs under 'the best Prince in the World' (p. 167), George I. Accordingly Defoe endeavoured to prove his steadfast support for 'Revolution principles', his zeal in the cause of 'Liberty and the Protestant Interest'. Yet another object was to defend Defoe's former 'benefactor', Robert Harley, who was in danger of impeachment. The 'True Account', then, for the most part related actual events but their presentation was governed by Defoe's overriding rhetorical aim: to convince his new employers of his integrity and loyalty.

An Appeal to Honour and Justice, &c.

I Hope the Time is come at last, when the Voice of moderate Principles may be heard; hitherto the Noise has been so great, and the Prejudices and Passions of Men so strong, that it had been but in vain to offer at any Argument, or for any Man to talk of giving a Reason for his Actions: And this alone has been the Cause why, when other Men, who, I think, have less to say in their own Defence, are appealing to the Publick, and struggling to defend themselves, I alone have been silent under the infinite Clamours and Reproaches, causeless Curses, unusual Threatnings, and the most unjust and injurious Treatment in the World.

I hear much of Peoples calling out to punish the Guilty; but very few are concern'd to clear the Innocent. I hope some will be inclin'd to Judge impartially, and have yet reserv'd so much of the Christian, as to believe, and at least to hope, that a rational Creature cannot abandon himself so as to act without some Reason, and are willing not only to have me defend my self, but to be able to answer for me where they hear me causlesly insulted by others, and therefore are willing to have such just Arguments put into their Mouths as the Cause will bear.

As for those who are prepossess'd, and according to the modern Justice of Parties are resolv'd to be so, *Let them go*, I am not arguing with them, *but against them*; they act so contrary to Justice, to Reason, to Religion, so contrary to the Rules of Christians and of good Manners, that they are not to be argued with, but to be expos'd, or entirely neglected. I have a Receipt against all the Uneasiness which it may be supposed to give me, and that is, to contemn Slander, and think it not worth the least Concern; neither should I think it worth while to give any Answer to it if it were not on some other Accounts, of which I shall speak as I go on.

If any Man ask me, why I am in such hast to publish this Matter at this time? Among many other good Reasons which I could give, these are some:

1. I think I have long enough been made *Fabula Vulgi*, and born the Weight of general Slander; and I should be wanting to Truth, to my Family, and to my Self, if I did not give a fair and true State of my Conduct for impartial Men to judge of, when I am no more in being to answer for my self.

2. By the Hints of Mortality, and by the Infirmities of a Life of Sorrow and Fatigue, I have Reason to think that I am not a great way off from, if not very near to the great Ocean of Eternity, and the time may not be long e're I embark on the last Voyage:[1] Wherefore, I think, I should *even Accounts* with this World before I go, that no Actions (Slanders) may lie against my Heirs, Executors, Administrators, and Assigns, to disturb them in the peaceable Possession of their Father's (Character) Inheritance.

3. I fear, *God grant I have not a second Sight in it*, that this lucid Interval of Temper and Moderation which shines, *tho' dimly too* upon us at this time, will be but of short Continuance, and that some Men, who know not how to use the Advantage God has put into their Hands with Moderation, will push, in spight of the best Prince in the World, at such extravagant Things, and act with such an intemperate Forwardness, as will revive the Heats and Animosities which wise and good Men were in hopes should be allay'd by the happy Accession of the King to the Throne.

It is and ever was my Opinion, that Moderation is the only Vertue by which the Peace and Tranquillity of this Nation can be preserv'd, even the King himself, *I believe his Majesty will allow me that Freedom*, can only be happy in the Enjoyment of the Crown by a moderate Administration, if his Majesty should be oblig'd, contrary to his known Disposition, to joyn with intemperate Councils; if it does not lessen his Security, I am perswaded it will lessen his Satisfaction. It cannot be pleasant or agreeable, and, *I think*, it cannot be safe to any just Prince to Rule over a divided People, split into incens'd and exasperated Parties: Tho' a skilful Mariner may have Courage to master a Tempest, and goes fearless thro' a Storm, yet he can never be said to delight in the Danger; a fresh fair Gale, and a quiet Sea, is the Pleasure of his Voyage, and we have a Saying worth Notice to them that are otherwise minded, *Qui amat periculum peribit in illo*.[2]

To attain at the happy Calm, which, as I say, is the Safety of *Britain*, is the Question which should now move us all; and he would Merit to be call'd the Nation's Physician that could prescribe the Specifick for it. I think I may be allow'd to say, a *Conquest of Parties* will never do it; *a Ballance of Parties MAY*. Some are for *the former*; they talk high of Punishments, letting Blood, revenging the Treatment they have met with, and the like:[3] If they, *not knowing what Spirit they are of*, think this the Course to be taken, let them try their Hands, I shall give them for lost, and look for their Downfal *from that time*; for the Ruin of all such Tempers slumbereth not.

It is many Years that I have profess'd my self an Enemy to all Precipitations in publick Administrations; and often I have attempted to shew, that hot Councils have ever been distructive to those who have made use of them:

Indeed they have not always been a Disadvantage to the Nation, as in King *James* II's Reign, where, as I have often said in Print, his Precipitation was the Safety of us all; and if he had proceeded temperately and politickly, we had been undone, *Felix quem faciunt.*[4]

But these things have been spoken when your Ferment has been too high for any thing to be heard; whether you will hear it now or not, *I know not*, and therefore it was that I said, *I fear* the perfect Cessation of Party-Arms will not hold long.

These are some of the Reasons why I think this is the proper Juncture for me to give some Account of my self, and of my past Conduct to the World; and that I may do this as effectually as I can, being perhaps never more to speak from the Press, I shall, as concisely as I can, give an Abridgement of my own History during the few unhappy Years I have employ'd my self, or been employ'd in Publick in the World.

Misfortunes in Business having unhing'd me from Matters of Trade,[5] it was about the Year 1694 when I was invited by some Merchants, with whom I had corresponded abroad, and some also at home, to settle at *Cadiz* in *Spain*, and that with Offers of very Good Commissions; but Providence, which had other Work for me to do, placed a secret Aversion in my Mind to quitting *England* upon any account, and made me refuse the best Offers of that kind, to be concern'd with some eminent Persons at home, in proposing *Ways* and *Means* to the Government for raising Money to supply the Occasions of the War then newly begun. Some time after this, I was, without the least Application of mine, and being then seventy Miles from *London*, sent for to be Accomptant to the Commissioners of the Glass Duty, in which Service I continued to the Determination of their Commission.[6]

During this time, there came out a vile abhor'd Pamphlet, in very ill Verse, written by one Mr. *Tutchin*, and call'd, THE FOREIGNERS: In which the Author, *who he was I then knew not*, fell personally upon the King himself, and then upon the *Dutch* Nation; and after having reproach'd his Majesty with Crimes, that his worst Enemy could not think of without Horror, he sums up all in the odious Name of FOREIGNER.

This fill'd me with a kind of Rage against the Book, and gave birth to a Trifle which I could hope should have met with so general an Acceptation as it did, I mean, *The True-Born-Englishman.*[7] How this Poem was the Occasion of my being known to his Majesty; how I was afterwards receiv'd by him; how Employ'd; and how, above my Capacity of deserving, Rewarded, is no Part of the present Case, and is only mention'd here as I take all Occasions to do for the expressing the Honour I ever preserv'd for the Immortal and Glorious Memory of that Greatest and Best of Princes, and who it was my Honour and Advantage to call Master as well as Sovereign, whose Goodness to me I never forgot, neither can forget; and whose Memory I never patiently heard abused, nor ever can do so; and who had he liv'd, would never have suffered me to be treated as I have been in the World.[8]

But Heaven for our Sins remov'd him in Judgment. How far the Treatment he met with, from the Nation he came to save, and whose Deliverance he finished, was admitted by Heaven to be a Means of his Death, I desire to forget for their sakes who are guilty; and if this calls any of it to mind, it is mention'd to move them to treat him better who is now with like Principles of Goodness and Clemency appointed by God, and the Constitution, to be their Sovereign; least he that protects righteous Princes, avenges the Injuries they receive from an ungrateful People, by giving them up to the Confusions their Madness leads them to.

And in their just acclamations at the happy accession of His present Majesty to the Throne, I cannot but advise them to look back, and call to mind who it was that first Guided them to the Family of *Hanover*, and to pass by all the Popish Branches of *Orleans* and *Savoy*, recognizing the just authority of Parliament, in the undoubted Right of Limiting the Succession, and Establishing that Glorious Maxim of our Settlement, (*viz.*) That *it is inconsistent with the Constitution of this Protestant Kingdom to be Govern'd by a Popish Prince*.[9] I say let them call to mind who it was that guided their Thoughts first to the Protestant Race of their own Kings in the House of *Hanover*, and that it is to King *William*, next to Heaven it self, to whom we owe the Enjoying a Protestant King at this time. I need not go back to the particulars of his Majesty's Conduct in that Affair, his Journey in Person to the Country of *Hanover*, and the Court of *Zell*; his particular management of the Affair afterwards at home, perfecting the Design, by naming the Illustrious Family to the Nation, and bringing about a Parliamentary Settlement[10] to effect it, entailing thereby the Crown in so effectual a manner as we see has been sufficient to prevent the worst Designs of our *Jacobite* People in behalf of the Pretender; a Settlement, together with the subsequent Acts which followed it, and the Union with *Scotland* which made it unalterable, that gave a compleat Satisfaction to those who knew and understood it, and removed those terrible apprehensions of the Pretender (which some entertain'd) from the minds of others who were yet as zealous against him as it was possible for any to be: Upon this Settlement, as *I shall shew presently*, I grounded my Opinion, *which I often express'd*, (*viz.*) that I did not see it possible the Jacobites could ever set up their Idol here; and I think my Opinion abundantly justify'd in the Consequences, of which by and by.

This Digression, as a debt to the Glorious Memory of King *William*, I could not in Justice omit, and as the Reign of his present Majesty is esteem'd Happy, and look'd upon as a Blessing from Heaven by us, it will most necessarily lead us to bless the Memory of King *William* to whom we owe so much of it; How easily could his Majesty have led us to other Branches, whose Relation to the Crown might have had large pretences? What Prince but would have submitted to have Educated a Successor of their Race in the Protestant Religion for the sake of such a Crown—? But the King, who had our Happiness in View, and saw as far into it as any humane sight could Penetrate, who knew we were not to be Govern'd by unexperienc'd Youths; that the Protestant Religion was not to be Establish'd by Political Converts; and that Princes under *French* Influence, or Instructed in *French* Politicks, were not proper Instruments to preserve the Liberties of *Britain*, fixt his Eyes upon the Family who now possesses the Crown, as not only having an undoubted Relation to it by Blood, but as being first and principally Zealous and Powerful assertors of the Protestant Religion and Interest against Popery; And *Secondly*, stored with a visible Succession of worthy and promising Branches, who appear'd equal to the Weight of Government, quallified to fill a Throne, and guide a Nation which, without Reflection, are not famed to be the most easy to Rule in the World.

Whether the Consequence has been a Credit to King *William*'s Judgment I need not say, I am not Writing Panegyricks here, but doing justice to the Memory of the King my Master, who I have had the Honour very often to hear express himself with great satisfaction, in having brought the Settlement of the Succession to so good an Issue; and to repeat his Majesty's own Words, *That he knew no Prince in* Europe *so fit to be King of* England, *as the Elector of* Hanover. I am persuaded, without any Flattery, that if it should not every way answer the Expectations his Majesty had of it, the fault will be our own: God Grant the King may have more Comfort of his Crown than we suffer'd King *William* to have.

The King being Dead, and the Queen Proclaim'd, the Hot Men of that Side, as Hot Men of all Sides do, Thinking the Game in their own Hands, and all other People under their Feet, began to run out into those mad Extreams, and precipitate themselves into such Measures, as according to the Fate of all intemperate Councils, ended in their own Confusions, and threw them at last out of the Saddle.

The Queen, who, tho' willing to favour the High Church Party, did not thereby design the Ruin of those who she did not Employ, was soon alarm'd at their wild Conduct, and turn'd them out, adhering to the moderate Councils of those who better understood, or more faithfully pursued her Majesty's and their Countries Interest.[11]

In this Turn fell Sir *Edw.˙Seymour*'s Party,[12] for so the High Men were then call'd; and to this Turn, we owe the Conversion of several other Great Men, who became *Whigs* upon that Occasion, which it is known they were not before; which Conversion afterwards begat that unkind Distinction of Old Whig, and Modern Whig,[13] which some of the former were with very little Justice pleased to run up afterwards to an Extreme very pernicious to both.

But I am gone too far in this Part. I return to my own Story. In the Interval of these Things, and during the Heat of the first Fury of High-flying, I fell a Sacrifice for writing against the Rage and Madness of that High Party, and in the Service of the Dissenters: What Justice I met with, and above all what Mercy, is too well known to need a Repetition.[14]

This Introduction is made that it may bring me to what has been the Foundation of all my further Concern in publick Affairs, and will produce a sufficient Reason for my adhering to those whose Obligations upon me were too strong to be resisted, even when many things were done by them which I could not approve; and for this Reason it is that I think it is necessary to distinguish how far I did, or did not adhere to, or joyn in or with the Persons or Conduct of the late Government: And those who are willing to judge with Impartiality and Charity, will see reason to use me the more tenderly in their Thoughts, when they weigh the Particulars.

I will make no Reflections upon the Treatment I met with from the People I suffer'd for, or how I was abandon'd even in my Sufferings, at the same time that they acknowledg'd the Service it had been to their Cause; but I must mention it to let you know, that while I lay friendless and distress'd in the Prison of *Newgate*, my Family ruin'd, and my self, without Hope of Deliverance, a Message was brought me from a Person of Honour, who, till that time, I had never had the least Acquaintance with, or Knowledge of, other than by Fame, or by Sight, as we know Men of Quality by seeing them on publick Occasions.[15] I gave no present Answer to the Person who brought it, having not duly weighed the Import of the Message; the Message was by Word of Mouth thus: *Pray ask that Gentleman, what I can do for him?* But in return to this kind and generous Message, I immediately took my Pen and Ink, and writ the Story of the blind Man in the Gospel, who follow'd our Saviour, and to whom our Blessed Lord put the Question, *What wilt thou that I should do unto thee?* Who, as if he had made it strange that such a Question should be ask'd, or as if he had said, *Lord, doest thou see that I am blind, and yet ask me what thou shalt do for me?* My Answer is plain in my Misery, *Lord, that I may receive my Sight.*[16]

I needed not to make the Application; and from this time, altho' I lay four Months in Prison after this, and heard no more of it, yet from this time, as I learn'd afterwards, this noble Person made it his Business to have my Case represented to Her Majesty, and Methods taken for my Deliverance.

I mention this Part, because I am no more to forget the Obligation upon me to the Queen, than to my first Benefactor.

When Her Majesty came to have the Truth of the Case laid before Her,[17] I soon felt the Effects of her Royal Goodness and Compassion. And first, Her Majesty declar'd, That She left all that Matter to a certain Person,[18] and did not think he would have used me in such a Manner. Perhaps these Words may seem imaginary to some, and the speaking them to be of no Value, and so they would have been if they had not been follow'd with farther and more convincing Proofs of what they imported, which were these, That Her Majesty was pleased particularly to enquire into my Circumstances and Family, and by my Lord Treasurer *Godolphin*, to send a considerable Supply to my Wife and Family, and to send me to the Prison Money to pay my Fine, and the Expences of my Discharge. Whether this be a just Foundation, let my Enemies judge.

Here is the Foundation on which I built my first Sense of Duty to Her Majesty's Person, and the indelible Bond of Gratitude[19] to my first Benefactor.

Gratitude and Fidelity are inseparable from an honest Man. But to be thus oblig'd by a Stranger, by a Man of Quality and Honour, and after that by the Sovereign, under whose Administration I was suffering, let any one put himself in my stead, and examine upon what Principles I could ever act against either such a Queen, or such a Benefactor; and what must my own Heart reproach me with, what blushes must have cover'd my Face when I had look'd in, and call'd myself ungrateful to him that sav'd me thus from distress? Or Her that fetch'd me out of the Dungeon, and gave my Family Relief? Let any Man, who knows what Principles are, what Engagements of Honour and Gratitude are, make this Case his own, and say what I could have done less or more than I have done.

I must go on a little with the Detail of the Obligation, and then I shall descend to relate what I have done, and what I have not done in the Case.

Being deliver'd from the Distress I was in, Her Majesty, who was not satisfy'd to do me Good by a single Act of her Bounty, had the Goodness to think of taking me into her Service, and I had the Honour to be employ'd in several honourable, tho' secret Services, by the Interposition of my first Benefactor, who then appear'd as a Member in the publick Administration.

I had the Happiness to discharge my self in all these Trusts, so much to the Satisfaction of those who employ'd me, tho' often times with Difficulty and Danger, that my Lord Treasurer *Godolphin*, whose Memory I have always honour'd, was pleas'd to continue his Favour to me, and to do me all good Offices with Her Majesty, even after an unhappy Breach had separated him from my first Benefactor: The Particulars of which may not be improper to relate; and as it is not an Injustice to any, so I hope it will not be offensive.

When upon that fatal Breach, the Secretary of State was dismiss'd from the Service, I look'd upon my self as lost, it being a general Rule in such Cases, when a great Officer falls, that all who came in by his Interest fall with him.[20] And resolving never to abandon the Fortunes of the Man to whom I ow'd so much of my own, I quitted the usual Applications which I had made to my Lord Treasurer.

But my generous Benefactor, when he understood it, frankly told me, That I should by no means do so; for, said he, in the most engaging terms, My Lord Treasurer will employ you in nothing but what is for the publick Service, and agreeable to your own Sentiments of Things: And besides, it is the Queen you are serving, who has been very good to you. Pray apply your self as you used to do; I shall not take it ill from you in the least.

Upon this I went to wait on my Lord Treasurer, who receiv'd me with great Freedom, and told me smiling, *He had not seen me a long while.* I told his Lordship very frankly the Occasion, That the unhappy Breach that had fallen out, had made me doubtful whether I should be acceptable to his Lordship. That I knew it was usual, when great Persons fall, that all who were in their Interest fell with them. That his Lordship knew the Obligations I was under, and that I could not but fear my Interest in his Lordship was lessen'd on that Account.[21] *Not at all Mr.* De Foe, reply'd his Lordship; *I always think a Man honest, till I find to the contrary.*

Upon this I attended his Lordship as usual, and being resolved to remove all possible Ground of Suspicion that I kept any secret Correspondence, I never visited, or wrote to, or any way corresponded with my principal Benefactor for above three Years;[22] which he so well knew the Reason of, and so well approv'd that punctual Behaviour in me, that he never took it ill from me at all.

In Consequence of this Reception, my Lord *Godolphin* had the Goodness not only to introduce me for the second time[23] to her Majesty, and to the Honour of kissing her Hand, but obtain'd for me the Continuance of an Appointment which Her Majesty had been pleas'd to make me in Consideration of a former special Service[24] I had done, and in which I had run as much risque of my Life, as a Grenadier upon the Counterscarp;[25] and which Appointment however was first obtain'd for me at the Intercession of my said first Benefactor, and is all owing to that Intercession, and Her Majesty's Bounty. Upon this second Introduction Her Majesty was pleased to tell me with a Goodness peculiar to Her Self, That she had such Satisfaction in my former Services, that she had appointed me for another Affair, which was something Nice, and that my Lord Treasurer should tell me the rest; and so I withdrew.

The next Day his Lordship having commanded me to attend, told me, That he must send me to *Scotland*; and gave me but three Days to prepare my self.

Accordingly I went to *Scotland*,[26] where neither my Business, nor the manner of my discharging it is material to this Tract, nor will it be ever any part of my Character that I reveal what should be concealed; and yet my Errand was such as was far from being unfit for a Sovereign to direct, or an honest Man to perform; and the Service I did on that Occasion, as it is not unknown to the greatest Man now in the Nation under the King and the Prince, so I dare say, his Grace was never displeased with the Part I had in it, and I hope will not forget it.

These things I mention upon this Account, and no other, (*viz.*) to state the Obligation I have been in all along to Her Majesty personally, and to my first Benefactor principally, by which, *I say I THINK*, I was at least obliged not to act against them even in those things which I might not approve. Whether I have acted with them farther than I ought, shall be spoken to by it self.

Having said thus much of the Obligations lay'd on me, and the Persons by whom, I have this only to add, That I think no Man will say a Subject could be under greater Bonds to his Prince, or a private Person to a Minister of State; and I shall ever preserve this Principle, that an honest Man cannot be ungrateful to his Benefactor.

But let no Man run away now with the Notion, that I am now intending to plead the Obligation that was upon me from Her Majesty, or from any other Person, to justify my doing any thing that is not otherwise to be justify'd in it self.

Nothing would be more injurious than such a Construction; and therefore I capitulate for so much Justice as to explain my self by this Declaration (*viz.*) That I only speak of these Obligations as binding me to a negative Conduct not to fly in the Face of, or concern my self in Disputes with those to whom I was under such Obligations, altho' I might not in my Judgment joyn in many things that were done. No Obligation could excuse me in calling Evil Good, or Good Evil; but I am of the Opinion, that I might justly think my self oblig'd to defend what I thought was to be defended, and to be silent in any thing which I might think was not.

If this is a Crime, I must plead guilty, and give in the History of my Obligation above mention'd as an Extenuation, at least, if not a Justification of my Conduct; suppose a Man's Father was guilty of several things unlawful and unjustifiable, a Man may heartily detest the unjustifiable thing, and yet it ought not to be expected that he should expose his Father. I think the Case on my side exactly the same. Nor can the Duty to a Parent be more strongly obliging than the Obligation laid on me: But I must allow the Case on the other side not the same.

And this brings me to the Affirmative, and to enquire what the Matters of

Fact are, what I have done, or have not done, on Account of these Obligations which I have been under.

It is a general Suggestion, and is affirm'd with such Assurance, that they tell me it is in vain to contradict it; That I have been employ'd by the Earl of O[xfor]d,[27] late Lord Treasurer, in the late Disputes about Publick Affairs, to write for him, or to put it into their own Particulars, have written by his Direction, taken the Materials from him, been dictated to, or instructed by him, or by other Persons from him, by his Order, and the like; and that I have receiv'd a Pension, or Sallery, or Payment from his Lordship for such Services as these.

If I could put it into Words that would more fully express the Meaning of these People, I profess I would do it.

One would think it was impossible; but that since these things have been so confidently affirm'd, some Evidence might be produc'd, some Facts might appear, some one Body or other might be found that could speak of certain Knowledge: To say things have been carry'd too closely to be discover'd, *is saying nothing;* for then they must own, *that it is not discover'd*: And how then can they affirm it, as they do, with such an Assurance, as nothing ought to be affirm'd by honest Men, unless they were able to prove it?

To speak then to the Fact: Were the Reproach upon *me only* in this Particular, I should not mention it; I should not think it a Reproach to be directed by a Man to whom the Queen had at that time entrusted the Administration of the Government. But as it is a Reproach upon his Lordship, Justice requires that I do Right in this Case. The Thing is true or false, I would recommend it to those who would be call'd honest Men, to consider but one Thing, (*viz.*) What if it should not be true? Can they justify the Injury done to that Person, or to any Person concern'd? If it cannot be prov'd, if no Vestiges appear to ground it upon, how can they charge Men upon Rumours and Reports, and joyn to run Men's Characters down by the Stream of Clamour.

Sed quo rapit impetus undæ[28]

In Answer to the Charge, I bear Witness to Posterity, that every Part of it is false and forg'd; and I do solemnly protest, in the *Fear* and *Presence* of him that shall Judge us all, both the Slanderers, and the Slandered, that I have not re-ceiv'd any Instructions, Directions, Orders, *or let them call it what they will of that kind*, for the Writing any Part of what I have written, or any Materials for the putting together, for the Forming any Book or Pamphlet whatsoever from the said Earl of O[xfor]d, late Lord Treasurer, or from any Person, by his Order, or Direction, since the Time that the late Earl of G[odolph]in was Lord Treasurer: Neither did I ever shew, or cause to be shew'd to his Lordship, for his Appro-bation, Correction, Alteration, or for any other Cause, any Book, Paper, or

Pamphlet, which I have Written and Publish'd before the same was Printed, work'd off at the Press, and Publish'd.[29]

If any Man living can detect me of the least Prevarication in this, or in any Part of it, I desire him to do it by all means; and I challenge all the World to do it—*And if they cannot*, then I appeal, *as in my Title*, to the Honour and Justice of my worst Enemies, to know upon what Foundation of Truth or Conscience they can affirm these things, and for what it is that I bear these Reproaches.

In all my Writing, I ever capitulated[30] for my Liberty to speak according to my own Judgment of Things; I ever had that Liberty allow'd me, nor was I ever imposed upon to write this way or that against my Judgment by any Person whatsoever.

I come now historically to the Point of Time when my Lord *Godolphin* was dismiss'd from his Employment,[31] and the late unhappy Division broke out at Court; I waited on my Lord the Day he was displac'd, and humbly ask'd his Lordship's Direction, what Course I should take? His Lordship's Answer was, *That he had the same good Will to assist me, but not the same Power; That I was the Queen's Servant, and that all he had done for me, was by Her Majesty's special and particular Direction; and that whoever should succeed him, it was not material to me, he supposed I should be employ'd in nothing relating to the present Differences: My Business was to wait till I saw things settled, and then apply my self to the Ministers of State, to receive Her Majesty's Commands from them.*

It occur'd to me immediately, as a Principle for my Conduct, that it was not material to me what Ministers Her Majesty was pleas'd to employ, my Duty was to go along with every Ministry, so far as they did not break in upon the Constitution, and the Laws and Liberties of my Country;[32] my Part being only the Duty of a Subject, (*viz.*) to submit to all lawful Commands, and to enter into no Service which was not justifiable by the Laws: To all which I have exactly oblig'd my self.

By this I was providentially cast back upon my Original Benefactor, who, according to his wonted Goodness, was pleased to lay my Case before Her Majesty, and thereby I preserv'd my Interest in Her Majesty's Favour; but without any Engagement of Service.

As for Consideration, Pension, Gratification, or Reward, I declare to all the World I have had none; except only that old Appointment which Her Majesty was pleased to make me in the Days of the Ministry of my Lord *Godolphin*: Of which I have spoken already, and which was for Services done in a foreign country some Years before. Neither have I been employ'd, or directed, or order'd, by my Lord T[reasure]r aforesaid, to do, or not to do, any thing in the Affairs of the unhappy Differences which have so long perplex'd us, and for which I have suffer'd so many, and such unjust Reproaches.

I come next to enter into the Matters of Fact, and what it is I have done, or not done; which may justify the Treatment I have met with. And first, for the Negative Part, what I have not done.

The first Thing in the unhappy Breaches which have fallen out, is the heaping up Scandal upon the Persons and Conduct of Men of Honour on one Side, as well as on the other; those unworthy Methods of falling upon one another by personal Calumny and Reproach. This I have often in print complain'd of as an unchristian, ungenerous, and unjustifiable Practice. Not a Word can be found in all I have written reflecting on the Persons, or Conduct of any of the former Ministry, I serv'd Her Majesty under their Administration, they acted honourably and justly in every Transaction in which I had the Honour to be concern'd with them; and I never publish'd, or said any thing dishonourable of any of them in my Life: Nor can the worst Enemy I have produce any such thing against me. I always regretted the Change, and look'd upon it as a great Disaster to the Nation in general, I am sure it was so to me in particular; and the Divisions and Feuds among Parties, which follow'd that Change, were doubtless a Disaster to us all.

The next Thing which follow'd the Change was THE PEACE: No Man can say that ever I once said in my Life, that I approv'd of the Peace. I wrote a publick Paper at that time, and there it Remains upon Record against me, I printed it openly, and that so plainly, as others durst not do; That I did not like the Peace, neither that which was made, nor that which was before a making; That I thought the Protestant Interest was not taken care of in either; That the Peace I was for, was such as should neither have given the *Spanish* Monarchy to the House of *Bourbon*, or the House of *Austria*; but that this Bone of Contention should have been·broken to Pieces, that it should not have been dangerous to *Europe* on any Account, and that the Protestant Powers, (*viz.*) *Britain*, and the *States*, should have so strengthen'd and fortify'd their Interest by their sharing the Commerce and Strength of *Spain*, as should have made them no more afraid either of *France*, or the *Emperor*: So that the Protestant Interest should have been superior to all the Powers of *Europe*, and been in no more Danger of exhorbitant Power, whether *French* or *Austrian*. This was the Peace I always argued for, pursuant to the Design of King *William* in the Treaty of Partition, and pursuant to that Article of the Grand Alliance, which was directed by the same glorious Hand at the Beginning of this last War (*viz.*) That all we should conquer in the *Spanish-West-Indies* should be our own.[33]

This was with a true Design that *England* and *Holland* should have turn'd their Naval Power, which were eminently superiour to those of *France*, to the Conquest of the *Spanish-West-Indies*, by which the Channel of Trade, and Return of

Bullion, which now enriches the Enemies of both, had been ours; and as the Wealth, so the Strength of the World had been in Protestant Hands. *Spain*, whoever had it, must then have been dependent upon us; the House of *Bourbon* would have found it so poor without us, as to be scarce worth fighting for; and the People so averse to them for want of their Commerce, as not to make it ever likely *France* could keep it.

This was the Foundation I ever acted upon with relation to the Peace. It is true, that when it was made, and could not be otherwise, I thought our Business was to make the best of it, and rather to enquire what Improvements were to be made of it, than to be continually exclaiming at those who made it; and where the Objection lies against this Part I cannot yet see.

While I spoke of things in this manner, I bore infinite Reproaches from clamouring Pens of being in the *French* Interest, being hir'd and brib'd to defend a bad Peace, and the like; and most of this was upon a Supposition of my Writing, or being the Author of Abundance of Pamphlets which came out every Day, and which I had no hand in. And indeed, as I shall observe again by and by, this was one of the greatest Pieces of Injustice that could be done me, and which I labour still under without any redress; that whenever any Piece comes out which is not liked, I am immediately charg'd with being the Author, and very often the first Knowledge I have had of a Books being publish'd, has been from seeing my self abused for being the Author of it, in some other Pamphlet publish'd in Answer to it.

Finding my self treated in this manner, I declin'd writing at all; and for a great Part of a Year never set Pen to Paper, except in the publick Paper call'd the *Review*. After this I was long absent in the *North of England*,³⁴ and observing the Insolence of the *Jacobite* Party, and how they insinuated fine things into the Heads of the Common People of the Right and Claim of the *Pretender*, and of the great Things he would do for us if he was to come in; of his being to turn a Protestant, of his being resolved to maintain our Liberties, support our Funds, give Liberty to Dissenters, and the like; and finding that the People began to be deluded, and that the *Jacobites* gain'd ground among them by these Insinuations, I thought it the best Service I could do the Protestant Interest, and the best way to open the Peoples Eyes to the Advantages of the Protestant Succession, if I took some Course effectually to alarm the People with what they really ought to expect if the *Pretender* should come to be King. And this made me set Pen to Paper again.

And this brings me to the affirmative Part, or to what really I HAVE DONE; and in this I am sorry to say, I have one of the foulest, most unjust, and unchristian Clamours to complain of, that any Man has suffer'd, I believe, since the Days of the Tyranny of King *James* the Second. The Fact is thus.

In order to detect the Influence of *Jacobite* Emissaries, as above, the first thing I wrote was a small Tract, call'd, *A Seasonable Caution:*[35]

A Book sincerely written to open the Eyes of the poor ignorant Country People, and to warn them against the subtle Insinuations of the Emissaries of the *Pretender*; and that it might be effectual to that Purpose, I prevail'd with several of my Friends to give them away among the poor People all over *England,* especially in the *North*; and several thousands were actually given away, the Price being reduced so low, that the bare Expence of Paper and Press was only preserv'd, that every one might be convinc'd, that nothing of Gain was design'd, but a sincere Endeavour to do a publick Good, and assist to keep the People entirely in the Interest of the Protestant Succession.

Next to this, and with the same sincere Design, I wrote Two Pamphlets, one entituled, *What if the* Pretender *should come?* The other, *Reasons against the Succession of the House of* Hanover.[36] Nothing can be more plain, than that the Titles of these Books were Amusements, in order to put the Books into the Hands of those People who the *Jacobites* had deluded, and to bring the Books to be read by them.

Previous to what I shall farther say of these Books, I must observe, that all these Books met with so general a Reception and Approbation among those who were most sincere for the Protestant Succession, that they sent them all over the Kingdom, and recommended them to the Peoples reading as excellent and useful Pieces, insomuch, that about Seven Editions of them were Printed, and they were Reprinted in other Places; and I do protest, had his present Majesty, then Elector of *Hanover*, given me a thousand Pounds to have written for the Interest of his Succession, and to expose and render the Interest of the *Pretender* odious and ridiculous, I could have done nothing more effectual to those Purposes than these Books were.

And that I may make my worst Enemies, to whom this is a fair Appeal, Judges of this, I must take leave by and by to repeat some of the Expressions in those Books which were direct, and need no Explication, and which, I think, no Man that was in the Interest of the *Pretender*, nay which no Man but one who was entirely in the Interest of the *Hanover* Succession, could write.

Nothing can be severer in the Fate of a Man than to act so between two Parties, that both sides should be provok'd against him. It is certain, the *Jacobites* curs'd those Tracts and the Author; and when they came to read them, *being deluded by the Titles according to the Design,* they threw them by with the greatest Indignation imaginable: Had the *Pretender* ever come to the Throne, I could have expected nothing but Death, and all the Ignominy and Reproach that the most inveterate Enemy, of his Person and Claim could be suppos'd to suffer.

On the other hand, I leave it to any considering Man to Judge, what a Surprize it must be to me to meet with all the publick Clamour that Informers could invent, as being Guilty of writing against the *Hanover* Succession, and as having written several Pamphlets *in Favour of the* Pretender.

No Man in this Nation ever had a more riveted Aversion to the *Pretender*, and to all the Family he pretended to come of, *than I*: A Man that had been in Arms under the Duke of *Monmouth*, against the Cruelty and Arbitrary Government of his pretended Father;[37] That for twenty Years had, to my utmost, opposed him, (King *James*) and his Party after his Abdication; That had serv'd King *WILLIAM* to his Satisfaction, and the Friends of the Revolution after his Death, at all Hazards and upon all Occasions; That had suffer'd and been ruin'd under the Administration of *Highflyers* and Jacobites, of whom some are, *at this Day, COUNTERFEIT Whigs*;[38] It could not be! the Nature of the Thing could by no means allow it, it must be monstrous; and that the Wonder may cease, I shall take leave to quote some of the Expressions out of these Books, of which the worst Enemy I have in the World is left to Judge, whether they are in Favour of the *Pretender*, or no; but of this in its Place.

For these Books I was prosecuted, taken into Custody, and oblig'd to give Eight hundred Pound Bail.

I do not in the least object here against, or design to reflect upon the Proceedings of the Judges which were subsequent to this: I acknowledg'd *then*, and *now* acknowledge *again*, that, upon the Information given, there was a sufficient Ground for all they did, and my unhappy entring upon my own Vindication in Print, while the Case was before their Lordships in a Judicial Way, was an Error which I neither understood, and which I did not foresee; and therefore, altho' I had great Reason to reflect upon the Informers, yet I was wrong in making that Defence in the Manner and Time I then made it, and which, when I found, I made no scruple afterward to Petition the Judges, and acknowledge, that they had just Ground to resent it: Upon which Petition and Acknowledgment, their Lordships were pleas'd, with particular Marks of Goodness, to release me, and not take the Advantage of an Error of Ignorance, as if it had been consider'd and premeditated.[39]

But against the *INFORMERS*, I think, I have great Reason to complain; and against the Injustice of those Writers, who, in many Pamphlets, charged me with writing for the *Pretender*; and the Government, with pardoning an Author who wrote for the *Pretender*; and indeed the Justice of those Men can be in nothing more clearly stated, than in this Case of mine; where the Charge, in their Printed Papers and Publick Discourse was brought, not that they themselves believ'd me Guilty of the Crime, but because it was necessary to blacken the Man; That a general Reproach might serve for an Answer to whatever he should say that was not for their Turn: So that it was the Person, not the Crime they fell upon, and they may justly be said to persecūte for the sake of Persecution, *as will thus appear.*

This Matter making some Noise, People began to enquire into it, and to ask what *De Foe* was prosecuted for, seeing the Books were manifestly written against the *Pretender*, and for the Interest of the House of *Hanover?* And my Friends expostulated freely with some of the Men who appear'd in it, who answer'd, *with more Truth than Honesty*, That they knew this Book had nothing in it, and that it was meant another way; but that *De Foe* had disoblig'd them in other things, and they were resolv'd to take the Advantage they had, both to punish and expose him. They were no inconsiderable People who said this; and had the Case come to a Tryal, I had provided good Evidence to prove the Words.

This is the Christianity and Justice by which I have been treated; and this Injustice is the thing that I complain of.

Now as this was a Plot of a few Men to see if they could brand me in the World for a *Jacobite*, and perswade rash and ignorant People that I was turn'd about for the *Pretender*, *I think they might as easily have prov'd me to be a Mahometan*; therefore, I say, this obliges me to state that Matter as it really stands, that impartial Men may Judge whether those Books were written for, or against the *Pretender*; and this cannot be better done, than by the Account of what follow'd after the first Information, which in few Words is thus:

Upon the several Days appointed, I appear'd at the *Queen's Bench-Bar* to discharge my Bail; and at last had an Indictment for High Crimes and Misdemeanours exhibited against me by Her Majesty's Attorney-General, which, as I was inform'd, contain'd two hundred Sheets of Paper.

What was the Substance of the Indictment I shall not mention here, neither could I enter upon it, having never seen the Particulars: But I was told, that I should be brought to Tryal the very next Term.

I was not ignorant that in such Cases it is easy to make any Book a Libel, and that the Jury must have found the Matter of Fact in the Indictment, (*viz.*) That I had written such Books, and then what might have follow'd I knew not: Wherefore I thought it was my only way to cast my self on the Clemency of her Majesty, whose Goodness I had had so much Experience of many ways; representing in my Petition, that I was far from the least Intention to favour the Interest of the *Pretender*, but that the Books were all written with a sincere Design to promote the Interest of the House of *Hanover*; and humbly laid before her Majesty, as I do now before the rest of the World, the Books themselves to plead in my behalf; representing farther, that I was maliciously inform'd against by those who were willing to put a Construction upon the Expressions different from my true Meaning, and therefore, flying to her Majesty's Goodness and Clemency, I entreated her Gracious PARDON.

It was not only the native Disposition of her Majesty to Acts of Clemency and Goodness, that obtain'd me this Pardon; but, as I was inform'd, her Majesty was pleas'd to express it in the Council, *She saw nothing but private Pique in the first Prosecution*; and therefore, I think, I cannot give a better and clearer Vindication of my self, than what is contain'd in the Preamble to the Pardon which her Majesty was pleas'd to grant me, and I must be allow'd to say, to those who are still willing to object, that, I think, what satisfy'd her Majesty might be sufficient to satisfy them; and I can assure them, that this Pardon was not granted without her Majesty's being specially and particularly acquainted with the things alledg'd in the Petition, the Books also being look'd in to find the Expressions quoted in the Petition. The Preamble to the Patent for a Pardon, as far as relates to the Matters of Fact, runs thus:

Whereas, in the Term of the Holy Trinity *last past, our Attorney General did exhibit an Information, in our Court of* Queens Bench *at* Westminster, *against* DANIEL DE FOE, *late of* London, *Gent. for Writing, Printing, and Publishing, and causing to be Written, Printed, and Published, THREE LIBELS, the one entituled,* Reasons against the Succession of the House of *Hanover*; *with an Enquiry, how far the Abdication of King* James, *supposing it to be legal, ought to affect the Person of the* Pretender. *One other entituled,* And what if the *Pretender* should Come? *Or some Considerations of the Advantages and real Consequences of the* Pretender's *possessing the Crown of* Great Britain. *And one other entituled,* An Answer to a Question that nobody thinks of (*viz.*) What if the Queen should Die?

And whereas the said Daniel De Foe *hath, by his humble Petition, represented to us, that he, with a sincere Design to propagate the Interest of the* Hanover *Succession, and to animate the People against the Designs of the* Pretender, *whom he always looked on as an Enemy to our Sacred Person and Government, did publish the said Pamphlets: In all which Books, altho' the Titles seem'd to look as if written in Favour of the* Pretender, *and several Expressions, as in all ironical Writing it must be, may be wrested against the true Design of the Whole, and turn'd to a Meaning quite different from the Intention of the Author, yet the Petitioner humbly assures us, in the solemnest Manner, that his true and only Design in all the said Books was, by an ironical Discourse of recommending the* Pretender, *in the strongest and most forcible Manner to expose his Designs, and the ruinous Consequences of his succeeding therein; which, as the Petitioner humbly represents, will appear to our Satisfaction by the Books themselves, where the following Expressions are very plain,* (viz.) *That the PRETENDER is recommended* as a Person proper to amass the *English* Liberties into his own Soveraignty, supply them with the Privileges of wearing WOODEN SHOES; easing them of the trouble of chusing Parliaments; and the Nobility and Gentry of the Hazard and Expence of Winter Journeys, by governing them in that more righteous Method of his ABSOLUTE WILL, and enforcing the Laws by a Glorious STANDING ARMY; paying all the Nations Debts at once by stopping the Funds, and shutting up the *Exchequer*; easing and quieting their Differences in Religion, by bringing them to the UNION of POPERY, or leaving them at Liberty to have no Religion at all: *That these were some of the very Expressions in the said Books which the Petitioner sincerely design'd to expose, and oppose as far as in him lies the* Interest *of the* Pretender, *and with no other Intention: NEVERTHELESS, the Petitioner, to his great Surprize, has been misrepresented, and his said Books misconstrued, as if written in Favour of the* Pretender, *and the Petitioner is now under Prosecution for the same; which Prosecution, if farther carried on, will be the utter Ruin of the Petitioner and his Family: Wherefore the Petitioner humbly assuring us of the Innocence of his Design, as aforesaid, flies to our Clemency, and most humbly prays our most Gracious and Free Pardon. WE taking the Premises, and the Circumstances aforesaid into our Royal Consideration, are graciously pleas'd,* &c.

Let any indifferent Man Judge whether I was not treated with particular Malice in this Matter, who was, notwithstanding this, reproach'd in the daily Publick Prints with having written treasonable Books, in behalf of the *Pretender*; nay, and in some of those Books, as before, the Queen her self, was reproach'd, *with having granted her Pardon to an Author who writ for the* Pretender.

I think I might with much more Justice say, I was *the first Man* that ever was oblig'd to seek a Pardon for writing for the *Hanover* Succession; and *the first Man* that these People ever sought to Ruin for writing against the *Pretender*: For if ever a Book was sincerely design'd to farther and propagate the Affection and Zeal of the Nation against the *Pretender*, nay, and was made use of, and that with success too, for that purpose, THESE BOOKS *were so*; and I ask no more Favour of the World to determine the Opinion of honest Men for or against me than what is drawn constructively from these Books. Let one Word, either written or spoken by me, either publish'd, or not publish'd, be produced, that was in the least disrespectful to the Protestant Succession, or to any Branch of the Family of *Hanover*, or that can be judg'd to be favourable to the Interest or Person of the *Pretender*, and I will be willing to wave her Majesty's Pardon, and render my self to Publick Justice, to be punish'd for it as I should well deserve.

I freely and openly Challenge the worst of my Enemies to charge me with any Discourse, Conversation, or Behaviour in my whole Life, which had the least Word in it injurious to the Protestant Succession, unbecoming or disrespectful to any of the Persons of the Royal Family of *Hanover*, or the least favourable Word of the Person, the Designs, or Friends of the *Pretender*.

If they can do it, let them stand forth and speak, no doubt but they may be heard; and I, for my part, will relinquish all Pleas, Pardons, and Defences, and cast my self into the Hands of Justice.

Nay, to go farther, I defy them to prove, that I ever kept Company, or had any Society, Friendship, or Conversation with any *Jacobite*; so averse have I been to the Interest, and to the People, that I have studiously avoided their Company upon all Occasions.

As nothing in the World has been more my Aversion than the Society of *Jacobites*, so nothing can be a greater Misfortune to me than to be accus'd, and publickly reproach'd with what is, of all things in the World, most abhorr'd by me, and which has made it the more afflicting is that this Charge arises from those very things, which I did, with the sincerest Design, to manifest the contrary.

But such is my present Fate, and I am to submit to it, which I do with Meekness and Calmness, as to a Judgment from Heaven, and am practising that Duty which I have studied long ago, of *Forgiving my Enemies*, and *praying for them that despitefully use me*.[40]

Having given this brief History of the Pardon, *&c.* I hope the Impartial part of the World will Grant me, That being thus Graciously Deliver'd a second Time from the Cruelty of my Implacable Enemies, and the Ruin of a Cruel and unjust Persecution, and that by the meer Clemency and Goodness of the Queen, my Obligation to her Majesty's Goodness, was far from being made less than it was before.

I have now run through the History of my Obligation to her Majesty, and to the Person of my Benefactor aforesaid. I shall state every thing that follow'd this with all the Clearness I can, and leave my self lyable to as little Cavil as I may; for I see my self assaulted by a sort of People who will do me no justice. I hear a Great Noise made of Punishing those that are GUILTY, but as I said before not one Word of Clearing those that are INNOCENT; and I must say in this Part, they Treat me not only as I were no Christian, but as if they themselves were not Christians. They will neither prove the Charge, nor hear the Defence, which is the unjustest thing in the World.

I foresee what will be alledged to the Clause of [41] my Obligation, *&c.* to Great Persons: And I resolve to give my Adversaries all the Advantage they can desire; by acknowledging beforehand. That *no Obligations to the QUEEN, or to any Benefactor, can justify any Man's acting against the Interest of his Country, against his Principles, his Conscience, and his former Profession.*

I think this will Anticipate all that can be said upon that Head, and it will then remain to state the Fact as I am, or am not Chargeable with it; which I shall do as clearly as possible in few words.

It is none of my Work to enter into the Conduct of the Queen or of the Ministry in this Case, the Question is not what *they have done*, but what *I have done?* And tho' I am very far from thinking of them as some other People think, yet for the sake of the present Argument, I am to give them all up, and Suppose, *tho' not Granting*, that all which is suggested of them by the worst Temper, the most censorious Writer, the most scandalous Pamphlet or Lampoon should be True, and I'll go through some of the Particulars, as I meet with them in Publick.

1st, That they made a Scandalous Peace, unjustly Broke the Allyance, Betray'd the Confederates, and Sold us all to the *French*.

God forbid it should be all Truth, in the manner that we see it in Print; But that, I say, is none of my Business.—*But what hand had I in all this?* I never wrote one word for the Peace *before it was made*, or to Justify it after *it was made*, let them produce it if they can; Nay, in a *Review* upon that Subject, while it was making I Printed it in plainer Words than other Men durst Speak it at that Time, That *I did not like the Peace*, nor did I like any Peace that was a making, since that of the PARTITION, and that the Protestant Interest was not taken Care of either in that or the Treaty of *Gertrudinburgh* before it.[42]

It is true, that I did say, That since the Peace was made, and we could not help it, that it was our Business and our Duty to make the best of it,[43] to make the utmost Advantage of it by Commerce, Navigation, and all kind of Improvement that we could, and this I SAY STILL; and I must think it is more our Duty to do so, than the Exclamations against the thing it self which it is not in our power to Retrieve. This is all that the worst Enemy I have can Charge me with: *After the Peace was made*, and the *Dutch* and the Emperor stood out, I gave my Opinion of what I foresaw would necessarily be the Consequence of that Difference, (*viz.*) That it would inevitably involve these Nations in a War with one or other of them; *any one* who was Master of Common Sense in the publick Affairs, might see that the standing out of the *Dutch* could have no other Event: For if the Confederates had Conquer'd the *French*, they would certainly have fallen upon us by way of Resentment, and there was no doubt, but the same Councils that led us to make a Peace, would Oblige us to maintain it, by preventing too great Impressions upon the *French*.

On the other hand, I alledged, that should the *French* prevail against the *Dutch*, unless he stopt at such Limitations of Conquest as the Treaty oblig'd him to do, we must have been under the same necessity to renew the War against *France*; and for this Reason, seeing we had made a Peace, we were oblig'd to bring the rest of the Confederates into it, and to bring the *French* to give them all such Terms as they ought to be satisfied with.

This way of Arguing was either so little Understood, or so much Malign'd, that I suffer'd innumerable Reproaches in Print, for having Written for a War with the *Dutch*, which was neither in the Expression, or ever in my Imagination:[44] But I pass by these Injuries as small and trifling compar'd to others *I* suffer under.

However one thing *I* must say of the Peace, *Let it be Good or Ill in its self*, I cannot but think we have all reason to Rejoyce in behalf of his Present Majesty, That at his accession to the Crown, He found the Nation in Peace; and had the Hands of the King of *France* tied up by a Peace, so as not to be able, without the most infamous breach of Articles, to offer the least Disturbance to his taking a Quiet and Leisurely possession, or so much as to Countenance those that would.

Not but that *I* believe, if the War had been at the height, we should have been able to have preserved the Crown for his present Majesty, its only Rightful Lord: But *I* will not say it should have been so Easy, so Bloodless, so Undisputed as now, and all the Difference must be acknowledged to the Peace, and this is all the Good *I* ever yet said of the Peace.

I come next to the general Clamour of *the Ministry being for the Pretender*; *I* must speak my Sentiments solemnly and plainly, as I always did in that matter, (*viz.*) That if it was so, *I* did not see it, nor did I ever see Reason to believe it; This *I* am sure of, that if it was so, *I* never took one step in that kind of Service, nor did *I* ever hear one Word spoken by any of the Ministry that *I* had the Honour to know or Converse with, that favour'd the Pretender: But have had the Honour to hear them all Protest that there was no Design to Oppose the Succession of *Hanover* in the least.

It may be Objected to me, That they might be in the Interest of the Pretender for all that: *It is true they might*; But that is nothing to me, *I* am not Vindicating their Conduct, but my own; as *I* never was Employ'd in any thing that way, so *I* do still protest, *I* do not believe it was ever in their Design, and *I* have many Reasons to confirm my Thoughts in that Case, which are not material to the present Case: But be that as it will, it is enough to me that *I* acted nothing in any such Interest, neither did *I* ever Sin against the Protestant Succession of *Hanover* in Thought, Word, or Deed; and if the Ministry did, *I* did not see it, or so much as suspect them of it.

It was a Disaster to the Ministry, to be driven to the Necessity of taking that set of Men by the hand, who, no body can deny, were in that Interest:[45] But as the former Ministry answer'd, when they were charg'd with a Design to overthrow the Church, because they favour'd, joyn'd with, and were united to the *Dissenters*; I say they answer'd, *That they made use of the* Dissenters, *but granted them nothing* (WHICH BY THE WAY WAS TOO TRUE:) So these Gentlemen Answer, *That it is true, they made use of* Jacobites, *but did nothing for them.*

But *this by the by.* Necessity is pleaded by both Parties for doing things which neither Side can justify. I wish both Sides would for ever avoid the Necessity of doing Evil; for certainly it is the worst Plea in the World, and generally made use of for the worst Things.

I have often lamented the Disaster which I saw, employing *Jacobites*, was to the late Ministry, and certainly it gave the greatest Handle to the Enemies of the Ministry to fix that universal Reproach upon them of being in the Interest of the *Pretender*: But there was no Medium. The *Whigs* refused to shew them a safe Retreat, or to give them the least Opportunity to take any other Measures but at the Risque of their own Destruction; and they ventur'd upon that Course, in hopes of being able to stand alone at last without help of either the one or the other, in which no doubt they were mistaken.

However, in this Part, as I was always assur'd, and have good Reason still to believe, that her Majesty was steady in the Interest of the House of *Hanover*, and that nothing was ever offer'd to me, or requir'd of me to the Prejudice of that Interest, On what Ground can I be reproach'd with the secret reserv'd Designs of any, if they had such Designs as I still verily believe they had not?

I see there are some Men who would fain perswade the World, that every Man that was in the Interest of the late Ministry, or employ'd by the late Government, or that serv'd the late Queen, was for the *Pretender*.

God forbid this should be true; and I think there needs very little to be said in Answer to it. I can answer for my self, that it is notoriously false; and I think the easy and uninterrupted Accession of his Majesty to the Crown contradicts it: I see no End which such a Suggestion aims at, but to leave an Odium upon all that had any Duty or Regard to her late Majesty.

A Subject is not always Master of his Sovereign's Measures, nor always to examine what Persons or Parties the Prince he serves Employs; so be it that they break not in upon the Constitution; that they govern according to Law, and that he is employ'd in no illegal Act, or have nothing desir'd of him inconsistent with the Liberties and Laws of his Country: If this be not right, then a Servant of the King's is in a worse Case than a Servant to any private Person.

In all these things I have not err'd, neither have I acted or done anything in the whole Course of my Life, either in the Service of her Majesty, or of her Ministry, that any one can say has the least Deviation from the strictest Regard to the Protestant Succession, and to the Laws and Liberties of my Country.

I never saw an Arbitrary Action offer'd at, a Law dispens'd with, Justice deny'd, or Oppression set up, either by Queen or Ministry, in any Branch of the Administration, wherein I had the least Concern.

If I have sin'd against the *Whigs*, it has been all NEGATIVELY, (*viz.*) that I have not joyn'd in the loud Exclamations against the Queen, and against the Ministry, and against the Measures; and if this be my Crime, my Plea is twofold.

1. I did not really see Cause for carrying their Complaints to that violent Degree.

2. Where I did see what, as before, I lamented and was sorry for, and could not joyn with, or approve, as joyning with *Jacobites*, the *Peace*, &c. My Obligation is my Plea for my silence.

I have all the good Thoughts of the Person, and good Wishes for the Prosperity of my Benefactor, that Charity, and that Gratitude, can inspire me with: I ever believ'd him to have the true Interest of the Protestant Religion, and of his Country in his view; if it should be otherwise, I should be very sorry. And I must repeat it again, that he always left me so entirely to my own Judgment in every thing I did, that he never prescrib'd to me what I should write, or should not write in my Life; neither did he ever concern himself to dictate to, or restrain me in any kind; nor did he see any one Tract that I ever wrote before it was Printed: So that all the Notion of my writing by his Direction, is as much a Slander upon him, as it is possible any thing of that kind can be; and if I have written any thing which is offensive, unjust, or untrue, I must do that Justice as to declare, He has had no hand in it; the Crime is my own.[46]

As the Reproach of his directing me to write, is a Slander UPON THE PERSON I am speaking of; so that of my receiving Pensions and Payments from him for writing, is a Slander UPON ME; and I speak it with the greatest Sincerity, Seriousness, and Solemnity that it is possible for a Christian Man to speak, That except the Appointment I mention'd before, which her Majesty was pleas'd to make me formerly, and which I receiv'd during the time of my Lord *Godolphin*'s Ministry, I have not receiv'd of the late Lord Treasurer, or of any one else by his Order, Knowledge, or Direction, one Farthing, or the Value of a Farthing, during his whole Administration; nor has all the Interest I have been suppos'd to have in his Lordship, been able to procure me the Arrears due to me in the time of the other Ministry. SO HELP ME GOD.

I am under no Necessity of making this Declaration. The Services I did, and for which her Majesty was pleas'd to make me a small Allowance, are known to the greatest Men in the present Administration; and some of them were then of the Opinion, and I hope are so still, that I was not unworthy of her Majesty's Favour. The Effect of those Services, however small, are enjoy'd by those Great Persons, and by the whole Nation to this Day; and I had the Honour once to be told, *That they should never be forgotten.* It is a Misfortune, that no Man can avoid, to forfeit for his Deference to the Person and Services of his Queen, to whom he was inexpressibly oblig'd: And if I am fallen under the Displeasure of the PRESENT Government, for any thing I ever did in Obedience to her Majesty in THE PAST, I may say it is my Disaster; but I can never say it is my Fault.

This brings me again to that other Oppression which as I said I suffer under, and which, I think, is of a Kind, that no Man ever suffer'd under so much as my self: And this is to have every Libel, every Pamphlet, be it ever so foolish, so malicious, so unmannerly, or so dangerous, be laid at my Door, and be call'd publickly by my Name. It has been in vain for me to struggle with this injury; It has been in vain for me to protest, to declare solemnly, nay, if I would have sworn that I had no hand in such a Book, or Paper, never saw it, never read it, and the like, it was the same thing.

My Name has been hackney'd about the Street by the Hawkers, and about the Coffee-Houses by the Politicians, at such a rate, as no Patience could bear. One Man will swear to the Style; another to this or that Expression; another to the Way of Printing; and all so positive, that it is to no purpose to oppose it.

I publish'd once, to stop this way of using me, that I would Print nothing but what I set my Name to, and I held it for a Year or Two;[47] but it was all one, I had the same Treatment. I now have resolv'd, for some time, to write nothing at all; and yet I find it the same thing. Two Books lately publish'd being call'd mine, for no other reason that I know of, than that, at the Request of the Printer, I revised two Sheets of them at the Press, and that they seem'd to be written in Favour of a certain Person;[48] which Person also, as I have been assur'd, had no Hand in them, or any Knowledge of them, till they were publish'd in Print.

This is a Flail which I have no Fence against, but to complain of the Injustice of it, and that is but *the shortest Way* to be treated with more Injustice.

There is a mighty Charge against me for being Author and Publisher of a Paper call'd, *The MERCATOR.* I'll state the Fact first, and then speak to the Subject.

It is true, that being desir'd to give my Opinion in the Affair of the Commerce with *France*, I did, as I often had done in Print many Years before, declare, That it was my Opinion we ought to have an open Trade with *France*, because I did believe we might have the Advantage by such a Trade; and of this Opinion I am still.[49] What Part I had in the *Mercator*, is well known; and would Men Answer with Argument, and not with personal Abuses, I would, at any time, defend every Part of the *Mercator* which was of my doing. But to say the *Mercator* was mine, is false; I neither was the Author of it, had the Property of it, the Printing of it, or the Profit by it. I had never any Payment or Reward for writing any Part of it; Nor had I the Power to put what I would into it: Yet the whole Clamour fell upon me, because they knew not who else to load with it.[50] And when they came to Answer, the Method was, instead of Argument, to threaten, and reflect upon me; reproach me with private Circumstances and Misfortunes, and give Language which no Christian ought to give, and which no Gentleman ought to take.

I thought any *Englishman* had the Liberty to speak his Opinion in such things; for this had nothing to do with the Publick. The Press was open to me as well as to others; and how, or when I lost my *English* Liberty of speaking my Mind, I know not; neither how my speaking my Opinion without Fee or Reward could authorize them to call me Villain, Rascal, Traytor, and such opprobious Names.

It was ever my Opinion, and is so still, that were our Wooll kept from *France*, and our Manufactures spread in *France* upon reasonable Duties, all the Improvement which the *French* have made in Woolen Manufactures would decay, and in the End be little Worth, and consequently the Hurt they could do us by them, would be of little Moment.

It was my Opinion, and is so still, that the Ninth Article of the Treaty of *Commerce*[51] was calculated for the Advantage of our Trade, let who will make it, *that is nothing to me*: My Reasons are, because it TYED up the *French* to open the Door to our Manufactures at a certain Duty of Importation THERE, and left the Parliament of *Britain* at Liberty to shut theirs out by as high Duties as they pleas'd HERE, there being no Limitation upon us as to Duties on *French* Goods; *but that other Nations should pay the same.*

While the *French* were thus bound, and the *British* free, I always thought we must be in a Condition to Trade to Advantage, or it must be our own Fault: This was my Opinion, and IS SO STILL, and I would venture to maintain it against any Man upon a publick Stage, before a Jury of fifty Merchants, and venture my Life upon the Cause, if I were assured of fair Play in the Dispute. But that it was my Opinion, That we might carry on a Trade with *France* to our great Advantage, and that we ought for that reason to Trade with them, appears in the Third, Fourth, Fifth, and Sixth Volume of the *Reviews*, above Nine Year[52] before the *Mercator* was thought of; it was not thought Criminal to say so then, how it comes to be Villainous to say so now God knows, I can give no account of it; I am still of the same Opinion, and shall never be brought to say otherwise, unless I see the state of Trade so altered, as to alter my Opinion; and if ever I do, I will be able to give good Reasons for it.

The Answer to these things, whether mine or no, was all pointed at me, and the Arguments were generally in the Terms of Villain, Rascal, Miscreant, Lyer, Bankrupt, Fellow, Hireling, Turn-Coat, *&c.* what the Arguments were better'd by these Methods, that I leave to others to Judge of. Also most of those things in the *Mercator*, for which I had such Usage, were such as I was not the Author of.

I do grant, had all the Books which have been called by my Name been written by me, I must of Necessity have exasperated every Side, and perhaps have deserved it; but I have the greatest Injustice imaginable in this Treatment, as I have in the perverting the Design of what really I have written. To sum up therefore my Complaint in few Words:

I was from my first entring into the Knowledge of publick Matters, and have ever been to this Day, a sincere Lover of the Constitution of my Country; zealous for Liberty, and the Protestant Interest; but a constant Follower of moderate Principles, a vigorous Opposer of hot Measures in all Parties: I never once changed my Opinion, my Principles, or my Party; and let what will be said of changing Sides, this I maintain, That I never once deviated from the Revolution Principles, nor from the Doctrine of Liberty and Property, on which it was founded.

I own I could never be convinc'd of the great *Danger* of the PRETENDER, in the Time of the late Ministry: Nor can I be now convinc'd of the great *Danger* of the CHURCH under this Ministry.[53] I believe the Cries of one was politically made use of then to serve other Designs; and I plainly see the like Use made of the other now. I spoke my Mind freely then, and I have done the like now, in a small Tract to that purpose not yet made publick; and which, if I live to publish, I will publickly own, as I purpose to do, every thing I write, that my Friends may know when I am abused, and they impos'd on.[54]

It has been the Disaster of all Parties in this Nation to be very HOT in their Turn, and as often as they have been SO, I have differed with them all, and ever must and shall do so. I'll repeat some of the Occasions on the *Whigs* Side, because from that Quarter the Accusation of my turning about comes.

The first Time I had the Misfortune to differ with my Friends, was about the Year 1683, when the *Turks* were besieging *Vienna*, and the *Whigs* in *England*, generally speaking, were for the *Turks* taking it; which I having read the History of the Cruelty and perfidious Dealings of the *Turks* in their Wars, and how they had rooted out the Name of the Christian Religion in above Threescore and Ten Kingdoms, could by no means agree with: And tho' then but a young Man, and a younger Author, I opposed it, and wrote against it;[55] which was taken very unkindly indeed.

The next Time I differed with my Friends was when King *James* was wheedling the *Dissenters* to take off the Penal Laws and Test, which I could by no means come into. And as *in the first* I used to say, I had rather the Popish House of *Austria* should ruin the Protestants in *Hungaria*, than the Infidel House of *Ottoman* should ruin both Protestant and Papist, by over-running *Germany*; So in the other, I told the *Dissenters* I had rather the Church of *England* should pull our Cloaths off by Fines and Forfeitures, than the Papists should fall both upon the *Church*, and the *Dissenters*, and pull our Skins off by Fire and Fagot.[56]

The next Difference I had with good Men, was about the scandalous Practice of *Occasional Conformity*, in which I had the Misfortune to make many honest

Men angry, rather because I had the better of the Argument, than because they disliked what I said.[57]

And now I have lived to see the *Dissenters* themselves very quiet, if not very well pleased with an Act of Parliament to prevent it.[58] Their Friends indeed laid it on; they would be Friends indeed if they would talk of taking it off again.

Again, I had a Breach with honest Men for their Male-treating King *William*; of which I say nothing: Because, I think, they are now opening their Eyes, and making what amends they can to his Memory.

The fifth Difference I had with them, was about the *Treaty of Partition*, in which many honest Men were mistaken, and in which I told them plainly then, That they would at last End the War upon *worse Terms*;[59] and so it is my Opinion they would have done, tho' the Treaty of *Gertrudenburgh* had taken Place.

The sixth Time I differed with them,[60] was when the *Old Whigs* fell upon the *Modern Whigs*; and when the Duke of *Marlborough* and my Lord *Godolphin* were used by the *Observator*[61] in a Manner worse, *I must confess for the Time it lasted*, than ever they were used since; nay, tho' it were by *Abel*[62] and the *Examiner*:[63] But the Success failed. In this Dispute my Lord *Godolphin* did me the Honour to tell me, *I had served him* and *his Grace also*, both *faithfully* and *successfully*. But his Lordship is Dead, and I have now no Testimony of it but what is to be found in the *Observator*, where I am plentifully abused for being an Enemy to my Country, by acting in the Interest of my Lord *Godolphin*, and the Duke of *Marlborough: What Weather-Cock can Turn with such Tempers as these!*

I am now in *the seventh* Breach with them, and my Crime now is, That I will not believe and say the same things of the Queen, and the late *Treasurer*, which I could not believe before of my Lord *Godolphin*, and the Duke of *Marlborough*, and which in Truth I cannot believe, and therefore could not say it of either of them; and which, if I had believed, yet I ought not to have been the Man that should have said it, for the Reasons aforesaid.

In such Turns and Tempers and Times a Man must be tenfold *a Vicar of* Bray, or it is impossible but he must one Time or other be out with every Body. This is my present Condition, and for this I am reviled with having abandon'd my Principles, turn'd *Jacobite*, and what not: God Judge between me and these Men. Would they come to any Particulars with me, what real Guilt I may have I would freely acknowledge; and if they would produce any Evidence, of the Bribes, the Pensions, and the Rewards I have taken, I would declare honestly, whether they were true or no. If they would give a List of the Books which they charge me with, and the Reasons why they lay them at my Door, I would acknowledge any Mistake, own what I have done, and let them know what I have not done. But these Men neither shew Mercy, or leave place for Repentance, in which they act not only unlike their Maker, but contrary to his express Commands.

It is true, good Men have been used thus in former times; and all the Comfort I have is, that these Men have not the last Judgment in their Hands, if they had, dreadful would be the Case of those who oppose them. But that Day will shew many Men and Things also in a different State from what they may now appear in; some that now appear clear and fair, will then be seen to be black and foul; and some that are now thought black and foul, will then be approved and accepted; and thither I chearfully appeal, concluding this Part in the Words of the Prophet, *I heard the Defaming of many; Fear on every side; Report*, say they, *and we will Report it; All my Familiars watch'd for my halting, saying, Peradventure he will be enticed, and we shall prevail against him, and we shall take our Revenge on him,* Jerem. 20. 10.

Mr. *Pool's Annotations*[64] has the following Remarks on these Lines, which, I think, are so much to that Part of my Case which is to follow, that I could not omit them. His Words are these.

'The Prophet, *says he*, here rendreth a Reason why he thought of giving 'over his Work as a Prophet; his Ears were continually filled with the Obloquies 'and Reproaches of such as reproached him; and besides, he was afraid on all 'Hands, there were so many Traps laid for him, so many Devises devised against 'him. They did not only take Advantage against him, but sought Advantages, 'and invited others to raise Stories of him. Not only Strangers, but those that 'he might have expected the greatest Kindness from; those that pretended most 'courteously, they watch, *says he*, for opportunities to do me Mischief, and lay 'in wait for my Halting, desiring nothing more than that I might be enticed to 'speak, or do something which they might find Matter of a colourable Accu-'sation, that so they might satisfie their Malice upon me. This hath always been the Genius of wicked Men; *Job* and *David*, both made Complaints much like 'this. These are Mr. *Pool's* Words.

And this leads me to several Particulars, in which my Case may, without any Arrogance, be likened to that of the Sacred Prophet; except only the vast Disparity of the Persons.

No sooner was the Queen Dead, and the King as Right required, proclaim'd, but the Rage of Men encreased upon me to that Degree, that the Threats and Insults I receiv'd were such as I am not able to express: If I offered to say a word in favour of the present Settlement, it was called fawning and turning round again; on the other hand, tho' I have meddled neither one way or other, nor written one Book since the Queen's Death,[65] yet a great many things are call'd by my Name, and I bear every Day the Reproaches which all the Answerers of those Books cast as well upon the Subject as the Authors. I have not seen or spoken to my Lord of *Oxford* but once since the King's Landing, nor receiv'd the least Message, Order, or Writing from his Lordship, or any other way Corresponded with him,[66] yet he bears the Reproach of my Writing in his Defence, and I the Rage of Men for doing it. I cannot say it is no Affliction to me to be thus used, tho' my being entirely clear of the Facts, is a true support to me.

I am unconcerned at the Rage and Clamour of *Party-men*; but I can not be unconcern'd to hear Men, who I think are good Men and good Christians, prepossess'd and mistaken about me: However I cannot doubt but some time or other It will please God to open such Mens Eyes. A constant, steady adhering to *Personal Vertue*, and to *Publick Peace*, which, I thank God, I can appeal to him, has always been my Practice; will AT LAST restore me to the Opinion of Sober and Impartial Men, and that is all I desire: What it will do with those who are resolutely Partial and Unjust I cannot say, neither is that much my Concern. But I cannot forbear giving one Example of the hard Treatment I receive, which has happened, even while I am Writing this Tract: I have six Children,[67] I have Educated them as well as my Circumstances will permit, and so as I hope shall recommend them to better Usage than their Father meets with in the World. I am not indebted One Shilling in the World for any part of their Education, or for any thing else belonging to bringing them up; yet the Author of the *Flying-Post*[68] Published lately, That I never pay'd for the Education of any of my Children. If any Man in *Britain* has a Shilling to demand of me for any part of their Education, or any thing belong to them, let them come for it.

But these Men care not what Injurious Things they Write, nor what they Say, whether Truth or Not, if it may but raise a Reproach on me, tho' it were to be my Ruine. I may well Appeal to the Honour and Justice of my worst Enemies in such Cases as this.

Conscia Mens Recti fama Mendacia Ridet.[69]

Conclusion by the Publisher[70]

While this was at the Press, and the Copy thus far finish'd, the Author was seiz'd with a violent Fit of an Apoplexy, whereby he was disabled finishing what he design'd in his farther Defence, and continuing now for above Six Weeks in a Weak and Lan-

guishing Condition, neither able to go on, or likely to recover, at least in any short time, his Friends thought it not fit to delay the Publication of this any longer; if he recovers, he may be able to finish what he began; if not, it is the Opinion of most that know him, that the Treatment which he here complains of, and some others that he would have spoken of, have been the apparent Cause of his Disaster.

FINIS

The Family Instructor   1715

Among Defoe's objections to a tax on printed matter (*Review*, VIII, 172, p. 672) was the harm it would cause to 'family instruction . . . a work so generally neglected by all sorts'. Three years later he made his own contribution to that *genre* in the work from which an extract is printed below. Published anonymously on 31 March the book was immediately popular; the second edition appeared in November, the eighth in 1720. The market for didactic works was obviously brisk; Defoe knew what would sell.

Sutherland suggests (*Defoe*, p. 211) that *The Family Instructor* may have been written to salve the conscience of a Puritan who had neglected the tenets it preached. What is certainly true is that evidence of a full personal commitment, of writing that springs from a multitude of urgently felt experiences, is missing. On the other hand the experience of creating characters in order to dramatize the issues involved in relationship between parents and children, masters and servants, husbands and wives, was valuable to Defoe the novelist. A significant part is played in the novels by the parent-child relationship, most obvious perhaps in *Robinson Crusoe*—published only four years later—where the hero recognizes that his rejection of parental advice is the 'Original Sin' which subsequently earns divine punishment.

The Family Instructor

The Fourth Dialogue

For the better understanding this Discourse, it is to be understood, that the Father and Mother, according to their Resolution in the last Dialogue, *had set effectually* about the Reformation of their Family, and about proper Methods for reducing their Children to an Obedience *to*, and Sence *of* their Duty.

Their Children were most of them grown up, and had run a great Length, they had been indulg'd in all possible Folly and Levity, such as *Plays, Gaming,* and *Loosness* of Life; *Irreligious* Behaviour, not immodest or dishonest, that they were not arrived to yet; but they were bred up with *Gayety* and *Gallantry,* as being of good Fortunes and Fashion; but nothing of Religion, more than just the common course of going to Church, which they did because it was the Custom and Fashion, rather than with any other View; and being thus unhappily Educated, we shall find the Instruction they were now to bear, met with the more Opposition in them, and we shall see how it had a various Effect according to the different Temper and Constitution of the Children.

Their eldest Daughter was about eighteen Years old, and her Mother, it seems, began with her first; the Mother found it a very difficult matter to deal with her: For when she came to tell her of laying by her foolish Romances and Novels, *of which she was mighty fond*; leaving off her Patches and Play-Books; refusing her going to the Park on the Sabbath-Days, *and the like*, she flew out in a Passion and told her Mother *in plain Words* she would not be hinder'd, she was past a Child, she would go to the Park, and to the Play, *and the like*, ay that she wou'd.

But *the Mother,* whose Resolutions were too well fix'd, *after such an Occasion as has been said,* to be conquer'd by her Daughter, *having try'd softer Methods to no purpose,* took her roundly to task, and told her, That as she took those Measures with her *for her good only,* and that she could not satisfie her own Conscience, to see her ruin'd *Body* and *Soul* together, so she was resolv'd to be obey'd, and that since she would not comply by fair means, she would take another Course; this Course, it seems, *besides other things which will appear in the following part of this Dialogue,* was *particularly,* that it being Sabbath Day after they came home from Church, when her Mother began this Discourse, her Daughter call'd for the Coach to go to the Park, as their Custom, it seems, had always been, but *her Mother* would not suffer her to stir out, and upon her being a little stubborn or resolute, had used some little Violence with her in shewing her Resentment, and threatened her with worse, *as will appear presently.*

Upon this Repulse she flings up Stairs into her Chamber, where she sat crying, when *her elder Brother,* whom the Father, it seems, had not yet begun with, came to her, between which Couple begins the following Dialogue.

Brother: Sister! what in Tears! what's the matter now?

She cries on, but makes no Answer.

Bro.: Dear Sister! tell me your Grievance, *I say tell me,* what is it troubles you?

And pulls her by her Cloaths.

Sis.: I wont; don't trouble me, *I won't tell you,* let me alone.

Sobs and cries still.

Bro.: Prethee what is the matter, *Sister?* Why, you will spoil your Face, you won't be fit to go to the Park; *come,* I came to have you *go out,* we will all go to the Park.

Sis.: Ay, so you may if you can.

Bro.: If I can! what do you mean by that? I have order'd *Thomas* to get the Coach ready.

Sis.: It's no matter for that, I can assure you *he won't do it.*

Bro.: I'll Cane the Rascal if he don't, *and that presently too*; come, do you wipe your Eyes, and don't pretend to go Abroad with a blubber'd Face.

Sis.: I tell you, *Thomas* will not obey you, he is otherwise order'd; you will find that neither you nor I are to go out to Night.

Bro.: Who will have the Impudence to hinder us!

Sis.: I have been hinder'd already, and my Mother has told me in so many Words, I not only shall not go *to Night,* but never no more of a Sunday, *tho' I think I shall fail her.*

Bro.: What does my Mother mean by that, *not go to the Park!* I must go, and I will go, as long as Sermon is done, what harm is there in't? *I warrant you we will go,* come get you ready, and wipe your Eyes.

Sis.: You'll find your self mistaken in my Mother, *I'll assure ye*; I told her I would go, *as you do me,* and she was in such a Passion with me, she struck me, which she never did in all her Life before, and then read me a long Lecture of the Sabbath-Day, and being against her Conscience, *and I know not what,* things I never heard her talk of in my Life before; I don't know what ails her to be in such a Humour.

Bro.: Conscience! *What does my Mother mean by that!* Why, have we not gone every Sunday to the Park, and my Mother always gone with us! What, is it against her Conscience now, and never was against her Conscience before! *that's all Nonsence*; I'll warrant you I'll go for all this new Bustle you make about it.

Sis.: I'd go with all my heart, but *I tell you* she is in such a Passion you had better let her alone, it will but make her worse.

Bro.: Prethee don't tell me, I will go to the Park if the Devil stood at the Door; what, shan't I have the Liberty to go out when I please! *Sure I am past a Boy,* a'n't I!

Sis.: I tell you, my Mother is very positive, and you had better let her alone, you will but provoke her; you may do as you will.

Bro.: Not I, I won't provoke her at all, for I won't ask her, I'll go without her.

Sis.: Then you will go without a Coach too; for I assure you, as I said before, you won't get *Thomas* to go.

Bro.: Then I'll take a Hackney, and go to the Mall.

Sis.: Come, Brother, we had better let it alone *for once,* my Mother will be better condition'd another time, *I hope this will be over.*

Bro.: Nay, I don't care, *come let's read a Book then:* Have you never a Play here? Come, I'll read a Play to you.

Sis.: Ay, what will you have?

Bro.: Any thing.

She runs to her Closet for a Play-Book, and finds her Plays, Novels, Song-books, and others of that kind taken all away.

Sis.: O Thieves! Thieves! I am robb'd!

Bro.: Robb'd! What do you mean, Sister?

He runs to her.

Sis.: All my Books are gone! they are all gone! all stole! I ha'nt a Book left! *Here you may suppose her taking God's Name in vain very much, and in a great Passion.*

Bro.: What, all your Books?

Sis.: Every one, that are good for any thing; here's nothing *but a Bible,* and an old foolish Book about Religion, *I don't know what.*

Her Brother looks.

Bro.: I think, *as you say,* they are all gone! *No, hold,* here's a Prayer Book, and here's the *Practice of Piety;*[1] and here's the *Whole duty of Man.*[2]

Sis.: Prethee what signifie them to me? But all my fine Books are gone; I had a good Collection of Plays, all the *French* Novels, all the modern Poets, *Boileau, Dacier,* and a great many more.

Bro.: What's the meaning of this!

Sis.: I'll lay *a hundred Pounds* this is my Mother.

Bro.: I believe so too; I wish my Mother be not mad: This is horrid! What can my Mother mean!

Sister falls in a great Passion of crying; the Second Brother comes up to them, and the Father had been talking to him.

2nd *Bro.*: What's the matter with *my Sister?* What, is she not well?

1st *Bro.*: I don't know what's the matter *very well*, but my Mother has been ruffling her a little, and put her out of Humour.

2 *Bro.*: What has she done?

1 *Bro.*: Why, She won't let her go to the Park; and when she said she *WOULD* go, *my Mother* struck her, and we find she has taken away all her Books, I can't imagine what the meaning of this is; I think my Mother is mad.

2 *Bro.*: No, *no, Brother*, my Mother is not mad, if she is mad, my Father is mad too; you won't want long to know what the Meaning of it is, for you will hear of it quickly *too* your self, *that I can assure you.*

1 *Bro.*: *I hear of it!* What, from my Father?

2 *Bro.*: Yes, *from my Father;* he has told me his Mind already, and the Reason and Occasion of it, and I know he is enquiring for you, *to do the like.*

1 *Bro.*: He may talk what he will to me, *but I'll do what I please* for all that.

2 *Bro.*: Hark! you are call'd just now; you will be of another Mind when you come back, *I'll warrant you.*

The eldest Son is call'd to come to his Father.

1 *Bro.*: Never *as long as I live.*

Goes out.

2 *Bro.*: If my Father's Reasons do not perswade him, *I can assure him,* his Authority will, *for* he is resolv'd upon the thing.

Sis.: *What thing is it, Brother?* What is our Father and Mother a going to do with us: For my part I cannot imagine what they mean!

2 *Bro.*: Why really, *Sister*, I find they have begun with the *Youngest* first; for *my Father* has been upon me, and *my Mother* has begun with my Sister *Betty*, but you will have your Turn too.

Sis.: I think *my Mother has begun with me already*; for I was but humming over a new Song this Afternoon, *tho' Church was done, and all over*, and every body come home; but my Mother was in such a Passion with me, *that* I never had so many Words with her in my Life; she would not let me go to the Park, and had much ado to keep her Hands off me.

2 *Bro.*: *I heard* she was angry at you, but, *it seems*, you answer'd her rudely.

Sis.: *I said nothing* but that I would go to the Park.

2 *Bro.*: Well, but you told her you would go *whether she would or no.*

Sis.: Why, *was that such a Crime?* And so I would say again.

2 *Bro.*: Well, *but if you did*, you would not say it was well done, *would you?* And, as it seems, she told you then, *so I can satisfie you now*, she will not take it from you, nor none of us, *as she has done.*

Sis.: *It may be so*, and I have found it otherwise already.

2 *Bro.*: *What*, has she not taken some Books *out of your Closet?*

Sis.: Some! No, she has only taken all my Books away.

2 Bro.: I warrant she has left your *BIBLE* and *Prayer-Books*, and such as those.

Sis.: Ay those! What does that signifie? She has taken away all my Plays, and all my Songs, and all the Books *that I had any Pleasure in.*

2 Bro.: Yes, I heard of it.

Sis.: But I will have them again, or I'll lead her such a Life she shall have *little Comfort of me.*

2 Bro.: Truly Sister, you may fancy you may have taken them again, *but I can satisfie you,* most of them are past Recovery, for I saw them upon the *Parlour-Fire* before I came up.

Sis.: THE FIRE! I'll go and pull them out *before her Face.*

Here she is raging, and in a violent Passion at her Mother, and makes as if she would run down Stairs.

2 Bro.: Come Sister, you had as good be easie, *for I find* both our Father and Mother are agreed in the thing; and *I must own* I begin to see they have reason for it; *for my part,* I am inclin'd to submit to all their Measures, for I think in my Conscience *we have all been wrong,* and if my Father and Mother see reason to have me alter my Conduct, *and especially* when I am convinc'd it is for the better too, I think it is my part to submit.

Sis.: I'll never submit.

The Sister cries again.

2 Bro.: Perhaps you will be perswaded when my Mother talks *a little calmly* to you; I believe *my Sister Betty* is of another Mind already.

Sis.: I have had talk enough already; *my Mother tells me* I shall not go to the Park, nor to the Playhouse, nor patch, nor play at Cards, *I think this is talk enough*; what does my Mother think to make a Nun of me.

2 Bro.: No, *I dare say* she does not.

Sis.: No, and if she does *she will be mistaken,* for I shall not be hinder'd of my innocent Diversions, let my Mother do what she pleases.

2 Bro.: But Sister, I do not think you will find my Mother unreasonable in what she desires, if you will but allow your self Leisure *to think of it* a little.

Sis.: Unreasonable in her Desires! *Prethee* can you tell me what it is she does desire? For I cannot imagine what my Mother would be at. . . .

2 Bro.: Dear Sister! I do not find that my Father or Mother is inclin'd to tax you in particular *any more than all of us,* but all of us together, nay, even our Father and Mother themselves have been negligent, godless, and graceless; and if *my Father* does now resolve to repent, and turn, and to carry himself after another manner, and to have us do the same, *pray what taxing can you call this?* Does not my Father say, he confesses he has been negligent, and has not done his Duty, *as well as any of us?* And what is all he desires of us *but only*, that as he begs Pardon of Almighty God for himself, *so* we should ask the same for our selves; *that as* he resolves to reform the Practice, *so we* should do also; and *that so* at last we may be a sober Family, and a reform'd Family, and may serve God for the future after another manner than we have done; *pray where's the Hardship of all this?*

Sis.: Well, you may go on with your Reformation, and Confessions, *and all that*, if you have a Mind, for my part I'll have *nothing to do with it*, let my Father and all of you go your own Way.

2 Bro.: Well, Sister, I am sorry for you; if you hold of this Mind, we are like to have *a foul House with you quickly*, for I know my Father will go thro' stitch³ with what he has begun.

Sis.: My Father may go on with what he will, I shan't hinder him; *he may let me alone*, and reform the rest of you, can't he? I need no Reformation, *as I know of.*

2 Bro.: I am not so sorry for the Difficulty my Father will meet with, *as for the Hazard you will run for your self*, and the Breach you will make in your own Happiness; but here comes my *Sister Betty*, I see by her Looks she has something to say upon the same Subject.

2d Sister.: How long have *you two* been together?

2d Bro.: A great while.

2 Sis.: I suppose I know *something of your Discourse*, at least, I guess at it by your looking so grave: *Pray*, how long have you been *here?*

2 Bro.: I told you a great while; *but since you would be answer'd particularly*, I believe we have been here *just as long* as you have been with my Mother, *for I know* she has been talking to you.

2 Sister.: That's true, my Mother and I have been talking.

1 Sis.: Talking! do you say? *or Fighting?*

2 Sis.: Fighting! What do you mean, *Sister?* Do you think I fight with my Mother!

1 Sis.: No, but it may be your Mother may fight with you; why not *with you* as well as *with other Folks?*

2 Sis.: My Mother never struck me in her Life, and I never gave her any Cause that I know of.

1 Sis.: That's more than I can say, and yet I think I never gave her any more Cause than you did.

2 Sis.: If my Mother has struck you, *certainly you must ha' given her more Cause than I have done;* for every body knows she loves you *to a distinction* above every Child she has.

1 Sis.: I don't believe a word of it, nor do I desire *such Love*.

2 Bro.: Well Sister, but you may tell us a little how you like things, and what Discourse my Mother has had *with you*, for we all know the Subject already.

2 Sis.: My Mother said nothing to me *but what I like very well*, and am very willing to comply with.

2 Bro.: I am very glad to hear you say so, *I wish we were all of the same Mind.*

2 Sis.: I hope we shall: I think what she proposes is so rational, and the Reasons of it so unanswerably good, that I see no room to object against it *in the least*, nor do I see the least thing design'd in it all, but what is for our Good.

2 Bro.: I am perfectly of your Opinion, and am glad to find you of my Opinion; *but here is my Sister MARY* quite of different Sentiments from us all.

1 Sis.: And *with a great deal of Reason*, for she has not been treated with the same Kindness that you have been treated with.

2 Sis.: Wherein, pray ?

1 Sis.: Why, I suppose my Mother has not been in your Chamber, and rifled your Closet, and taken all your choice Books, and your Plays, and your Songs, and your Novels, *&c.* and carried them away, and thrown them into the Fire.

2 Sis.: No, my Dear! For what my Mother said to me was *so* affecting, *so* fully convincing, and *so* unanswerable, that I immediately fetch'd them all down my self, and put them into the Fire *with my own Hands*, before her Face.

1 Sis.: A pretty complying, easie Fool, *I warrant she kiss'd thee*, and call'd thee *dear Child*, and cry'd over thee, did she not, for thy pains, *my Dear?*

2 Sis.: I am asham'd to hear you talk so of *my Mother*, Sister; sure you ha'n't lost your *Manners*, and *Duty*, as well as Respect, and Religion, *Sister!* I beseech you what is the Matter with you !

1 Sis.: And have you really burnt all your Plays to please a Humour ?

2 Sis.: Indeed I have burnt them, but not to please a Humour, I have done it to oblige the best Mother in the World, and I have done it from a Sence of its being very fit to be done.

1 Sis.: A fine Child! And are not you a deal the wiser for it; do you not repent it already ?

2 Sis.: No, Sister! So far from repenting it, that I never did a thing in my Life that gave me more Satisfaction, and *if I were to do it again*, I should now do it with ten times the Pleasure I did it then; and if God give me Grace to keep my Resolution, I never design to see a Play, or read a Play more.

1 Sis.: Pretty Child! Thorowly reform'd *at once*; this is a mighty sudden Conversion, and may hold accordingly, *I suppose*, as most such hasty things do.

2 Sis.: It will hold, I hope, longer than your Obstinacy against it.

1 Sis.: When it has *as good Reasons* I may think so too.

2 Sis.: I shall debate that with you hereafter, when you have heard the same Reasons for it that I have heard.

1 *Sis.:* Well, but come, *pray let's have a few of your Reasons* just now, if you can spare them; pray, what harm is there in seeing or reading a Play? Is there any sufficient Mischief in them to justifie your burning them, and to justifie my Mother's using me about them *as she has done?*

2 *Sis.: In the first place,* Sister, the Time we have before us, compar'd to the Eternity that is to be prepar'd for, is *so* little, and *so* short, that if it be possible to employ it better, there is none to spare for what has so little Good in it *as a Play.*

1 *Sis.:* I have learnt a great deal *of Good* from a Play.

2 *Sis.:* But might you not have learnt more from the Scriptures?

1 *Sis.:* It may be not.

2 *Sis.:* You would have been a bad Scholar then.

1 *Sis.: Well,* and what's next?

2 *Sis.: In the second place,* the little Good which you *can pretend* is to be found in them, is mix'd with *so much Evil,* attended with *so much lewd, vicious and abominable Stuff,* that no sober Person will bear with the *wicked part* for the sake of the *good part,* nor can any one justifie it, that the good Part is such, *or so great,* that so much Hazard should be run for it.

1 *Sis.: Very well;* so you are afraid you should be tempted *when you go to the Play,* I suppose that is because you are so tempting your self.

2 *Sis.: No Sister,* I am in no more danger, *I hope,* than another; but sure, if I am to pray to God, as in the Lord's Prayer, *Lead me not into Temptation,* I must not *lead my self* into it.

1 *Sis.:* And is this *all you have to say* for throwing the best Collection of Plays the whole Town has, in the Fire.

2 *Sis.:* I have many more Reasons which I shall bestow on you *when you have answer'd these,* but there is one more which I will bestow upon you now, which you may give an Answer to before the rest, if you please, *viz.* That it is my *Mother*'s Desire and Resolution, that I should do so; and that she declares, it is against her Conscience to permit me the use of these things *as formerly,* and therefore desires, and in *one kind* commands, that I should do thus, and I am bid in the Scripture many ways to obey; *Children obey your Parents in all things,*[4] &c.

1 *Sis.:* That is the best Reason you have given yet.

2 *Sis.:* I think not, *neither;* for the other Reasons *are better,* as they are drawn from the Nature and Authority of God, *and this* but from the Authority of my Mother; which, tho' it is great, and ought to be very prevalent *with me,* and ever shall be so, yet not quite equal, or up to the Authority of him that made us all; nor will my Mother think hard that I say so.

2 *Bro.:* Sister, *indeed I think* my Sister *Betty* has fully answer'd you there.

1 *Sis.: Yes, yes,* you are two fine new Converts.

2 *Bro.*: Which I hope we shall never be asham'd of.

1 *Sis.*: *Well*, and pray what said you to her about going to the Park a Sundays? Had you nothing to say about that?

2 *Sis.*: Yes, yes, my Mother shewed her Dislike of it, and said it was a plain Violation of the Commands of God; *I mused a little while about it*, and being convinc'd that it was so, I presently resolved never to go any more.

1 *Sis.*: So, and you had not a Box on the Ear then?

2 *Sis.*: I gave my Mother no Occasion for that, *Sister*, as I understand *you did*.

1 *Sis.*: *No, no*, You are a mighty good, obedient thing.

2 *Sis.*: I am not asham'd to own *that I obey my Mother*, and am willing to do so in every thing; *especially* every thing that is right, *more especially* in every thing that is for my own Good, and *most of all*, where my Duty to God joins with it; if you think it below you to do so, I am sorry for it, I cannot follow you in that Example; for the Scripture says expressly, *Children obey your Parents in all things*, much more where the Command of God, and the Command of our Parents *concur together*, as it does in this Case.

1 *Sis.*: You preach nicely, *Sister*, You shall Marry a Parson, and when you turn *Quaker* you shall be *a speaking Sister*.

2 *Sis.*: Any thing rather than a Rebel to God and my Parents, break the Commandments of the first, and abuse the Tenderness of the last.

1 *Sis.*: You are mighty Mannerly *to your Sister*.

2 *Sis.*: Much more to you, *than you* to my Mother; *I love my Sister very well*, but I know neither *Brother* nor *Sister* when they rise up against my Mother, and that *such a Mother* as ours is; who, I must tell you, *Sister*, deserves other things at your Hands; and unless you behave better, you will find the whole Family against you, *as well as I*, for every body says, you treated my Mother *very rudely*, the very Servants speak of it with Abhorrence, and of you with Contempt; for *every body must despise you* if you carry it so to your Mother.

1 *Sis.*: With all my Heart; if *every body* despises me, *I'll despise every body*, and so I'll be even with you all.

2 *Sis.*: You'll be soon tir'd of that.

1 *Sis.*: If *I am*, I'll bear my Affliction with Patience.

2 *Sis.*: You are like to be a Martyr in the worst Cause *that ever Saint suffered in*; no doubt but you will suffer for Conscience sake; two excellent Points in Divinity you maintain, *viz. Contempt of Religion*, and *Rebellion against your Parents*: I wonder what *Evil Spirit* is your Instructor.

1 *Sis.*: You are very pert, *Madam*, and shew abundance of Affection and Respect.

2 *Sis.*: I follow *your own Example still*, Sister, but I'll be very honest to you, I'll neither have *Respect* nor *Affection* to you, or any body, that shall carry it to

my Mother as you have done; I would not load you, *or add to your sorrows*, but no body in this House can do otherwise, who have such a Father, and such a Mother as we have.

1 *Sis.*: I have no Sorrow about it, *and am resolved* I will have none.

2 *Sis.*: I think the best way to deal with you, is to do, *as I fear God has done with you*, leave you; your Crime will be your sufficient Punishment: But I must tell you *before I go*, which I should have told you *at first*, that my Business was *not to visit you now*, but to call you to my Father and Mother, who want to speak with you *in the Parlour*, and where, I suppose you will hear more of it.

1 *Sis.*: I won't go.

2 *Sis.*: *As you please, Sister, for that;* I have delivered my Message.

1 *Sis.*: *Ay*, and you may carry that for an Answer.

2 *Sis.*: No, Sister, I'll *have no hand in your Misfortunes*; besides, I believe here comes another Messenger from them.

A Servant comes up Stairs, and tells the eldest Lady that her Father and Mother waited to speak with her.

1 *Sis.*: I am indisposed, *tell my Mother*, I can't come, I am upon the Bed.

Servant.: If you won't go, *Madam*, I doubt they will come to you.

1 *Sis.*: Go you, and deliver your Message.

2. *Sis.*: And are you so resolute against your self, *Sister!* Can nothing perswade you to your own Good! Certainly you will be wiser.

1 *Sis.*: What would you have me do? *What is the matter with you all?*

2 *Sis.*: *Nay, Sister*, I am not fit to give you Advice, who are my elder Sister; *but* methinks you do not want Advice to go down when you are sent for.

1 *Sis.*: I won't.

2 *Sis.*: What shall I say to them? *I dare not say* you won't, *for your own Sake.*

1 *Sis.*: Tell them, *I a'n't well, can't you?* that I am upon the Bed, and have shut my Door, and won't be spoke with; *tell them any thing*: Don't you see I an't fit to be spoke to?

2 *Sis.*: As the Maid said, *I am certain* they'll come up *to you*, for they know your Distemper; I would fain have you go down, *I dare say*, you will be treated very tenderly and kindly, perhaps better than you can expect, if you do not force them to treat you ill.

1 *Sis.*: Yes! after they have burnt all my Books; robb'd me of what they knew was my Delight; refus'd me the Liberty of going Abroad; and given me a Blow in the Face for nothing; now they'll treat me kindly, *will they!* I desire none of their Kindness: *I won't go.*

2 *Sis.*: Well, *Sister*, then they must wait upon you, *I suppose.*

1 *Sis.*: If they do, I won't speak to them,* or open the Door.

She cries vehemently.

2 *Sis.:* I hope you will alter your Mind, *I'll leave you to think of it.*
The 2nd Sister withdraws, and the other claps the Door after her.

This Dialogue needs no Observations, save on the different Temper between Children dutifully submitting to Family-Government, and affectionately complying with their Parents just Desires; and on the other hand, Children obstinately adhering to the Dictates of their Passions, and this will appear to every common Reader; and much of this *whole first Part* being Historical, and the Family known, I forbear farther Observations on the particular Conduct of the Persons. The Design of this work being rather to instruct other Families, than to reproach those who may think themselves concern'd: The Author leaves these Dialogues therefore without particular Remarks, and leaves room for abler Hands to Annotate upon them hereafter, when the Persons concern'd may be gone off the Stage, and then it may rather appear as a general Reproach to those that are guilty, than a particular Satyr upon Persons or Families; which he conceives will also tend more to the Usefulness of the Work.

End of the Fourth Dialogue

Letter to Charles de la Faye[1]

26 April 1718

Sir

Tho' I doubt Not but you have Accquainted My Ld Stanhope[2] with what Humble Sence of his Ldpps goodness I Recd The Account you were Pleased to Give me, That My Little Services are Accepted, and That his Ldpp is Satisfyed to go on Upon the Foot of Former Capitulations[3] &c., yet I Confess Sir I have been Anxious On Many Accounts, with Respect as Well to the Service it Self, as to my Own Safety, Least My Lord May Think himself ill Served by me, Even when I may have best Perform'd My Duty:

I Thought it therefore Not Onely a Debt to my Self, But a Duty to his Ldpp that I should give his Ldpp a Short Account as Clear as I can, How far my former Instructions Empowred me to Act, and in a Word what this Little Peice of Secret Service is for which I am So much a Subject of his Ldpps Present Favour and Bounty.

It was in the Ministry of My Lord Townshend,[4] When My Ld Chief Justice Parker to whom I stand Obliged for the favour, Was pleased So farr to state my Case, That Notwithstanding the Missrepresentations Under which I had Suffred, and Notwithstanding Some Mistakes which I was the first to Acknowledge,[5] I Was So happy as to be believ'd in the Professions I made of a Sincere attachmt to The Intrest of the Present Governmt; and speaking with all Possible Humillity, I hope I Have not Dishonourd My Ld Parkers Recommendation.

In Considring after this which Way I might be Rendred Most usefull to the Government, It was proposed By My Lord Townshend That I should still appear as if I were as before under the Displeasure of the Governmt; and Seperated From the Whiggs; and That I might be more Servicable in a kind of Diguise, Than If I appeared openly; and Upon this foot a Weekly Paper which I was first Directed to Write, in Opposition to a Scandalous paper called the Shif shifted,[6] was Lay'd aside: and The first thing I Engaged in was a Monthly Book called Mercurius Politicus[7] of which Presently.

In the Intervall of This, Dyer[8] The News Letter Writer haveing been Dead, and Dormer his Successor being Unable by his Troubles to Carry on that Work, I had an Offer of a share in The Property as Well as in the Mannagemt of that Work.

I Imediately Accquainted my Ld Townshend of it, who by Mr Buckley[9] let me know, it Would be a Very Acceptable Peice of Service; for that Letter Was Really Very Prejudiciall to the Public, and the most Difficult to Come at in a judiciall way, in Case of Offence Given; My Ld was pleased to Add by Mr Buckley that he would Consider[10] my Service in that Case as he afterwards did.

Upon This I Engaged in it, and That So far, that Tho' the Property was not wholly my Own, yet the Conduct, and Governmt of the stile and News, was So Entirely in Me, that I Ventur'd to assure his Ldpp the sting of that Mischeivous Paper should be Entirely Taken out, Tho' it was Granted that the stile should Continue Tory, as it was, that the Party might be Amused, and Not Set up another, which Would have destroy'd the Design, and This Part I therefore Take Entirely on my Self still.

This Went on for a year, before My Ld Townshend Went Out of The Office;[11] and his Ldpp in Consideration of This Service, Made me the Appointment which Mr Buckley knows of, with Promise of a Further allowance as Service Presented.

My Ld Sunderland[12] to whose Goodness I had Many yeares agoe been Obliged when I was in a Secret Commission Sent to scotland,[13] was pleased to approve and Continue this Service, and the Appointmt Annexed; And with his Ldpps Approbation, I Introduced my Self in the Disguise of a Translator of the Forreign News to be So farr Concernd in This Weekly Paper of *Mists*,[14] as to be able to keep it within the Circle of a Secret Mannagement, also, prevent the Mischievous Part of it, and yet Neither Mist or any of those Concerned with him have the least Guess or Suspicion By whose Direction I do it.

But here it becomes Necessary to Accquaint My Lord (as I hinted to you Sir) That This paper called the Journall is not in My Self in Property, as the Other;[15] Onely in Mannagemt; with this Express Difference, that if anything happens to be put in without my knowledge, which may Give Offence; Or if any thing slips my Observation which may be ill Taken; His Ldpp shall be Sure allways to kno', whether he has a Servant to Reprove, or a stranger to Correct.

Upon the whole However, this is the Consequence, that by this Mannagemt The Weekly Journall and Dormers Letter as Also the Mercurius Politicus, which is in the Same Nature of Mannagemt as The journall, Will be allwayes kept (mistakes Excepted) To Pass as Tory Papers, and yet be Dissabled and Ennervated, So as to do no Mischief or give any Offence to the Governmt.

I Beg leav to Observ Sir one Thing More to his Ldpp in my Own behalf, And without which Indeed I May one Time Or other Run the hazard of fatall Missconstructions: I am Sir for This Service, Posted among Papists, Jacobites, and Enraged High Torys, a Generation who I Profess My Very Soul abhorrs; I am Oblig'd to hear Trayterous Expressions, and Outrageous Words against his Majties Person, and Governmt, and his Most faithfull Servants; and Smile at it all as if I Approv'd it; I am Oblig'd to take all the Scandalous and Indeed Villainous papers that Come, and keep them by Me as if I Would gather Materialls from Them to Put them into the News; Nay I often Venture to Let things pass which are a little shocking that I may not Render my Self Suspected.

Thus I bow in The House of *Rimmon*; and must Humbly Recommend my Self to his Lordpps Protection, or I may be Undone the Sooner, by how much the more faithfully I Execute The Commands I am Under.

I forbear to Enlarge. I beg you Sir to Represent these Circumstances to his Ldpp in Behalf of a faithfull Servant That Shall allways Endeavour to approve his fidellity by actions Rather Than Words.

I am, Sir, Your Most Humble Servt

De Foe

Newington, April 26. 1718

P.S. I Send you here One of the Letters stopt at the Press as I Mention'd to you. As to the Manuscript of Sultan Galga,[16] another Villainous Paper, I Sent the Coppy to my Ld Sunderland; if the Originall be of any Service it is Ready at your first orders.

Memoirs of a Cavalier 1720

'I have followed ... the method of Defoe's *Memoirs of a Cavalier* ... in which the author hangs the chronicle and discussion of great military and political events upon the thread of the personal experiences of an individual.' Sir Winston Churchill's remark (*The Gathering Storm*, 1948, p. vii) not only pays tribute to one of Defoe's most vivid narratives but also draws attention to the interplay in it between fact and fiction. The Cavalier is fictional—A. W. Secord has demonstrated that the manuscript which Defoe claims was secured as plunder at the battle of Worcester (1651) never existed (*Robert Drury's Journal and Other Studies*, Urbana, 1961, pp. 72–133); but the narrative rests on careful documentation from works such as *The Swedish Intelligencer*, Clarendon's *History of the Rebellion*, and Sir Bulstrode Whitelocke's *Memorials of the English Affairs*. Defoe at once claimed and confessed as much in the preface to the first edition:

> Almost all the facts, especially those of moment, are confirmed for their general part by all the writers of those times. If they are here embellished with particulars, which are nowhere else to be found, that is the beauty we boast of.

Defoe was careful in his selection of facts both about the German campaigns of Gustavus Adolphus and the English Civil War; he introduced details of his own (such as the part played by the sergeant in the second extract below, and the whole episode in the third), and brilliantly kept them in harmony with those which are authentic; but his creative energy was principally devoted to the portrayal of human figures in action. The generous, courageous Gustavus Adolphus, the initiative and resource of the common soldiery, or the bravery of the cavalier-hero—these were Defoe's paramount concerns.

The extracts are printed from the fifth (Newark) edition, 1782.

Memoirs of a Cavalier

Part First

It may suffice the reader, without being very inquisitive after my name, that I was born in the county of *SALOP*, in the year 1608;[1] under the government of what planet I was never astrologer enough to examine; but the consequences of my life may allow me to suppose some extraordinary influence affected my birth. If there be any thing in dreams also, my mother, who was mighty observant that way, took minutes, which I have since seen in the first leaf of her prayer-book, of several strange dreams she had while she was pregnant of her second son, which was me.—Once she noted, that she dreamt of being carried away by a regiment of horse, and delivered in the fields of a son, that as soon as it was born had two wings came out of its back, and in half an hour's time flew away from her: and the very evening before I was born, she dreamed of being brought to bed of a son, and that all the while she was in labour, a man stood under her window beating on a kettle-drum, which discomposed her very much.

My father was a gentleman of a very plentiful fortune, having an estate of above 5000l. per annum, of a family nearly allied to several of the principal nobility, and lived about six miles from the town: and my mother being at —— on some particular occasion, was surprised there at a friend's house, and brought me very safe into the world.

I was my father's second son, and therefore, was not altogether so much slighted as younger sons of good families generally are. But my father saw something in my genius which particularly pleased him, and caused him to take extraordinary care of my education.—I was instructed therefore, by the best masters that could be had, every thing that was needful to accomplish a young gentleman for the world; and at seventeen years old, my tutor told my father an academic education was very necessary for a person of quality, and he thought me very fit for it: my father, in consequence, entered me of —— college, *Oxford*, where I was three years.

A collegiate life did not suit me at all, though I loved books very well. It was never designed that I should be either a lawyer, physician or divine. I thought I had been long enough at college, for a gentleman, and wrote to my father, that I was desirous, by his leave, to pay him a visit.

During my stay at *Oxford*, though I passed through the proper exercises of the house,[2] yet my chief reading were history and geography, as those pleased my mind best, and supplied me with ideas most suitable to my genius: by one I understood what great actions had been done in the world; and by the other, I understood where they had been done.

*　　　*　　　*　　　*

This march of the King broke all *Tilly's* measures, for now was he obliged to face about, and leaving the *Upper Palatinate*, to come to the assistance of the Duke of *Bavaria*; for the King being 20000 strong, beside 10000 foot and 4000 horse and dragoons which joined him from the *Duringer Wald*, was resolved to ruin the Duke, who now lay open to him, and was the most powerful and inveterate enemy of the protestants in the empire.

Tilly was now joined with the Duke of *Bavaria*, and might together make about 22000 men, and in order to keep the *Swedes* out of the country of *Bavaria*, had planted themselves along the banks of the river *Lech*, which runs on the edge of the Duke's territories; and having fortified the other side of the river, and planted his cannon for several miles at all the convenient places on the river, resolved to dispute the King's passage.

I shall be the longer in relating this account of the *Lech*, being esteemed in those days as great an action as any battle or siege of that age, and particularly famous for the disaster of the gallant old General *Tilly*; and for that I can be more particular in it than other accounts, having been an eye-witness to every part.

The King being truly informed of the disposition of the *Bavarian* army, was once of the mind to have left the banks of the *Lech*, have repassed the *Danube*, and so setting down before *Ingolstat*, the Duke's capital city, by the taking that strong town to have made his entrance into *Bavaria*, and the conquest of such a fortress, one entire action; but the strength of the place and the difficulty of maintaining his leaguer in an enemy's country, while *Tilly* was so strong in the field, diverted him from that design; he therefore concluded that *Tilly* was first to be beaten out of the country, and then the siege of *Ingolstat* would be the easier.

Whereupon, the King resolved to go and view the situation of the enemy; his Majesty went out the 2d of *April* with a strong party of horse, which I had the honour to command; we marched as near as we could to the banks of the river, not to be too much exposed to the enemy's cannon, and having gained a little height, where the whole course of the river might be seen the King halted, and commanded to draw up. His Majesty alighted, and calling me to him, examined every reach and turning of the river by his glass, but finding it run a long and almost a straight course, he could find no place that he liked, but at last turning himself north, and looking down the stream, he found the river fetching a long reach, doubles short upon itself, making a round and very narrow point,

"There's a point will do our business, (says the King) and if the ground be good I will pass there, let *Tilly* do his worst."

He immediately ordered a small party of horse to view the ground, and to bring him word particularly how high the bank was on each side and at the point; and he shall have 50 dollars, says the King, that will bring me word how deep the water is. I asked his Majesty leave to let me go, which he would by no means allow; but as the party were drawing out, a sergeant of dragoons[3] told the King, if he pleased to let him go disguised as a boor, he would bring him an account of every thing he desired. The King liked the motion very well, and the fellow being well acquainted with the country, puts on a ploughman's habit, and went away immediately with a long poll upon his shoulder; the horse lay all this while in the woods, and the King stood undiscerned by the enemy on the little hill aforesaid. The dragoon with his long poll comes down boldly to the bank of the river, and calling to the centinels which *Tilly* had placed on the other bank, talked with them, asked if they could not help him over the river, and pretended he wanted to come to them; at last, being come to the point where, as I said, the river makes a short turn, he stands parlying with them a great while, and sometimes pretended to wade over, he puts his long poll into the water, then finding it pretty shallow, pulls off his hose and goes in, still thrusting his poll in before him, till being got up to the middle, he could reach beyond him, where it was too deep, and so shaking his head, comes back again. The soldiers on the other side laughing at him, asked him if he could swim? He said no. Why you fool you, says one of the centinels, the channel of the river is 20 feet deep. How do you know that, says the dragoon. Why our engineer, says he, measured it yesterday. This was what he wanted, but not yet fully satisfied; ay, but, says he, may be it may not be very broad, and if one of you would wade in to meet me till I could reach you with my poll, I would give him half a ducat to pull me over. The innocent way of his discourse so deluded the soldiers, that one of them immediately strips and goes in up to the shoulders, and our dragoon goes in on this side to meet him; but the stream took the other soldier away, and he being a good swimmer, came over to this side. The dragoon was then in a great deal of pain for fear of being discovered, and was once going to kill the fellow, and make off; but at last resolved to carry on the humour, and having entertained the man with a tale of a tub,[4] about the *Swedes* stealing his oats, the fellow being cold wanted to be gone, and he as willing to be rid of him, pretended to be very sorry he could not get over the river, and so makes off.

By this, however, he learned both the depth and breadth of the channel, the bottom and nature of both shores, and every thing the King wanted to know; we could see him from the hill by our glasses very plain, and could see the soldier naked with him: he is a fool, says the King, he does not kill the fellow and run off; but when the dragoon told his tale, the King was extremely well satisfied with him, gave him 100 dollars, and made him a quarter-master to a troop of cuirassiers.

The King having further examined the dragoon, he gave him a very distinct account of the ground on this side, which he found to be higher than the enemy's by 10 or 12 feet, and a hard gravel.—Hereupon the King resolves to pass there, and in order to it gives, himself, particular directions for such a bridge as I believe never army passed a river on before or since.

His bridge was only loose planks laid upon large tressels in the same homely manner I have seen bricklayers raise a low scaffold to build a brick wall; the tressels were made higher than one another to answer to the river as it became deeper or shallower, and was all framed and fitted before any appearance was made of attempting to pass.—When all were ready the King brings his army down to the bank of the river, and plants his cannon as the enemy had done, some here and some there, to amuse them.

At night, *April* 4th, the King commanded about 2000 men to march to the point, and to throw up a trench on either side, and quite round it with a battery of six pieces of cannon at each end, beside three small mounts, one at the point and one at each side, which had each two pieces upon them. This work was begun so briskly, and so well carried on, the King firing all night from the other parts of the river, that by daylight all the batteries at the new work were mounted, the trench lined with 2000 musqueteers, and all the utensils of the bridge lay ready to be put together.

Now the *Imperialists* discovered the design, but it was too late to hinder it, the musqueteers in the great trench, and the five new batteries, made such continual fire that the other bank, which, as before, lay 12 feet below them, was too hot for the *Imperialists*; whereupon *Tilly*, to be provided for the King at his coming over, falls to work in a wood right against the point, and raises a great battery for 20 pieces of cannon, with a breast-work, or line, as near the river as he could, to cover his men,[5] thinking that when the King had built his bridge he might easily beat it down with his cannon.

But the King had double prevented him, first by laying his bridge so low that none of *Tilly's* shot could hurt it; for the bridge lay not above half a foot above the water's surface, by which means the King, who in that shewed himself an excellent engineer, had secured it from any batteries being made within the land, and the angle of the bank secured it from the remoter batteries, on the other side, and the continual fire of the cannon and small shot, beat the *Imperialists* from their station just against it, they having no works to cover them.

And in the second place, to secure his passage he sent over about 200 men, and after that 200 more, who had orders to cast up a large ravelin[6] on the other bank, just where he designed to land his bridge; this was done with such expedition too, that it was finished before night, and in a condition to receive all the shot of *Tilly's* great battery, and effectually covered his bridge. While this was doing the King on his side lays over his bridge. Both sides wrought hard all day and all night, as if the spade, not the sword, had been to decide the controversy, and that he had got the victory whose trenches and batteries were first ready; in the mean time the cannon and musquet bullets flew like hail, and made the service so hot, that both sides had enough to do to make their men stand to their work; the King in the hottest of it, animated his men by his presence, and *Tilly*, to give him his due, did the same; for the execution was so great, and so many officers killed, General *Attringer*[7] wounded, and two sergeant-majors killed, that at last *Tilly* himself was obliged to be exposed, and to come up to the very face of our line to encourage his men, and give his necessary orders.

And here about one o'clock, much about the time that the King's bridge and works were finished, and just as they said he had ordered to fall on upon our ravelin with 3000 foot, was the brave old *Tilly* slain with a musquet bullet in the thigh; he was carried off to *Ingolstat*, and lived some days after, but died of the wound the same day that the King had his horse shot under him at the siege of that town.

We made no question of passing the river here, having brought every thing so forward, and with such extraordinary success, but we should have found it a very hot piece of work if *Tilly* had lived one day more; and if I may give my opinion of it, having seen *Tilly's* battery and breast-work, in the face of which we must have passed the river, I must say, that whenever we had marched, if *Tilly* had fallen in with his horse and foot, placed in that trench, the whole army would have passed as much in danger as in the face of a strong town in the storming a counterscarp. The King himself, when he saw with what judgment *Tilly* had prepared his works, and what danger he must have run, would often say, that day's success was every way equal to the victory of *Leipsick*.

Tilly being hurt and carried off, as if the soul of the army had been lost, they began to draw off; the Duke of *Bavaria* took horse and rode away as if he had fled out of battle for life.

*   *   *   *

The country being by this time alarmed, and the rout of our army every where known, we foresaw abundance of difficulties before us; we were not strong enough to venture into any great towns, and we were too many to be concealed in small ones. Upon this we resolved to halt in a great wood about three miles beyond the place, where we had the last skirmish, and sent out scouts to discover the country, and to learn what they could, either of the enemy, or of our friends.

Any body may suppose we had but indifferent quarters here, either for ourselves or for our horses; but however, we made shift to lie here two days and one night. In the interim I took upon me, with two more, to go to *Leeds* to learn some news; we were disguised like country ploughmen; the cloaths we got at a farmer's house, which for that odd occasion we plundered; and I cannot say no blood was shed in a manner too rash, and which I could not have done at another time; but our case was desperate, and the people too surly, shot at us out of the window, wounded one man and shot a horse, which we counted as great a loss to us as a man, for our safety depended upon our horses. Here we got cloaths of all sorts enough for both sexes, and thus dressing myself up *a la paisant*, with a white cap on my head, and a fork on my shoulder, and one of my comrades in the farmer's wife's russet gown and petticoat, like a woman; the other with an old crutch like a lame man, and all mounted on such horses as we had taken the day before from the country. Away we set off for *Leeds* by three several ways, and agreed to meet upon the bridge. My pretended country woman acted her part to the life, though he was a gentleman of good quality of the Earl of *Worcester's* family, and the cripple did as well as he; but I thought myself very awkward in my dress, which made me very shy, especially among the soldiers. We passed their centinels and guards at *Leeds* unobserved, and put up our horses at several houses in the town, from whence we went up and down to make our remarks.[8] My cripple was the fittest to go among the soldiers, because there was less danger of being pressed.[9] There he informed himself of the matters of war, particularly, that the enemy sat down again to the siege of *York*; that flying parties were in pursuit of the cavaliers; and there he heard that 500 horse of Lord *Manchester's* had followed a party of cavaliers over *Bramhammoor*; and, that entering a lane, the cavaliers, who were 1000 strong, fell upon them, and killed all but about 50. This, though it was a lie, was very pleasant for us to hear, knowing it were our party, because of the other part of the story, which was thus; that the cavaliers had taken possession of such a wood, where they rallied all the troops of their flying army; that they had plundered the country as they came, taking all the horses they could get; that they had plundered *Goodman Thomson's* house, which was the farmer I mentioned, and killed man, woman and child; and that they were about 2000 strong.

My other friend in women's cloaths got among the good wives at an inn, where she set up her horse, and there she heard the sad and dreadful tidings; and that this party was so strong, none of the neighbouring garrisons durst stir out; but that they had sent expresses to *York* for a party of horse to come to their assistance.

I walked up and down the town, but fancied myself so ill disguised, and so easy to be known, that I cared not to talk with any body. We met at the bridge exactly at our time, and compared our intelligence, found it answered our end of coming, and that we had nothing to do but to get back to our men; but my cripple told me, he would not stir till he bought some victuals: so away he hops with his crutch, and buys four or five great pieces of bacon, as many of hung beef, and two or three loaves; and, borrowing a sack at the inn (which I suppose he never restored) he loads his horse, and getting a large leather bottle, he filled that of *aquavitæ* instead of small beer; my woman comrade did the like.

I was uneasy in my mind, and took no care but to get out of the town, however we all came off well enough; but it was well for me I had no provisions, as you will hear presently. We came, as I said, into the town by different ways, and so we went out; but about three miles from the town we met again exactly where we had agreed: I being about a quarter of a mile from the rest, met three country fellows on horseback; one had a long pole on his shoulder, another a fork, the third no weapon at all, that I saw; I gave them the road very orderly, being habited like one of their brethren; but one of them stopping short at me, and looking earnestly, calls out, "Hark thee, friend (says he, in a broad north country tone) whar hast thou thilk horse?" I must confess, I was in the utmost confusion at the question, neither being able to answer it, or speak in his tone; so I seemed as if I did not hear him, and went on. "Na, but ye's not gang foa," says the boor, and comes up to me, and took hold of the bridle to stop me; at which, vexed at heart that I could not tell how to talk to him, I reached him a great knock on the pate with my fork, and fetched him off his horse, and then began to mend my pace. The other clowns, though it seems they knew not what the fellow wanted pursued me, and finding they had better heels than I, I saw there was no remedy but to make use of my hands, and faced about. The first that came up with me was he that had no weapons, so I thought I might parly with him; and, speaking as country like as I could, asked him what he wanted? "Thou'st know that soon (says *Yorkshire*) and Ise but come at thee." "Then keep awa' man (said I) or Ise brain thee." By this time the third man came up, and the parly ended; for he gave me no words but laid at me with his long pole, and that with such fury, that I began to be doubtful of him: I was loath to shoot the fellow, though I had pistols under my grey frock, as the noise of a pistol might bring more people in, the village being on our rear; and also because I could not imagine what the fellow meant, or would have; but at last finding he would be too many for me with that long weapon, and a hardy strong fellow, I threw myself off my horse, and running in with him, stabbed my fork into his horse; the horse being wounded, staggered awhile, and then fell down, and the booby had not the sense to get down in time, but fell with him; upon which, giving him a knock or two with my fork, I secured him. The other, by this time, had furnished himself with a great stick out of a hedge, and, before I was disengaged from the last fellow, gave me two such blows, that if the last had not missed my head, and hit me on the shoulder, I had ended the fight and my life altogether. It was time to look about me now, for this was a madman; I defended myself with my fork, but it would not do; at last, in short, I was forced to pistol him, and get on horse-back again, and, with all the speed I could make, to the wood to our men.

If my two fellow spies had not been behind, I had never known what was the meaning of this quarrel of the three countrymen, but my cripple had all the particulars; for he being behind us, as I have already observed, when he came up to the first fellow, who began the fray, he found him beginning to come to himself; so he gets off, pretends to help him, and sets him upon his breech, and being a very merry fellow, talked to him, "Well, and what's the matter now" (says he to him) "ah, waes me, (says the fellow) I is killed!" "Not quite, mon" (says the cripple). "O that's a fau thief," says he, and thus they parlied. My cripple got him on his feet, and gave him a dram of his *aquavitæ* bottle, and made much of him, in order to know what was the occasion of the quarrel. Our disguised woman pitied the fellow too, and together they set him up again upon his horse, and then he told them that that fellow was gone upon one of his brother's horses who lived at *Wetherby*. They said the cavaliers stole him, but it was like such rogues; no mischief could be done in the country, but it was the poor cavaliers must bear the blame, and the like; and thus they jogged on till they came to the place where the other two lay. The first fellow they assisted as they had done the other, and gave him a dram out of the leather bottle; but the last fellow was past their care, so they came away: for when they understood that it was my horse they claimed, they began to be afraid their own horses might be known too, and then they had been betrayed in a worse pickle than I, and must have been forced to have done some mischief or other to have got away.

I had sent out two troopers to fetch them off, if there was any occasion; but their stay was not long, and the two troopers saw them at a distance coming towards us, so they returned.

I had enough of going for a spy, and my companions had enough of staying in the wood; for other intelligence agreed with ours, and all concurred in this, that it was time to be going; however, this use we made of it, that while the country thought us so strong we were in the less danger of being attacked, though in the more of being observed; but all this while we heard nothing of our friends, till the next day. We heard Prince *Rupert*, with about 1000 horse, was at *Skipton*, and from thence marched away to *Westmoreland*.

We concluded now, we had two or three days good; for, since messengers were sent to *York* for a party to suppress us, we must have at least two days march of them, and therefore, all concluded we were to make the best of our way. Early in the morning, therefore, we decamped from those dull quarters; and as we marched through a village, we found the people very civil to us, and the women cried out, "God bless them, it is pity the roundheads should make such work with brave men," and the like. Finding we were among our friends, we resolved to halt a little and refresh ourselves; and, indeed, the people were very kind to us, gave us victuals and drink, and took care of our horses. It happened to be my lot to stop at a house where the good woman took a great deal of pains to provide for us; but I observed the good man walked about with a cap upon his head, and very much out of order, I took no great notice of it, being very sleepy, and having asked my landlady to let me have a bed, I lay down and slept heartily: when I awaked I found my landlord on another bed beside me groaning very heavily.

I came down stairs, and found my cripple talking to the landlady; he was now out of his disguise, but we called him cripple still; and the other, who put on the woman's cloaths, we called *Goody Thompson*. As soon as he saw me, he called me out, "Do you know (says he) the man of the house you are quartered in?" "No, not I," (replied I). "No, that I believe, nor they you (says he) if they did, the good wife would not have made you a posset, and fetched a white loaf for you." "What do you mean" (says I). "Have you seen the man?" (says he). "Seen him (replied I) yes, and heard him too; the man's sick, and groans so heavily, that I could not lie upon the bed any longer for him." "Why this is the poor man (says he) that you knocked down with your fork yesterday, and I have all the story out yonder at the next door." I confess it grieved me to have been forced to treat one so roughly who was one of our friends, but to make some amends, we contrived to give the poor man his brother's horse; and my cripple told him a formal story, that he believed the horse was taken away from the fellow by some of our men; and if he knew him again, if it was his friend's horse, he should have him. The man came down upon the news, and I caused six or seven horses, which were taken at the same time, to be shewn him; he immediately chose the right, so I gave him the horse, and we pretended a great deal of sorrow for the man's hurt; and that we had knocked the fellow on the head as well as took away the horse. The man was so overjoyed at the revenge he thought was taken on the fellow, that we heard him groan no more. We ventured to stay all day and the next night at this town, and got guides to lead us to *Blackstone-Edge*, a ridge of mountains which part this side of *Yorkshire* from *Lancashire*.

Early in the morning we marched, and kept our scouts very carefully out every way, who brought us no news for this day; we kept on all night, and made our horses do penance for the little rest they had, and the next morning we passed the hills, and got into *Lancashire*, to a town called *Littlebury*; and from thence to *Rochdale*, a little market-town. And now we thought ourselves safe as to the pursuit of enemies from the side of *York*; our design was to get to *Bolton*, but all the county was full of the enemy in flying parties, and how to get thither we knew not. At last we resolved to send a messenger to *Bolton*; but he came back and told us, he had with lurking and hiding, tried all the ways that he thought possible, but to no purpose; for he could not get into the town. We sent another, but he never returned; and some time after we understood was taken by the enemy. At last one got into the town, but brought us word, they were tired with our constant alarms, had been straitly blocked up, and every day expected a siege, and therefore, advised us either to go northward, where Prince *Rupert* and Lord *Goring*[10] ranged at liberty; or to get over *Warrington* bridge, and so secure our retreat to *Chester*.

This double direction divided our opinions; I was for getting into *Chester*, to recruit myself with horses and with money, both which I wanted, and to get refreshment, which we all stood in need of; but the major part of our men were for the north. First they said, there was their general, and it was their duty to the cause, and the King's interest obliged us to go where we could do best service; and there were their friends, and every man might hear some news of his own regiment; for we belonged to several regiments; besides, all the towns to the left of us, were possessed by Sir *William Brereton*;[11] *Warrington* and *North-wich*, garrisoned by the enemy, and a strong party at *Manchester*; so that it was very likely we should be beaten and dispersed before we could get to *Chester*. These reasons, and especially the last, determined us for the north, and we had settled to march the next morning, when other intelligence resolved us to more speedy resolutions. We kept our scouts continually abroad, to bring us in news of the enemy, whom we expected on our backs, and also to keep an eye upon the country; for as we lived upon them something at large, they were ready enough to do us any ill turn that lay in their power.

The first messenger that came to us, was from our friends at *Bolton*, to inform us, that they were preparing at *Manchester* to attack us. One of our parties had been as far as *Stockport*, on the edge of *Cheshire*, and was pursued by a party of the enemy, but got off by the help of the night. Thus all things looking black to the south, we had resolved to march northward in the morning, when one of our scouts from the side of *Manchester* assured us, Sir *Thomas Middleton*,[12] with some of the parliament forces, and the country troops, making above 1200 men, were on their march to attack us, and would certainly beat up our quarters that night. Upon this advice we resolved to be gone; and getting all things in readiness, we began to march about two hours before night: and having got a trusty fellow for a guide, a fellow that we found was a friend to our side, he put a project into my head, which saved us all for that time; and that was, to give out in the village, that we were marched back to *Yorkshire*, resolving to get into *Pontefract* castle; and accordingly, he leads us out of the town the same way we came in; and taking a boy with him, he sends the boy back just at night, and bade him say he saw us go up the hills at *Blackstone-Edge*; and it happened very well, for this party were so sure of us, that they had placed 400 men on the road to the northward, to intercept our retreat that way, and had left no way for us, as they thought, to get away, but back again.

About ten o'clock at night, they assaulted our quarters, but found we were gone; and being informed which way, they followed upon the spur, and travelled all night, being moonlight, they found themselves the next day about 15 miles east, just out of their way; for we had by the help of our guide, turned short at the foot of the hills, and through blind, untrodden paths, and with difficulty enough, by noon the next day, had reached almost 25 miles north near a town called *Clithero*. Here we halted in the open field, and sent out our people to see how things were; it was a country almost impassable, and walled round with hills, but indifferently quiet, and we got some refreshment for ourselves, but very little horsemeat, and so went on; we had not marched far before we found ourselves discovered; and the 400 horse sent to lie in wait for us as before, having understood which way we went, followed us hard; and by letters to some of their friends at *Preston*, we found we were beset again.

Our guide began now to be out of his knowledge, and our scouts brought us word, the enemy's horse were posted before us, and we knew they were in our rear. In this exigence we resolved to divide our small body, and so amusing[13] them, at least one might get off, if the other miscarried. I took about 80 horse with me, among which were all that I had of our own regiment, amounting to above 32, and took the hills towards *Yorkshire*. Here we met with such impassable hills, vast moors, rocks and stony ways, as lamed all our horses, and tired our men; and sometimes I was ready to think we should never be able to get over them, till our horses failing, and jack-boots being but indifferent things to travel in, we might be starved before we should find any road or towns, for guide we had none, except a boy who knew but little, and would cry when we asked him any questions. I believe neither man nor horse ever passed in some places where we went, and for 20 hours we saw not a town or a house, excepting sometimes from the top of mountains, at a vast distance. I am persuaded we might have encamped here, if we had had provisions, till the war had been over, and have met with no disturbance; and I have often wondered since, how we got into such horrible places, as much as how we got out. That which was worse to us than all the rest, was, that we knew not where we were going, nor what part of the country we should come into, when we got out of these desolate crags.

At last, after a terrible fatigue, we began to see the western parts of *Yorkshire*, some few villages, and the country at a distance, looked a little like *England*; for before I thought it looked a little like *Old Brennus*[14] hill, which the *Grisons* called the grandfather of the *Alps*. We got some relief in the villages, which indeed some of us had so much need of, that they were hardly able to sit their horses, and others were forced to help them off, they were so faint. I never felt so much of the power of hunger in my life; for having not eaten in 30 hours, I was ravenous as a hound; and if I had had a piece of horse-flesh, I believe I should not have had patience to waited the dressing of it, but fallen upon it raw, and have eaten it as greedily as a *Tartar*.

However, I eat very cautiously, having often seen the danger of men's eating heartily after long fasting. Our next care was to enquire the way. *Halifax*, they told us, was on our right; there we dare not think of going; *Skippon*[15] was before us, and there we knew not how it was; for a body of 3000 horse, sent out by the enemy in pursuit of Prince *Rupert*, had been there but two days before, and the country people could not tell us, whether they were gone or not: and *Manchester's*[16] horse, which were sent out after our party, were then at *Halifax*, in quest of us, and afterward marched into *Cheshire*. In this distress we would have hired a guide, but none of the country people would go with us; for the round-heads would hang them, they said, when they came there. Upon this I called a fellow to me, "Harke ye friend (says I) dost thee know the way so as to bring us into *Westmoreland*, and not keep the great road from *York?*" "Ay merry (says he) I ken the way weel enou;" "and you would go and guide us (says I) but that you are afraid the roundheads will hang you?" "Indeed would I" (says the fellow). "Why then (says I) thou hadst as good be hanged by a roundhead as a cavalier; for if thou wilt not go, I'll hang thee just now." "Na, and ye sarve me soa (says the fellow) Ise ene gang wi' ye; for I care not for hanging; and ye'll get me a horse, Ise gang and be one of ye, for I'll nere come heame mere." This pleased us still better, and we mounted the fellow; for three of our men died that night with the extreme fatigue of the last service.

Next morning, when our new trooper was mounted and cloathed, we hardly knew him; and this fellow led us by such ways, such wildernesses, and yet with such prudence, keeping the hills to the left, that we might have the villages to refresh ourselves, that without him, we had certainly either perished in those mountains, or fallen into the enemy's hands. We passed the great road from *York* so critically, as to time, that from one of the hills he shewed us a party of the enemy's horse, who were then marching into *Westmoreland*. We lay still that day, finding we were not discovered by them, and our guide proved the best scout we could have had; for he would go out ten miles at a time, and bring us in all the news of the country. Here he brought us word, that *York* was surrendered upon articles,[17] and that *Newcastle*, which had been surprised by the King's party, was besieged by another army of *Scots* advanced to help their brethren.

Along the edges of those vast mountains we passed by the help of our guide, till we came into the forest of *Swale*; and finding ourselves perfectly concealed here, for no soldier had ever been here all the war, nor perhaps would not, if it had lasted 7 years; we thought we wanted a few days rest, at least for our horses, so we resolved to halt, and while we did so, we made some disguises, and sent out some spies into the country; but as here were no great towns, nor any post road, we got very little intelligence.—We rested four days, and then marched again; and indeed having no great stock of money about us, and not very free of that we had, four days were enough for those poor places to be able to maintain us.

We thought ourselves pretty secure now; but our chief care was how to get over those terrible mountains; for having passed the great road that leads from *York* to *Lancaster*, the crags the farther northward we looked, appeared still worse, and our business was all on the other side. Our guide told us, he would bring us out, if we would have patience, which we were obliged to, and kept on this slow march, till he brought us to *Stanhope*, in the county of *Durham*; where some of *Goring's* horse, and two regiments of foot, had their quarters. This was 19 days from the battle of *Marston-moor*. The Prince who was then at *Kendal* in *Westmoreland*, who had given me over as lost, when he had news of our arrival, sent an express to me, to meet at *Appleby*. I went thither accordingly, and gave him an account of our journey, and there I heard the short history of our men, whom we parted from in *Lancashire*.

The Complete English Tradesman
1725

In this book—first published in 1725, with a second volume added in 1727—Defoe wrote some of his most lucid and urgent prose. Characteristically he was giving advice; he was drawing on his own experience as a tradesman and trying to protect his readers from the business failures he had undergone. His audience for the first volume—the second was directed to more experienced tradesmen—was clear in his mind:

> We are speaking now to a tradesman who, 'tis suppos'd, must live by his business; a young man who sets up shop, or warehouse, and expects to get money; one that would be a rich tradesman, rather than a poor, fine, gay man; a grave citizen, not a peacock's feather; for he that sets up for a *Sir Fopling Flutter*, instead of a *compleat tradesman*, is not to be thought capable of relishing this discourse; neither does this discourse relish him. (p. 142.)

So rigorous was Defoe's advice that Charles Lamb was provoked to ask:

> Was the man in earnest, when he could bring such powers of description, and all the charms of natural eloquence, in commendation of the meanest, vilest, wretchedest degradations of the human character? Or did he not rather laugh in his sleeve at the doctrines which he inculcated, and retorting upon the grave Citizens of London their own arts, palm upon them a sample of disguised Satire under the name of wholesome instruction? (*Works*, ed. E. Lucas, I (1903), 132.)

But there can be no doubt about Defoe's seriousness. The integrity, relentless industry, reliability, knowledge, and satisfaction in active achievements which he required of his 'complete tradesman' were essential qualifications for the 'true-bred merchant' whom he celebrates in the *Review* (see above, p. 120). Furthermore the book is a manifesto of the aims and an earnest of the success of the new trading gentry of wealth who could no longer be safely ignored by the established aristocracy. From this point of view the *Complete English Tradesman* and the *Compleat English Gentleman* were companion books.

With the exception of the final one, all extracts given below are taken from Volume I.

The Complete English Tradesman

Letter III   Of the Trading Stile

Sir,

In my last I gave you my thoughts for the instruction of young tradesmen in writing letters with orders, and answering orders, and especially about the proper stile of a tradesman's letters, which I hinted should be plain and easy, free in language, and direct to the purpose intended; give me leave to go on with the subject a little farther, as I think 'tis useful in another part of the tradesman's correspondence.

I might have made some apology to you for urging tradesmen to write a plain and easy stile; let me add to you, that the tradesmen need not be offended at my condemning them *as it were* to a plain and homely stile; easy, plain, and familiar language is the beauty of speech in general, and is the excellency of all writing, on whatever subject, or to whatever persons they are we write or speak. The end of speech is that men might understand one another's meaning; certainly that speech, or that way of speaking which is most easily understood, is the best way of speaking, If any man was to ask me, which would be supposed to be a perfect stile, or language, I would answer, that in which a man speaking to five hundred people, of all common and various capacities, idiots or lunaticks excepted, should be understood by them all in the same manner with one another, and in the same sense which the speaker intended to be understood, this would certainly be a most perfect stile.

ALL exotic sayings, dark and ambiguous speakings, affected words, and as I said in my last, abridgment, or words cut off, as they are foolish and improper in business, so indeed are they in any other things; hard[1] words and affectation of stile in business, is like bombast in poetry, a kind of rumbling nonsense, and nothing of the kind can be more ridiculous.

THE nicety of writing in business, consists chiefly, in giving every species of goods their trading names; for there are certain peculiarities in the trading language, which are to be observ'd as the greatest proprieties, and without which the language your letters are written in would be obscure, and the tradesmen you write to would not understand you: for example, if you write to your factor at *Lisbon*, or at *Cadiz*, to make your returns in *hard ware*, he understands you, and sends you so many bags of pieces of eight. So if a merchant comes to me to hire a small ship of me, and tells me 'tis for the pipin trade; or to buy a vessel, and tells me he intends to make a *pipiner* of her, the meaning is, that she is to run to *Seville* for oranges, or to *Malaga* for lemons. If he says he intends to send her for a lading of fruit, the meaning is, she is to go to *Alicant*, *Denia*, or *Xevia*, on the coast of *Spain*, for raisins of the sun, or to *Malaga* for *Malaga* raisins. Thus in the home trade in *England*, if in *Kent* a man tells me he is to go among the *night riders*, his meaning is he is to go a carrying wool to the sea-shore; the people that usually run the wool off in boats, are called *owlers*; those that steal customs, smugglers; and the like. In a word, there is a kind of a cant in trade, which a tradesman ought to know, as the beggars and strollers know the gypsy cant, which none can speak but themselves; and this in letters of business is allowable, and indeed they cannot understand one another without it.

A brickmaker being hired by a brewer to make some bricks for him at his country-house, wrote to the brewer that he could not go forward unless he had two or three load of *spanish*; and that otherwise his bricks would cost him six or seven chaldron[2] of coals extraordinary, and the bricks would not be so good and hard neither by a great deal, when they were burnt.

THE brewer sends him an answer, that he should go on as well as he could for three or four days, and then the *spanish* should be sent him: accordingly, the following week the brewer sends him down two carts loaded with about twelve hogsheads or casks of *molasses*; which frighted the brickmaker almost out of his senses. The case was this, the brewers formerly mixt *molasses* with their ale, to sweeten it, and abate the quantity of malt, *molasses* being at that time much cheaper in proportion; and this they call'd *spanish*, not being willing that people should know it. Again, the brickmakers all about *London*, do mix sea-coal-ashes, or laystal-stuff, as we call it, with their clay of which they make brick, and by that shift save eight chaldron of coals out of eleven, in proportion to what other people use to burn them with; and these ashes they call *spanish*.

Thus the receiv'd terms of art in every particular business are to be observed; of which I shall speak to you in its turn: I name them here to intimate, that when I am speaking of plain writing in matters of business, it must be understood with an allowance for all these things: and a tradesman must be not only allowed to use them in his stile, but cannot write proper without them; it is a particular excellence in a tradesman to be able to know all the terms of art in every separate business, so as to be able to speak or write to any particular handicraft or manufacturer in his own dialect; and it is as necessary as it is for a seaman to understand the names of all the several things belonging to a ship.

THIS therefore is not to be understood when I say that a tradesman should write plain and explicit, for these things belong to, and are part of the language of trade.

BUT even these terms of art, or customary expressions, are not to be used with affection, and with a needless repetition, where they are not called for.

Nor should a tradesman write those *out of the way* words, tho' 'tis in the way of the business he writes about, to any other person, who he knows, or has reason to believe, does not understand them; I say, he ought not to write in those terms to such, because it shews a kind of ostentation, and a triumph over the ignorance of the person they are written to, unless at the very same time you add an explanation of the terms, so as to make them assuredly intelligible at the place, and to the person to whom they are sent.

A tradesman, in such cases, like a parson, should suit his language to his auditory; and it would be as ridiculous for a tradesman to write a letter fill'd with the peculiarities of this or that particular trade, which trade he knows the person he writes to is ignorant of, and the terms whereof he is unacquainted with, as it would be for a minister to quote *Chrysostome* and St. *Austin*, and repeat at large all their sayings in the *Greek* and the *Latin*, in a country church among a parcel of plowmen and farmers. Thus a sailor writing a letter to a surgeon, told him he had a swelling on the North-East side of his face, that his windward leg being hurt by a bruise, it so put him out of trim that he always heel'd to starboard when he made fresh way, and so run to leeeward till he was often forced aground; then he desired him to give him some directions how to put himself into a sailing posture again. Of all which the surgeon understood little more than that he had a swelling on his face, and a bruise in his leg.

It would be a very happy thing, if tradesmen had all their *lexicon technicum* at their fingers ends; I mean, (for pray remember that *I observe my own rule*, not to use *a hard word without explaining it*,) that every tradesman would study so the terms of art of other trades, that he might be able to speak to every manufacturer or artist in his own language, and understand them when they talk'd one to another; this would make trade be a kind of universal language, and the particular marks they are oblig'd to, would be like the notes of music, an universal character, in which all the tradesmen in *England* might write to one another in the language and characters of their several trades, and be as intelligible to one another as the minister is to his people, *and perhaps much more.*

*   *   *   *

Among the many turnings and by-lanes which, as I say, are to be met with in the strait road of trade, there are two as dangerous and fatal to their prosperity as the worst, tho' they both carry an appearance of good, and promise contrary to what they perform; these are,

I. Pleasures and Diversions, especially such as they will have us call *innocent Diversions.*

II. Projects and Adventures, and especially such as promise mountains of profit *in nubibus,* and are therefore the more likely to ensnare the poor eager avaritious tradesman.

1. I am now to speak of the first, *viz.* pleasures and diversions. I cannot allow any pleasures to be innocent, when they turn away either the body or the mind of a tradesman from the one needful thing which his calling makes necessary, and that necessity makes his duty; I mean, the application both of his hands and head to his business; those pleasures and diversions may be innocent in themselves, which are not so to him: there are very few things in the world that are simply evil, but things are made circumstantially evil when they are not so in themselves: killing a man is not simply sinful; on the contrary, 'tis not lawful only, but a duty, when justice and the laws of God or man require it; but when done maliciously, from any corrupt principle, or to any corrupted end, is murther, and the worst of crimes.

PLEASURES and diversions are thus made criminal, when a man is engaged in duty to a full attendance upon such business as those pleasures and diversions necessarily interfere with, and interrupt; those pleasures, tho' innocent in themselves, become a fault in him, because his legal avocations demand his attendance in another place. Thus those pleasures may be lawful to another man, which are not so to him, because another man has not the same obligation to a calling, the same necessity to apply to it, the same cry of a family, whose bread may depend upon his diligence, as a tradesman has.

SOLOMON, the royal patron of industry, tells us, *He that is a lover of pleasure, shall be a poor man;*[3] I must not doubt but *Solomon* is to be understood of *tradesmen* and *working men,* such as I am writing of, whose time and application is due to their business, and who in persuit of their *pleasures,* are sure to neglect their shops, or employments, and I therefore render the words thus, to the present purpose, *The tradesman that is a lover of pleasure, shall be a poor man.* I hope I do not wrest the scripture in my interpretation of it, I am sure it agrees with the whole *tenor* of the wiseman's other discourses.

WHEN I see young shop-keepers keep horses, ride a hunting, learn dog-language, and keep the sportsmens brogue upon their tongues, I will not say I read their destiny, for I am no *fortune-teller;* but I do say, I am always afraid for them; especially when I know that either their fortunes and beginnings are below it, or that their trades are such as in a particular manner require their constant attendance; as to see a barber abroad on a *Saturday,* a corn-factor abroad on a *Wednesday* and *Friday,* or a *Blackwell-hall* man[4] on a *Thursday,* you may as well say a country shop-keeper should go a hunting on a market-day, or go a feasting at the fair-day of the town where he lives; and yet riding and hunting are otherwise lawful diversions, and in their kind very good for exercise and health.

I am not for making a galley-slave of a shop-keeper, and have him chain'd down to the oar; but if he be a wise, a prudent and a diligent tradesman, he will allow himself as few excursions as possible.

BUSINESS neglected is business lost; 'tis true, there are some businesses which require less attendance than others, and give a man less occasion of application; but in general, that *tradesman* who can satisfy himself to be absent from his business, must not expect success; if he is above the character of a diligent tradesman, he must then be above the business too, and should leave it to somebody that having more need of it will think it worth his while to mind it better.

NOR indeed is it possible a tradesman should be master of any of the qualifications which I have set down to denominate him *complete*, if he neglects his shop and his time, following his pleasures and diversions.

I'LL allow that the man is not vicious and wicked, that he is not addicted to drunkenness, to women, to gaming, or any such things as those, for those are not woundings, but murther, downright killing; a man may wound and hurt himself sometimes, in the rage of an ungovern'd passion, or in a frenzy or fever, and intend no more; but if he shoots himself thro' the head, or hangs himself, we are sure then he intended to kill and destroy himself, and he dies inevitably.

FOR a tradesman to follow his pleasures, which indeed is generally attended with a slighting his business, leaving his shop to servants or others, 'tis evident to me that he is indifferent whether it thrives or no; and above all, 'tis evident, that his heart is not in his business; that he does not delight in it, or look on it with pleasure. To a complete tradesman there is no pleasure equal to that of being in his business, no delight equal to that of seeing himself thrive, to see trade flow in upon him, and to be satisfied that he goes on prosperously: He will never thrive, that cares not whether he thrives or no: As trade is the chief employment of his life, and is therefore called, by way of eminence, *his business*; so it should be made the chief delight of his life: The tradesman that does not love his business, will never give it due attendance. . . .

IN short, pleasure is a *thief* to business: how any man can call it innocent, let him answer that does so; it robs him every way, as I have said above; and if the tradesman be a christian, and has any regard to religion and his duty, I must tell him, that when, upon his disasters, he shall reflect, and see that he has ruin'd himself and his family, by following too much those diversions and pleasures which he thought innocent, and which perhaps in themselves were really so, he will find great cause to repent of that which he insisted on as innocent; he will find himself lost, by doing lawful things, and that he made those innocent things sinful, and those lawful things unlawful to him. Thus, as they robb'd his family and creditors before of their just debts, (for maintenance is a tradesman's just debt to his family, and a wife and children are as much a tradesman's real creditors, as those who trusted him with their goods;) I say, as his innocent pleasures robb'd his family and creditors before, they will rob him now of his peace, and of all that calm of soul which an honest, industrious, tho' unfortunate tradesman meets with under his disasters.

I am ask'd here, perhaps, how much pleasure an honest-meaning tradesman may be allow'd to take? for it cannot be suppos'd I should insist that all pleasure is forbidden him, that he must have no diversion, no spare hours, no intervals from hurry and fatigue; that would be to pin him down to the very floor of his shop, as *John Sheppard*5 was lock'd down to the floor of his prison.

THE answer to this question every prudent tradesman may make for himself; if his pleasure is in his shop, and in his business, there is no danger of him; but if he has an itch after exotick diversions, I mean such as are foreign to his shop, and to his business, and which I therefore call *exotick*, let him honestly and fairly state the case between his shop and his diversions, and judge impartially for himself; so much pleasure, and no more, may be innocently taken, as does not interfere with, or do the least damage to his business, by taking him away from it.

EVERY moment that his trade wants him in his shop, or ware-house, &c. 'tis his duty to be there; 'tis not enough to say, I believe I shall not be wanted; or, I believe I shall suffer no loss by my absence; he must come to a point, and not deceive himself, if he does, the cheat is all his own: if he will not judge sincerely at first, he will reproach himself sincerely at last; for there is no fraud against his own reflections, a man is very rarely an hypocrite to himself.

THE rule may be, in a few words thus: Those pleasures or diversions, and those only, can be innocent, which the man may or does use, or allow himself to use, without hindrance of, or injury to, his business and reputation.

*   *   *   *

HAVING thus done a particular piece of justice to ourselves, in the value we put upon trade and tradesmen in *England*, it reflects very much upon the understandings of those refin'd heads, who *pretend to* depreciate that part of the nation, which is so infinitely superiour in number and in wealth to the families who call themselves gentry, or quality, and so infinitely more numerous.

As to the wealth of the nation, that undoubtedly lies chiefly among the trading part of the people; and tho' there are a great many families rais'd within few years, in the late war by great employments, and by great actions abroad, to the honour of the *English* gentry; yet how many more families among the tradesmen have been rais'd to immense estates, even during the same time, by the attending circumstances of the war? such as the cloathing, the paying, the victualling and furnishing, &c. both army and navy? And by whom have the prodigious taxes been paid, the loans supplied, and money advanced upon all occasions? By whom are the Banks and Companies carried on? And on whom are the Customs and Excises levied? Has not the trade and tradesmen born the burthen of the war? And do they not still pay four millions a year interest for the publick debts? On whom are the funds levied, and by whom the publick credit supported? Is not trade the inexhausted fund of all funds, and upon which all the rest depend?

As is the trade, so in proportion are the tradesmen; and how wealthy are tradesmen in almost all the several parts of *England*, as well as in *London?* How ordinary is it to see a tradesman go off of the stage, even but from mere shop-keeping, with, from ten to forty thousand pounds estate, to divide among his family? when, on the contrary, take the gentry in *England* from one end to the other, except a few here and there, what with excessive high living, which is of late grown so much into a disease, and the other ordinary circumstances of families, we find few families of the lower gentry, that is to say, from six or seven hundred a year downwards, but they are in debt and in necessitous circumstances, and a great many of greater estates also.

ON the other hand, let any one who is acquainted with *England*, look but abroad into the several counties, especially near *London*, or within fifty miles of it: How are the ancient families worn out by time and family misfortunes, and the estates possess'd by a new race of tradesmen, grown up into families of gentry, and establish'd by the immense wealth, gain'd, as I may say, behind the counter; that is, in the shop, the warehouse, and the compting-house? How are the sons of tradesmen rank'd among the prime of the gentry? How are the daughters of tradesmen at this time adorn'd with the ducal coronets, and seen riding in the coaches of the best of our nobility? Nay, many of our trading gentlemen at this time refuse to be Ennobled, scorn being knighted, and content themselves with being known to be rated among the richest Commoners in the nation: And it must be acknowledg'd, that whatever they be as to court-breeding, and to manners, they, generally speaking, come behind none of the gentry in knowledge of the world.

AT this very day we see the son of Sir *Thomas Scawen*[6] match'd into the ducal family of *Bedford*, and the son of Sir *James Bateman*[7] into the princely house of *Marlborough*, both whose ancestors, within the memory of the writer of these sheets, were tradesmen in *London*; the first Sir *William Scawen*'s apprentice, and the latter's grandfather a P—— upon, or near, *London-Bridge*.

How many noble seats, superior to the palaces of sovereign Princes (in some countries) do we see erected within few miles of this city by tradesmen, or the sons of tradesmen, while the seats and castles of the ancient gentry, like their families, look *worn out*, and fallen into *decay*; witness the noble house of Sir

John Eyles,[8] himself a Merchant, at *Giddy-hall* near *Rumford*; Sir *Gregory Page*[9] on *Black-heath*, the son of a *Brewer*; Sir *Nathanael Mead*[10] near *Weal-green*, his father a *Linen-Draper*, with many others, too long to repeat; and to crown all, the Lord *Castlemain's*[11] at *Wanstead*, his father Sir *Josiah Child* originally a Tradesman.

IT was a smart, but just repartee of a *London* tradesman, when a gentleman, *who had a good estate too*, rudely reproach'd him in company, and bad him hold his tongue, for he was no Gentleman; *No, Sir*, says he, *but I can buy a Gentleman*, and therefore I claim a liberty to speak among Gentlemen.

AGAIN, in how superior a port or figure (as we now call it) do our tradesmen live, to what the middling gentry either do or can support? An ordinary tradesman now, not in the city only, but in the country, shall spend more money by the year, than a gentleman of four or five hundred pounds a year can do; and shall encrease and lay up every year too; whereas the gentleman shall at the best stand stock still, just where he began, nay, perhaps decline; and as for the lower gentry, from an hundred pounds a year to three hundred, or thereabouts, *though they are often as proud and high in their appearance as the other*; as to them, I say, a *Shoemaker* in *London* shall keep a better house, spend more money, cloath his family better, and yet grow rich too: It is evident where the difference lies, *an Estate's a pond*, but *a Trade's a spring*; The first, if it keeps full, and the water wholesom, by the ordinary supplies and dreins from the neighbouring grounds, 'tis well, and 'tis all that is expected; but the other is an inexhausted current, which not only fills the pond, and keeps it full, but is continually running over, and fills all the lower ponds and places about it.

THIS being the case in *England*, and our trade being so vastly great, it is no wonder that the tradesmen in *England* fill the lists of our nobility and gentry; no wonder that the gentlemen of the best families marry tradesmen's daughters, and put their younger sons apprentices to tradesmen; and how often do these younger sons come to buy the elder sons estates, and restore the family, when the elder, and head of the house, proving rakish and extravagant, has wasted his patrimony, and is obliged to make out the blessing of *Israel's* family, where the younger son bought the birth-right, and the elder was doom'd to serve him?[12]

TRADE is so far *here* from being inconsistent with a Gentleman, that *in short* trade in *England* makes Gentlemen, and has peopled this nation with Gentlemen; for after a generation or two the tradesmen's children, or at least their grand-children, come to be as good Gentlemen, Statesmen, Parliament-men, Privy-Counsellors, Judges, Bishops, and Noblemen, as those of the highest birth and the most antient families; and nothing too high for them: Thus the late Earl of *Haversham*[13] was originally a Merchant, the late Secretary

Craggs[14] was the son of a *Barber*; the present Lord *Castlemain's* father was a Tradesman; the great grandfather of the present Duke of *Bedford*[15] the same, and so of several others: Nor do we find any defect either in the genius or capacities of the posterity of tradesmen, arising from any remains of mechanick blood, which 'tis pretended should influence them; but all the gallantry of spirit, greatness of soul, and all the generous principles, that can be found in any of the antient families, whose blood is the most untainted, as they call it, with the low mixtures of a mechanick race, are found in these; and, as is said before, they generally go beyond them in knowledge of the world, which is the best education.

* * * *

THE Compleat Tradesman, I say, should be a Man of Sense; what if it is not absolutely necessary he should be what we call a Man of Parts? He should, nay, he must, have Knowledge competent to his Business. As to Learning, it is not absolutely necessary he should understand *Greek* and *Latin*; but 'tis absolutely necessary he should understand Trade and Business: Tho' he need not be a Man of Letters, he ought to be a Man of Figures; as a Carpenter need not understand Mr. *Whiston's* Astronomical Tables,[16] yet he ought to be Master of *Gunter's Scale*,[17] and know how to measure by his Rule and his Compass.

THERE are many Studies as remote from a Tradesman as the *Greek Grammar* is from the *English Primmer*; but it does not follow, therefore, that the Tradesman must know nothing but his Weights and Measures: As I say in my Title, he need not be a *Wit*, but he should not be a *Dunce*: He need not be a Poet or a Pedant; but he should not be a dull sleepy Thing, that has no Genius to any Thing, but just what he has before him; he should have some Spirit and Life in his Business.

THERE are *thin-headed* Fellows, who are all Flutter and Fancy, that are too volatile for a Shop or Warehouse, and are fitter for Dancing Masters than Tradesmen; and there are *thick-headed* Fellows on the other hand, who must have every Thing beaten into them, as Men cleave Blocks, with Beetle and Wedges.

THE Compleat Tradesman is the Middle among these Extremes; he knows more than he has an immediate Use for, and is capable of learning more than he knows; he loves Knowledge enough to make him seek it, and knows he wants it enough to make him love it; he has Knowledge enough to make him diligent, and not so much as to make him loose and aspiring.

ONE of the best Parts of Knowledge the Tradesman in good Business can have, is to know *when he is well*; be contented to go on where he is, keep the Road, not straggling into unknown By-paths of Trade, which he has never travelled in before, and where he does not know the Way in, or the Way out, but may be lost before he can look around him. Over much searching after more Business, when he has enough already, grasping when he has his Hands full, and hatching more, when he is as full as he can hold, is a trading Evil, and generally is fatal to the Tradesmen; 'tis like a Sow bringing forth more Pigs than she can suckle, or a Hen laying more Eggs than she can cover.

THE ploding fair-driving Tradesman, that goes on safe and sure, and is always moving; he, I say, is the Man that bids fairest to be rich: The Coach and the Chariot gallop, and drive, and the Posts[18] whip and spur; but the Plowman and the Carrier go soft and fair, and yet the last come with the greatest Certainty to the End of their Journey, and draw or carry the greatest Burden.

THE *English* Carriage, which we use in drawing the greatest Burdens or Loads, I mean such as draw Timber, and are, in our modern Usage, call'd a Wain or Carriage, are in *Kent* and *Sussex* called a *Tug*, from the old *Saxon* Language, signifying Hard Labour; and the *Waggon* has its Derivation from the same Language, wherein the Words are usually expressive of the Manner or Thing which they are used for; as the *Waggon* is a Carriage, which being heavy loaden, does but just WAG ON; but still 'tis observ'd, it keeps wagging, and it always goes on; and as softly as it goes, we see some of our Carriers come as far as from *Exeter*, a hundred and fifty Miles to *London*, with forty to fifty Hundred Weight, and make their Journeys constantly, wet or dry, dark or light, blow high, blow low, still, according to their true original Name, and the Meaning of it, they WAG ON.

THUS the prudent Tradesman, that goes on carefully and gently, lets no Irons burn, and yet lets no Irons cool; he truly drives his Trade, but does not push it; keeps it going, but does not over-run it; keeps in his own Orbit, and within the Circle of his own diurnal Revolution: This is in a Word the Compleat Tradesman.

Now, as I said, this Tradesman should neither be a Wit or a Fool: My Reason is this; I do not think a Man can have too much Wit, let his Calling or Employment be what it will, provided there is a due Weight of Judgment and Experience to ballance this Wit; for there is a manifest Difference between Wit and Judgment, not in the Nature of them only, but in their Operation also; and indeed, they will neither of them be able to shew their Value alone. Like *Spanish* Wool in the *English* Manufacture, they are too fine to work by themselves; and, as Silver, is too brittle to work without its Aloy: There must be a Mixture of Judgment to keep the Wit solid.

> *Wit, without Sense, is like the laughing Evil,*
> *While Sense unmix'd with Fancy, is the Devil.*[19]

WIT, like Mercury and Quicksilver, is of Use to make the Silver Ore run, and separate the Sterling from the Dross; but bring it to the Crucible by itself, it flies up into the Air, like a true Spirit, and is lost at once, and who can fix it again afterwards.

A Wit, turn'd Tradesman! what an incongruous Part of Nature is there brought together, consisting of direct Contraries? No Apron Strings will hold him; 'tis in vain to lock him in behind the Compter, he's gone in a Moment; instead of Journal and Ledger, he runs away to his *Virgil* and *Horace*; his Journal Entries are all Pindaricks, and his Ledger is all Heroicks; he is truly dramatick from one End to the other, through the whole Scene of his Trade; and as the first Part is all Comedy, so the two last Acts are always made up with Tragedy; a Statute of Bankrupt is his *Exeunt omnes*, and he generally speaks the Epilogue in the *Fleet Prison* or the *Mint*. Again, take the Fool-Tradesman, the thick-headed Wretch, that has nothing bright about him;[20] no Genius neither for one or other; he should have been the Manufacturer, not the Factor; he should have stood by the Shuttle and the Warping-Mill, not come to the Buying and Selling; indeed he is a kind of natural Mechanick, *viz*. Nature cut him out to be a meer Mechanick, not a Tradesman; to make the Work, not buy and sell it; and he is out of his Element when he is out of the Loom.

INDEED, when you see him in the Shop or the Warehouse, he seems to be a little like the Shuttle that the Weaver throws backward and forward, he is ever going just the same Pace, and keeps the same Road: This backward and forward is the only Motion, for ought I know, in all Natures Engines, that is not circular; 'tis the Pendulum of the Manufacture, which regulates and measures the rest of its Motions, and makes all the circular Motions be exact.

THIS Man is no more fit for a Tradesman than the fluttering Shuttlecock-Tradesman mentioned above as a Wit: If the Tradesman is a Man of Wit, a Man of bright Thoughts, has a Touring Fancy, a Profusion of polite Ideas, let him make it his Business to keep all those fine Parts of Nature's Imagery within Bounds; let him make use of them like fine Paintings, to be hanged up in his Hall, and grace the Entrance; let him garnish his Soul with them as much as he pleases, and shew them as much as he finds Occasion, but not take them down, and displace them.

THE finest Accomplishments of Nature may do the Tradesman no Harm, if he can keep this Magazine of Gunpowder from the Fire; but if he brings the Candle to it, or brings the Powder to the Candle, he is gone, he is sure to be blown up: Pictures taken down from the Wall, and set one before another, with their painted Sides inward, are the worst Furniture in the House, and like a fine brocaded Silk, are beautiful on one Side, but all Rags and Ends on the other.

THE Brightness of the Tradesman's Head, the Clearness of his Thought, the

Elevation of his Fancy, they are all *out-of-the-way Things* to the poor Man in his Business, and serve only to set him up in a Station above himself; make him fancy himself framed by Nature for other Things than the Compter or the Compting-House; and so set his Pride a tip-toe, bloating it up into Conceit; and thus the Man is undone. . . .

AMBITION and aspiring Thought are Plagues and Diseases to a Tradesman: When they work in his Mind, his Friends should get his Head shav'd, and put him into a dark House[21] for a little while, administring proper Physick to him, to keep him from the Vapours; and that the Cure might be wrought upon his Understanding, it should be first wrought upon his Body, for the desir'd Effect.

THE Tradesman should be wise rather than witty; he should be as wise as he can in his Business; and though he passes for *no Body* among the Beaus, and Wits of the Town, Nature's Weather-Cocks, and the Froth and Flutter of the Creation, he will be *some Body* in his own Way, and build upon a Foundation, that his Posterity may have Room to value themselves upon; and if he cannot be a Gentleman, he may be able to buy a Gentleman, and that's enough to him.

BUSINESS is a Thing suited to a staid Head; it does not require the polite Part of human Understanding, or call for a liberal Education; and it is the Tradesman's Mercy that it is so: But at the same Time he knows little of Business, who thinks a Tradesman may be a Fool, an Idiot, or a Natural.[22]

IT is a poor Pittance of human Nature, that these Men will allow to a Tradesman, that they will allow him neither Sense or Honesty; that he need not be a wise Man, and is bound to be a K[nave]; that he needs no Wit, and can have no Honour: But such Men forget that the Honesty and the Wit are Assistants to one another, and that the Tradesman that is a K[nave], is generally so for want of Sense: I do confess 'tis very hard for the Fool-Tradesman to be an honest Man, and there I believe the Scandal began; but if he is a Man of Sense, that Sense is the Protection of his Principles, and he is honest because he is wise, as he is rich because he is diligent.

The History of the Pyrates   1728

Defoe's interest in rogues of various kinds is clear: *Moll Flanders*, *Roxana* and *Colonel Jack* provide evidence enough. But piracy held a particular fascination not least because, about 1683, he had been captured by Algerian pirates; Robinson Crusoe is held prisoner by Moorish pirates and Captain Singleton has a successful career as a pirate. Defoe's love of excitement, adventure, travel, as well as commerce found a special satisfaction in tales of piratical exploits. A more profound interest was also satisfied by the opportunity to study human responses to a situation in which normal governmental or social disciplines were withdrawn; a similar fascination obviously operates in *Robinson Crusoe* where man in a state of nature is compelled to develop laws and government for himself. Furthermore *The History of the Pyrates* enabled Defoe to satirize English society in a way that recalls Gay in *The Beggar's Opera* (1728): social outcasts comment by word and deed on the corruptions practised by the ruling class in England, often showing themselves motivated by higher ideals of justice and equity, and certainly revealing greater courage. In the account of the life of Captain Misson (ed. M. Novak, Augustan Reprint Society, 1961), for example, Defoe shows a man who abhorred unnecessary violence, proposed to use his power of command 'for the publick Good only', held that the rôle of men in authority was as 'Guardians of the Peoples Rights and Liberties', and refused to trade in slaves because 'no Man had Power of the Liberty of another . . . he had not exempted his Neck from the galling Yoak of Slavery, and asserted his own Liberty, to enslave Others'. Misson is an idealized figure in many respects, but the kind of thinking embodied in him also lies behind the extract printed below.

Volume I, *The General History of the Pyrates*, was published in 1724; Vol. II, *The History of the Pyrates*, from which *Captain Bellamy* is taken, appeared in 1728. The pseudonymous author of both volumes is 'Capt. Charles Johnson'.

The History of the Pyrates

Of Capt. Bellamy

As we cannot, with any Certainty, deduce this Man from his Origin, we shall begin where we find him first a declared Enemy to Mankind. Capt. *Bellamy* and *Paul Williams*,[1] in two Sloops, had been upon a *Spanish* Wreck, and not finding their Expectation answered, as has been mentioned in former Parts of this History, they resolved not to lose their Labour, and agreed to go upon the Account,[2] a Term among the Pyrates, which speaks their Profession. The first, who had the Misfortune to fall in their Way, was Captain *Prince*, bound from *Jamaica* to *London*, in a Galley built at that Port, whose Cargo consisted of Elephants Teeth, Gold Dust, and other rich Merchandize. This Prize not only enrich'd, but strengthened them; they immediately mounted this Galley with 28 Guns, and put aboard 150 Hands of different Nations; *Bellamy* was declared Captain, and the Vessel had her old Name continued, which was *Whidaw*: This happen'd about the latter End of *February*, 1717. They, now thus fitted for the continuing of their desperate Resolution, shaped their Course for *Virginia*, which Coast they very much infested, taking several Vessels: They were upon shifting this Station, when they were very near, as the Psalmist expresses it, *going quick down into Hell*,[3] for the Heaven's beginning to lowre, prognosticated a Storm; at the first Appearance of the Sky being likely to be overcast, *Bellamy* took in all his small Sails, and *Williams* double reefed his main Sail, which was hardly done when a Thunder Shower overtook them with such Violence, that the *Whidaw* was very near over-setting; they immediately put before the Wind, for they had no other Way of working, having only the Goose Wings of the Fore-Sail to scud with; happy for them the Wind was at *West* and by *North*, for had it been Easterly, they must have infallibly perish'd upon the Coast. The Storm encreased towards Night, and not only put them by all Sail, but obliged the *Whidaw* to bring her Yards aportland, and all they could do with Tackles to the Goose Neck of the Tiller, four Men in the Gun Room, and two at the Wheel, was to keep her Head to the Sea, for had she once broach'd to,[4] they must infallibly have founder'd. The Heavens, in the mean while, were cover'd with Sheets of Lightning, which the Sea by the Agitation of the saline Particles seem'd to imitate; the Darkness of the Night was such, as the Scripture says, as might be felt;[5] the terrible hollow roaring of the Winds, cou'd be only equalled by the repeated, I may say, incessant Claps of Thunder, sufficient to strike a Dread of the supream Being, who commands the Sea and the Winds, one would imagine in every Heart; but among these Wretches, the Effect was different, for they endeavoured by their Blasphemies, Oaths, and horrid Imprecations, to drown the Uproar of jarring Elements. *Bellamy* swore he was sorry he could not run out his Guns to return the Salute, meaning the Thunder, that he fancied the Gods had got drunk over their Tipple, and were gone together by the Ears: They continued scudding all that Night under their bare Poles, the next Morning the Main-Mast being sprung in the Step,[6] they were forced to cut it away, and, at the same time, the Mizzen came by the Board. These Misfortunes made the Ship ring with Blasphemy, which was encreased, when, by trying the Pumps, they found the Ship made a great Deal of Water; tho' by continually plying them, it kept it from gaining upon them: The Sloop as well as the Ship, was left to the Mercy of the Winds, tho' the former, not having a Tant-Mast,[7] did not lose it. The Wind shifting round the Compass, made so outrageous and short[8] a Sea, that they had little Hopes of Safety; it broke upon the Poop, drove in the Taveril,[9] and wash'd the two Men away from the Wheel, who were saved in the Netting. The Wind after four Days and three Nights abated of its Fury, and fixed in the North, North East Point, hourly decreasing, and the Weather clearing up, so that they spoke to the Sloop, and resolv'd for the Coast of *Carolina*; they continued this Course but a Day and a Night, when the Wind coming about to the Southward, they changed their Resolution to that of going to *Rhode Island*. All this while the *Whidaw*'s Leak continued, and it was as much as the Lee-Pump could do to keep the Water from gaining, tho' it was kept continually going. Jury-Masts[10] were set up, and the Carpenter finding the Leak to be in the Bows, occasioned by the Oakam spewing out of a Seam, the Crew became very jovial again; the Sloop received no other Damage than the Loss of the Main-Sail, which the first Flurry tore away from the Boom. In their Cruise off *Rhode Island*, the Beginning of *April*, they took a Sloop commanded by Capt. *Beer*, belonging to *Boston*, in the Lat. of *South Carolina*, 40 Leagues from Land; they put the said Captain on Board the *Whidaw* Commodore, while they rifled and plundered his Vessel, which *Williams* and *Bellamy* proposed returning to him, but the Crews being averse to it, they sunk her, and put the Captain ashore upon *Block Island*.

I can't pass by in Silence, Capt. *Bellamy*'s Speech to Capt. *Beer*. *D[am]n my Bl[oo]d, says he, I am sorry they won't let you have your Sloop again, for I scorn to do any one a Mischief, when it is not for my Advantage; damn the Sloop, we must sink her, and she might be of Use to you. Tho', damn ye, you are a sneaking Puppy, and so are all those who will submit to be governed by Laws which rich Men have made for their own Security, for the cowardly Whelps have not the Courage otherwise to defend what they get by their Knavery; but damn ye altogether: Damn them for a Pack of crafty Rascals, and you, who serve them, for a Parcel of hen-hearted Numskuls. They villify us, the Scoundrels do, when there is only this Difference, they rob the Poor under the Cover of Law, forsooth, and we plunder the Rich under the Protection of our own Courage; had you not better make One of us, than sneak after the A[rse]s of these Villians for Employment?* Capt. Beer told him, that his Conscience would not allow him to break thro' the Laws of God and Man. *You are a devilish Conscience Rascal, d[am]n ye, replied* Bellamy, *I am a free Prince, and I have as much Authority to make War on the whole World, as he who has a hundred Sail of Ships at Sea, and an Army of* 100,000 *Men in the Field; and this my Conscience tells me; but there is no arguing with such snivelling Puppies, who allow Superiors to kick them about Deck at Pleasure; and pin their Faith upon a Pimp of a Parson; a Squab, who neither practices nor believes what he puts upon the chuckle-headed Fools he preaches to.——* The Pyrates wanting neither Provision nor Water, and the *Whidaw*'s Damage being repaired, they past their Time very jovially. One of the Crew had been a Stroler, a Fellow who had pass'd thro' a great many real as well as fictitious Scenes of Life, the stroling Business not answering the Greatness of his Soul (as he expressed it) he thought it more profitable, and less fatiguing, to turn Collector.[11] Accordingly in *Yorkshire* he borrowed an excellent Gelding, (I make Use of his own Terms) with a hunting Saddle and Bridle, and with a Case of Pocket Pistols, which he before had, he set out to seek Adventures, without taking Leave of his Company; he met, he said, with several Knights Errant, whom as they declined the Combat, he spoiled and sent to offer themselves at the Feet of his *Dulcinea*,[12] but being under the Influence of some malicious Enchanter, who envied his glorious Feats of Arms, and fear'd they would eclipse by the Brightness of their Lustre, those of some favourite Knight whom he protected; or otherwise, knowing by his Skill, that he should one Day succumb under the Weight of his irresistable Arm, by his magical Power, threw him into a loathsome Dungeon loaded with Irons, whence the wise Man, who had Care of his Affairs, and was destined to write the History of his heroick Deeds delivered, and putting him on board a Ship, transported him to the famous Island of *Jamaica*; and after various Turns of Fortune, link'd him in Society with these Marine Heroes, the Scourge of Tyrants and Avarice, and the brave Asserters of Liberty.

This whimsical Fellow made a Play whilst he was on Board, which he called the *Royal Pyrate*; and this (which to see once would make a Cynick laugh) was acted on the Quarter-Deck with great Applause, both of the Actors and Poet; but an Accident which turn'd the Farce into Tragedy, occasioned an Order of Council to forbid its being play'd a second Time. The Case was thus; *Alexander* the Great, environ'd by his Guards, was examining a Pyrate who was brought before him: The Gunner, who was drunk, took this to be in earnest, and that his Mess-Mate was in Danger, and hearing *Alexander* say,

> Know'st thou that Death attends thy mighty Crimes,
> And thou shall'st hang to Morrow Morn betimes.

Swore by G[o]d he'd try that, and running into the Gun Room where he left three Companions over a Bowl of Rum Punch as drunk as himself, told them, they were going to hang honest *Jack Spinckes*; and if they suffered it, they should be all hang'd one after another, but by G[o]d, they should not hang him, for he'd clear the Decks; and taking a Grenade with a lighted Match, followed by his Comrades with their Cutlash, he set Fire to the Fuze and threw it among the Actors. The Audience was on the Gang Ways and Poop, and falling in with their Cutlash, poor *Alexander* had his left Arm cut off, and *Jack Spinckes* his Leg broke with the bursting of the Shell: The Ship was immediately in an Uproar and the Aggressors seiz'd, who else would have made Havock with the Guards, or have been cut to Pieces by them, for they had all Cutlashes. *Alexander* the Great revenged the Loss of his Arm by the Death of him who deprived him of his Limb. The Gunner and two surviving Comrades were that Night clapp'd into Irons, and the next Day at a Court-Marshal, not only acquitted but applauded for their Zeal. *Alexander* and his Enemies were reconciled, and the Play forbad any more to be acted.

A Fortnight after the setting Capt. *Beer* ashore, *Williams* boarded and took a Vessel off *Cape Cod*, laden with Wine; the Crew of which encreased the Number of their Prisoners: They put seven Men on Board the Prize, with Orders to keep Company with the Ship and Sloop, commanded by *Bellamy* and *Williams*, and left aboard her the Master.

As the Ship and Sloop had been long off the *Carreen*,[13] they stretch'd away to the Northward, and made the best of their Way to *Penobscott* River, which lies between *Nova Scotia* and the Province of *Main*, where they designed to heave down. This Tract of Land is along the Coast about 190 Miles from West to East, reckoning from the Province of *Main* to St. *Croix*; and about 200 Miles over from North to South, counting from the River *Quebeck* to the Sea. King *Charles* the Second made a Grant of it in 1663, to his Royal Highness *James* Duke of *York*,[14] who made a Settlement at *Pemaquid*; it abounds in all Sorts of Timber, and would bear excellent Hemp and Flax, and all Sorts of Naval Stores; is rich in Copper, Lead, and Iron Ore; and the Seas are stock'd with Whales, Cod, Sturgeon, Herrings, Mackrel, Salmon, Oysters, Cockles, &c. the Soil produces all Sort of *European* Grain and Fruits; and the Woods shelter a great Number of Deer, as Elks, Red and Fallow Deer, &c. and this Country, if settled, would certainly be of great Advantage to *England*. I hope the Reader will pardon this small Digression which the Interest I take in every Thing, which may tend to the enriching or extending the Dominions of our glorious *Britain*, my dearly loved Country, forced me into: But to return, when they were at the Mouth of this River, it was thought more eligible to careen in the River *Mechisses*; they entered it as agreed, and run up about two Miles and a half, when they came to an Anchor, with their Prizes. The next Morning all the Prisoners were set ashore with Drivers, and Orders to assist in the building Huts; the Guns were also set ashore, and a Breast Work raised, with Embrazures, for the Canon on each Side of the River, this took up four Days: A Magazine was dug deep in the Earth, and a Roof rais'd over it by the poor Slaves the Prisoners, whom they treated after the same Manner as the Negroes are used by the *West-India* Planters. The Powder being secured, and every Thing out, they hove down the Sloop, cleaned her, and when she had all in again, they careened the *Whidaw*, by the largest Prize. Here the Stroler told the two Commanders, that they might lay the Foundation of a new Kingdom, which, in time, might subject the World, and extend its Conquests beyond those of the *Roman* Empire. *I am, it is true, said he, by Birth, the Son of a Miller, but I have Ambition, Avarice, and Learning enough, to be a Secretary of State, for I was a Servitor at* Oxford *before I turn'd Stroler; and if you think fit to erect this Tract of Land into an Empire, and your joint Imperial Majesties will employ my Abilities, don't question but I will prove a true Patriot; that is, by the Figure I will make, I will be a Credit to your Court, and by the squeezing your Subjects (whom under the specious Pretence of Liberty, I will keep in abject Slavery) drain such Sums as shall ever keep them poor, and your and my Treasury full.* Rome, *the Mistress of the World, was founded by a couple of Sheep-Stealers, and peopled by run-away Slaves and insolent Debtors; how much more advantageously might you two undertake the erecting of a new Monarchy, whose Subjects are no Strangers to the Art of War, who are not environ'd as they were with invidious Neighbours, and who may encrease your Power, and propagate the Species, by taking into your Protection the* Indians *of these Parts, and the discontented and desperate People of the neighbouring* English *and* French *Colonies? To strengthen your selves, raise every useful Man to some Dignity in the State, and share the Prisoners (I mean such as won't swear Allegiance) as so many Slaves unworthy of Liberty among your great Men; build more Vessels, keep them constantly on the Cruize, and force all the the Prisoners either by fair or foul to acknowledge your Sovereignty; it was thus the greatest Empires of the World were founded; superior Force was always acknowledged a just Title; and the Ancients ever esteem'd the Prisoners they made, whose Lives were in their Power by the Law of Arms, lawful Slaves; and the employing their Lives in the Service of the Conqueror, but a grateful Retribution for preserving of them. I leave it to the mature Deliberation of your great Wisdom, whether it is not more eligible to found here an Empire, and make War by a lawful Authority derived from your Royal selves, than lie under the opprobrious Appellations of Robbers, Thieves, profligate Rogues and Pyrates; for begging Pardon of your Majesties, for that Freedom of Speech, which my Zeal for your Royal Service, and the publick Good oblige me to; the World treats you and your Subjects with no softer Terms. But, when you have once declared your selves lawful Monarchs, and that you have Strength enough to defend your Title, all the Universities in the World will declare you have a Right Jure Divino;* [15] *and the Kings and Princes of the Earth, will send their Ambassadors to court your Alliance.*

Bellamy and Williams told him, *They would consider on his Proposal, and they would let him know what they should in their great Wisdom conclude upon. In the mean while, they thank'd him for his Advice, promis'd when they began to found their Monarchy, (should they find it expedient,) to make him Prime Minister, or Quarter-Master ashore; and when he had enriched himself and Family, by the fleecing their Subjects, they assured him they would pass an Act of Indemnity for his Security;* and concluded with ordering a Bowl of Punch for every Mess.

The *Whidaw* being clean'd, they thought of cruizing again, and accordingly steer'd for *Fortunes Bay* in *Newfoundland*; they made some Prizes on the Banks, forced all the Men, and sunk the Vessels.

They had not been long on this Coast before they were separated by a Storm, which held some Days. Off the Island of St. *Paul* the *Whidaw* spied a Sail, which she immediately gave Chase to; the Ship brought to and lay by for her, she prov'd a *French* Man of 36 Guns, carrying Soldiers to *Quebeck*. The *Whidaw* engag'd with great Resolution, and the *French* did not shew less, for he boarded the *Whidaw*, and was twice put off, with the Loss of Men on both Sides. *Bellamy* after two Hours Engagement thought the *Frenchman* too hard a Match, and was for shaking him off; but his Enemy was not as willing to part with him, for he gave Chase, and as he sail'd altogether as well as *Bellamy*, the latter had certainly been taken and had received the due Punishment of his Crimes, had not the Night coming on favour'd his Escape: He lost in this Engagement 36 Hands, beside several wounded, the poor Minister of State, our before-mentioned Stroller, was in the Number of the slain.

The *Whidaw* returned to the Coast of *Newfoundland*, and off *Placentia* Bay met with his Consort and the Prize.

They resolved to visit again the Coast of *New England*, the *Whidaw* being much shatter'd in the late Engagement, having receiv'd a great many Shot in her Hull; they ran down this Coast, and between St. *George*'s Banks and *Nantuket's* Shoals, took the *Mary Anne*.

The Master of the Vessel, taken formerly off *Cape Cod*, was left on board her, and as he was very well acquainted with the Coast, they order'd him to carry the Light and go a-head; and the Pyrates commonly kept him at Helm: He upon a Night of publick Rejoicing, seeing all the Pyrates drunk, laid hold on the Opportunity, and run his Vessel ashore about Midnight, near the Land of *Eastham*, out of which he alone escap'd with Life. The *Whidaw* steering after the Light, met with the same Fate; the small Vessel ran into a sandy Bay, and the Men got ashore without Difficulty.

When the *Whidaw* struck, the Pyrates murder'd all their Prisoners, that is, all their forced Men; as is concluded, from the mangled Carcasses which were wash'd ashore; but not a Soul escaped out of her or *Williams'*, who was also lost.

The Pyrates, to the Number of seven who escaped, were seiz'd by the Inhabitants, and on the Information of the Master who escap'd, and on their own Confession, were imprison'd, condemn'd, and executed. They were all Foreigners, very ignorant and obstinate; but by the indefatigable Pains of a pious and learned Divine, who constantly attended them, they were, at length, by the special Grace of God, made sensible of, and truly penitent, for the enormous Crimes they had been guilty of. As the Trial of these Pyrates, and their Behaviour while under Sentence, and at the Place of Execution, was printed at *Boston*, and is to be had in Town, I shall refer the curious Reader to that small Tract.

The Compleat English Gentleman [1728-9]

This work, one of Defoe's last, was not published until over 160 years after its composition. Only one proof-sheet was run off by Defoe's printer, John Watts, in September 1729 (*Letters*, p. 473); complete publication was delayed until Karl D. Bülbring's edition in 1890.

Defoe's starting-point is essentially Lockean: 'Nature's production is a *Charte Blanche*, and the soul is plac'd in him like a peice of clean paper, upon which the precepts of life are to be written by his instructors, and he has the charge of keeping it fair lay'd upon himself' (Bülbring, *op. cit.*, p. xiv). The accident of birth, then, has little to do with the 'compleat gentleman' who must be 'a Person of Merit and Worth; a Man of Honour, Virtue, Sense, Integrity, Honesty, and Religion' (p. 21); and these qualities will be fostered only by instruction and example. Defoe rejected Shaftesbury's view that civilization corrupts the natural goodness of man; he was convinced that, without education, man would be a fool. Hence his contempt for men who despised learning and his admiration for those who—like Colonel Jack with the aid of his tutor in Maryland—embellished natural qualities 'with a fund of learning and acquir'd knowledg' (p. 4).

Like the majority of Defoe's publications, this too was a tract for the times. The eighteenth century was in many ways the age of the '*novus homo*' (as Burke later described himself), the man who made his mark in consequence of personal achievement, learning, and experience, without the advantages of noble birth—the age of Swift, Pope, Johnson, Garrick, and Defoe himself.

The Compleat English Gentleman

Introduccion

That I may begin with the same brevity that I purpose to go on with, I shall onely observ here by way of introduccion that there are two sorts of classes of men who I am to be understood to speak of under the denomination of gentlemen:

1. The born Gentleman,
2. The bred Gentleman.

The complete gentleman I am to speak of will take them in both; and neither of them, singly and abstractedly considred, will stand alone in the class of a compleat gentleman without some thing that may be said to comprehend both.

The born gentleman is a valuable man if bred up as a gentleman ought to be, that is, educated in learning and manners suitable to his birth. This I must insist on as a preliminary, that I may not be censur'd and condemn'd unread, and bring upon me a clamour from the numerous party of old women (whether male or female), idolators who worship escutcheons and trophyes, and rate men and families by the *blazonry* of their houses, exclusiv of learning or virtue, and of all personall merit.

On the other hand, the son of a mean person furnish'd from Heaven with an originall fund of wealth, wit, sence, courage, virtue, and good humour, and set apart by a liberall education for the service of his country; that distinguishes himself by the greatest and best actions; is made acceptable and agreeable to all men by a life of glory and true fame; that hath the naturall beauties of his mind embellish'd and set off with a vast fund of learning and accquir'd knowleg; that has a clear head, a generous heart, a polite behaviour and, in a word, shews himself to be an accomplish'd gentleman in every requisite article, that of birth and blood excepted: I must be allowd to admit such a person into the rank of a gentleman, and to suggest that he being the first of his race may possibly raise a *roof tree* (as the antients call it) of a noble house and of a succession of gentlemen as effectually as if he had his pedigree to show from the Conqueror's army or from a centurion in the legions that landed with Julius Caesar.

Out of the race of either of these, the compleat gentleman I am to describe is to be deriv'd. How to reconcile the antient line to this and bring them, however degenerate, to embrace the modern line, tho' exalted by the brightest virtue and the most valuable accomplishments of a man of honour, is the difficult case before me.

I am resolv'd however to giv antiquity its due homage; I shall worship the image call'd antient lineage as much as possible without idolatry; I shall giv it all the reverence and respect that it can pretend to claim, search for all the glories of birth and blood, and place them in full proportion: no lustre of antient gentry shall be ecclypst by me, onley with this excepcion, that I must intreat the gentlemen who are to value themselves chiefly upon that advantage, that they will *stoop so low* as to admit that vertue, learning, a liberal educacion, and a degree of naturall and accquir'd knowledge, are necessary to finish the born gentleman; and that without them the entitul'd heir will be but the shaddow of a gentleman, the opaac, dark body of a planet, which can not shine for want of the sun communicating its beams, and for want of being plac'd in a due posITION, to reciev and reflect those beams when they are communicated and reciev'd.

In condicioning for so small an advance in the favour of true merit, and insisting upon its being, as I said, absolutely necessary, I think we differ upon so small a point, that I can not doubt of reconciling it all in the end of this discourse and bringing the blood and the merit together; so we shall soon produce the best and most glorious peice of God's creation, a complete gentleman; which is the deserv'd subject of the whole work.

*   *   *   *

I should be very unwilling to treat the English gentlemen rudely, when they are so civil to themselves. Nothing is more affronting to a gentleman than to contradict him when he takes the affirmatio upon him, and if he assures me then that he is a man of sence, that he has a fund of brains and a stock of wit, whether it be mother-wit or clergy,[1] it matters not; good manners say I am oblig'd to believ it, and while I submit to the popery of it, how can I go about to undeciev him? that would be popery indeed of another kind, (viz.) to preach one thing and profess another.

Here a man is embarrasst in an inextricable labrinth: he is bound on one hand to see the fool (nature forbids shutting our eyes against the light), and he is bound on the other hand to recognize the wit; and, which is the part particularly perplexing, both these center in the same object, yet it must be done, the laws of Nature command one, and the rules of decency, which is nature in a gentleman, oblige the other. Thus he submits to worship the idol when the deity is absent, as our people bow to the candles upon the altar when they deny the Reall Presence, a sort of popery that every body may not think of.

I must say, however, 'tis something hard that, when Coll. Ch[arteris] rattles at W[hite's]s[2] and talks so ridiculously that the very foot-men grin and sneer at it, I must sit by and say *yes* and *no* just as his brains jingle, and accquisce in what every body that hears him knows to be the worst of nonsence onely because he weares a red coat and a sword, and, it may be, has two or three orderly men, corporalls or sergeants allways at his heels, who will knock a man down with their halberds, if we should not let him knock us down with his toungue.

I once met casually with one of those sons of ignorance in a country coffee-house. He had in his company two clergy-men and his younger brother. One of the clergy-men was the chapline of the family, the other a divine of some note in the next town, who, however, enjoy'd a living by the gift of those two gentlemen's father, who was yet alive, tho' the sons were both of them then grown.

The two brothers had a warm discourse about learning and wit, and it was as much as both the clergy-men could do to keep them from quarrelling.

The younger brother had been bred at the University, and had acquir'd a good stock of learning, which he had the felicity to graft upon a noble stock of originall sence. He had a genius above the common rate, and, as it was improv'd by a liberall educacion, it made him extremely valued by the best men, and particularly quallify'd by a polite conversation for the best company. The elder brother was a gentleman, that is, he was heir to an estate of about 3000 pounds a year, and expected to be chosen Parliament man at an eleccion which was then at hand. He had been a hunting early that morning, and his man stood at the coffee house door with the French horn in his hand; and the mustering being just ready to go home, the park and mansion house being about a mile out of the town, but meeting with his younger brother in the town, with the two clergy men, they came all together to the coffee house to read the news. When every one taking a severall paper in his hand, the gentleman happens to read a paragraph telling us that such a gentleman was made Commissioner in some business or other, I do not remember whether of the Customes or Excise or some other employment under the Government; at which he threw down the paper in a kind of passion:

"D[amn] 'em," says he, "what fool must he be now that they have given him a place!"

"Who is it?" sayes the brother.

"Why, there," sayes he, "look, 'tis that beggarly fellow, Sir Tho——."

"Why, brother?" sayes the younger, "he is a very pretty gentleman I assure you, a man of merit, and fit for any employment whatsoever."

"A gentleman and a man of merit, what d'ye mean by that? What family is he of? Why, his grandfather was a citizen, a tradesman! he a gentleman!"

Younger: "I don't kno' what his father was, or his grandfather; but I assure you he has all the quallifications of a——"

Elder brother: "Of a what? of a scoundrel. I tell you he is but one remove from a shopkeeper, his father was a——"

Younger: "Nay I must interrupt you now, brother, as you did me. Let his father be what he will, his merit will make a gentleman of him in spite of family; besides he is a baronet by birth."

Elder: "A baronet? yes, his father got money by bubbling[3] and tricking and jobbing, and bought a patent of a poor gentleman that was starving."

Younger: "Let the patent be bought by who it will; he inherits it, he didn't buy it."

Elder: "Well that does not make him a gentleman; you kno' what King Charles said, that he could make a knight, but could not make a gentleman."

Younger: "But I tell you, Sir Thomas was a gentleman before he was a knight."

Elder: "How do ye make out that, Doctor, with all your schollarship?"

Younger: "Don't be so witty upon your younger brother: I am no doctor, and yet I can make out that well enough. He was a man of vertue and modesty, had a universall knowledge of the world, an extraordinary stock of sence, and withall is a compleat schollar."

Elder: "And those things, you suppose, make a gentleman, do ye?"

Younger: "They go a great way towards it, in my opinion, I must confess."

Elder: "Not at all! they may make him a good man perhaps and a good Christian; nay, they may make him good company, but not a gentleman, by no means. I can't allow that."

Younger: "Then I don't know what a gentleman is at all, or what it means."

Elder: "Then I am sorry for your head. Have you gone all this while to school, and don't know what a gentleman is?"

Younger: "I am mighty willing to learn, especially of my elder brother."

Elder: "Why then your elder brother may teach you. I take him to be a gentleman that has the blood of a gentleman in his veins. Nothing can be a gentleman but the son of a gentleman."

Younger: "And vertue, parts, sence, breeding, or religion, have no share in it."

Elder: "Not at all. They may constitute a good man, if you will, but not a gentleman. He may be the D[evil] if he will, he is still a gentleman."

Younger: "Well then let me be the good man, and you shall be the gentleman. But I tell you, Sir Thomas has a thousand good things in him, and above all I take him to be that good man too; for he is a very religious gentleman."

Elder: "Very good then; he would have made a good parson, it may be, or a bishop; but what's that to a gentleman?"

Here the minister put in, tho' modestly too: "Sir," sayes he, "I hope you will allow a clergy-man may be a gentleman."

Elder: "What, do I touch your cloth too, Doctor? I don't allow it I assure you. A parson a gentleman? No, I assure you I allow no tradesmen to be gentlemen."

Then the chaplain spoke: "That's too hard, Sir," sayes he, "upon our cloth. I hope you don't call us tradesmen neither."

Elder brother: "Not tradesmen? why, what are you? Is it not your business to work for your bread, and is not that your trade? Is not the pulpit your shop, and is not this your apron, Mr Book Beater?"—Here he took up [the] chaplain's scarf and gave it a twirle into his face, at which both the clergy-men rose up, as if they would be gon.

*　　　*　　　*　　　*

" 'I cannot think but that, tho' we were not made schollars when we were boys, we need not go block-heads to the grave. Is there nothing to be learnt now, because we learn't nothing then? Is there no learning in the world, cousin, but Greek and Latin?'

"He answer'd after some very modest apologies for talking so to me: yes, there was certainly a great many good things to be learn't that had no great relacion to the tongues; that, 'tis true, the tongues were usefull helps, but that there were severall things very needfull for the knowlege of a gentleman that allways, or at least generally, were taught in English, and that some of the greatest masters of them in their time had not so much as understood Latin or Greek.

" 'Well, nephew,' said I, 'now you come to me. Pray then, without any ceremony, or appology, be so free with me as to tell me what those things are; what is the properest method to apply to them, and which of them are proper for, and most usefull to, a gentleman; for since I have not been taught what I should have learnt in the time of it, I am resolv'd to learn what I can, tho' out of season.'

" 'Sir,' said my nephew, 'it is true that custome has prevail'd so at our Universities in favour of the tongues, that all the publick exercises in the schooles are perform'd in the learned languages, but it is acknowleg'd there is not an absolute necessity of it other than that of preserving the use and knowledge of those tongues in the schollars that perform them. But 'tis certain that a course of phylosophy as well naturall as experimental, as also of the mathematicks, of astronomy and of most of the sciences properly so called, is to be taught in the English tongue, if the tutor or master please to read his lectures in those sciences in English to his pupils.'

" 'Say you so, nephew?' said I, 'and is there then no such tutor to be found that will read his lectures, as you call them, in the English tongue? and may I not make my self master of some degree of knowlege in the world, tho' I do not meddle with Latin and Greek.'

" 'Yes, Sir,' sayes he, 'without doubt, you may; besides there are some things, as I said before, which are never taught in Latin or Greek, or very rarely, and which are in themselves noble studyes and very agreeable to the genius and temper of a gentleman, extremely usefull to him in conversation, and suited to his inclinacion as a man of quallity, and especially as a man of sence.'

" 'Pray, what are they, cousin?' said I.

" 'Sir,' sayes he, 'the first and most valuable is the use of the globes, or to speak more properly the study of Geography, the knowlege of mapps, as also so much of Astronomy as may giv him a theory of the universe, particularly as far as relates to the motion and distances of the heavenly bodies, the eclypses, conjunctions, revolutions, and influences of the planets, comets, fix'd starrs, and other phænomena of nature.'

" 'May all these be learned in English?' said I.

"He return'd: 'Sir, as I said before, they are very seldome taught in Latin except in the Universities, and there it is done so meerly as it was the antient custome, and I think none of the best customes neither.'

" 'Why so, nephew?' said I.

" 'Because, Sir,' said he, 'it seems to confine the knowledge of those usefull studies to the schooles and to the men of letters exclusiv of other men, whereas abundance of men do, and more might, understand them who are not train'd up at the colleges, and whose fortunes would not admitt a liberall education; and confining these most necessary branches of science to those onely who can read and understand Latin is tying up knowledge to a few, whereas Science being a publick blessing to mankind ought to be extended and made as difusiv as possible, and should, as the Scripture sayes of sacred knowlege, spread over the whole earth, as the waters cover the sea.'

" 'I think you are very right there, nephew,' said I, 'and in particular your discourse is very agreeable to me; for according to your notion, then, I may learn all these things still, tho' I don't go to school again like a boy.'

" 'Sir,' answer'd my nephew, 'so far from going to school again like a boy, that these things are seldome learnt till we are men; and as the seafaring men are generally well acquainted with these studyes, let any one examine how few of them understand Latin or Greek; nay, the very Masters that teach them do not allwayes understand those tongues and have no occasion for it, as I think I hinted before; and if Latin and Greek was necessary to a study of Astronomy, Navigation, and, in generall, severall other branches of the Mathematicks, what would become of Navigation in generall; for where is there a sea-faring man in twenty that understands Latiñ, and yet some of them the compleatest artists in the world.'

" 'Well; but, cousin,' said I, 'you intimated, I think, that there were two reasons why you thought the custome of the Universities in confining their schollars to read all the systems in the Latin tongue was not the best method: pray, what was the other reason ?'

" 'Truly, Sir, my other reason was because it throws the English tongue so entirely out of use among them, excluding it from all the Colleges, and out of every course of their teachings, that many gentlemen come from the University excellently well skill'd in the sciences, Masters, nay, criticks, in the Oriental languages and in most parts of usefull learning, and can hardly spell their mother tongue, at least 'tis frequent that, tho' all their performances are at last to issue in the original mother English, yet being lost out of all their school readings and out of all the lectures of their tutors and all their own performances, they have no stile, no diction, no beauty or cadence of expression, but are so dull, so awk-ward and so heavy in delivring themselves, that 'twould be a shame to hear one of them declaim in English, who, perhaps, would gain an universall applause if it were perform'd in the Latin tongue.'

" 'This is still o' my side, cousin,' said I, 'and 'tis a very great satisfaction to me to hear it; for by your account of the thing 'tis very possible for me, tho' not a boy, and tho' I have no Greek or Latin, to be master of some parts of learning, at least; if I can not be a schollar I need not be a fool.'

" 'Sir,' says my nephew, 'I am of opinion that the world has a very wrong notion of what they call a schollar.

... A man may be a schollar in their sence and be good for nothing, be a meer pedant, a Greek and Latin monger. I think our meer schollars are a kind of mechanicks in the schools, for they deal in words and syllables as haber-dashers deal in small ware. They trade in measure, quantityes, dactyls, and spondaes, as instrument-makers do in quadrants, rules, squares, and compasses; etymologyes, and derivations, prepositions and terminations, points, commas, colons, and semicolons, etc., are the product of their brain, just as gods and devils are made in Italy by every carver and painter; and they fix them in their proper stations in perspectiv, just as they do in nitches and glass windows.'

" 'You make strange fellows of them, indeed,' said I.

" 'I make nothing of them,' said my nephew, 'but what they are. They are meer pædagogues, they seem to be form'd in a school on purpose to dye in a school.

... We must distinguish between a man of polite learning and a meer schollar: the first is a gentleman and what a gentleman should be; the last is a meer book-case, a bundle of letters, a head stufft with the jargon of languages, a man that understands every body but is understood by no body, a creature buryed aliv in heaps of antients and moderns, full of tongues but no languages, all sence but no wit, in a word, all learning and no manners.'

" 'But what then should I be, cousin,' said I; 'for I would fain be some thing that I am not.'

"He answer'd, 'I see nothing you want, Sir, but a little reading.'

" 'I differ from you there, cousin,' said I, 'I doubt you are mistaken; 'tis a great deal I want. I would be glad to read a little.'

" 'Perhaps, Sir,' said he, ' 'tis not so much as you imagine. I distinguish, as I said, between a learned man and a man of learning, as I distinguish between a schollar and a gentleman. You have a polite educacion as a gentleman allready.'

" 'An ignorant education, cousin,' said I, 'do you call that polite ?'

" 'No, Sir,' said he, 'all that you call ignorance would vanish presently with a little application to books.'

" 'What can I do,' said I, 'and what will reading do for me that can read nothing but English.'

" 'Reading, Sir, in English,' said he, 'may do all for you that you want. You may still be *a man of reading*, and that is in a large part of the sence of that word, *a man of learning*; nay, it is the more gentlemanly part: you may in a word be *a gentleman of learning*.' "

*   *   *   *

No gentleman ought to throw up the point and grow desperate because he was not sent to school, as he ought to have been, in his childhood, and been made master of the learned languages in the time of it, seeing it is never too late; and he may still form his genius with the sublimest studyes, and store himself with all the learning necessary to make him a complete gentleman.

If he had not travell'd in his youth, has not made the grand tour of Italy and France, he may make the tour of the world in books, he may make himself master of the geography of the Universe in the maps, attlasses, and measurements of our mathematicians. He may travell by land with the historian, by sea with the navigators. He may go round the globe with Dampier and Rogers,[4] and kno' a thousand times more in doing it than all those illiterate sailors. He may make all distant places near to him in his reviewing the voiages of those that saw them, and all the past and remote accounts present to him by the historians that have written of them. He may measure the latitudes and distances of places by the labours and charts of those that have survey'd them, and know the strength of towns and cityes by the descripcions of those that have storm'd and taken them, with this difference, too, in his knowlege, and infinitely to his advantage, viz., that those travellers, voiagers, surveyors, soldiers, etc., kno' but every man his share, and that shar but little, according to the narrow compass of their owne actings. But he recievs the idea of the whole at one view.

The studious geographer and the well read historian travells with not this or that navigator or traveller, marches with not this or that generall, or making this or that campaign, but he keeps them all company; he marches with Hannibal over the Alps into Italy, and with Caesar into Gaul and into Britain, with Belisarius into Affric, and with Emperor Honorius into Persia. He fights the battle of Granicus with Alexander, and of Actium with Augustus; he is at the overthro' of the great Bajazette by Tamerlain, and of Tomombejus and his Mamaluks by Selymus; he sees the battle of Lepanto, with the defeat of the Spanish Armada with Drake; with Adrian he views the whole Roman Empire and, in a word, the whole world; he discovers America with Columbus, conquers it with the great Cortez, and replunders it with Sir Francis Drake,

Nothing has been famous or valuable in the world, or even the ruines of it, but he has it all in his view; and nothing done in the world but he has it in his knowledge, from the seige of Jerusalem to the siege of Namure, and from Titus Vespasian to the greater King William: he has it all at the tip of his tongue.

Nor are these studyes profitable onely and improving, but delightfull and pleasant too to the last degree. No romances, playes, or diverting storyes can be equally entertaining to a man of sence; nay, they make a man be a man of sence; they give him a tast who had none before; they teach him how to relish superior knowlege as he looks up to the heavenly bodyes, whose mocions he learns to understand in his astronomicall readings; he is charm'd with the harmony of the system and with seeing their direct, as well as retrograde mocions conform exactly with the calculacions of them by books.

When he sees the ecclypses, conjunccions, and oppositions of the plannets, those solemn testimonyes of the verity of Astronomy, happen exactly in time and quantity, situacion, and degree, I say exactly to the moment foretold by the artists, he is fir'd with desires of searching farther into the glorious circle of wonders, the hemisphere, the arch of which appeares continually revolving in the most beautiful order, exactly as describ'd by his Ephimeris[5] and as he can read it upon the celestial globe.

He has the like delightfull view of the terrestrial globe when reading all the most antient, as well as modern histories of the world; he can turn to his maps and see the very spot where every great accion was done, however remote either in place or in time. Every scene of glory is there spread before him, from the great overthro' of Senacharib's army at the gates of Samaria, or from the defeat of the Ethiopian army of a thousand thousand to the yet more well fought battles of Leipsick, Blenheim, and Malplaquet.

How agreeable a diversion is it to him to read the public prints with his colleccion of maps and charts before him, where he can see the British Squadron blocking up the Spanish Plate Fleet at Porto Belo, and imediately turn his eye and see another British Squadron, awing the Russian Navy at Revell and Narve, and they, tho' double in number, not daring to put to sea to succour the Spaniards. The next moment he has turn'd over a leaf, and the like chart presents Gibraltar to his view, and the Spaniards battering themselves to peices instead of the town, and wasting their army in a fruitless, unskillfull seige without so much as comeing near enough to draw a sword in the whole war. There also he sees another English Squadron keeping the seas open and convoying troops and relief dayly to the place and assisting that one small town in overmatching all the forces of Spain, whether by land or by sea.

When armies march or fleets sail he can trace them with his eye, see all their mocions, and some of them even before they are begun, can tell where they are to day, and make a probable judgement where they will be to morrow.

I might enlarge experimentally upon the delightfull search into naturall history and the rarityes discover'd daily in the vegitativ world, like wise into experimental as well as naturall phylosophy the most agreeable as well as profitable study in the world.

All these things lye before him; he may turn his head to them as he sees fit; his having been abused in his child-hood and not having been sent to school may present nothing discouraging to him for these are the studyes of men, not of boys. The ladyes can not put him off of them by saying they are below his birth; for these are improvments for gentlemen, not mechanicks, nay, even for the highest rank of men.

But to go farther yet, the inquiries and improvements of this kind are fitted for the brightest genius, the most clear understanding, the most discerning heads; men exalted in their curious search after knowledge above the ordinary sort of people look into such things as these. The king himself might glory in the accquirement, nor is it beneath the dignity of an emperor to understand them.

Letter to Henry Baker

12 August 1730

Dear Mr Baker,

I have your very kind and affectionate Letter of the 1st: But not come to my hand till the 10th; where it had been delay'd I kno' not. As your kind Manner, and Kinder Thought, from which it flows, (for I take all you say to be as I always believed you to be, sincere and Nathaniel like, without Guile,) was a particular Satisfaction to me; so the stop of a Letter, however it happened, depriv'd me of that Cordial too many Days, considering how much I stood in need of it, to support a Mind sinking under the Weight of Affliction too heavy for my Strength, and looking on myself as Abandon'd of every Comfort, every Friend, and every Relative, except such only as are able to give me no Assistance.[1]

I was sorry you should say at the Beginning of your Letter, you were debarred seeing me. Depend upon my Sincerity for this, I am far from debarring you. On the contrary, it would be a greater Comfort to me than any I now enjoy, that I could have your agreeable Visits with Safety, and could see both you and my dear Sophia, could it be without giving her the Grief of seeing her Father *in tenebris*, and under the Load of insupportable Sorrows. I am sorry I must open my Griefs so far as to tell her, it is not the Blow I recd from a wicked, perjur'd, and contemptible Enemy,[2] that has broken in upon my Spirit; which as she well knows, has carryed me on thro' greater Disasters than these. But it has been the injustice, unkindness, and, I must say, inhuman dealings of my own Son,[3] which has both ruin'd my Family, and, in a Word, has broken my Heart; and as I am at this Time under a weight of very heavy Illness, which I think will be a Fever, I take this Occasion to vent my Grief in the Breasts who I know will make a prudent use of it, and tell you, that nothing but this has conquered or could conquer me. *Et tu! Brute*. I depended upon him, I trusted him, I gave up my two dear unprovided Children[4] into his Hands; but he has no Compassion, but suffers them and their poor, dying Mother[5] to beg their Bread at his Door, and to crave, as if it were an Alms, what he is bound under Hand and Seal, besides the most sacred promises, to supply them with; himself, at the same Time, living in a profusion of Plenty. It is too much for me. Excuse my Infirmity, I can say no more; my Heart is too full. I only ask one Thing of you as a dying request. Stand by them when I am gone, and let them not be wrong'd, while he is able to do them right. Stand by them as a Brother; and if you have anything within you owing to my Memory, who have bestow'd on you the best

Gift I had to give, let them not be injured and trampled on by false Pretences, and unnatural Reflections. I hope they will want no help but that of Comfort and Council; but that they will indeed want, being too easie to be manag'd by Words and Promises.

It adds to my Grief that it is so difficult to me to see you. I am at a distance from London in Kent; nor have I Lodging in London, nor have I been at that Place in the Old Bailey, since I wrote you I was removed from it. At present I am weak, having had some fits of a Fever that have left me low. But those Things much more.

I have not seen Son or Daughter, Wife or Child, many Weeks, and kno' not which Way to see them. They dare not come by Water, and by Land there is no Coach, and I kno' not what to do.

It is not possible for me to come to Enfield,[6] unless you could find a retired Lodging for me, where I might not be known, and might have the Comfort of seeing you both now and then; Upon such a circumstance, I could gladly give the days to Solitude, to have the Comfort of half an Hour now and then, with you both, for two or three Weeks. But just to come and look at you, and retire immediately, 'tis a Burden too heavy. The Parting will be a Price beyond the Enjoyment.

I would Say, (I hope) with Comfort, that 'tis yet well. I am so near my Journey's end, and am hastening to the Place where the Weary are at Rest, and where the Wicked cease to trouble; be it that the Passage is rough, and the Day stormy, by what Way soever He please to bring me to the End of it, I desire to finish Life with this temper of Soul in all Cases: *Te Deum Laudamus.*

I congratulate you on the Occasion of your happy advance in your Employment. May all you do be prosperous, and all you meet with pleasant; and may you both escape the torments and troubles of uneasie Life. May you Sail the dangerous Voyage of Life with *a forcing Wind*, and make the Port of Heaven *without a Storm.*

It adds to my Grief that I must never see the pledge of your mutual Love, my little Grandson.[7] Give him my Blessing, and may he be to you both your Joy in Youth, and Your Comfort in Age, and never add a Sigh to your Sorrow. But, alas! that is not to be expected. Kiss my dear Sophy once more for me; and if I must see her no more, tell her this is from a Father that loved her above all his Comforts, to his last Breath.

Your unhappy,
D. F.

About two Miles from Greenwich, Kent,
Tuesday, Augst 12, 1730

P.S. I wrote you a Letter some Months ago, in answer to one from you, about selling the House; but you never signified to me whether you received it. I have not the Policy of Assurance; I suppose my Wife, or Hannah, may have it.

Idem.
D. F.

Notes

An Essay Upon Projects

1 *Clippers* A clipper was 'one who debased coin by cutting' (Johnson).
2 *Protection* A grant of immunity from arrest.
3 *Mint or Friars* The Mint, Southwark, and Blackfriars, were both sanctuaries.
4 *Nascitur ... mus* Horace, *Ars Poetica*, l.139.
5 *Saltpeter-Maker ... Houses* Probably a jocular reference to contemporary methods of obtaining saltpetre from 'earths moistened or manured with the excrements of animals ... and ... in France, by boiling in water the matter of old walls, the old plaster of ruined buildings, and the earths of stables and other places where animals have fed' (*A New and Complete Dictionary of Arts and Sciences*, 1764). A 'Tom Turd's Man' was a nightman who emptied cess-pools, etc.

[Projects for banks, highways, and insurance are omitted; the section 'Of Seamen' forms one part of the project 'Of Friendly Societies'.]

6 *Friendly-Society* Originally the name of a particular fire-insurance company which came to have general application. (Defoe's use of the term antedates the earliest usage recorded in *O.E.D.*)
7 *An Eye 25l.* etc. A comparative standard is supplied by Defoe's estimate of the cost of building a cottage (in the essay on highways) as £40.

[Essays on a pension-office, the treatment of the insane, and bankruptcy are omitted.]

8 *The French ... Europe* The French Academy was incorporated in 1635.
9 *Roscommon* Wentworth Dillon, 4th Earl of Roscommon (1633?–1685). The quotation is from his *Essay on Translated Verse* (1684), ll.51–4.
10 *And if ... Gaiety* Defoe is probably intending Boileau or St. Evremont as the 'greatest Critick'. His remark parallels Dryden's (made also in 1697) in the dedication to the *Aeneis*: 'The French have set up purity for the standard of their language; and a masculine vigour is that of ours. Like their tongue is the genius of their poets, light and trifling in comparison of the English; more proper for sonnets, madrigals, and elegies, than heroic

poetry. The turn on thoughts and words is their chief talent; but the epic poem is too stately to receive those little ornaments.'

11 *King of England* Defoe's veneration of William III (whom he claimed to know personally) is frequently expressed throughout his writings; for example the number of the *Review* published nearest to November 7th (the King's birthday) was always dedicated to his memory. William's 'Greatness of spirit' in war was caught in the portrait of the King on horseback by Sir Godfrey Kneller.

12 *'twere to ... Capacity* Cf. *The Compleat English Gentleman*, below, p. 249.

13 *Whoredoms and ... Appetite* Defoe is here, and in the following paragraph, less willing to sympathize with the causes of vice than in *Moll Flanders* or *Colonel Jack*, for example. See also *A True-Born Englishman*, ll. 614-15, and *Review*, below, p. 131.

14 *Two Theatres* Drury Lane and Lincoln's Inn Fields.

15 *I need ... Education* One instance occurs in *The Compleat English Gentleman*, below, pp. 250-52.

16 *Ingenious Lady* Mary Astell (1668-1731) whose book is entitled *A Serious Proposal to the Ladies for the Advancement of their True and Great Interest* (1694).

An Argument Shewing, that a Standing Army, ...

1 *This we ... Argument* Defoe is probably referring to [Andrew Fletcher], *A Discourse concerning Militias and Standing Armies*, 1697, and to Walter Moyle, *The Second Part of an Argument shewing that a Standing Army is inconsistent with a Free Government*, 1697.

2 *Prince of Parma* Alexander Farnese, duke of Parma (1545-1592) who, when Governor-General of the Netherlands, was ordered by Philip II to prepare the 'Invincible Armada' against England.

3 *Rochel* La Rochelle, the Huguenot stronghold. Charles attempted to relieve the inhabitants, 1627-8, but had to give up in view of Louis XIII's determination to subdue them.

4 *Rhe* The isle of Rhé, off La Rochelle; it was seized by Richelieu from the Huguenots in 1625 and unsuccessfully attacked in 1627 by English forces under Buckingham.

5 *Peace of Nimeguen* Signed between France and Holland, August 1678.

6 *the Dutch ... 1672* Holland was invaded on 7 April 1672 by 120,000 French under Condé and Turenne; they very swiftly captured most of the principal towns.

7 *Count Colocedo* Count Don Carlos Coloma was the Spanish ambassador in England during James I's reign.

8 *Count Mansfield* Count Ernst von Mansfield, a soldier of fortune; he led an English army to help the Dutch secure independence, in 1625.

9 *Tho' his . . . tremble* Andrew Marvell, *A Dialogue between the Two Horses* (1689), ll.139–40.

10 *Claim of Right* The declaration of the rights and liberties of the subject presented to William III when the throne was offered to him in February 1689; it was embodied in a statute passed in November 1689.

11 *I'll suppose . . . 1680* Parliament carried a resolution, in December 1697, that all land forces raised since 29 September 1680 should be disbanded. The army was thereby reduced to about 8,000 men (in place of the 30,000 William III thought essential).

12 *Purbeck fancied Invasion* No reference to such an invasion-scare has been traced. Defoe may be referring to the futile attempt of James II and French forces to invade in May 1692, or to a later attempt in 1696.

13 *Battel of Newport* Prince Maurice of Orange (1567–1625), with the support of English troops, conducted a successful campaign against the Spanish in the Netherlands. A major victory was won at Nieuwport, 1600.

14 *Consent of . . . Judge* The Bill of Rights declared it illegal to raise a standing army in time of peace *without* consent of Parliament.

15 *Duke D'Alva* Ferdinand, Duke of Alba (1507–1582) became captain-general in the Netherlands in 1567. He tried to introduce the *Alcabala*, a Spanish tax on all sales; the opposition to this tax stiffened the resistance to Spanish domination and eventually led Alba to request his own recall in 1573.

16 *Coat and Conduct Money* A tax laid on the counties to defray the cost of clothing the troops levied, and their travelling expenses.

17 *Quo Warrantoes* A legal term denoting a Crown writ against one who claims or usurps any office or prerogative (e.g. the right to hold a public market) to enquire by what authority he supports his claim.

18 *In the . . . vain* Sir John Moore (1620–1702)—'Ziloah' in Dryden's *Absalom and Achitophel*—was induced by court influence to use the Lord Mayor's privilege (long in abeyance) of nominating one of the Sheriffs. He nominated Dudley North; Ralph Box was the other court candidate; and Moore declared them elected. The election was challenged. When the poll was examined the whig candidates Thomas Papillon and Dubois were found to have a large majority, but a further poll was ordered and eventually the court party achieved their purpose.

The True-Born Englishman   Cf. *Richard II*, I, iii, 309

1   *Times of Peace*   The Treaty of Ryswick had been signed in 1697.

2   *Golden Key*   The symbol of the office of Lord Chamberlain. The Earl of Sunderland had resigned the office in December 1697.

3   *Bubbl'd*   i.e. deceived, cheated.

4   *Wherever God ... there*   This proverb is to be found in Burton's *Anatomy of Melancholy* (1621), III, iv, 1, and in George Herbert's *Jacula Prudentium* (1640), No. 670. Morley (*Earlier Life*, p. 186) claims that Defoe was the first to versify the proverb and to add the rider in the couplet following.

5   *Wealth which ... undo*   Cf. Pope, *Moral Essays*, III, 351–2:
      'But Satan now is wiser than of yore,
          And tempts by making rich, not making poor.'

6   *D'avenant*   Charles Davenant (1656–1714), political economist. Published *A Discourse upon Grants and Resumptions* (1700).

7   *Dr. Sherl[ock]*   William Sherlock (1641?–1707), at first a prominent non-juror but, in 1690, he convinced himself that since William and Mary were, at least since the Battle of the Boyne, *de facto* in authority, their sovereignty was also rightful and could command the allegiance of Christians. (See Macaulay, *History of England*, ed. Firth, IV (1914), 2012–8.)

8   *David at Hackelah*   See 1 Samuel, XXIII, 19; XXVI, 3.

9   *Bold Strafford ... Lisle*   Thomas Wentworth, Earl of Strafford, executed 1641; James Hamilton, 2nd Earl of Cambridge, led a Scottish army into England, executed 1649; Arthur Capel (1st Baron Capel), Sir Charles Lucas, and Sir George Lisle, royalist leaders, all put to death after the surrender of Colchester, 1648.

10   *Six Bastard ... Reign*   They were Southampton, Grafton, and Northumberland (sons of Castlemaine); Richmond (son of Portsmouth); Monmouth (son of Lucy Walter); and St. Albans (son of Nell Gwynn).

11   *C[astlemai]n*   Barbara Villiers (1641–1709); her husband was made Earl of Castlemaine and she, in 1668, Duchess of Cleveland.

12   *P[ortsmout]h*   Louise Renée de Keroualle (1649–1734), made Duchess of Portsmouth in 1673.

13   *Tabby S[co]t*   Probably Nell Gwynn (1650?–1687).

14   *Cambrian*   Probably Lucy Walter (1630–1658) who was Welsh by origin.

15   *S[chomber]g*   Frederick de Schomberg (1615–1690), a close friend of William III, who was made Earl of Brentford and Duke of Schomberg in 1689.

16   *P[ortlan]d*   William Bentinck (1649–1709), another of William's close associates; he was created Earl of Portland in 1689.

17 *Blewcoat . . . Bridewell* Christ's Hospital was founded (in 1552) as a school for 'fatherless children and other poor men's children'; the pupils' traditional dress is a blue coat and yellow stockings—hence the name 'Bluecoat'. Bridewell Royal Hospital was a school for homeless apprentices, later partly used as a prison (see Hogarth, *Harlot's Progress*, Plate IV).

18 *Tarpaulin Lords* Naval commanders who had worked their way from the ranks to positions of distinction, but who retained the rough manners of their origin. (See Macaulay, *op. cit.*, I (1913), 294.)

[p. 66. The lines omitted chiefly satirize English drunkenness.]

19 *Seldom contented . . . long* Reminiscent of lines from Dryden's portrait of Zimri, *Absalom and Achitophel*, Pt. I, ll.547–8. (Tutchin's poem to which Defoe is replying, was an imitation of Dryden's manner in *Absalom*.)

20 *Tells you . . . despise* A constant complaint in Augustan satire cf. Pope, *Moral Essays*, III; Johnson, *London*, ll.176–81.

21 *For where . . . Inclination* Cf. *Essay upon Projects* above, p. 31, and note.

22 *Shamwig* John Tutchin (1661?–1707). See headnote. A supporter of the Monmouth rebellion, Tutchin was sentenced to whipping and only by bribing Judge Jeffreys was he pardoned. On William's accession he published *An Heroic Poem upon the late Expedition of his Majesty to rescue England from Popery, Tyranny, and Arbitrary Government* and *The British Muse: or Tyranny Exposed*. He obtained a clerkship in the Victualling Office (1692) but in 1695 he accused the commissioners of cheating the King of vast sums; the accusation was not proved and he was dismissed. In 1696 appeared his *Pindarick Ode in praise of Folly and Knavery*. On 1 August 1700, in *The Foreigners*, he attacked the King whom he 'panegyrick't' before. (From the 9th edition of his poem onwards Defoe omitted the thirty lines on Tutchin.)

23 *In this . . . heard* In Tutchin's *Foreigners* (imitating Dryden) the English are Israelites, the Dutch 'Gibeonites'.

[p. 71. Approximately 70 lines, mainly satire on the clergy, are omitted.]

24 *trepann'd* i.e. ensnared, beguiled.

25 *S[underland]* Robert Spencer, 2nd Earl of Sunderland (1640–1702), former Lord President of the Council and Lord Chamberlain. He was accused by some contemporaries of having ruined James II to benefit William. 'Sot' here means 'fool'; Sunderland was not a drunkard.

26 *No Man . . . undo* Self-defence was a cardinal feature in Defoe's ethical system.

[p. 76. ll.931–1024—emphasizing England's ingratitude to men who have served her well—are omitted.]

27 *Godolphin* Sidney, Baron Godolphin (1645?–1712), was first Lord of the Treasury under William but maintained treacherous links with James II; he was compromised by the attempted assassination of William in 1696.

28 *First to . . . Fleet* In 1693 nearly 400 richly-laden ships, supposedly protected by the English and Dutch navies, were captured or routed by the French under Tourville in the Bay of Lagos. The Whigs blamed treacherous mismanagement.

29 *And Injur'd . . . Camaret* In 1694 British troops under General Talmash tried to land at Camaret Bay (near Brest) in order to prevent further sorties by Tourville from Brest. The French knew the plan; the attack failed; and Talmash was fatally wounded.

30 *A Modern . . . Note* Sir Charles Duncombe (d. 1711) was of mean origin; he was apprenticed to Alderman Edward Backwell (d. 1683), a leading city goldsmith, but managed to avoid involvement when Backwell met financial ruin. He gradually established himself as a prominent goldsmith and banker; was elected Sheriff and knighted in 1699; and later (1708) became Lord Mayor. At a cost of £600 he erected 'a curious dyall' in the Church of St. Magnus. (He is mentioned briefly in *Colonel Jack*, I, 78.)

31 *Mobile* Mob. Duncombe released many prisoners from debtors' prisons while he was Sheriff.

32 *Sir C[harle]s . . . Speech* This title became 'His Fine Speech' in the 9th edition, thus blunting the attack on Duncombe.

33 *Ziba* A servant of Mephibosheth; he obtained half his master's property by accusing him of treachery. See 2 *Samuel*, IX, XVI, XIX.

34 *And so . . . B[il]l* In February 1698 Duncombe was expelled from Parliament on a charge of having forged endorsements on treasury bills. A Bill of Pains and Penalties against him was rejected by the Lords; in 1699 he was tried before the King's Bench but acquitted on a legal technicality.

35 *Banditti* The trained-bands.

36 *The King . . . ye* In 1698 the King instructed the magistrates (by royal proclamation) to punish severely all persons guilty of 'dissolute, immoral, or disorderly practices'.

37 *Miss——* 1716 edition gives 'Miss M——n'.

38 *Jeffery* Sir Jeffrey Jeffreys, Sheriff of London with Duncombe, 1699–1700.

Legion's Memorial

1 *J[oh]n H[o]w* Commonly known as Jack Howe (1657–1722), the Tory M.P. for Gloucestershire whose attack on the Partition Treaty negotiated

by William III was so savage that the King declared he would have demanded satisfaction were it not for the disparity of rank.

2 *Our Name . . . many* See *Mark*, V, 9.

The Shortest-Way with the Dissenters

1 *Sir Roger . . . another* *Fables of Aesop* (1692) No. 439.

2 *the purest . . . World* Sacheverell, in his Oxford sermon, 10 June 1702, had referred to the Church of England as possessing 'the Purest and most Apostolical Religion in the World' (2nd edn., 1710, p. 23).

3 *Act of Tolleration* The Act of 1689 which declared that penal statutes against Protestant Dissenters should not be enforced. Protestant nonconformity was officially 'recognised' by the Act.

4 *having sworn . . . -Government* A reference to the 'non-jurors'; they argued that James remained the anointed King and refused to take the new oaths of fidelity to William and Mary.

5 *The first . . . Collony* On 16 July 1604 Puritan clergy within the Church were required to conform by 30 November on pain of expulsion. The *Mayflower* sailed for New England on 6 September 1620.

6 *King Charles . . . Conscience* Charles II unconstitutionally suspended penal laws against nonconformists and recusants in 1672.

7 *Rye-Plot* An attempt, in 1683, to seize and perhaps to kill the King and Duke of York on their way from Newmarket. The plot was the pretext for establishing a reign of terror; Lord Russell and Algernon Sidney were executed for complicity.

8 *Duke of Monmouth* The 'Protestant Duke'—Dryden's 'Absalom' and Charles's favourite son—landed at Lyme Regis on 11 June 1685 to raise a rebellion; he was defeated, and executed on 11 July. The irony of Defoe (himself a supporter of Monmouth) is underlined not only by mentioning Judge Jeffreys and the Bloody Assize, but also by recalling that on 20 June 1685 the lords-lieutenant in the south-west were ordered to arrest disaffected persons, especially Dissenters.

9 *universal Liberty* Through Declarations of Indulgence, 1687 and 1688.

10 *crope* Obsolete form of 'crept'.

11 *there they . . . Government* Episcopacy was abolished by an Act of 22 July 1689.

12 *the Observator* A Whig journal (founded April 1702)—in the form of a dialogue between 'Observator' and 'Countryman'—edited by John Tutchin (see above, p. 265).

13   *Treatise of . . . Scotland* [Anon], *A late letter, giving a full account of the Sufferings of the Episcopal Clergy in Scotland*, 1691.

14   *the French . . . once* Louis XIV revoked the Edict of Nantes in 1685; thousands of Protestants left France as a result.

15   *I am . . . pretended* In the *Review*, 20 September 1712, Defoe estimated the number of Dissenters at about two millions.

16   *Old-Money* To stop the export of 'clippings' from English silver coinage to the continent, the Commons agreed in December 1695 that there should be a complete recoinage of silver money. After May 1696 clipped coins ceased to be legal tender; they were melted down at the Treasury.

17   *Shaftsburys* Anthony Ashley Cooper (1621–1683)—Dryden's 'Achitophel' —was made Earl of Shaftesbury in 1672; he supported Monmouth, was indicted for high treason, 1681, and fled to Holland where he died in exile.

18   *Argiles* Archibald Campbell, 9th Earl of Argyle (d. 1685), in a concerted effort with Monmouth, landed in Scotland with 300 men in May 1685; he was seized on 18 June and executed twelve days later.

19   *experimentally* i.e. as the result of experience.

20   *Post est . . . Calvo* Ps. Cato, *Distichs*, 2, 26 ('. . . calva').

21   *Her Majesty . . . England* See headnote.

22   *the Church . . . danger* 'The Church is in danger' was a popular Tory rallying-cry in the early years of the century.

23   *What will . . . for* Song of Solomon, VIII, 8.

24   *De Heret. Comburendo* Under the Act *De Heretico Comburendo* (1382) a diocesan bishop alone could pronounce sentence of heresy and require the sheriff to burn the offender without royal consent.

25   *as Scipio . . . Carthago* It was Cato who believed and kept on declaring that Carthage should be destroyed; Scipio Nasica thought it should be preserved. (See Florus, *Epitome*, I, xxxi. Florus was a popular author in schools in the seventeenth and eighteenth centuries.)

26   *Moses was . . . Idolatry* Possibly a deliberate exaggeration: the figure varies from 3,000 (*Exodus*, XXXII, 28) to 24,000 (*Numbers*, XXV, 9), but 33,000 has no authority.

27   *they that . . . Mayors* To qualify for public office Dissenters 'occasionally conformed' by taking communion in an Anglican church.

28   *One of . . . Conformity* Defoe published *An Enquiry into the Occasional Conformity of Dissenters* (1698), urging Dissenters not to compromise by occasional conformity or—if public office were a serious consideration— to join the Established Church. A Preface to the second edition of the *Enquiry* provoked a reply from Rev. John How, a leading minister among

the Occasional Conformists. (Defoe answered How in a further pamphlet, 1701.)

29 *Three the ... differences* Presumably a reference to Articles nos. 34, 35, 36 (on tradition, the homilies, and bishops) to which, under the Toleration Act, 1689, nonconformists were not compelled to subscribe.

30 *another Dutch turn* i.e. if Queen Anne were to be succeeded by a monarch like William III, support for the High Church party would cease.

31 *Enthusiast* An abusive term applied to Protestant Dissenters (cf. Swift, *A Tale of a Tub*).

A Hymn to the Pillory

1 *Bastwick ... Pye* Presumably all men who had suffered in the pillory: John Bastwick (1593–1654), anti-episcopal writer; William Prynne (1600–1669), Puritan pamphleteer; no details of Hunt, Hollingsby, or Pye have been traced with any certainty.

2 *Oats and Fuller* Titus Oates (1649–1705) and William Fuller (1660–1717), both notorious perjurers who stood in the pillory.

3 *Selden* John Selden (1584–1654), famous jurist; imprisoned 1629–1631.

4 *S[achevere]ll* See headnote to *The Shortest-Way*.

5 *Wise ... Press* Sacheverell's sermon was published as *Political Union, a Discourse Shewing the Dependence of Government on Religion in England* (Oxford), 1702; it was licensed by the Univerity (see Defoe's *Letters*, ed. Healey, p. 52) through its Vice-Chancellor, Roger Mander. Defoe's point in the lines which follow is that, press censorship in advance of publication having been discontinued in 1696, Sacheverell's work received a supererogatory 'puff' from the Vice-Chancellor because a licence to publish was no longer needed.

6 *Juno's ... Billingsgate* The famous fish-market, notorious for abusive language. In *Review*, VII, 114, p. 455, 'Juno's Royal Academy' is identified with Billingsgate.

7 *They ... Blest* Baron de Pointis, an able French naval commander, besieged Cartagena in 1697; the English fleet arrived after the city had fallen and the French had left. De Pointis safely reached Brest despite efforts to intercept him. (He published his *Account of the Taking of Carthagena*, 1698.)

8 *Those ... Camaret* See *True-Born Englishman*, ll.1039–40 and n.

9   *Who ... soon* Admiral Edward Russell, Earl of Orford, proposed in 1695 to attack Toulon and the French fleet based there; political disagreement weakened his resolve and the squadron continued freely to harass British shipping.

10 *Their ... done* A naval force under the Duke of Ormonde and Admiral Rooke, proposing to attack Cadiz on 12 August 1702, decided first to seize the open villages of Rota and Porta Santa Maria. The action was militarily irrelevant and Ormonde's troops 'plundered Santa Maria to the bare walls, sacked the churches with heretical glee, raped women, and even nuns' (G. M. Trevelyan, *Blenheim* (1945 edn.), p. 265).

11 *Vigo men* A fleet of Spanish treasure galleons, protected by French ships, put into Vigo Bay in northern Spain; they were vigorously attacked by the fleet under Rooke, and by Ormonde's troops. The whole enemy fleet was destroyed but comparatively little treasure was taken; the Spaniards saved some, much was sunk, and it is not known how much was stolen.

12 *Pampalone* The word has not been traced. It might be a corruption of *fanfarón* (a braggart) or of *gonfalone* (an ensign), or a conflation of these two terms. Some connection with Pamplona in Spanish Navarra is also possible.

[In the lines omitted Defoe continues to indict prominent individuals and groups who should, in his view, share the indignity of the pillory.]

13 *The ... Wife* See *True-Born Englishman*, l.229 and n. The accusation that Sherlock's change of heart resulted from his wife's expostulations was frequently made; in contemporary ballads she was portrayed as Delilah shearing Samson, Eve tempting Adam, etc. (Macaulay quotes a fragment from one such ballad, *History of England*, IV, 2018 n.)

14 *Mene Tekel* See *Daniel*, V, 25.

15 *Furbulo's* Furbelows were showy trimmings on female dress. (This usage antedates the earliest recorded in *O.E.D.*)

16 *Knight o' th' Post* A professional perjurer.

Letter [May–June 1704?]

1   *the Goodness ... Dear* She had—through the Treasurer, Godolphin— paid his fine over *The Shortest-Way*, and given some financial relief to his family; Defoe had been taken into the Government's secret service.

2   *Tis True .. Expect* See J. Sutherland, 'Some Early Troubles of Defoe', *R.E.S.*, IX (1933), 275–90.

3   *I was ... Once* His flight and imprisonment in 1703 caused the ruin of his pantile business at Tilbury.

4 *Good House* At Hackney.
5 *when my . . . her* The story that Nottingham insulted Mary Defoe and tried to bribe her to betray Defoe's secrets is doubted by Trevelyan (*Blenheim* (1930), p. 336 n.).
6 *[symbol]* Defoe regularly used a symbol instead of his own signature in letters to Harley.
7 *Enclos'd* Acknowledgements to the Queen and Godolphin.

A Review
Vol. II, No. 26

1 *We have . . . Westminster* 'The Queen's New Theatre in the Haymarket' was built by Vanbrugh and opened on 9 April 1705. Thirty people subscribed £100 each to provide capital.
2 *In short . . . Employments* Cf. Johnson's *Prologue at the Opening of Drury Lane* (1747):
> 'The stage but echoes back the public voice;
> The drama's laws, the drama's patrons give,
> For we that live to please, must please to live.'
3 *Clenching* i.e. fastening securely.
4 *Prologue* Written by Sir Samuel Garth; spoken by Mrs Bracegirdle.
5 *By Beauty founded* The foundation stone was inscribed 'The little Whig' in honour of the beautiful Lady Sunderland (Colley Cibber, *Apology*, ed. R. W. Lowe, I (1889), 320 n.).
6 *Lay-stall* A dung heap.
7 *Salt Assembly* Lecherous or salacious audience.

Vol. III, No. 2

1 *I wonder . . . Trade* Cf. *Complete English Tradesman*, below, pp. 232–35.

Vol. V, No. 31

1 *Rochester, Shadwell . . . Oldham* Satirists of the preceding (Restoration) age: John Wilmot, 2nd Earl of Rochester (1648–80), for whose poems Defoe had a particularly high regard; Thomas Shadwell (1642?–92); Thomas Otway (1652–85); John Oldham (1653–83).
2 *sike* i.e. such.
3 *Dottrel* i.e. a foolish person, a dotard.

Vol. VIII, No. 75

1 *Benefit of Clergy* For certain offences any person able to read could plead exemption from sentence.
2 *Gazette* Names of bankrupts—those who 'break'—were (and still are) recorded in the *London Gazette*.
3 *let him . . . fall* I Corinthians, X, 12.
4 *Give me . . . Steal* Cf. *Moll Flanders*: 'let none read this part without seriously reflecting . . . how they would grapple with want of friends, and want of bread; it will certainly make them think . . . of the wise man's prayer, "*Give me not poverty lest I steal*" ' (I, 266). The 'wise man' was Agur (see *Proverbs*, XXX, 8–9; see also *Colonel Jack*, I, 251).

A True Relation

1 *It was . . . Worded* The statement conflicts with Defoe's normal practice of re-writing or adapting the available factual information.
2 *very sober . . . Gentlewoman* Possibly Lucy Lukyn whose letter concerning Mrs Veal is printed by Sir Charles Firth, 'Defoe's *True Relation . . .* ', *R.E.S.*, VII (1931), pp. 3–4. It is proper that she should have 'attested' the discourse; her father was a well-known notary in Canterbury (see Dorothy Gardiner, 'What Canterbury knew of Mrs Veal and her Friends', *R.E.S.*, VII (1931), p. 195).
3 *whole Life . . . Piety* Some evidence exists to substantiate the claim (see Gardiner, *op. cit.*, pp. 192–3).
4 *she is . . . Friend* Defoe may have known some of the Veal family (see J. R. Moore, *Daniel Defoe*, p. 169).
5 *impertinence* i.e. an irrelevance or incongruity.
6 *Drelincourt upon Death* See headnote.
7 *Dr. Sherlock* See *True-Born Englishman* l.229, above, and note.
8 *Dr. Horneck* Anthony Horneck, *The happy Ascetick*, 1681.
9 *Mr Norris* John Norris, *A Collection of Miscellanies*, 1687, contains the poem referred to: 'Damon and Pythias, or Friendship in perfection'.
10 *the face . . . Market* A rare factual error. (See Gardiner, *op. cit.*, p. 191.)
11 *Escocheons* The hatchment or funeral escutcheons, of a deceased person affixed to the front of his house.
12 *her Sister . . . expiring* Probably the 'Bro: and Sister Hazlewood' whom Lukyn's letter describes as arriving in Dover when 'ye Bell was ringing for Mrs Veal, she was just dead' (Firth, *op. cit.*, p. 3).
13 *four times Printed* Drelincourt's book, originally published in French, was in a 4th English edition by 1701.

Letter [13 September 1706]

1 *Ordr to Dispatch*   For Scotland to promote the Union.
2 *heads of the Treaty*   The Treaty of Union consisted of 25 Articles.
3 *what has . . . Observ*   The Scottish Commissioners had met their English colleagues in London and, by 22 July, had agreed on a tentative Treaty which was to be laid before the Edinburgh Parliament first.
4 *Parted with . . . thing*   As a result of his bankruptcy in August.
5 *Cantabit Vacuus*   Juvenal, X, 22.
6 *Mr Bell*   John Bell, Postmaster at Newcastle, was the intermediary through whom Harley communicated with his agents in the North.
7 *I have . . . Otherwise*   The Union provided material for many *Reviews*, beginning on 26 September.
8 *Alexa Goldsmith*   One of Defoe's pseudonyms.
9 *Coningham*   Perhaps James Coningham, a dissenting Minister, who was one of Defoe's agents.
10 *the positiv . . . Down*   The Scottish Estates convened on 3 October.

Letter [6 December 1710]

[Harley was again leading the Ministry and Defoe was once more in Scotland on his behalf. Defoe sometimes considered it necessary to communicate with his patron in code.]

1 *Bateman*   Probably Thomas Bateman, an associate of Harley's.
2 *in 212 . . . [Pretender]*   See *Parliamentary History*, VI, 930.
3 *Maitland*   James Maitland, Commander of Fort William.
4 *Oldfield*   Probably Joshua Oldfield (1656–1729), famous Presbyterian preacher and writer, who visited Edinburgh about this time.
5 *Ambassador*   Probably Oldfield.
6 *C Guilot*   One of Defoe's pseudonyms.

And what if the Pretender Should Come?

1 *Author of the Review*   This pamphlet was published anonymously; Defoe was therefore able to use, for the purpose of irony, his own arguments from the *Review*.
2 *Scanderberg*   Properly Iskander-beg ('Prince Alexander'), the Turkish name of George Castriot (1414–1467), the patriot chief who won Albanian freedom from the Turks. (Cf. Jonson, *Every Man in his Humour*, I, iii, 22.)

3 *Amusement* i.e. distraction or bewilderment.

4 *New Treaties . . . Guarantee* A group of treaties first negotiated in 1709 between England and Holland; the Dutch promised military support to the Hanoverian Succession in return for a guarantee of the barrier forts on the Netherlands-French border. Negotiations were not finally completed until 1715 in which year the Dutch supplied 6,000 troops to aid in defeating the Jacobite rebellion.

5 *Grandson of . . . Spain* Philip V of Spain, grandson of Louis XIV.

6 *In the . . . King* The irony of such references to French power would be evident to Defoe's contemporaries who had witnessed the victories of Blenheim and Ramillies, and the military (if not the diplomatic) success at Malplaquet.

7 *Gewgaws* i.e. paltry trivialities.

8 *grutch* A form of 'grudge'.

9 *for it . . . enjoy* Cf. Swift's satire on the 'nominal Christianity' of his contemporaries in the *Argument against Abolishing Christianity*, 1708.

10 *we shall . . . Nation* By 1713 many people considered the Union (created by the Act of 1707) a failure; had it not been for Queen Anne's death, the two countries might well have separated (Trevelyan, *The Peace and the Protestant Succession* (1946 edn.), p. 232). Opposition to the Union was growing in Scotland when Defoe was writing his pamphlet.

11 *the present . . . Abjuration* An abjuration of the Pretender was a condition of toleration under the Toleration Act, 1712. The Presbyterians objected to being compelled to swear an oath by the English 'prelatic parliament' as a condition of their ministry.

12 *Lord Hav[er]sham* Sir John Thompson, 1st Baron Haversham (1647–1710) opposed any concession to the Scots; in December 1704, in Parliament, he accused the Government of betraying the interests of England and the Hanoverian Succession. (Defoe had attacked Haversham in a pamphlet of 1706.) Nottingham, Defoe's old enemy, had supported Haversham in denouncing the recalcitrant Scots.

13 *but even . . . Manner* Arising from the case of the Duke of Hamilton whom the Queen had created a Peer of Great Britain as the Duke of Brandon, the House of Lords declared in 1711 'that no patent of Honour, granted to any Peer of Great Britain, who was a Peer of Scotland at the time of the Union, can entitle such a Peer to sit and vote in Parliament or to sit upon the trial of Peers' (Trevelyan, *op. cit.*, p. 235). The Scottish peers, who had been active in promoting the Union, suffered this indignity until 1782.

14 *a Halter* i.e. the gallows.

15 *This we . . . James II* Cf. *Review*, 20 May 1710 (vol. VII, p. 90): 'When the Inhabitants of *Carlisle*, in their famous Address, *Ann* 1686 . . . gave the late King James Thanks in *Totidem Verbi*, for his standing Army . . . Blessed him for his Care of, and Concern for the Protestant Interest, and for his assurance of upholding the Church of *England*—Will any Man believe, King *James* was so Weak, as not to see they Jested and Wheedled with him, and in effect Banter'd him—When they could not but see, that he was preparing that Standing Army to pull down that Church, and had done several things even then, that almost *down-right* acknowledg'd it.'

16 *to Nose with* i.e. to reproach or confront with.

17 *Feather-caps* Probably a derogatory term for militia units which were invariably raised under local patronage and wore distinctive emblems—often plumes in the men's hats—devised by their commanders.

18 *Trophy-Money* A tax raised by the county for the militia's ammunition and other necessities.

19 *Nor shall . . . Hall* Pro-Jacobite sympathizers had strongly opposed the founding of the Bank (1694); it was feared they might attack the Grocers' Company Hall which was used as the Bank's premises from October 1694 until 1734. (These fears were realized on 29 May 1715.)

20 *Exchange-Alley . . . -Skin* Stock-jobbers who buy bargains on the stock exchange.

21 *Quam si . . . Ausis* Ovid, *Metamorphoses*, II, 328.

An Appeal to Honour and Justice

1 *By the . . . Voyage* Like the Conclusion to the work, this pious language seems an attempt to engage the reader's sympathy. It is possible that Defoe had recently suffered a severe illness—a letter of 28 October 1713 refers to 'violent' indisposition; he was certainly ill at ease regarding his future.

2 *Qui amat . . . illo* *Ecclesiasticus* (Vulgate), III, 26.

3 *Some are . . . like* Probably an allusion to the Tories who had been almost completely excluded from George I's first Ministry.

4 *Felix quem faciunt* Part of a saying ('Felix quem faciunt aliena pericula cautum') in Cyllenus's *Tibullus* (1493).

5 *Misfortunes in . . . Trade* He went bankrupt for £17,000 in 1692 after the failure of various business enterprises.

6 *to be . . . Commission* One of the 'eminent Persons' was Dalby (later Sir Dalby) Thomas to whom Defoe dedicated his *Essay upon Projects*. In 1695

Dalby became a Commissioner of the Glass Duty; Defoe was appointed accountant to the Commissioners, a post he held until the repeal of the duty in 1699.

7 *During this . . . -Englishman* See headnote to *The True-Born Englishman*.

8 *How this . . . World* There is no evidence beyond Defoe's own statements to support his claim of intimacy with William III. He refers (in 1704) to 'the late King's bounty' which had enabled him to set up his brickworks at Tilbury (*Letters*, p. 17), and he tells Harley that he used to give advice to the King (*ibid.*, p. 68). Defoe seized every opportunity to record his affection for William.

9 *that Glorious . . . Prince* In the *Review*, 6 September 1705, Defoe claimed to have seen Hampden appear before the House of Lords to announce the resolution passed by the Commons in the words here italicised. He re-iterated the claim on 23 September 1710 (*Review*, VII, 308).

10 *Parliamentary Settlement* By the Act of Settlement, 1701, the succession after Princess Anne and her descendants was limited to the Electress Sophia of Hanover and her descendants.

11 *The Queen . . . Interest* In 1702 the Tories' majority was nearly two to one; the Whigs gained a majority in 1705 and increased it considerably in 1708. The leading 'moderate' was Harley.

12 *Sir Edw. . . . Party* Edward Seymour (1633–1708), an extreme and arrogant Tory became Comptroller of the Household on Anne's accession; he was abruptly dismissed from office in April 1704 at the instigation of Harley and Godolphin.

13 *Old Whig . . Whig* Cf. *Review*, I [IX], 13, p. 25 (14 September 1712): 'By *New Whig* was meant the Court Whigs, or in short, the Ministry; and by *Old Whigs*, the *Whig-Lords* who separated from the Interest of the Treasurer [Godolphin] and the General [Marlborough], and set up for themselves, and whom others knew by the Name of the *Junto* at that Time.

14 *I fell . . . Repetition* See headnote to *The Shortest-Way*.

15 *while I . . . Occasions* Defoe is referring to the imprisonment he suffered on account of *The Shortest-Way*, July–November 1703. The 'Person of Honour' was Robert Harley (1661–1724), then Speaker of the House of Commons; he seems deliberately to have delayed Defoe's release, possibly to secure his services and to 'keep him under the power of an obligation' (Harley to Godolphin, 20 September 1703, quoted in Moore, *Defoe*, p. 145).

16 *I gave . . . Sight* Moore (*Defoe*, p. 144) suggests that William Penn (1644–1718) may have been the messenger; he had tried to save Defoe from the pillory (*Letters*, p. 7 n.) and was also a close friend of Harley. The biblical reference is to *Luke*, XVIII, 41.

17 *When Her . . . Her* On 26 September 1703 Godolphin told Harley that he had informed the Queen of Harley's views on Defoe's willingness 'to serve' her.

18 *certain Person* The Earl of Nottingham.

19 *the indelible . . . Gratitude* Defoe never forgot his indebtedness to Harley; one of his first acts on leaving prison was to write to Harley (9 November 1703), comparing himself to the one leper who returned to thank his Saviour (*Letters*, p. 10).

20 *When upon . . . him* Harley resigned as Secretary of State on 10 February 1708; the Earl of Godolphin (1645–1712) succeeded him. Defoe wrote to Harley on 10 February: 'I Sir Desire to be The Servant of your Worst Dayes . . . in Duty and Gratitude to Offer my Self to you Against all your Enemies' (*Letters*, p. 250).

21 *That his . . . Account* Godolphin knew of Defoe's service to Harley and had seen many of his reports. Defoe served as his agent 1708–10; on Harley's resumption of office Defoe resumed his duties to his 'generous Benefactor'.

22 *I never . . . Years* Defoe wrote to Harley on 20 February 1708 and then again on 17 July 1710 when a regular correspondence was resumed.

23 *second time* Defoe was first introduced to the Queen in August 1704 and now again in March 1708.

24 *former special Service* His work in Scotland, 1706–7, to promote the Union. (Cf. letter, pp. 144–45, above.)

25 *Counterscarp* The outer wall or slope of the ditch which supported the covered way in military fortifications.

26 *I went to Scotland* Probably about 22 March 1708; he arrived in Edinburgh on 17 April after some mishaps *en route*.

27 *Earl of O[xfor]d* Harley was created Earl of Oxford and Earl Mortimer on 24 May 1711; he became Lord Treasurer in the same month.

28 *Sed quo . . . undæ* Ovid, *Metamorphoses*, XI, 530 ('. . . ruit impetus undæ').

29 *In Answer . . . Publish'd* There is no evidence to disprove this assertion. (See headnote to *Review*.)

30 *capitulated* i.e. stipulated.

31 *the Point . . . Employment* On 8 August 1710.

32 *my Duty . . . Country* Some self-interest was involved; having supported a moderate Whig policy under Godolphin, Defoe then supported Harley's moderate Toryism.

33 *No Man . . . own* Defoe certainly wrote in the *Review* in support of Harley's efforts to finish the war, and on 6 October 1711 (7 weeks before Swift's *Conduct of the Allies*) he published *Reasons why this Nation ought to*

put a Speedy End to this Expensive War. He could also justly claim that he declared his disapproval of the negotiations for the peace of Utrecht (e.g. *Review*, 8 December 1711; 20 May 1712). The 'publick Paper' he alludes to was probably *The Felonious Treaty: Or An Enquiry Into The Reasons Which moved his late Majesty King William* ... *To enter into a Treaty at Two several Times with the King of France for the Partition of the Spanish Monarchy. With An Essay, Proving* ... *That the Spanish Monarchy should never be United in the Person of the Emperor.* It was published on 6 December 1711.

34 *I was* ... *England* He was in the north of England and in Scotland on Harley's behalf from October 1712 (see *Letters*, p. 388) to January 1713.

35 *A Seasonable Caution A Seasonable Warning and Caution Against the Insinuations of Papists and Jacobites in Favour of the Pretender,* 1712.

36 *Two Pamphlets* ... *Hanover* See headnote to *And What if the Pretender should come?*

37 *A Man* ... *Father* Defoe was in Somerset with Monmouth's forces June–July 1685.

38 *suffer'd and* ... *Whigs* A reference to his persecution on account of *The Shortest-Way.* Defoe's former Tory enemy, Nottingham, joined the Whigs in 1711.

39 *I do* ... *premeditated* After the publication of Defoe's *Answer to a Question that nobody thinks of,* April 1713, three Whig journalists—William Benson, Thomas Burnet, and George Ridpath—complained to the Lord Chief Justice, Sir Thomas Parker, that the three pamphlets on the Succession were treasonable. The printer, Richard Janeway, disclosed the author's name; a warrant was issued for Defoe's arrest and he was seized at Stoke Newington on 11 April. Through Harley's assistance he was released on bail on 13 April (see *Letters*, pp. 405–8). The informers had acted maliciously against Defoe; they were also determined to embarrass the Government. The Chief Justice was a Whig; it would be claimed that the pamphlets were hostile to the Hanoverian Succession; and thus the Government could not openly protect Defoe. Defoe exacerbated the difficulties by vigorous protests in the *Review*, 16 and 18 April; on 22 April Parker committed him to prison for libel; and his release (on 2 May) came only when he apologized to the court (having printed his apologies in the *Review*, 28 April). Defoe petitioned the Queen for a general pardon to quash the original indictment; the pardon was signed by Bolingbroke for the Queen in November.

40 *praying for* ... *me Luke*, VI, 28.

41 *to the Clause of* i.e. among the provisos in.

42 *Nay, in . . . it* Defoe wrote frequently in the *Review*, late 1711 and early 1712, on the negotiations for the Treaty of Utrecht (cf. p. 278 above), e.g. VIII, 143, p. 575 (21 February 1712): 'I have been unjustly traduc'd by a Mob of Writers and others, as favouring an ill Peace, but I thank God it is unjustly; a Peace I am for, but a good Peace or no Peace, is the utmost I am for.' Negotiations to make peace were undertaken at Gertruydenberg, March–July 1710; they broke down because of excessive Allied demands on France.

43 *It is . . . it* See *Review*, I [IX], 24 (21 October 1712).

44 *for having . . . Imagination* Defoe was prepared to see peace made, if necessary, without Dutch consent. In a letter to Harley, 5 June 1712, he mentions a pamphlet (probably his *Farther Search into the Conduct of the Allies*) which, 'farr from Exciting the people against The Dutch', urged— what Defoe felt was Harley's view—that 'it seems Necessary . . . to have the Dutch Friends and Not Masters; Confederates not Governors; and to keep us from a Dutch as well as a French Mannagement' (*Letters*, p. 377).

45 *It was . . . Interest* In 1711–12 Harley was leading a coalition government but losing ground within it to Bolingbroke who was supported by a group of about 150 extreme Tories known as the 'October Club'. Some of them were alarmingly Jacobite in their statements. (Defoe ridiculed the Club in his *Secret History of the October Club*, published in two parts in 1711; Swift, in his *Letter to the October Club* (1712), appealed to the Tories to remain loyal to Harley.)

46 *And I . . . own* The claim may be substantially accurate; nevertheless in a letter to Harley, 27 May 1712, Defoe seems to offer to write about a current furore according to Harley's dictates: 'If your Ldpp please but to hint your Commands . . . by a Single *yes* or *No*, it is Enough to be Understood by me.' Also it is strange to find him reiterating the claim about his freedom of action, in a later letter to Harley himself (*Letters*, p. 379). Defoe seems to protest too much.

47 *I publish'd . . . Two* Several works—especially some published 1702–5— carry on their title-pages, 'By the Author of the True-Born Englishman', and occasionally, 'By the Author of the Shortest-Way with the Dissenters', but Defoe's claim to have printed nothing anonymously for 'a Year or Two' is a gross exaggeration.

48 *Two Books . . . Person* Parts I & II of Defoe's *Secret History of the White Staff*, 1714. The 'certain Person' was Harley.

49 *It is . . . still* He argued in favour of trade with France in the *Review* and *Mercator* during 1713.

50 *But to . . . it* Another claim which seems false. *Mercator: or, Commerce Retrieved* appeared twice a week, 26 May 1713–20 July 1714; its object was to popularize the Ministry's free-trade policy. Moore (*Checklist*, p. 232) believes it 'certainly Defoe's throughout'; at the least Defoe was responsible for many issues. On 21 May 1714 he told Harley that 'Ever Since Lady day Last . . . I perform it [*Mercator*] wholly without any Appointmt for it, or benefit by it; which I do Singly as I hope it is of Service, and That it may be agreeable to your Ldpp to have it Continued' (*Letters*, p. 441). Sutherland (*Defoe*, p. 201) shows that during the first seven months of 1714 Defoe received £500 from secret service funds; part of this may well have been for conducting the *Mercator* in a way that was 'of Service' to Harley.

51 *Treaty of Commerce* One of the series of treaties negotiated at Utrecht.

52 *Nine Year* More accurately, seven years.

53 *the great . . . Ministry* 'The Church in danger' was a High-Church rallying cry, especially likely to be raised for political ends under a Whig Ministry. George I's first Ministry was, with one or two exceptions, composed entirely of Whigs.

54 *a small . . . on* Defoe may be referring to *Some Considerations on the Danger of the Church From her own Clergy*, which he published in 1715. He 'publickly' owned neither this nor many subsequent publications.

55 *I. opposed . . . it* This is the only evidence for the existence of such a pamphlet by Defoe; no copy of it has been traced.

56 *So in . . . Fagot* In *A Letter to a Dissenter from his Friend at the Hague* [1688], Defoe says: 'You had better keep your *Penal Laws*, than fall under the lash of a *Popish Supremacy*.'

57 *The next . . . said* Defoe's opposition to the practice was responsibly argued in *An Enquiry into the Occasional Conformity of Dissenters, In Cases of Preferment* [1698].

58 *an Act . . . it* An 'Act for preserving the Protestant Religion', directed against the practice of occasional conformity, was passed in December 1711.

59 *The fifth . . . Terms* Possibly a reference to *The Felonious Treaty*. See above, p. 278.

60 *The sixth . . . them* In early 1708 Marlborough and Godolphin were faced with a choice: either they had to join the Queen and Harley, or accept the alliance of Sunderland and other 'Old Whigs' to force Harley's dismissal. They chose the second course.

61 *the Observator* See above, p. 267.

62 *Abel* Abel Roper (1665–1726), a Tory journalist who edited *The Post Boy* from 1695. His level of journalism is indicated by a remark of Swift in the *Journal to Stella*, 17 November 1712, and by Defoe's comment in the *Review*, 30 August 1712: 'his Paper is not only capable of having one or two false things in it, but is one Universal Lump of Falshood and Fiction.'

63 *Examiner* Swift was severely ironic at Marlborough's expense in this journal. See Nos. 16, 17, 27.

64 *Pool's Annotations* The extract—which is substantially accurate—is taken from Matthew Poole's (unpaginated) *Annotations upon the Holy Bible*, 1685, Vol. II.

65 *nor written . . . Death* This is almost certainly false. Moore's *Checklist* includes several works which were at any rate *published* between August 1714 and the appearance of the *Appeal* in February 1715.

66 *I have . . . him* George I landed on 18 September 1714; the last extant letter from Defoe to Harley is dated 28 September.

67 *six Children* Two sons and four daughters survived beyond infancy of the eight children born to Defoe's wife.

68 *the Author . . . -Post* The Whig *Flying Post* was written by George Rid-path, one of the informants against Defoe in 1713 (see above, p. 278). He had himself been found guilty of libel: the 'Scotch rogue' as Swift called him (*Journal to Stella*, ed. H. Williams, II (Oxford, 1948), 568) fled to France.

69 *Conscia Mens . . . Ridet* Ovid, *Fasti* 4, 311 ('. . . famae . . .').

70 *Conclusion* Sutherland (*Defoe*, p. 210) and Moore (*Checklist*, p. 122) both suspect, with good reason, that this overt appeal for sympathy was the work of Defoe himself.

The Family Instructor

1 *Practice of Piety* The *Practise of Pietie, directing a Christian how to walke that he may please God* (1612), by Lewis Bayly, Bishop of Bangor.

2 *Whole Duty of Man* A popular devotional work, published in 1659, and attributed to Richard Allestree, Regius Professor of Divinity.

3 *go thro' stitch* A West Yorkshire expression—to accomplish something thoroughly.

4 *Children obey . . . things* *Colossians*, III, 20.

Letter [26 April 1718]

[Defoe was once again in the secret service, this time under a Whig ministry. His mission was chiefly, by pretending still to be a Tory, to manage certain Tory newspapers in such a way that they would not damage the Whig interest.]

1 *De La Faye* Under-Secretary to Stanhope (see below).
2 *Stanhope* James, 1st Earl Stanhope (1673–1721), Secretary of State for the Northern Department.
3 *Capitulations* i.e. agreements.
4 *Townshend* Charles, 2nd Viscount Townshend (1674–1738), had been Northern Secretary 1714–16.
5 *Ld. Chief . . . Acknowledge* Defoe refers to the case over the three pamphlets of 1713. (See *Appeal to Honour and Justice*, p. 180 & n., above.)
6 *Shif shifted* A Jacobite weekly edited by George Flint.
7 *Mercurius Politicus* It ran May 1716–December 1720.
8 *Dyer* John Dyer, author of the Tory *News-letter* and Defoe's old enemy, died on 6 September 1713.
9 *Buckley* Samuel Buckley, editor of the Whiggish *Daily Courant* since 1702. Defoe and Buckley, former enemies, were now co-operating.
10 *Consider* i.e. recompense.
11 *My Ld. . . . Office* Early December 1716; he was succeeded by Stanhope.
12 *Sunderland* Charles Spencer, 3rd Earl of Sunderland (1674–1722), became Northern Secretary on 15 April 1717.
13 *scotland* In 1708.
14 *Mists* Nathaniel Mist's *Weekly Journal* was a very influential Tory newspaper. Defoe was instrumental in moderating its Toryism for a time, 1717–18.
15 *the Other* Dormer's *News-letter*.
16 *Sultan Galga* Nothing is known of this publication.

Memoirs of a Cavalier

1 *I was . . . 1608* Arthur Secord (*Robert Drury's Journal*, p. 78) believes it possible that Defoe may have had in mind as his narrator the man whom the eighteenth century tried to identify as the author-hero, Hon. Colonel Andrew Newport. Historically Newport could not have been the hero; born in 1623 he would have been under 10 years old when Defoe's cavalier was in Germany.

2 *house* A common Oxford term for 'College'.

[The cavalier leaves for Europe, April 1630; he joins the Imperial army under Count Tilly and witnesses the massacre at Magdeburg; but, disgusted by the behaviour of Tilly's troops, he enlists with Gustavus Adolphus. He gives a vivid account of the rout of Tilly near Leipzig (1631); the description of the crossing of the Bavarian river Lech (April 1632) follows.]

3 *sergeant of dragoons* It is historically true that Gustavus Adolphus made careful reconnaissances of the river; he exchanged badinage with Tilly's sentries (M. Roberts, *Gustavus Adolphus*, II (1958), 700); but the part played by the sergeant is Defoe's invention.

4 *tale of a tub* i.e. an apocryphal yarn.

5 *as near . . . men* A tactical blunder: 'instead of defending the river with his army, [Tilly] fell into the error of trying to defend his army with the river' (Roberts, *op. cit.*, II, 701).

6 *ravelin* Two embankments which form a salient angle in front of a fortified position.

7 *Attringer* Johan von Aldringen.

[The cavalier is eventually captured by the enemy, spends two years wandering in Germany, and finally makes his way to England (1635). Later he joins Charles I's army against the Scots. He describes the battle of Edgehill, Prince Rupert's northern campaign, and then Marston Moor. The extract that follows recounts his flight after Marston Moor to rejoin Charles or Rupert; the episode is completely original to Defoe.]

8 *remarks* i.e. observations.

9 *pressed* i.e. forced into military service.

10 *Goring* George, Baron Goring (1608–1657) commanded the left-wing of the royalist forces at Marston Moor.

11 *Brereton* Sir William Brereton (1604–1661) commanded all parliamentary forces in Cheshire and neighbouring southern counties.

12 *Middleton* Sir Thomas Myddleton (1586–1666) was appointed sergeant-major general of the parliamentary forces in North Wales (in 1643); he decisively defeated the Royalists at Montgomery in 1644.

13 *amusing* i.e. confusing.

14 *Brennus* It appears to have been one of the summits (almost continually covered in snow) near the Brenner Pass; the name is no longer used.

15 *Skippon* i.e. Skipton.

16 *Manchester* Edward Montagu (1602–1671) succeeded to the earldom of Manchester in 1642; a parliamentary leader, he was associated with Cromwell and Fairfax in eastern and northern campaigns.

17 *articles* i.e. terms or conditions.

The Complete English Tradesman

1 *hard* i.e. obscure. 'Hard words' was a technical term in lexicography.

2 *chaldron* A measure of 36 bushels (used only for coals from the seventeenth century).

3 *He that . . . man* Proverbs, XXI, 17.

4 *Blackwell-hall man* A man who had a 'pitch' or stall for selling his woollen goods in Bakewell or Blackwell Hall, the exclusive market for woollen cloths and manufactures.

5 *John Sheppard* Notorious for the frequency of his escapes from prison. He escaped from the condemned cell in August 1724, was recaptured and chained to two iron staples in the floor; once more he got free, was recaptured, and executed on 16 November 1724. (Defoe had published *The History of the Remarkable Life of John Sheppard* [1724].)

6 *Scawen* A London alderman and Governor of the Bank of England.

7 *Bateman* London Merchant; his son William (later Viscount) Bateman married Anne, granddaughter of Marlborough, in 1720.

8 *Eyles* A London haberdasher; M.P. for Chippenham (1713–27); bought Gidea Hall in Havering, Essex; died 1745.

9 *Page* The son of Sir Gregory Page, formerly a brewer; he succeeded to the baronetcy in 1720; died 1775.

10 *Mead* He inherited large estates from his Quaker father, William Mead 1628–1713), a wealthy linen-draper.

11 *Castlemain* Sir Richard Child—created Viscount Castlemain in 1718—was the son of Sir Josiah Child (1630–1699) who began as a merchant's apprentice, became victualler to the Navy, and bought Wanstead Abbey in 1673.

12 *the blessing . . . him* Genesis, XXV, 31–3.

13 *Haversham* See above, p. 274.

14 *Craggs* James Craggs (1686–1721), Secretary of State, the son of James Craggs whose early occupation, while perhaps not that of a barber, was certainly humble.

15 *the great . . . Bedford* The 2nd Duke of Bedford married Elizabeth Howland, daughter of John Howland the East Indian merchant.

16 *Mr Whiston's . . . Tables* William Whiston, *Astronomical Lectures . . .* [and] *a Collection of Astronomical Tables*, 1715.

17 *Gunter's Scale* An early version of the slide-rule invented by the mathematician, Edmund Gunter (1581–1626).

18 *Posts* Couriers.

19 *Wit, without . . . Devil* Possibly Defoe's own composition.

20 *take the . . . him* In *Roxana* (1724) the heroine suffers from marrying a fool.
21 *dark House* It was considered proper to confine a madman in a dark house or room.
22 *Natural* A half-wit.

The History of the Pyrates

1 *Paul Williams* A section of Vol. II of the *History* is devoted to his career.
2 *to go . . . Account* Obsolete colloquialism: to turn pirate.
3 *the Palmist . . . Hell* Psalms, LV, 15.
4 *broach'd to* i.e. veered suddenly and turned the side of the ship into wind.
5 *the Darkness . . . felt* Exodus, X, 21.
6 *the Step* The block containing the heel of the mast.
7 *Tant-Mast* An excessively tall mast.
8 *short* i.e. choppy.
9 *Taveril* Probably a version of 'taffrail', a rail round the stern of a ship.
10 *Jury-Masts* Temporary masts to replace those carried away.
11 *Collector* Highwayman.
12 *his Dulcinea* i.e. his mistress (from Dulcinea del Toboso, Don Quixote's 'mistress').
13 *off the Carreen* Their hulls were in need of cleaning and repair.
14 *King Charles . . . York* Presumably a reference to the grant of land (known as the New Netherlands) made by Charles to James in March 1664.
15 *Jure Divino* The irony here reminds one that, in 1706, Defoe had published a long satirical poem entitled *Jure Divino*.

The Compleat English Gentleman

1 *clergy* i.e. learning. (Proverb: 'An ounce of mother-wit is worth a pound of clergy.')
2 *Coll. Ch[arteris] . . . W[hite']s* Francis Charteris (1675–1732), one of the most notorious debauchees and gamblers of the period. (Cf. Pope, *Moral Essays*, III, 20 & n.) White's was the celebrated gambling club in St James's Street.
3 *bubbling* i.e. cheating.
[p. 252. In the pages omitted Defoe continues to attack the neglect of education

among the gentry, demonstrating their barbarous ignorance and its consequences. Then, in chapter five, he offers a practical solution, a self-educational
programme. It is partly set out in this extract, in the conversation reported
between an elderly man (the opening speaker), unlearned but eager for self-
improvement, and his nephew, a man of intelligence and polite learning.]

4 *Dampier and Rogers* William Dampier (1652–1715) and Woodes Rogers
(d. 1732) whose accounts of their voyage were published in 1697 (*New
Voyage Round the World*) and 1712 (*A Cruising Voyage Round the World*)
respectively.

5 *Ephimeris* 'a book in which places of the heavenly bodies and other
astronomical matters are tabulated in advance for each day of a certain
period; an astronomical almanac' (*O.E.D.*).

Letter [12 August 1730]

[This is Defoe's last extant letter. It was written to the husband of his youngest
daughter Sophia.]

1 *sinking under . . . Assistance* Defoe, a fugitive from a persistent creditor
and separated from his family and friends, writes from an undisclosed
hiding-place.

2 *a wicked . . . Enemy* The creditor, probably Mary Brooke. (See Sutherland, *Defoe*, pp. 272–3.)

3 *Son* Daniel Defoe junior. (See Sutherland, *Defoe*, p. 273.)

4 *my two . . . Children* His unmarried daughters, Hannah and Henrietta.

5 *Mother* She died in 1732.

6 *Enfield* Where Baker lived.

7 *Grandson* David Erskine Baker, b. 30 January 1730.